Wonder City

Wonder City

How to Reclaim Human-Scale Urban Life

Lynn Ellsworth

EMPIRE
STATE
EDITIONS

AN IMPRINT OF FORDHAM UNIVERSITY PRESS
NEW YORK   2025

Copyright © 2025 Fordham University Press

All rights reserved. No part of this publication may be reproduced, stored in a retrieval system, or transmitted in any form or by any means—electronic, mechanical, photocopy, recording, or any other—except for brief quotations in printed reviews, without the prior permission of the publisher.

Fordham University Press has no responsibility for the persistence or accuracy of URLs for external or third-party Internet websites referred to in this publication and does not guarantee that any content on such websites is, or will remain, accurate or appropriate.

Fordham University Press also publishes its books in a variety of electronic formats. Some content that appears in print may not be available in electronic books.

Visit us online at www.fordhampress.com/empire-state-editions.

For EU safety / GPSR concerns: Mare Nostrum Group B.V., Mauritskade 21D, 1091 GC Amsterdam, The Netherlands, gpsr@mare-nostrum.co.uk

Library of Congress Cataloging-in-Publication Data available online at https://catalog.loc.gov.

Printed in the United States of America

27 26 25   5 4 3 2 1

First edition

CONTENTS

1. Competing Visions of the City and Urban Life   1
2. The Failure of Trickle-Down Housing Supply Theory   36
3. The Costs of Towerization and the Problem of Density   67
4. Economics of the Urban Commons   97
5. The Curse of New York: The Real Estate Lobby as the Demolition Machine   133
6. How Big Real Estate Stays on Top   173
7. Demonizing Historic Districts and the Capture of the Landmarks Preservation Commission   209
8. The Architecture of Rupture and Nihilism   251
9. What Policies for a Human-Scale City?   286

    Acknowledgments   319

    Notes   321

    References   327

    Index   359

Wonder City

Chapter 1

Competing Visions of the City and Urban Life

DURING THE PAST THIRTY YEARS, residents of successful historic cities such as New York have lived through escalating battles over demolition of old buildings and over the scale and design of new towers in their historic core neighborhoods. Residents cry "overdevelopment." They lament the loss of the city's spectacular economic and social diversity, the loss of a once-dizzying array of unique small businesses, and the destruction of historic architecture that connected residents to the city's rich past. Someone is killing the thing we love.

The real estate industry and its dependent technocrats insist that the concerns of residents are mere nostalgic nonsense. They hurl contempt at what they deem a misguided desire of an uneducated citizenry to "preserve the city in amber."

In New York City, residents mostly lose these battles. The industry clobbers the opposition with an embarrassingly simple playbook. First, it dangles the promise of more construction jobs and "more and higher real estate taxes." Then it delivers the battle's coup de grace by uttering the magic phrase "affordable housing." At the sound of that phrase, all remaining waffling politicians miraculously fold. Lax campaign finance laws and a profitable revolving door between city hall and real estate make these industry victories laughably predictable. Politicians know better than to bite the hand that feeds them.

From my home in Lower Manhattan, I have witnessed and participated in many frontline battles about overdevelopment in all five of New York's boroughs. During that time, I sat through over a hundred public hearings. I presented testimony in nearly as many and learned that these are not fair fights. Anyone can see that the real estate industry has mustered into permanent war footing a vast army of highly paid publicists, lobbyists, lawyers, architects, technocrats, planners, builders, dependent labor unions, and even a new pretend grassroots lobby group called "Open New York." This real estate army demands the right to build a new city of bristling towers of immense height. They insist that their vision of a new tower city—one inspired by Dubai, Beijing, Hong Kong, and Singapore—is the only way to infinitely grow New York and make it attractive to the world's wealthy. Towerization, they insist, is the only way to make New York City competitive in what they tell politicians is a Darwinian battle to attract corporate headquarters and, in the familiar coup de grace, the only way to make the city "affordable." I call their towerization vision "hyper-density." Its proponents are intent on remaking already dense New York into a city that conforms to their vision, a place akin to the Disney fantasy city depicted in the film *Tomorrowland*.

On the losing side of the battlefield is a disorganized array of underfunded, under-organized volunteer residents of the city's human-scale

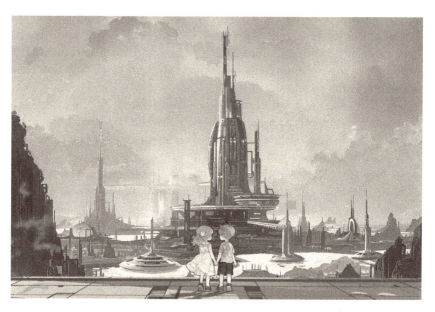

Figure 1.1. Inspired by the Disney film *Tomorrowland*, children contemplate the world adults make for them. Image provided by Daria Boryensova.

neighborhoods. They are voters, taxpayers, renters, homeowners, and lovers of New York's uniqueness. They arrive on the field of conflict armed with little more than metaphorical pitchforks and a vague, nearly folk memory of Jane Jacobs's fight with Robert Moses in the 1950s. They have no staff and no money. They put together weak, volunteer-based neighborhood organizations. Tiny, understaffed, nonprofit organizations operating on minuscule budgets stand with them from time to time. The volunteer residents who respond to the call to arms for any given development fight have little time to dedicate to it. They work at other jobs and are busy paying their rents and mortgages. Many are raising kids. They do not have the budget to hire lobbyists or lawyers. Theirs is an army of Davids without the means or time to play the long game against a well-funded, patient Goliath.

Nevertheless, even though they keep losing, New York residents show up for these battles in the hundreds. They love their historic and human-scaled city and want to protect it. They pay taxes, vote, join local political clubs, clean up their parks, plant tulips, and are appalled at the spectacle of corruption around real estate fights, corruption they only find out about too late. They are good people. They raise their kids in the urban world and worry about public schools. They want their children to grow up in the city and make their future homes in the city that they know and love—and fear losing to irrational overdevelopment. Few have country homes to escape to. They are not the wealthy elite of the city.

The real estate lobby likes to portray these New Yorkers as narrow-minded, greedy homeowners obsessively trying to raise and protect their property values. That insulting narrative is so prevalent that public hearings have lost their link to a democratic process and have become pointless theater: The politicians are either absent or don't even pretend to listen as they text away on smartphones behind their protected tables during the proceedings, clearly conducting more pressing business. But residents stick it out, waiting patiently, often for many hours, for their turn to speak for their legally allotted two minutes, to speak to an empty council or hearing chamber. Newcomers to these fights imagine idealistically that someone is listening. More experienced hands are resigned to speak their bit to some future historian who might listen to the archived recordings of the hearings. The sad truth is that New Yorkers have never been more marginalized in city politics—and incorrectly and insultingly—dismissed as NIMBYs ("Not In My Backyard") and categorized as selfish obstructionists who do not understand the greater good that the real estate industry is fostering upon the city. To anyone who pays close attention, the accusation is absurdly false. In fact, the solutions residents offer to the city's problems are often clever, considered, and better than the plans the real estate developers offer or the feeble, superficial compromises that the politicians devise.

Residents in New York City favoring a human-scaled vision of development rarely reject new construction. Instead, they seek a human-scaled, incremental build-out of the city, inspired by the great examples of the vast, dense, four-to eight-story historic neighborhoods they have seen in Paris, Barcelona, the Edwardian parts of London, and in their own historic neighborhoods of Jackson Heights, SoHo, Park Slope, Inwood, or the Lower East Side. They want their city to support the thriving of ordinary residents. They understand that thriving depends on the presence of a great public realm of schools and parks and swimming pools and a great subway system. Their vision includes places that support children, small businesses, plants, and animals. It is the very opposite of the towerized hyper-dense proposals of the real estate industry. Listening to their testimony, it is obvious that the human-scaled city supporters are the descendants of the great urbanist writer, Jane Jacobs, whose 1961 book *The Death and Life of Great American Cities* defended New York against its demolishers and which celebrated beauty and life in the historic city.

At the heart of these endless battles is a conflict over competing visions of what a city should be and what an urban way of life should look like. Human-scale city supporters know there is a balance to be struck: Nobody wants to be packed in like sardines, and at the same time, nobody wants to live in the grassy, car-dependent suburbs. They seek a Goldilocks "just right" density and height. They want to share the sky as a public asset rather than hand it over to developers. They value historic preservation and would rather advocate for adaptive reuse of old buildings than mourn their demolition. They favor incremental projects on small sites rather than massive rebuilding on huge sites. They want to stop the endless displacement of anyone who is not rich. They want an end to the misguided "luxury city" policy that New York's politicians formally adopted when Michael Bloomberg became mayor in 2002. These men and women want a vibrant public common made up of sky, parks, sidewalks, schools, libraries, streets, and plazas. They seek an end to the privatization of those spaces. They believe the city's public schools and universities ought to rival the renowned private institutions for the city's rich. And they want great public transit.

The real estate industry's vision of the city could not be more different. Theirs is a world filled with rich people working in tech or finance walking to work from clean, shiny new glass towers while sending their kids to private schools and not burdening the public education system. It markets each tower as a separate, suburban world onto itself with dazzling, utterly private "amenities" such as swimming pools, bowling alleys, and private parks for the tower's wealthy residents, a world of internal gated communities where the messiness of real urban life is absent. To the real estate industry, the old urban life of yore that Jane Jacobs wrote about, the one that took place in the public realm, is irrelevant to their hyper-dense tower vision. They just give lip service to that older, human-scale vision.

This chapter reviews the origins of these competing visions of the city and the arguments used to promote each. It contrasts the urban policies each vision proposes and examines who might win or lose under those policies. All of this sets the stage for what this book seeks to be: a multi-pronged defense of the human-scaled vision of great urban life and a critique of the real estate industry's toxic, towerized alternative.

The Wonder City

New York as the great Wonder City of the world exploded into existence between the end of the Civil War (1865) and the onset of the Great Depression in 1929. Within sixty years, millions of immigrants landed. Vast neighborhoods of tenements, row houses, and elegant apartment buildings sprang up with astonishing speed. The largest produce market in the world pulled in food from the prospering hinterland of small farms across North America and around the world. Small businesses of every stripe opened their doors—or set up pushcarts—in a period unprecedented in world history. Many of these small businesses morphed into the huge corporations that are today's household names. Municipal government, despite its corruption, did many good things: For example, it facilitated and sometimes outright built the massive subway system. And in the same period, the city industrialized—right in Lower Manhattan, where not that long ago everything from iron to refrigeration equipment was made. New York as the Wonder City emerged as a world center not only for business and industry, but for cuisine, dance, art, music, and theater. What made it so wonderful was not just its astonishing architecture but the sheer diversity of how so many people managed in so many different ways, in so many unique neighborhoods, to live cheek-by-jowl and share the public realm together.

The city's density, variety, and physical magnificence awed everyone. Picture books and postcards titled "The Wonder City" abounded. The writer W. Parker Chance coined the Wonder City name and described New York as "big, great, astounding, marvelous!" (Chase 1932). Visitors gawked not just at skyscrapers, but at row house neighborhoods, libraries, bridges, hospitals, churches, mosques, synagogues, piers, buses, and even school buildings and the subway system. These things were a source of amazement for visitors from the rest of still rural and small-town America. Moreover, the streets of the city pulsed with opportunity. There were districts of every kind: clothing, fabrics, furs, radios, fish, diamonds, flowers, jewelry, pets, and music. Ethnic enclaves made the hearts of visitors and residents alike race with interest and excitement. Gifted writers like Alfred Kazin and Joseph Mitchell of the *New Yorker* magazine walked around in a state of permanent astonishment exploring and writing about the great urbanity of the Wonder City, just as writers had done a century before in Paris (Kazin 1951; Mitchell 2008). The pleasure of wandering the city's spice district even conquered Joseph Mitchell's famous bouts of depression.

But that great Wonder City is gone now. Much of it was deliberately demolished. The elite in charge of finance and banking wanted to rid the city of manufacturing and the working waterfront. The elite demonized the flexible loft buildings as well as tenements of the poor and working class and sought to create a new city for a wealthier class of people.

The first wave of large-scale demolition arrived with planner Robert Moses and Mayor La Guardia at the helm. The pair had the support of housing reformers who wanted to demolish the tenement and row house neighborhoods where the poor lived. At the same time, the modernist architecture movement began to attack the very idea of a city made of local brick and stone. The movement hated a city made of anything local. Modernists sought to remake New York into a world of glass, steel, and concrete. In another blow to the Wonder City, the federal government after World War II had a national policy to subsidize the movement of white soldiers to the suburbs. That changed the very dynamic of urban living. The virtues of urbanity were forgotten. Writers began to demonize the city, as in the 1946 novel *The Street*, by Ann Petry. The entire country's dream became a single-family home, a picket-fence fantasy of how to live the good life, as in the family dream portrayed in the famous play, *A Raisin in the Sun*.

As America entered the late 1960s, New York City as the Wonder City faded. In the national consciousness it became instead a place of poor Black and Brown people who didn't have the option of suburban living with a yard and a garage. Nobody saw the city as a place suitable for anyone who aspired to middle-class status. Then, in the 1970s, the city went through terrible financial challenges. Even greater numbers of people left in pursuit of that suburban dream, and the city languished and even burned.

But in the 1980s, in an amazing turnaround, New York City rose phoenix-like from its ashes. People and businesses returned; demand for housing soared. However, during that renewal, the city fell, bit by bit, into the grip of the growing power of the real estate industrial complex that sought to transform the city into the tower vision and rid it of its history.

Two Conflicting Visions

These two visions—a hyper-dense city of towers, on one hand, and, on the other, a human-scaled vision of urban life—still compete for the future and soul of New York City. The struggle between the two has been going on long enough that different parts of the city now embody each vision. For example, the recently completed Hudson Yards project in Manhattan, Trump City in the West 60s, the supertalls now lining 57th Street, and the glass towers now dominating the neighborhood around Grand Central Station crystallize the hyper-dense vision. Yet their canyons are cold, windy, and dark; their streetscapes as bleak as can be. In contrast, the human-scale vision is represented by any of our historic neighborhoods such as Inwood, Jackson Heights, Park Slope, SoHo, the East Village, the West Village, Morningside Heights, Bed-Stuy, or Sugar Hill in Harlem. These neighborhoods have parks and grass. They have views of their brick and limestone buildings. The sky is visibly present overhead. Their streets are lined with small businesses who bring to the public the great dynamic diversity of street life for which New York was once so famous.

Advocates of the hyper-dense vision of towers have been around since the 1910s but emerged as an influential political force in New York during the mayoralty of Michael Bloomberg. Architects make up a significant part of those advocates and are represented in this chapter by the well-known architect, Vishaan Chakrabarti. Harvard economist Edward Glaeser was also extremely influential—his ideas will be treated in Chapter 2.

Two distinct features of the ideology of hyper-density are essential to note as we go along. One is a belief in high-rise towers as the natural, evolutionary future of the city, as if God (and not humans) had made the decision to demolish and rebuild New York into the sky. The second feature is a profound contempt for historic preservation and a hostility to the past in general. For example, Edward Glaeser, an outspoken hyper-density proponent mentioned above, baldly stated that any postwar building under ten stories in New York should be demolished and replaced with at least a forty-story tower (Jenkins 2015a).

Despite empirical evidence to the contrary, supporters of the hyper-dense vision for the city believe that towerization is the only way to satisfy the demand for more affordable housing. In making this argument, hyper-density fans rely on a libertarian, anti-regulatory ideology. Get rid of regulations they say: "Let loose the developers," and "build it now." They have also managed to convince journalists, architectural critics, and the curious public that the painful clash of styles and building heights that hyper-density produces is merely a delightful and inevitable part of "the condition of modernity." (See Figure 1.2.)

Figure 1.2. A painful clash of styles is supposed to be celebrated as "modernity" rather than the pain that it is. Photo of a landmarked building on Thomas Street in Lower Manhattan next to a tower known as 105 Duane. Photo provided by Robert A. Ripps.

COMPETING VISIONS OF THE CITY AND URBAN LIFE · 9

Figure 1.3. Architect Minoru Yamasaki's Pruitt-Igoe housing project (now demolished) is one popular and famous vision of hyper-density. Yamasaki was also the architect of the World Trade Center's Twin Towers in Lower Manhattan. The Twin Towers were anti-urban buildings that were widely disliked by the architectural cognoscenti and residents alike, all well before popular deification of the towers after the 9/11 attacks. Photo from the U.S. Geological Survey.

The city's mainstream press seems to have bought into these views and treats with silence the social costs of excessive scale. It ignores topics such as historic preservation, optimal densities for livability, height limits to preserve the sky, or design regulations to maintain neighborhood architectural integrity.

Let me pause for a second and be clear what I am talking about when I say "hyper-density." Crudely, it refers to a cityscape with tall towers everywhere, built mostly of glass and of at least ten stories, but usually far higher. If built for residential uses, hyper-density means at least 100 housing units per acre, but in truth its advocates talk about supporting dramatically greater numbers, such as 600, 1,000, or even 1,200 apartments per acre. The towers are often designed to be part of a superblock—a large block with its own internal pathways. New York variations of hyper-dense towers also include a unique type of skyscraper that has a smidgen of a public space around it called a "public private plaza" as well as the odd-duck building form planners call a "tower on base," which means a building of six to ten stories with a pencil-like skyscraper stuck on top of it.

Of course, beware. "Ten stories" with "100 housing units per acre" is merely a crude indicator of a threshold to suggest when we might be

1.4. A real "tower on base" building style, known as the Hearst Tower in Manhattan. Photo from author.

entering the realm of hyper-density. But I am not alone in thinking it a reasonable threshold. For example, when an influential group of London architects wrote public manifestos about density, they made a distinction between "super-density" and "hyper-density" (Bishop 2007; Derbyshire et al. 2015). They defined super-density as a range between 60 and 139 housing units per acre and hyper-density as anything above 100 units per acre. They argued that London should be planned around the lower range of super-density. To them, the historic Edwardian six- or seven-story apartment blocks scattered throughout historic London are the model for "just right" Goldilocks urban density. I agree with their instincts on this and suggest that New York adopt the same idea.

The Origins of the Hyper-Dense Vision

> By this immense step in evolution, we burn our bridges and break with the past ... and set ourselves against the past ... and shut our eyes to what exists.
> —Le Corbusier, *The City of Tomorrow*

Even though you can see ten-story residential buildings of obvious antiquity in Naples or in the medieval architecture of Yemen, the hyper-dense vision for how to build cities has its origins in the writings of the famed modernist architect self-named "Le Corbusier." He wrote manifestos about his vision for cities after World War I. He was responding to a growing set of architectural dreams of his time, particularly the fantasy images produced by the Italian futurist Antonio Sant'Elia. Le Corbusier's first manifesto was called *Towards a New Architecture*. It was rapidly followed by a second, titled *The City of Tomorrow and Its Planning* (Le Corbusier 1923; Le Corbusier and Etchells 1929). In them, Corbusier proposed a "City of Towers" to replace the historic core of Paris. It established him as one of the early gurus of the modernist architectural movement that was soon to sweep the world.

Le Corbusier's story and views are well known to architects and planners, as are the intense debates over his disputed legacy. For those who are not from the architectural world, I'll give a summary and crib sheet, as it is impossible to understand where we are today without some idea of what Le Corbusier wanted. His ideas are just so visible in the proposals of many contemporary planners and architects, as we shall see shortly in the case of Vishaan Chakrabarti, one of the proselytizers of the hyper-dense vision mentioned above.

Le Corbusier advocated for remaking cities into the form of tall towers. Ironically, his conversion to this vision took place in Paris, that epitome of human-scaled cities. In this oft-cited quote, you can see his opportunistic belief in the power of the new and destruction of the old:

> On that 1st day of October, on the Champs Elysée, I was assisting at the titanic reawakening of a comparatively new phenomenon ... traffic. Motor [cars] in all directions, going at all speeds. I was overwhelmed, an enthusiastic rapture filled me. Not the rapture of the shining coachwork under the gleaming lights, but the rapture of

power. The simple and ingenuous pleasure of being in the center of so much power, so much speed. We are a part of it. We are part of that race whose dawn is just awakening. We have confidence in this new society, which will in the end arrive at a magnificent expression of its power. We believe in it. Its power is like a torrent swollen by storms, *a destructive fury. The city is crumbling, it cannot last much longer; its time is past. It is too old.* The torrent can no longer keep to its bed. It is a kind of cataclysm. (Le Corbusier and Etchells 1929; emphasis mine)

Instead of reacting to the spectacular traffic on a Parisian boulevard with a spirit of resistance as current biking advocates do, Le Corbusier tells us here to instead adopt a spirit of opportunism: Align with the newly encountered power of the car.

Like many of his time, Le Corbusier also held himself in thrall to the idea of "modernity" and thought it a wonderful thing. But what was "modernity" exactly? Reading Le Corbusier—and the other modernists of his time—it is hard not to conclude that he (and they) equated modernity with *capitalism*. Like Marxists and many other followers of the German philosopher Hegel, Le Corbusier thought that capitalism imposed a total rupture with the past. The fuel of that rupture was capitalism's most visible manifestation: industry. Industry, Le Corbusier correctly believed, would end up "overwhelming us like a flood which rolls on towards its destined ends" (Le Corbusier 1923). He figured it best to not just go with the flow but be part of it.

Le Corbusier wanted to make architecture a tool of this powerful capitalist, industrial force. To do that, he decided that everything to do with traditional, vernacular, and craft architecture must be killed off and reinvented. "By this immense step in evolution," he wrote, "we burn our bridges and break with the past." He insisted we "set ourselves against the past" and "shut our eyes to what exists." A new architecture must arise to embody what he thought would be a thrilling "machine age," one symbolized by the very car whose carbon emissions have brought our planet to its present crisis. By necessity, Le Corbusier demanded, the new architecture should be "brutal," "plain," "pitiless," and unromantic, qualities that mirrored his idea of the qualities of capitalism. He pushed the envelope even further, declaring: "If we set ourselves against the past, we are forced to the conclusion that the old architectural code, with its mass of rules and regulations evolved during four thousand years, is no longer of any interest; it no longer concerns us" (Le Corbusier 1923).

To those who disagreed with Le Corbusier's desire to ignore thousands of years of urban and architectural experience for what he dubbed "a march towards order," Le Corbusier told his opponents that they were "reactive" and full of "misplaced sentimentalism," which he claimed was "dangerous and criminal." This ad hominem insult to opponents remains typical of the discourse of many modernists. We'll see that same attitude again in the writings of Vishaan Chakrabarti and Edward Glaeser.

However silly they might seem now, Le Corbusier's ideas became the consensus over time, especially in the postwar period when socialist-dominated governments decided to invest in public housing. That was a unique time in history and high modernist architects like Le Corbusier saw in it their chance. They went after government contracts and won them, not because they nobly shared some vague socialist desire to act in the public good, but because they saw a chance to realize their ideas with the backing of an excellent client: government. The ugly modernist public housing tower-slabs that proliferate the world were thus born of two parents: big government and high modernism. But don't be fooled by the do-good rhetoric of modernists: The public good part of all this came from governments seeking to build housing, not from the modernist clan hired to do the design work for the resulting slabs.

Much like the Marxist visionaries who preceded him, Le Corbusier thought the new machine age required government, capitalists, and like-minded architects to engage in a special kind of project to create a new type of human. He urged these powers to muster "the will" to require mankind to "submit to the harness the new age required" (Le Corbusier 1923), implying that resisters to his vision would be run over. And Le Corbusier got right to the point about kick-starting the new age: "The [historic] center city must be demolished. It must be thrown away and replaced." Skyscrapers would replace historic city centers.

For those who are not architects, here is a cheat sheet of the elements of Le Corbusier's vision. It is a summary of the rules he dictated to architects. I have tried to use his own words wherever possible in quotes, taken from both of his manifestos cited above, *The City of Tomorrow* and *Towards a New Architecture*:

- The crooked streets and irregular roofs of old Rome and Paris must go. Architects, ordered Le Corbusier, "will dispense with dormers, eaves, mansards and the rest," to be replaced by "a pure and simple line" and streets with "right angles". The new buildings must also be without color (except for white) and must all have "flat roofs."

- In demolished central Paris there should arise at least "twenty skyscrapers over 500 feet in length and 600 feet in height." The new buildings must be "enormous and square built" and "twenty, forty, and sixty stories high" and above all, "severe and pure" and built to a scale that "ravishes" (meaning, carry away by force).
- Le Corbusier had confused ideas about how to deal with man's need for nature and human-scaled objects. On the one hand, he thought of nature as a scary "chaos," something men "struggled with" every day (Hardy 2019), and there is very little nature in his ideas and designs. He decreed at one point that a few trees be planted in his newly constructed vison of the city, but just in between the big towers. Moreover, cities he thought, should rather be surrounded by green belts rather than have parks inside them. The existing suburbs should be nonchalantly moved further out to make way for those greenbelts. There might be private terraces in the new tower buildings, upon which residents might have plants. In his second book, he decided that in front of the bleak row of skyscrapers, he might allow a row of trees and a row of one-story houses, "for the eye to feed on." But in his city of the future there were to be no parks in the sense of Central Park, Hyde Park, or the Luxembourg Gardens. Instead, he advocated for grassy, modestly treed spaces with exercise fields between the towers, dubbed disingenuously "towers in the park." His discomfort with nature is symbolized by his famous concrete rooftop "garden" (pictured in Figure 1.6) for children resident in the "Unité d'Habitation" in Marseille. It has no trees or greenery whatsoever and is as bleak as possible.
- He promised that erecting sixty-story buildings would increase the value of the land and result in a windfall for the government's finances (through real estate taxes, I presume), a habit the real estate industry has adopted.
- Le Corbusier knew that the resulting towers would be "magnificent," but also "terrifying, pitiless." He thought the quality of "pitilessness" important to demonstrate "a phenomenon of power" that reflected the true nature of modernity or capitalism. This notion comes up again and again from modernist architects.
- Hyper-density was essential: The towers should fit 1,200 inhabitants to the acre (although he did note that at the time of his writing, the average density at the core of Paris was only 146 inhabitants per acre and the overcrowded neighborhoods had 213 inhabitants per acre).

COMPETING VISIONS OF THE CITY AND URBAN LIFE · 15

- The towers were to be raised onto tall unornamented columns called "pilotis." The ground level space thus created was reserved for water pipes and electrical infrastructure—not for walking and shopping streets. The site of the former streets would become an uninhabitable, unwalkable "forest of pillars" occupied solely by heavy trucks making deliveries. In the tower basements, there must be "vast and sheltered public parking spaces" with each tower housing 3,000 cars.
- It wasn't just the pilotis that would transform the city. Le Corbusier declared "cafes and places for recreation would no longer be that fungus which eats up the pavements of Paris: they would be transferred to the flat roofs" (Le Corbusier 1923).
- Since the delivery trucks and pillars were to occupy the ground level, personal cars would be allowed to move at great one-way speeds on new, elevated highways. He designed cloverleaf highways for the 3,000 parked cars he imagined would be mostly used for weekend use so that urbanites might happily drive out to the countryside to enjoy access to a nature not known in the city itself.
- To his credit, Le Corbusier acknowledged that the severity of the new towers would result in a city not fit for children. To solve that perplexing dilemma, he announced: "Family life will be banished from the center of our city." It is also possible he just didn't like children: He famously did not put windows in the children's rooms of his *"Unité d'Habitation"*—the aforementioned concrete apartment block meant for the working class in Marseille (Curl 2018).
- The new towers were to be ephemeral and deliberately "cheap," "mass produced," with "thin partitions of glass or brick" preferably with "artificial" rather than "natural materials," all in keeping with the new machine age. They should have "the glitter of steel" or else be built of "poured cement." The emphasis on cheap quality might have been inspired by the Italian Futurist Antonio Sant'Elia, who argued that cities should be torn down "every 20 years without remorse"—so that they could be replaced by whatever new architectural fashion or "spirit" had arrived (Sant'Elia 1914).

In Figure 1.7 is the famous illustration of the hyper-dense tower city that Le Corbusier thought should replace central Paris, drawn in the grand architectural tradition of imaging a city without people. As anyone flying over New York City can see, most of the public housing estates and Mitchell-Lama complexes in our region look exactly like Le Corbusier's

1.5a and 1.5b. A human-scaled Lower Manhattan streetscape contrasted with hyper-dense Trump City on Manhattan's West Side. Lower Manhattan photo by author. Trump City photo reproduced under Creative Commons license.

Figure 1.6. Brutal rooftop "playground" for kids at Le Corbusier's housing project in Marseille called the "Unité d'Habitation." Image reproduced under Creative Commons license.

aerial vision. His vision can be found throughout the world, just not in central Paris.

The Modernists Hated Cities and Urban Life

Le Corbusier and the architects who followed him in the modernist movement argued that the big cities the world had inherited in 1920 were so filthy and overcrowded that they needed to be rebuilt entirely. They also believed with religious zeal that all architectural styles that existed before their modernist designs were "dead" (see Chapter 7), and therefore argued that the old cities and the old architecture should be destroyed and replaced with high towers of housing separated by grassy areas. Government must take charge and do this based on modernist plans that required the seizure of private property to demolish and then create the new city the modernists envisaged. All this was laid out in the core of their bible, known as *The Athens Charter* (Jeanneret-Gris 1973).

Le Corbusier and his followers particularly hated buildings that directly fronted the street. The street, to them, was a toxic sewer full of fumes and worse—other people. Streets irritated the modernists when the distances between street intersections were "too short." This dislike of street life stands in obvious contradiction to urbanist Jane Jacobs's point that in great

Figure 1.7. Le Corbusier's "Let's Demolish Everything and Rebuild" plan for central Paris called "le Plan Voisin." Image reproduced under Creative Commons license.

cities, successful blocks were short and sidewalks immense relative to the roadway so as to make them interesting to humans. Unsurprisingly, Le Corbusier and his followers also hated vernacular architecture—meaning architecture built in a local or regional style with local materials. Le Corbusier famously proposed a complete demolition of the magnificent vernacular city of Algiers and its replacement with his designs.

But more than anything, Le Corbusier and his modernist movement hated the past. The erasure of the past, the overt hostility to it, and the insistence that the past is dead—rather than a living, ongoing cultural tradition that sustains us and inspires us as we face the unknowable future—is a hallmark of modernist architectural thinking and common to all its forms and subsequent iterations, including the vision of the hyper-dense city. What modernists looked to, instead, was The Future as They Imagined It. That meant embracing the car. Le Corbusier and other modernists proposed a great deal of infrastructure for cars in their designs: driveways, highways, parking lots, and big parking garages. Streets were to be widened, sidewalks shrunken (and elevated into the sky if necessary) to fit more cars. Le Corbusier even fantasized in another book, *The Radiant*

City, that everyone in the new modern city would live miles apart and be compelled happily to drive everywhere. He waxed rhapsodic: "We shall use up tires, wear out road surfaces and gears, consume oil and gasoline" (Le Corbusier's words from *Radiant City*, cited in Mehaffy 2010).

Sigfried Giedion, an architectural historian famous for his relentless cheerleading on behalf of Le Corbusier and the modernist movement and the author of one the movement's primary textbooks, in 1941 summed up modernist architecture's hostility to the historic cities:

> The question arises whether the large city as it has been inherited from the nineteenth century, with its chaotic intermingling of functions, should not be allowed to die. One opinion is that the metropolis cannot be saved and must be broken up, and the other that instead of being destroyed it must be *transformed in accordance with the structure and genius of our times*. (Giedion 1980, 819; emphasis mine)

One of the modernist manifestos of that postwar period was a diatribe against urban life called *Can Cities Survive?* by Le Corbusier's formalized movement, called the International Congress for Modern Architecture (CIAM) (Sert 1947). The book's color cover shows humans packed miserably into a sardine can. Within it was a celebration of the demolition of the historic city and its replacement with Le Corbusier's vision of towers in the park.

If you want further visual proof of this city-hating tendency and the contempt for the historic city within modern architecture, look at the photos in Figures 1.8–1.14. These are famed modernist designs for a new city to replace the old.

Figure 1.8a. Postcard of the old city of Algiers.

Figure 1.8b. Le Corbusier's proposal to replace Algiers with a city of Le Corbusier's imagination. Images reproduced under Creative Commons license.

Figure 1.9. *High Rise City, Hochhausstade*, by Ludwig Hilberseimer. 1924. Image from Art Institute of Chicago.

Figure 1.10. Le Corbusier's *Ville Radieuse* fantasy. Image reproduced under Creative Commons license.

Figure 1.11. Photomontage, aerial view of the Illinois Institute of Technology 1941 campus master plan by Ludwig Mies van der Rohe, superimposed on the neighborhood. Note its complete separation from the surrounding historic city. Image from Illinois Institute of Technology.

Figure 1.12. Designer Noman Bel Geddes's diorama vision of the "City of Tomorrow," sponsored by Shell Oil at the 1936 World's Fair. Photo by Richard Garrison.

Figure 1.13. General Motors' anti-urban "Future City" being sold to crowds across America in a traveling sideshow, 1956, with the old city referred to as "the muddle." Image from Futureliner.org.

Figure 1.14. A new city for Turkey by Zaha Hadid, Kartal Masterplan, proposed in a design competition. 2006. Photo by Zaha Hadid architects.

What does one notice in looking at these images? One sees a wiping out of the historic context of the city and its replacement by the architect's imaginary world, hostile to the previous one, a world without history or a street life. Humans are infinitesimal, practically erased. These are also places that are obviously hostile to children and birds, uninhabitable for them both. These are cities without life. These visionaries of a hyper-dense city are insisting, as architectural theorist Christopher Alexander has pointed out with brilliant exactitude, on the architecture of death (Alexander and Neis 2012) instead of the architecture of life. These imaginary places are also, in the words of urban sociologist Saskia Sassen, "mere agglomerations," not cities as we have thought of them in the Jane Jacobs tradition (Sassen 2015).

Let's now look at a contemporary modernist's vision for hyper-density to see how similar it is to the vision that Le Corbusier laid out. We will see that Le Corbusier has never really gone away.

Chakrabarti's Hyper-dense City as a Variant of Le Corbusier's

Vishaan Chakrabarti, the contemporary architect now with the architectural firm he calls "PAU" and formerly of the firm calling itself "SHoP Architects" [sic], laid out his vision for hyper-density in his influential book, *A Country of Cities: A Manifesto for an Urban America*. Chakrabarti worked for Mayor Bloomberg at the New York City Planning Commission after having done a stint with one of the larger real estate developers of the city, the Related Company. He has been deeply involved in nearly all the big money planning projects New York City has embraced, from the Brooklyn Waterfront to Sunnyside Yards to the proposals for Penn Station. In his book, Chakrabarti enthusiastically advocates for—and warns of the dangers of not embracing—the ideology of hyper-density for cities. His ideas are remarkably like those of Le Corbusier. But in marked contrast, Chakrabarti senses that the excessive scale Le Corbusier favored often looks off-putting to non-architects. Instead, Chakrabarti opens the doors to the hyper-density idea by use of a clever bait-and-switch tactic. First, he reels us in by writing that "city" and "hyper-density" are interchangeable words that refer to "densities greater than or equal to 30 units of housing per acre." Note that this is far less than the 100 units per acre mentioned at the beginning of this chapter. However, if Chakrabarti's reader continues into his manifesto, he will realize that the reference to 30 units of housing per acre quickly morphs into discussion of the immense densities of Hong Kong of 1,000 units or more per acre.

It is a clever rhetorical strategy. For urbanists and planners, the figure of 30 housing units per acre is so unexceptional that it is like Grandma's apple pie. What urban planner would quibble with 30 units of housing per acre? None. You can find beautiful, livable, human-scaled neighborhoods in great historic cities, where there is still a sunny side of the street, with up to 80 or 100 units per acre. So, 30 units an acre sounds extremely low. The catch is that Chakrabarti doesn't really mean 30 housing units per acre: He wants us to embrace towers with much greater density than that. To get to the higher number, he first heaps contempt on the great, historic, dense cities of Europe. "It is unrealistic," he declares, "and irresponsible for any true urbanist to embrace European capitals as models for future development when they are among the most segregated urban centers on earth and have increasingly unstable finances characterized by debt-driven *grand projets*" (Chakrabarti 2013, 129), a critique that could equally be lobbed at many non-Western cities.

With the entire European tradition of great urbanity shunted aside, Chakrabarti pushes instead for densities of many hundreds of units per acre such as is commonly found in Shanghai, Hong Kong, Beijing, and Singapore. Don't look to Europe, he says; look instead to Asia, to the cities of China and Singapore as the ideal models.

In illustration after illustration in *A Country of Cities*, Chakrabarti praises the idea of combining housing units to create a hyper-dense tower, often one in a small park in the Le Corbusier manner. In one illustration, we see a tower-in-the-park with the caption that echoes Le Corbusier, "More height allows for the maximization of open-space uses . . . and the vertical intensification of amenities." In another, he holds out the gentrified Lafayette Park Towers in Detroit (a complex of anti-urban slab apartments built on top of a demolished Black urban neighborhood) as a model of success. Later, he opines that the equally infamous public housing towers of Pruitt-Igoe in St. Louis were unfairly maligned in the press. The only problem with Pruitt-Igoe towers, says he, is not that they were depressing, ugly, segregated, violent, anti-urban, and anti-human, but merely that they weren't dense enough or properly maintained (Chakrabarti 2013, 187).

It is in his discussion of the Pruitt-Igoe housing project that we encounter the first clue that Chakrabarti does not think much of 30 housing units per acre. The Pruitt-Igoe towers were built as 50 units per acre. Since he felt they weren't dense enough, Chakrabarti is clearly not pushing for a world of 30 housing units per acre, or even of 50 units per acre, but some much greater figure. But what figure exactly?

Chakrabarti finally gives a big shout-out for Hong Kong as the urban model we should all emulate. Hong Kong is composed of very tall,

COMPETING VISIONS OF THE CITY AND URBAN LIFE · 23

Figure 1.15a. A rendering of a viewing platform and a vision for the Grand Central Station area that Skidmore, Owings, and Merrill (SOM) proposed for Grand Central Station in 2012. Note the burying of the old under glass and steel. Image provided by SOM.

Figure 1.15b. Hudson Yards. Photo provided by Robert A. Ripps.

hyper-dense towers of hundreds of units per acre surrounded by a zone of protected forests. We are now talking about at least 150 housing units per acre if not 300–1,200 housing units per acre in this kind of speculative dream. Chakrabarti also likes the complete separation of real nature from the city as in Hong Kong. He'd happily get rid of parks in the historic core altogether to get more density into the core of a city. Chakrabarti dislikes the idea of concentrating modernist towers in clustered districts, as Paris did with its skyscraper district known as La Defense. Chakrabarti says that towers should instead be clustered around each subway stop or transit point so that we get a kind of high-low, roller-coaster skyline when you look at it from a distance. Chakrabarti does not talk about what it is like to experience such a city from the ground—that kind of rumination is more typical of the human-scaled city advocates. Here is the Chakrabarti vision of hyper-dense urbanity summarized in a nutshell:

- Densities of 800–1,200 units per acre should be copied from Hong Kong, Beijing, Dubai, and Singapore. Those models are to be honored as "forward thinking." Those who do not like these models and prefer those of European cities are accused of "parochialism" and of thinking that "only Western Civilization can—and will—produce superior urbanism" (Chakrabarti 2013, 129), even though many urbanists admire the dense vernacular hutongs of China as a successful urban model. (The term hutong means "street" but refers to the networks of alleyways that characterize the traditional, low-rise residential neighborhoods of older cities in China.)
- We should build in superblocks with integrated parking and interior facilities like gyms, pools, and golf simulators so people don't have to go outside into the streets. See a photo of Chakrabarti's idea for a mixed-use superblock for the Atlantic Yards project of Brooklyn in Figure 1.17.
- We should build in a "high-low" roller-coaster pattern: very high around subway stops, a bit less high farther from the subway.
- We should impose a rule that developers must build 20–30 percent of the units in the new towers as "affordable." This sounds like a lollipops and rainbows idea, giving Chakrabarti's hyper-dense pitch, a dangerous Trojan Horse allure, since who objects to affordable housing? Alas, "affordable" is a slippery concept, as we shall see in Chapter 2.
- If developers are freed from zoning rules and regulations, Chakrabarti suggests, there will be a construction boom as developers respond to the new, unregulated situation. During this imagined boom, the city should invite new residents from around the world to buy the new luxury housing, particularly young unmarried graduates from top universities. The virtue of that demographic is that modernists imagine this group will be highly paid in the finance and tech industries. This would allow the city to be able to further raise real estate taxes, thereby pocketing more tax revenue in a virtuous cycle of ever-increasing municipal revenue (Keenan and Chakrabarti 2013).
- Labor unions will be tasked with assembling cheap, prefabricated modular housing made in China. Remember, houses are no longer

Figure 1.16. Lafayette Towers in Detroit, built on top of a demolished Black neighborhood. Architect Vishaan Chakrabarti holds this out as a good thing for cities, when it is hard to see the outcome as urban at all. Photo by Corine Vermeulen.

Figure 1.17. A widely circulated and published proposal for Atlantic Yards in Brooklyn by SHoP Architects. Image by SHoP.

beautiful, crafted things, but "machine age" constructions, same as in the Le Corbusier vision. Chakrabarti's book even illustrates a union member raising his hands in joy at the prospect of an unskilled existence assembling buildings from China, while being supervised by someone holding a "quality control" device.

- Historic preservation is to be abandoned. Neighborhood associations are accused of "parochialism" and told (without any evidence) that they "fear change" and must be "made to pay" for their "false claims of historic merit" that prevent new "denser, mixed-use development." Zoning in any form is "overregulation" (Chakrabarti 2013, 143).

It should be clear by now that the hyper-dense city of towers that Chakrabarti advocates for is astonishingly like Le Corbusier's vision for cities. It supports replacing the older city with a new one. Chakrabarti also shares with Le Corbusier a contempt for historic preservation and anything that is not new and designed in the modernist paradigm.

The Human-Scaled Vision of Cities and Urban Life

In the history of ideas, Austrian urban planner Camillo Sitte might be called the father of the human-scaled vision of urbanity. His vision stands in stark contrast to the hyper-dense vision put forward by such contemporary modernists as Chakrabarti. Sitte defended the curved streets and other virtues of medieval, Renaissance, and Baroque street plans in his famed 1899 book, *City Planning According to Artistic Principles*. He argued that historic cities had much to commend them and that planners need not destroy old buildings to accommodate a city's modernization and physical growth. Forty years later, the British townscape movement, which was active from the 1940s to the 1960s, echoed similar ideas (Cullen 1961).

Sitte was dismayed at the pace of the destruction of the historic core of so many German and Austrian towns and the way that destruction was legitimized in the name of modernization. He created intricate black and white eagle's-eye maps of the physical layouts of historic cities that he considered Europe's patrimony at the turn of the nineteenth century to illustrate their virtues. He saw the destruction of a city's historic core as senseless and argued for planners to borrow from what was already known to work in the historic parts of the city.

Urban planning, Sitte believed, should concern itself not just with transport and infrastructure but the artistic arrangement of public buildings to create a variety of differently shaped plazas and parks. There, citizens could congregate and conduct parts of their social, civic, cultural, and business lives. These non-symmetrical outdoor spaces were essential to his vision. The goal was to serve people and public civic life: "Only freedom in the composition of plazas can instill life and movement into the total architecture of the city" (Sitte 1946, 271). For him, one of the most important goals of planning and city design was to produce a multiplicity and variety of such enclosed plazas.

Sitte insisted that city planning could be learned through the study of "what worked" in successful older cities in terms of their layouts. These old places, he thought, were beautiful. They made the urban experience an artistic experience. They embodied lessons about how to live in a city. He liked the idea of living with your heritage. His rules were simple: Avoid strict grid layouts of streets and instead favor natural street layouts that follow the shape of the landscape itself. Curved streets should be tolerated, even encouraged. Planners needed to allow for views as seen by pedestrians at street level: "Irregularities of terrain, existing waterways, and roads should not be forcibly eliminated simply to achieve a banal rectangularity but should instead be preserved as a welcome excuse for crooked streets and other diversities." Moreover, he pointed out, "various large and small edifices could be planned as needed and they could be grouped in accordance with the principle of perspective concavity so that effective public squares would be produced instead of dark and deserted interior courtyards." That said, Sitte also suggested that some residential buildings would do well to have large, inner courtyards to allow for substantial gardens. "Endless repetition of one and the same plan unit should be avoided on principle," for "it is a lack of imagination on the part of planners which condemns us modern city dwellers to pass our lives in formless apartment house blocks and unbroken frontage lines." For Sitte, green space as a bit of access to nature was essential: "Several public gardens should be placed at an equal distance from each other, if possible," with long building frontages for commercial use.

Sitte did not like freestanding buildings separated from the rest of the city as stand-alone art objects. Instead, he asked for an appreciation of how earlier cities grew organically without great ruptures and contradictions in style on any street. He thought buildings needed to be planned and designed in context and relation to each other on the streetscape. He did not like superblocks and advocated minor variations in building heights and cornice lines, all in the strongest possible contrast to the thinking of Le Corbusier. Alas, Sitte's ideas were overwhelmed by the popularity of the modernist movement whose followers turned away from the street and urbanism in general, instead idolizing the car and individual buildings as art objects. But good ideas like Sitte's don't really die out.

In the United States, New Yorker and urbanist Jane Jacobs emerged as the great voice of the human-scaled city and the inheritor of Sitte's ideas. In 1961, Jacobs published *The Death and Life of Great American Cities*.

The book is a sustained critique of the destruction of the city during the tragic phase of urban renewal promoted by the federal government. Jacobs decries the replacement of successful neighborhoods with over-scaled mega-projects and towers-in-the-park public housing in the manner of Le Corbusier. Her book is also a closely observed anthropological analysis of what makes great neighborhoods work. In the annals of urban planning, hers is often the only book that must be read and is among the most frequently cited books on cities ever written.

Great urban neighborhoods, she argued, ought to be judged by how well they create the qualities of safety, "vitality," "convenience," and "diversity." By "vitality" Jacobs meant the proliferation of a bustling street life, brought into being by thriving small businesses and (in her famous words) the "ballet" of many different people going about their business on the streets and sidewalks at different times of the day. By "convenience" Jacobs meant walkability for the purpose of conducting errands and getting to work. She implied that convenience included access to public transportation. She did not mean the presence of national chain stores, which would only have created regimentation and homogeneity, qualities she disliked. Unlike Le Corbusier, Jacobs liked street trees and disliked cars, recognizing that successful streets in older cities were not built for cars. She lamented the habit of New York's Department of Transportation (DOT) of incrementally narrowing sidewalks throughout Manhattan to give cars more room. She wanted the widest possible sidewalks for a multiplicity of activities: errand running, domino tables, neighborly schmoozing, teenage flirtations, and child's play.

By "diversity" Jacobs meant something different from what we hear today when that word comes up. She meant diversity of several things all at once: a visual variety of building sizes, a variety of building ages (although she said more than once that good neighborhoods had "mostly old" buildings), a diversity of businesses and professions renting space on the street, diversity in the types of housing and in the purpose of buildings (rooming houses, row houses, schools, churches, tenement walk-ups, and elevator apartment buildings), and last, a diversity of economic classes.

Jacobs wanted constant stimulation of all the senses so that a neighborhood had "interest." She did not like neighborhoods that were dominated by "the Great Blight of Dullness" and were characterized by "visual monotony." Giant, homogenous housing blocks and enormous buildings—be they for rich or poor—did not provide this desirable quality of "interest." Jacobs was very much opposed to "standardization" of buildings and opposed to gigantism. Her books are full of decisively argued rants against both.

To illustrate what she meant by liveliness, safety, convenience, and diversity in a residential neighborhood, she described in detail her "ideal street": 11th Street in Greenwich Village between Fifth Avenue and Sixth Avenue. It was not the block she lived on, but it was a short distance away. On that short block she counted fifty-one buildings. At the extremes, the array included just one single-story building and just one fourteen-story building. Most of the buildings (twenty-five) were four-story buildings, followed by ten three-story buildings, nine five-story buildings, and three six-story buildings. Most (85 percent) of the buildings she enumerated were between three and six stories, and about half (49 percent) were four-story buildings. That block included a graveyard, a nursery school, a university library (with windows at ground floor looking onto the street), a restaurant, a bar, a single-story candy/newspaper shop, and two churches that were about three stories high if one counted the steeples.

Jacobs's emphasis on diversity, liveliness, and the visual impact that the streetscape had on humans took urban planning by storm. Jacobs launched what I refer to as the Jane Jacobs School of Urban Planning. Her book become required reading for aspiring planners everywhere. It induced a vast literature on Jacobs. To simplify her many insightful and complex ideas, here is a non-comprehensive crib sheet of her ideas for New York City, culled from her various books and articles:

- Make an end to massive urban renewal plans. She liked more incremental plans that involved adaptive reuse and renovation of old buildings.
- Jacobs favored heights that allowed people to see and recognize people on the street. Her "eyes on the street" phrase was to assure resident engagement with the civic world and safety in the outdoor spaces.
- Her "do not do" list of mistakes and disasters to avoid was simple. Avoid "architectural exhibitionism" or what we call starchitecture these days. Avoid giant expensive projects. Build no monolithic superblocks or towers-in-the-park. Avoid regimentation and monotony in design. Do not ignore the way the ground floor of a building interacts with the sidewalk and street and the humans walking there. Do not build for cars. She preferred to have a variety of buildings of different ages with a good proportion of old buildings.

- Like Sitte, she suggested creating and preserving visual closures that allowed for bends and irregularities in the street grid.
- Buildings should create a lively and interesting wall of buildings that interface with the street (the "streetwall") by means of "porosity" meaning visual variety and small businesses with plenty of "pores" in the form of windows, stores, stoops, décor, porches, and other ways for the building to interact, attract, intrigue, and visually interest the people on the street.
- Blocks ought to be short, not long, with frequent opportunities for the pedestrian to turn.
- Buildings and neighborhoods should have mixed uses: residences and businesses combined.
- There should be enough density so that there are people outside at different times of the day patronizing ground floor retail and using the public spaces. This ensures safety. For Jacobs, there was no specific magic number for the right density: It depended on the surrounding economy (see subsequent chapters).
- Make sure parks are designed such that the sun shines on them. Avoid parking lots and the taking over of the city by cars.

Jacobs did not test much of her theorizing at an empirical level, but Danish architect Jan Gehl took her ideas and decided to do just that. He went out into the streets of Europe and studied how people used cities and places, just like his American counterpart, William H. Whyte. Gehl grounded his work in empirical analysis about what people do and see in the street and how the built environment helped or hindered them in their wants. He has advocated a good number of human-scaled design principles for cities, and now his firm consults around the world promoting those ideas. They will sound familiar now to what Jacobs and Sitte proposed, but Gehl is summarizing the results of his own empirically oriented studies of how people use urban space, joining a growing chorus. Here are some of them (Gehl 2010):

- Plan and design the city at the eye level of the average human. Don't design from airplane views and other planning models that trivialize the human experience from inhuman heights. (Readers might note for future reference that when starchitect Frank Gehry designed the giant tower at 8 Spruce Street in New York, he did so from a high floor studio so he could study the skyline rather than experience the streets of New York.)

- Six- to eight-story buildings are best. Gehl cites Paris and Copenhagen as great, dense cities, in direct contrast to Chakrabarti.
- Smaller spaces should be placed in front of larger spaces.
- Build for humans, not for cars. Make cars go slowly. Don't give streets over to cars. Make streets useful places for pedestrians and bicyclists. Have lots of seating with backrests. Avoid overpasses and pedestrian bridges. If you need them, you've been building for cars, not for people.
- Avoid tall, freestanding buildings that create wind tunnels and block sun and air.
- Avoid buildings with smooth, faceless facades. He suggested that planners avoid "overly large modern buildings placed more or less at random," such as one now finds at the site of the World Trade Center in Lower Manhattan.
- Encourage the building of irregular, rough, tactile facades with lots of niches, details, and ornamentation that people can look at, recalling the porosity idea of Jacobs. He urges the construction of building entrances that vary with steps, stoops, windows, balconies, and terraces not too high up so that the users can see and even interact with people on the street itself.
- Like Jacobs, Gehl thought the ground floor of buildings should intersect the sidewalk or street with windows and niches for a variety of smaller shops to occupy the human eye. He even recommends having a different small shop every ten or twelve feet as one walks along the street wall (instead of having one massive retailer occupying the entire space).
- Like Sitte, Gehl thinks a human-scaled city needs to have many closed squares, plazas, and parks where people can congregate. He agrees with Sitte that the great dense and successful historic European cities are full of lessons on how to have a great urban experience.
- The outdoor spaces around buildings should be places people wish to slow down and linger in, not places where people rush through to get someplace more pleasant, or places workers merely endure because they have no other choice.

Ideas similar to those of Gehl and Jacobs can be found among advocates for vernacular and traditional architecture, historic preservationists, and among some of the supporters of the charter for the Congress for the New Urbanism (a movement of planners and architects founded by architect

Andrés Duany). For example, Charles Siegel argues specifically for mid-rise buildings averaging seven stories (Siegel 2010). Robert Freedman, the former director of Urban Design for the City of Toronto has been a supporter of zoning regulations to encourage new construction that is human-scaled (Freedman 2014). Freedman has written about the successful experience Toronto had in imposing such mid-rise zoning rules.

These Visions Have Contrasting Worldviews and Policy Regimes

The hyper-dense tower city and the human-scaled city present radically different visions of urban life. The only thing they seem to have in common is some degree of agreement that adherence to a good streetwall is important and that mixed-use buildings are better than single-use buildings. After that, the differences are stark.

Human-scale advocates talk about a balanced range of Goldilocks densities—people per square acre. The aim is to create livability and liveliness, but not a sardine can. Hyper-density fans believe that densities of well over 100, such as 300 and even 600 or 800 units per acre are necessary, and that skyscrapers are the way to achieve this density.

At the core of human-scale urbanism is not an architectural fantasy but concern for the emotional and physical well-being of citizens participating in an ancient tradition of urbanity and civic culture, one that includes a vibrant street life composed of multiple public and civic spaces, including pedestrian-filled sidewalks and streets and plazas. It is clearly a humanist vision, alien to the Le Corbusian and Chakrabarti way, which rejects literally four thousand years of urban experience as irrelevant to "modernity." Oddly, the hyper-dense vision reduces and simplifies the public realm to bike lanes and relegates many urban functions to indoor gyms, pools, playrooms, and bowling alleys, which are now privatized "amenities" to be built inside luxury towers. Urban life on the sidewalks of New York has little value to hyper-density manifesto writers. By contrast, Sitte, Gehl, and Jacobs see the public spaces and institutions as the heart of how residents experience urbanity. Beauty and a tactile, immediate connection to history also matter to the human-scale idea of urbanity. Preservation of historic neighborhoods matters. In the human-scaled vision, the recycling of old buildings through adaptive reuse is encouraged. Stand-alone "starchitecture" and architecture that deliberately creates rupture with the existing context are negatives. New buildings are not judged as stand-alone sculptures but for how they contribute to the public experience of street level urbanity, how they fit the context around them, their ecological footprint, and whether they are better than what they replaced. Glass towers are questioned for their ecological sustainability, their faceless facades, and the carbon footprint and tendency to shadow all around them by seizing and privatizing the sky.

In the human-scale way of thinking, cities become competitive by being desirable places to live, not because they are agglomerations of glass towers for corporate headquarters or places for investors to park their real estate portfolio. Zoning and regulations are meant to protect the public good and solve problems of market failure, externalities, and to prevent social costs being inflicted on the public. Light, air, and views in the human-scale universe have public value for producing shared common benefits. Incremental development and small-scale solutions are seen as useful. In the human-scale worldview, economic development should be driven by investment in the public realm, which includes the sky, public education, and public buildings (not just the roadway as the bike advocates do), as well as in small businesses and good public transport.

The hyper-dense value system and political economy could not contrast more with what I have just described. In the hyper-dense universe, the human experience at ground level is ignored and what gets discussed is square footage, housing units, and developer profits. Light and air and views are up for sale. Common property resources like the skydome are not to be celebrated and passed on to future generations but are resources for developers to appropriate for private gain at the expense of the public. In the hyper-dense political economy, the role of the state is to facilitate this privatization and expropriation of the public natural capital. In various versions of trickle-down and supply-side economic theory (explored at length in the following chapter), the hyper-dense city boils down to the idea that what is profitable for developers is good for the city. There is no such thing as market failure. Zoning and regulations are seen as bad things because they slow developers down and might sometimes (very rarely in New York City) even stop them altogether. In the hyper-dense worldview, the modernist architecture movement insists upon rupture with the historic context. Historic districts and neighborhoods are objects of contempt, treated as irritating realities that stand in the way of building more skyscrapers or modernist-style buildings.

To hyper-dense city fans, the competitiveness of cities is seen as an exercise in counting flashy skyscrapers. Mega-developments, giant schemes, tallest-building-in-the-world-boosterism, and parametric architectural silliness are the objects of delight in this system. The policy agenda for government of hyper-density centers on freeing up air rights and ridding the

Figure 1.18. Human-scale nineteenth-century Lower Manhattan. Photo by Robert A. Ripps.

city of regulatory constraints on building upward and liberating protected areas from rules that prevent demolition. By contrast, the policy agenda of the human-scaled vision is about how to regulate efficiently so that light, air, and views are dispersed fairly among citizens; how to channel normal developer greed into building at a human-scale in areas with too low a density; and avoiding excessive density where there is already enough. It is a policy agenda that gives weight to planning and creating public infrastructure around transit, housing, and office development. It is also an agenda that talks about using the affordable housing problem as an opportunity to channel human-scaled profits to a wider middle class of small homeowners and contractors, rather than concentrate the opportunity into the hand of big developers who build towers. The last chapter expands on this policy discussion. By contrast, affordable housing in hyper-density comes through small micro-units built as a percentage of a skyscraper's units. The skyscraper developer gets extra height to accommodate a few of these affordable units. But the streets will be darker, and that's okay to partisans of that approach to urban life.

It should be obvious who are the winners in the hyper-dense tower vision: the Big Developers, and not the small fry among them, since building very tall buildings in New York requires mobilizing vast amounts of capital.

In contrast, the human-scaled partisans think low- and mid-rise buildings with densities with a range of 30 to 120 units per acre are the way to go. A human-scaled affordable housing policy, discussed in the last chapter, would change zoning to allow single and two-family homeowners in the low-density boroughs to add basement, attic, and garage rental apartments.

Incrementalism would be the guiding framework, not the explosion into neighborhoods of what economists call "supply shocks" (meaning towers everywhere). The winners in the human-scaled vision would be smaller developers and ordinary New Yorkers whose neighborhoods get a reprieve from the wrecking ball. Small-scale homeowners would also win, as they would get a chance to monetize extra space for "granny flats," "basement apartments," and "auxiliary units" and solve the affordable housing concerns in a dispersed way.

But how is one to decide between these two visions? Each pushes developers, planners, and architects towards opposite ways of building out a city, so a choice must be made. Will developers make that choice through their dependent politicians? Or will the voices of New York's residents matter at all?

Chapter 2

The Failure of Trickle-Down Housing Supply Theory

THE AFFORDABLE HOUSING PROBLEM has always been with us, for as long as there have been poor and middle-class people in Wonder Cities like New York, Paris, and London. For the unlucky many, the rent is forever too high given their low wages. Even for the wealthy, there is a limited supply of successful urban neighborhoods in locations that have the qualities they seek. It is a problem as old as time and one without miracle solutions.

From the beginning in New York City, property owners and the nascent industry of speculative homebuilders did respond to the problem. First, they converted Lower Manhattan's tiny federal row houses to boardinghouses while the original homeowners were migrating north to new and bigger digs. They built mostly row houses in the expanding street grid of Manhattan. Many builders also constructed the first generation of five- to seven-story tenement buildings, a history beautifully documented in Zachary Violette's 2019 book, *The Decorated Tenement*. In a frenzied burst of activity spurred on by regulation, builder-landlords constructed an improved version of tenement housing all over the Upper East Side, Harlem, Upper Manhattan, the Bronx, Brooklyn, Queens, and Newark. In the farther reaches of what was once farmland they also built neighborhoods of single-family homes. As time went on, and more and more people came, developers began to demolish Manhattan's row-house blocks and replace them with larger apartment, factory, and office buildings all over Hell's Kitchen, the East 50s, and the Upper West and Upper East Sides, and finally, everywhere (see Figure 6.4 in Chapter 6). New York City became very dense, especially Manhattan and Downtown Brooklyn, places where the civic infrastructure of schools, parks, transit, and ease of access to work in the business districts gave them high locational value.

For their part, residents responded to the permanent affordability problems in ways that varied by income level. Those with the least money crowded themselves into the cheapest housing possible, in the doing creating the crowded, famed immigrant neighborhoods of Harlem, Yorkville, Hell's Kitchen, and the Lower East Side. Others resigned themselves to long commutes from remoter corners of the city and the Tri-State region. And those with the most money—if they even stayed in the city—soon accepted the emerging lifestyle of multistory apartment living, although row-house living remains a primary aspiration to this day. That said, the city's first generation of elite row-house owners quickly found their spacious homes too costly: Within a generation they began to subdivide the single-family row houses into rooming houses and smaller apartments. Boardinghouses and single-room occupancy hotels served every demographic and remained thick on the ground across most of the boroughs until the 1980s. As time went on and excessive density made life too difficult in the densest parts of Manhattan, many residents of the historic core moved to the suburbs or outer boroughs into spacious single-family homes, or into big apartment buildings in the Bronx or farther out in Queens and Brooklyn.

For their part, city and state government responded to the housing affordability problem with a strange mix of policies, which amounted to filling a bucket while at the same time punching holes in it. To its credit, the city facilitated the explosion of mass transit that spread housing around the Tri-State metro area. Streetcars, trains, subways, and ferries knitted the region together to bring workers into the historic core to work in the booming business, waterfront, and manufacturing districts. The city even supported rent control as early as the 1920s—over the objections of the real estate industry, and eventually, rent stabilization (in the 1960s). Nonetheless, starting just before World War II, the city began to destroy as much affordable housing as it could in misguided slum clearance projects. The city demolished immense vibrant neighborhoods of great urbanity and replaced them with badly built, mostly high-rise public housing and highways. In the 1970s, the city also developed policies to replace single-room occupancy (SRO) hotels and incentivized the conversion of low-cost rental housing into more expensive co-op ownership structures. In the 1960s and 1970s, the city also engaged in a planned shrinkage policy that allowed large areas of affordable housing in poorer neighborhoods to burn (Flood 2011). Everything happened in an overlapping manner, so it is no surprise that city government also flip-flopped in the policy realm and ultimately just eroded one of New York's bedrock affordable housing mechanisms: rent control and stabilization. All these contradictory actions made the affordable housing market a maelstrom, and within it, the stock of affordable housing was continuously shrinking.

In the 2000s, a conservative economist named Edward Glaeser entered the city's policy scene. We look at his ideas in this chapter because politicians as disparate as Donald Trump, Barack Obama, Elizabeth Warren, and Joe Biden adopted them. In New York, Glaeser's influence grew in the Bloomberg "luxury city" years when Glaeser wrote popular manifestos like *Triumph of the City* and marketed articles in *The Atlantic* such as "How Skyscrapers Can Save the City." He proclaimed to be in possession of a solution to New York's eternal affordable housing "crisis." Journalists loved his pitch: a Harvard Economist with a recipe for success that was merely (in his words) "Econ 101." When the mayor who followed Bloomberg, Bill de Blasio, named one of Glaeser's colleagues and academic co-authors as deputy mayor for housing, it seemed clear that Glaeser had accomplished the full conquest of New York's housing policy scene. Glaeser-inspired housing policy has continued into the administration of New York's new mayor as of this writing, Eric Adams. It dominates policy discussion with glib phrases like "let's be a City of Yes." Glaeser's victory in the city's policy world was no accident. He was a frequent keynote speaker at real estate industry gatherings and had the full backing of the ultra-conservative Manhattan Institute, all of which facilitated the spread of his ideas (Peck 2016).

The problem in New York, Glaeser told everyone, is that *height restrictions* in Manhattan cause the city's high housing prices. His solution is to get rid of zoning and height regulations, deregulate New York's housing market, and unleash real estate developers to build upward to create a massive housing "supply shock." In pushing his policy, Glaeser has been relentless in pointing out that the historic city will need to be demolished and the Landmarks Preservation Commission removed from relevance. Glaeser and his followers promise that if we do what they say and build enough tower housing in the historic core of Manhattan, New York's historic housing affordability problem will be solved.

Glaeser's views reflect his training at the economics department of the University of Chicago, a libertarian hot spot. That school of thought holds that "free" markets always give the best solution to all problems. Libertarians also think government cannot possibly do regulation right, that ham-fisted bureaucrats will inevitably make things worse. The libertarian bent is in marked contrast to the rest of the economics discipline that recognizes a different reality: Markets are almost always imperfect and rarely generate optimal solutions; hence regulation is an inevitable necessity. But more on that later.

Consider Glaeser's vision in his own words:

- "Cities need to be torn down to build up" (Leonhardt 2011, 2).
- "Nothing would be lost in NY's DNA by replacing 10-story post-war buildings with 40-story buildings. I will defend that to my grave . . ." (Jenkins 2015a).
- "In the most desirable cities, whether they're on the Hudson River or the Arabian Sea, height is the best way to keep prices affordable and living standards high" (Glaeser 2011).
- "Manhattan will get more affordable only if it permits a lot of really high structures" (Glaeser, Gyourko, and Saks 2003).
- "A city of 20 million people occupying a tiny landmass could be housed in corridors of skyscrapers" (Jenkins 2015a).
- Landmarking buildings amounts to "a massive expropriation of private property" and "I hope that the mayor and city council will rein the [landmarks] commission in" (Glaeser 2006).
- Historic districts are "freezing up large tracts of land rendering them unable to accommodate the thousands of people [in high-rises] who would like to live in Manhattan but cannot afford to" (Glaeser 2010).
- "The natural thing is to have tall buildings in the center, where demand is greatest, not on the edge" (in a statement criticizing the way Paris created a high-rise business district on the outskirts of the historic city called "La Defense") (Jenkins 2015).
- "More attractive neighborhoods in a free market would end up having taller buildings" (Glaeser, Gyourko, and Saks 2003, 11).
- "As long as building in the high-rise district is sufficiently unfettered . . ." prices will trickle down (Glaeser 2011).
- "High productivity, high amenity places are *underbuilt*" and should be replaced with towers, such as found in Shanghai or Dubai (Glaeser, Gyourko, and Saks 2003, 7).
- Less productive, less attractive places with cheaper land should have fewer people (Queens, the Bronx, and Staten Island) and more people should be moved to the attractive "high amenity" places in Manhattan where there are "attractive," historic, and "core" neighborhoods that he thinks are "underbuilt" (Glaeser, Gyourko, and Saks 2003).

I call Glaeser's theory "trickle-down housing supply fundamentalism." This chapter is about what is wrong with Glaeser's theory. These pages examine his ideas, explore what other critics have said about them, and refute the theory with historical information as to the cause of the affordability problem in New York City. The upshot is that trickle-down housing supply fundamentalism is based on overly simplistic economic ideas and has no place in affordable housing policy for the city. The policy is deeply destructive in older, complex cities like New York that have an intact urban DNA that includes vast historic fabric and human-scale neighborhoods. This chapter focuses on a series of working papers Glaeser produced between 2002 and 2005 (the Bloomberg period) when Glaeser set out the core ideas that have come to define trickle-down housing supply fundamentalism.[1]

Introduction to Trickle-Down Housing Supply Fundamentalism

Trickle-down housing supply fundamentalism turns out to be exactly what you imagine it to be: If we "unfetter" private developers to do what they want without regulation, we'll get a boom in the construction of luxury tower apartments. (In the preceding chapter we saw architect Chakrabarti echoing that idea.) And then, fundamentalists promise, luxury housing prices will start to fall. Soon thereafter, housing prices at the next price tier will fall and so on down the "housing ladder." In the unspecified long run, lower prices will "trickle down" to those at the very bottom of the housing market. Readers may recall this kind of trickle-down, libertarian-inflected economic theory became popular when President Ronald Reagan supported it in 1981.

Part of the theory includes the notion of "filtering." Upward filtering is a process in which the rich move from older housing to new "better" towers, freeing up the older housing for poorer households. There is also downward filtering. That happened in many historic districts of New York when artists, the middle class, and Hollywood movie stars left the Upper West and East Sides and sought out decaying row houses, historic lofts, and warehouses as homes. In New York, when downward filtering happened, the old apartment buildings on the Upper West and East Sides got filled up instead with equally prosperous people from around the city, country, and world who appeared to have an insatiable appetite for Manhattan real estate. A large segment of the prospering gentry of New York continue to aspire to owning the city's shrinking pool of human-scale row houses, including Mayors Bloomberg (who bought two of them) and De Blasio, and even Deputy Mayor for Housing Vicki Been (who sold her spectacular single-family Village townhouse for $19 million in 2022, as announced in the *Real Deal*).

Glaeser posits the existence of a powerful coalition of allied groups who stand in the way of his vision: white people living in "unfairly" rent-stabilized apartments; "blue-haired" co-op and condo owners; and "villainous" preservationists (the words in quotes are words fundamentalists like to use). Glaeser sees this coalition as squatting like a dog in a manger atop low-rise buildings in the historic centers of high-growth city centers such as Manhattan, preventing their buildings from being demolished and replaced with glass towers for lower-income people (Glaeser, Gyourko, and Saks 2003; Jenkins 2015; Glaeser 2012, 151; Been 2018). The fundamentalist storyline maintains that Manhattan and brownstone Brooklyn homeowners are motivated by the goal of increasing their property values and to that end manipulate politicians and zoning codes to prevent new construction. Fundamentalists support this storyline without data—beyond a few cherry-picked anecdotes—but it makes for a good story.

Fundamentalists don't leave it at that. In one influential simulation model produced by economists of the fundamentalist persuasion, "the misallocation" of unemployed Rust Belt labor "stuck in Detroit" inside what Glaeser dubs "loser" cities (places where the jobs were lost to China or the union-free South) is the cause of trillions of dollars of imaginary lost Gross Domestic Product (GDP) growth (Hsieh and Moretti 2018). Fundamentalists believe high housing prices in Manhattan block the movement of those unemployed Rust Belt workers into the city, since those unemployed steelworkers can't afford to move to expensive Manhattan apartments lining Central Park. This "blocking" implies a loss of the GDP that these workers might have been producing if only they left Detroit and Ohio and made themselves productive in the financial and tech industries of Manhattan.[2] In the same way, supply fundamentalists speculate that high housing prices in Manhattan might also block the timeless career moves of high-wage Ivy League college graduates into New York City, thus preventing them from also serving as GDP producers for Manhattan's tech and financial industries. In the fundamentalist framework of perfect markets, wageworkers move around the country in search of cheap housing prices instead of searching for jobs. That part of their story is contrary to the facts in New York City. But it is a popular line of thought.

Within the Glaeser camp is a large network of political bloggers and activists who peddle a libertarian, Yes In My Backyard, YIMBY-style fundamentalism sometimes called "market urbanism." They agitate on social media that zoning must be done away with to combat the "exclusionary sentiment of wealthy enclaves they believe prevents cities from becoming more equitable" (Raskin 2018). In New York City, there are now real estate–funded YIMBY groups with wealthy donors. One donor gave the group $1.5 million to hire full-time lobbyists from the pool of City Council staffers, a move that tempered their bellicose and bullying behavior at hearings but made them more successful.[3]

The popularity of the fundamentalist anti-regulatory analysis and their take-no-prisoners agenda (Upzone! Demolish! Build now!) has led to much crudity in analysis and policy discussion. For example, fundamentalists often lump together places as historically, physically, and economically distinct as the Virginia and New Jersey suburbs, Las Vegas, Detroit, New Orleans, New York City, Los Angeles, and San Francisco (Glaeser and Gyourko 2003).

To understand Glaeser, it helps to have some context for his supply-side rhetoric. Econ 101 textbooks describe a world where suppliers of a thing (such as builders of housing) and demanders (such as the renters and buyers of homes) interact in an invisible auction to determine the final price of a commodity such as housing. Econ 101 tells us that the buyers and sellers will reach an equilibrium point at a magical price where no more demanders exist who are willing to buy the product at that price and no more suppliers exist who are willing to sell the product at the same price. The marketplace has "cleared" or emptied. Supply-siders believe that the interesting price-determining action inside these market auctions is among the suppliers, not the demanders.

Glaeser and his colleagues point out that they are interested in the supply side of the market since "other" academics "ignore the supply side" (Glaeser, Gyourko, and Saks 2005, 2) and thus they are only rectifying a gap in theory. Glaeser and his team note in one paper that "it is noteworthy that we do not focus on the housing demand side" (Glaeser and Gyourko 2002, 4; Glaeser, Gyourko, and Saks 2003). Ignoring the demand-side of the market frees Glaeser to put out his oft-repeated hypothesis that "housing is expensive because of artificial limits on construction created by the regulation of new housing." In another paper he declares the same hypothesis in a different way: "Homes are expensive in high-cost areas primarily because of government regulation, i.e., zoning" (Glaeser, Gyourko, and Saks 2003, 5).

Sometimes Glaeser introduces into his Manhattan arguments a straw-man puzzle: Developers are making huge profits in Manhattan, far above what Glaeser thinks are the actual costs of construction. Why, he wonders, are developers not tearing everything down and rebuilding like crazy so that profits get driven down to zero like Econ 101 ideas would suggest? He seems blind to the empirical reality that the pace of demolition has been furious in New York City for decades. For example, between 1985 and 2018, 44,622 buildings have been demolished (New York City Rent Guidelines Board 2019, 23), which makes for about four buildings demolished every single day for thirty-two years, the bulk of them in Manhattan.

Moreover, ignoring the demand for Manhattan real estate as an investment asset leads Glaeser and his followers to a strange conclusion borrowed from the literature on suburban housing markets. They insist that the fault for excessive zoning and regulation must lie with those creatures that planners and journalists loathe: "NIMBYs." In the planning literature, NIMBYs are those people in the suburbs who oppose the construction of apartment buildings and who want big zoning lots for single-family homes instead. Glaeser and his co-authors bring this argument right into Manhattan; to wit, high housing prices in Manhattan are:

> The consequence of an increasingly restrictive regulatory environment. In Manhattan and in other parts of the country, local homeowners have become more and more competent in blocking new development which they presumably oppose because the new development would reduce the value of their property either because of increased supply or because of congestion-related externalities. (Glaeser, Gyourko, and Saks 2003, 3)

Glaeser puts together an algebraic model to illustrate these core ideas, with the usual troubling assumptions common to this kind of model. Sidebar 2.1 provides a list of those problematic assumptions. I discuss the most important of these problems below.

Problem: Ignoring Demand Is a Breathtaking Error

Readers and policymakers should strongly object to a one-sided supply-side theory from the get-go. It leaves out too many other causes. Glaeser does admit in an aside that in places like Manhattan it could be that "high wages and attractive amenities made demand for the space understandable" (notably among the worldwide investor class), but he doubles down on the notion that "increases in the demand for housing *need not always* create such large price increases" (Glaeser, Gyourko, and Saks 2003, 2; emphasis mine).

This supply obsession is a blind spot. Worldwide demand of investors for NYC housing as an investment asset is an immense part of the city's

Sidebar 2.1
Summary of Problematic Assumptions in Glaeser's Trickle-Down Theorizing on NYC Housing Supply

1. Regulations and the regulatory state are bad things. The "free market" will always provide the best solution, if only we would "unfetter" real estate developers.
2. NYC real estate industry is a "textbook case of perfect competition."
3. Housing consumers are alike ("homogeneous" in the economic sense, see elsewhere in this chapter for details).
4. Developer profits can be redefined as a "regulatory tax."
5. Density is a "normal good" for consumers.
6. The only regulations that might affect housing prices are those having to do with height or that prevent historic districts from being demolished and replaced.
7. We can accurately measure how zoning affects prices.
8. The deliberate destruction of affordable housing at the low end of the market is irrelevant to housing prices. (Fundamentalists ignore the problem that city politicians, at the behest of the real estate industry, have purposefully induced a housing shortage at the bottom of the market over an eighty-year period.)
9. The assumption that demand is irrelevant to housing prices implies that the following four demand factors are irrelevant to the price of housing in NYC:
    a) Manhattan's geographic reality as an island that is already densely built out.
    b) Poverty—when some 20 percent of the city's population lives on less than $25,000 a year.
    c) The presence of a parallel housing market of one million rent-stabilized housing units.
    d) The tsunami of international real estate capital seeking to invest in NYC that has long been crowding out local consumers and inflating prices, a problem abetted by the excessive "financialization" of housing.
10. NIMBYs are in control of zoning such that the real estate "growth machine" is out of power and residents in NYC behave like monopolists trying to raise the price of their housing.
11. The skydome over the city and with it the light, air, and direct access to sunlight are all free resources that are infinitely elastic and can be handed over to developers without significant negative externalities. Indeed, the social costs and negative externalities of his policy proposal to towerize the city are assumed to be minimal, or in his words, "trivial," or "insignificant."
12. Housing units and human density can grow infinitely without regard to the underlying carrying capacity of the natural and physical infrastructure, or the common resource of great urbanity.
13. The theories about racist exclusionary zoning that are popular among analysts of housing supply in the single-family home world of suburbia can be usefully adapted to theorizing about Manhattan's housing market.
14. The social welfare of an imagined future upper middle class of high-tax-paying residents is worth more than the social welfare of current residents.

housing market. The financial press even describes world investor demand for New York real estate as a "tsunami" that has clearly raised housing prices for locals, in a price climb widely "fueled by speculation and exuberance" (Martin 2019; 2016). This has long been happening in NYC and is a frequent topic of delight in the real estate press (Solomont and Sun 2019). It is odd that Glaeser chooses to ignore the phenomenon. But policymakers should not ignore it. The indicators of the scale of international investment demand are many. *The Real Deal* reported that according to the latest U.S. Census Bureau data, a whopping 60 percent of residences in a fourteen-block tract of Midtown East between 49th and 56th streets (mostly new towers) were "seasonally vacant" between 2013 and 2017. This is a large indicator of investor demand for new tower housing. StreetEasy's economist for New York City reported that "nearly 30% of the condos built since 2013 have been listed for rent on StreetEasy" rather than occupied by their owners (Long 2018), another indicator of investor demand. Real estate financier Robert Knakal pointed out that foreign investors poured an average of $3.9 billion a year into New York's real estate market between 2007 and 2014, about "16% of the total capital deployed into the market" and that foreign investment tripled over the subsequent three years (2015–2018) such that it eventually made up "42% of capital deployed" in the city's real estate market. Knakal also pointed out that even after the industry recognized that the market for luxury condos and rental units was oversaturated, the annual average of foreign investment into the real estate sector since 2018 continued to rise to a whopping $6.23 billion (Knakal 2019). All this took place before the more recent flood of capital that the new "opportunity funds" have unleashed upon the city.[4]

It is impossible to imagine that investment demand of this scale for hard assets has not had the effect of raising the prices of housing, crowding out locals from the market, and explaining the huge profits that real estate developers have been getting in the "hot" markets of the city. The astonishing speculative churn may also explain the finding (reported to the NYC Department of Housing Preservation, and Development) that the hot markets of the city in the historic core had a "yield on capital" of 93 percent if invested in luxury condos.[5]

The upshot is that income-constrained New York City residents cannot compete with the world's Real Estate Investment Trusts (REITs) and foreign investors pouring into New York City looking for a place to park capital. Developers are supplying an asset for the world's rich, not the local middle class, let alone the poor, and there has been no sign in New York City that prices are falling in the infamous trickle-down effect despite a spectacular pace of demolition and reconstruction.

It is also disturbing how much of the profit from all this activity ends up leaving New York City. The case of just one of the large REITs invested in NYC, Equity Residential, illustrates the point. The Chicago-based firm owns 10,007 housing units in New York, mostly in newly built glass towers in Manhattan. Equity Residential brags to its shareholders about the wealth of its tenants and reports that it drains nearly *half a billion dollars in rents out of New York City* every year—$466,646,424 to be exact (Mandzy 2017). At least old school tenement slumlords lived in New York City and spent their haul locally!

By ignoring demand factors, fundamentalists are imposing such stringent boundary conditions (meaning rules about where the model can apply) on their model that their conclusions end up baked into the creation of the model itself. Assuming away every other demand explanation for high housing prices, or simply ignoring them and brushing aside the entire empirical messiness of how New York's housing market works, does not make for useful explanations. With all demand explanations dismissed, fundamentalists conclude that zoning regulations are limiting the ability of developers to towerize the city into a competitive equilibrium. That means, if they were allowed to towerize, prices would trickle down lower and developer's profits would, if you believe Econ 101 fairy tale versions of economic theory, fall to zero. Got that?

Last, why ignore the problem that is presented by the weak market power of the city's population of low-income families? As of 2017, some 24 percent of the city's households earn less than $25,000 a year (Baruch College 2017). They don't have enough money to jump into the housing market and have "their" demand for housing affect what suppliers of housing build, a fact well established since the 1910s by housing reformers.

Problem: Casting Price Markups as a Regulatory Tax Is Obfuscation

In constructing his argument, Glaeser and co-authors make an interesting rhetorical decision to never use the word "profit." They refer instead to "price markups" and then are puzzled when these markups exceed the actual cost of building a unit of housing in New York City. Why aren't these "price markups" falling to zero as economic theory suggests they should be in perfect markets of Econ 101? Glaeser and his co-authors decide that price "markups" are a "regulatory tax" (Glaeser, Gyourko, and Saks 2003, 5)—which they might be if there was proof that their excess profits were caused by regulation, but we don't have that proof. They do not consider that the markups—meaning excess profits—might be due to market structure, special characteristics of the Manhattan market like the grid or monopoly power or barriers to entry, macro-economic conditions, or some other demand-side consideration. This is a brilliant oratorical leap, for it transforms developer profits into a flaw of regulatory government, not a flaw in the economist's theorizing or in the structure of the market.

Problem: Perfect Competition among Developers Is Not a Credible Assumption and New York Development Field Is Full of Barriers to Entry

Glaeser and colleagues describe NYC's real estate industry as "a textbook case of perfect competition," claiming it "is a highly competitive industry with almost no natural barriers to entry" (Glaeser, Gyourko, and Saks 2003, 1). Hence, they are surprised at the existence of excessive profits, which of course can exist, as Glaeser notes, "when monopoly power is present." They prefer to get rid of that stumbling block by claiming that monopoly power is just "not relevant to the home-building industry" (Glaeser, Gyourko, and Saks 2003, 5).

But hold on there! The assumption of perfect competition requires all kinds of conditions to exist, few of which are present in New York's housing market. For example, all buyers and sellers must have perfect and equal information about the market; there can be no barriers for housing firms to enter the market; all buyers must make choices over differentiable preference functions (obviously not happening in housing); all housing units must just be varieties of apples—meaning perfect substitutes for each other—all the inputs into building have to be perfectly mobile and elastically available so that suppliers can make the product quickly, and nobody can be powerful enough to set prices. Yet the only evidence Glaeser gives to justify the perfect housing market is his observation that there were 1,000 registered multi-home builders in New York State (Glaeser, Gyourko, and Saks 2003, 4). That is a head-scratcher: The number of firms with contractor licenses in New York State does not imply that the industry is competitive.

There is also evidence—not just in New York—that the perfect competition assumption in the real estate industry more generally is just not realistic. As early as 1978, Martin Mayer reported on near-monopoly conditions in the single-family home industry of Dallas. There, the homebuilder Fox & Jacobs had already built "65% of all the new homes in the lower and lower-middle end of the price spectrum." A competing builder complained that he had to abandon the market there "because he ran into the power of Fox & Jacobs." The CEO of Fox & Jacobs even admitted that he used his market position to "under-build a little so as to get continuity" of demand (Mayer 1978, 230). Other economists have found that for the real estate industry as a whole, "increasing concentration in the past decade has led to lower production volume, fewer units in the production pipeline, and greater unit price volatility" (Cosman and Quintero 2018). In the same vein, Somerville (1999) notes that homebuilders in the United States are better regarded as "monopolistically competitive," not perfectly competitive. Michael Porter, one of Glaeser's competitors for Harvard Guru status, notes that the average return on invested capital to homebuilding in the U.S. is 15 percent, well above average for any industry, a red flag for monopolistic conditions. He notes that barriers to entry in homebuilding have been rising, and that the industry underwent a huge consolidation in the 1990s (Porter 2003).

Industry insiders to New York have also long commented on the oligarchic, familial, and dynastic character of the city's unique real estate development industry (Brenzel and McHugh-Chiappone 2017) and (Pincus 2013). In that vein, note that the real estate press reported in 2018 that just three property owners control 75 percent of Manhattan's office space: SL Green, Vornado, and Brookfield (Schram 2019; Small 2018). In a related data point, the *Real Deal* found that the five largest landlords in NYC have about 40,000 apartments among them (Sun 2018) and that the largest twenty landlords (all big corporate entities) control at least 152,000 apartments among them, about 15 percent of the "market rate" housing stock in NYC. Those numbers, according to the author of the report, are biased downward because of how ownership remains shrouded in secrecy laws that disguise building ownership within limited liability corporations.

Perfect competitiveness also implies a nimble industry, able to react quickly to changes in prices, including prices to inputs like steel, concrete, glass, and labor. Yet StreetEasy's economist reported that despite a glut of 25 percent of unsold condos built since 2013, more than 5,617 additional luxury units, were still in the construction pipeline or already listed for rent on StreetEasy, hardly an indicator of nimbleness (Long 2018).

Another indicator of lack of competitiveness is a finding from industry analyst and insider Nancy Packes. She reports that during the 2018 supply glut of new luxury apartments, prices of the luxury rental units nonetheless kept rising. How so? She found that developers were using "concessions to stabilize and grow gross rents" such that "lower net rents sped absorption so that on average during the years of the supply glut, gross rents kept rising" (Packes 2018, 3). What this puzzle means is that developers gave away things like free move-ins, free access to building amenities for a temporary period, an elimination of security deposits, or more famously, reimbursement for the punishing 15 percent "brokers fee" that New York renters have had to pay for generations (one regulation that surely could be eliminated), but rents did not fall.

Financing of new towers in the historic core of New York City is unquestionably a significant barrier to entry. The real estate press such as the *Real Deal* and *Commercial Observer* often report on the length of time it takes for financing dramas to play out among the big skyscraper builders. For example, mega-developer Gary Barnett took three years to close on a $530 million loan for one of his Brooklyn towers (Gourarie 2018). In a similar case, Vornado (one of the country's largest real estate firms) took fourteen years to build a supertall skyscraper on 57th Street. Those included years of negotiating a $1.1 billion loan to pay for the construction. In Vornado's case, the firm had to first buy the existing twenty-story building on the site and evict all the tenants before demolishing it. The tenants did not want to leave. It is worth pointing out that the only real constraint Barnett faced wasn't a regulatory one, but the resistance of another mega-developer who wanted in on Barnett's profits and decided to be stubborn about selling the underground parking garage on the site (Hudson 2019). Mobilizing this amount of capital is obviously a huge barrier to entry as is Manhattan's famous problem of assembling a site big enough to build a tower.

Warehousing is another practice that suggests a lack of competition. *The City* reported in October 2022 about a state agency housing memo that noted that New York City had more than 60,000 empty apartments that property owners were withholding from the rental market, and not just to conduct renovations. The same report noted that 95,000 rent-stabilized units were mysteriously "lost" to the rent-stabilization program just one year after the 2021 rent reforms took place. Tenant groups speculate that the scale of this warehousing effort may be a concerted effort by landlords to nudge the city to a greater than 5 percent vacancy rate, at which point the "housing emergency" would be officially over, thus ending the reason for rent stabilization's existence (Rabiyah 2020).

Stepping back from a specific case, "perfect" competition in almost any industry is impossible. Economists assume the existence of perfect competition to allow the use of differentiable mathematical functions—essential for them to illustrate their theoretical ideas in academic journals. But it does not follow that they are describing a meaningful reality that is relevant to policy. One of the discipline's Nobel laureates, Joseph Stiglitz, found that imperfect information among market participants can render the quest for equilibrium or "optimality" pointless because in the real world, imperfect information is always present in markets. Stiglitz has long called for economists to reorient the way they theorize in consequence of his theoretical and empirical insights into imperfect information. In his own humorous summary of the problem, Stiglitz explained in an interview that the imperfections in markets mean that "the invisible hand is invisible because it is not there" (Stiglitz 1991, 5).

Problem: Density Is Not Infinitely Desirable as a "Normal" Good in Economic Terms and Cannot Be Expanded Infinitely

Fundamentalists (and most urban planners and architects) are deeply confused in their thinking about density (see subsequent chapters for more on this). In one place, Glaeser and colleagues assume density is a "normal good," meaning that as people get richer, they want more density. But this is clearly not the case, given the strong national preference for single-family homes in the suburbs, as depressing as that fact is to urbanists everywhere. In another paper, Glaeser and his co-authors declare without any evidence that much new residential building in Manhattan "has occurred at fairly low densities" which is a meaningless and inaccurate generalization given that much new residential construction has happened at spectacularly high densities, such as on the Upper East Side or among some of the skyscrapers in Battery Park City. Glaeser's vagueness on density leads him to make breathtakingly wrong statements about New York City's neighborhoods, one of them being that "even adding a large number of housing units and people [in Manhattan] will not change the basic nature of the place" (Glaeser, Gyourko, and Saks 2003, 30).

Empirically, density has a Goldilocks quality. Too low a density means the opposite of cities: big yards and garages and driveways and the inability to support street-level businesses. Too high a density leads to overcrowding and the many evils associated with being packed in like sardines, as the *New York Times* reported about Hong Kong (Stevenson and Wu 2019). Moreover, seekers of housing across income levels and ages have a range of attitudes toward density. Young people may love density at the beginning of their careers, but once more prosperous or married and with a second child on the way, they may find urban density an inferior good and seek out suburban life.

Problem: The Zoning Code Has Over 3,000 Pages, So Which Regulations Are We Talking about Anyway?

In the Glaeser story, even if we are hostile to regulation, only two things about regulations are important. First is the idea that the only zoning regulations that might affect price are those that concern height. The second is the notion that we can empirically connect a specific zoning rule about height to housing prices in New York City. Glaeser knows these are big problems, admitting, "Regulation of the housing market is extremely challenging to quantify" (Glaeser, Gyourko, and Saks 2003, 3) and that "we cannot measure the price impact of any specific [zoning] policy" (Glaeser, Gyourko, and Saks 2003, 4). Nonetheless, that is exactly what he claims to be attempting. He mashes together all zoning and building codes and state laws into that one word, "zoning," which he casts as a "bad" while ignoring the reality of how zoning works in New York City and the puzzle of what specific regulations might affect housing prices, and whether the price effect is positive or negative or even policy relevant.

The zoning resolution in New York runs over 3,000 pages. Which of those pages are guilty of raising housing prices in NYC? Might it be the ones requiring parking or windows in bedrooms? And wait, there are also regulations related to construction safety for workers, fire codes, and even the Multiple Dwelling Law of New York State, which isn't in the zoning code. The latter is the law that created successful "new law" tenement buildings, one of the most affordable kinds of housing ever built in New York. How do you disentangle which of the regulations are having cost-increasing consequences of a fatal, eliminate-the-regulation-at-all-costs urgency? The answer is you can't.

The fundamentalist framework also misses the point of how malleable and pro-developer zoning is in New York City. As we shall see in other chapters, developers and real estate insiders have had a heavy hand in the drafting of the zoning code to the point that informed insiders believe the final product presents no obstacle at all to developer ambitions. City Planning routinely pushes through spot rezonings on top of multiple procedures to get "special permits," "discretionary approvals," and "variances" that allow developers to break the public interest rules. Subsequent chapters elaborate in detail on these points.

Finally, fundamentalists have failed to accurately measure the relationship between zoning regulations and housing prices in a complicated city like New York. The task might be easier in the sprawling McMansion-world of the Virginia suburbs where availability of farmland, lot size, and single-family rules are likely the only things slowing down housing production. But New York is not the suburbs. So, what to do? In one paper, Glaeser and his co-authors try to measure the evil of "zoning" with a proxy variable: the number of permits issued each year by the Department of Buildings. But NYC building permits are easily granted, manipulated by minor bribes (according to at least one developer who spoke in confidence to this author), and more reflective of wider market conditions than they are of regulatory overreach. Moreover, 80 percent of all development in New York is as of right and comes with no zoning oversight beyond a building permit. In another paper, Glaeser relies on the Wharton Regulatory Index to be a stand-in for the evils of zoning overreach. But that is also a deeply flawed creation. It is created from responses of real estate insiders and planners to a questionnaire about their perceptions of regulatory problems. As anyone who has witnessed the long line of real estate lobbyists complaining about regulations at a NYC public hearing can testify, this is quite possibly the most biased group possible on the subject.

Problem: New York's Sky Is Being Treated Like Infinitely Available Free Commons That Nobody Owns and Is Just There for Developers to Take

Trickle-down housing supply theory requires land to be infinitely "elastic" and thus available to developers in any scalable amount. This is clearly not the case. How can that be? Glaeser cites the case of greater Las Vegas, which met excess demand for single-family housing by making available thousands of acres of empty land for vast new McMansion suburbs. Obviously, in Las Vegas, land was, for a short time, "elastically supplied" due to the unique geographic and historical circumstances of having a large desert to expand into. But even then Glaeser is incorrect, as the Las Vegas suburbs were soon flooded with international investors who speculated quite ruthlessly there (Chinco and Mayer 2014).

And obviously, Manhattan is not Las Vegas. There is no longer anything resembling a buildable hinterland. It was long ago built-out to every parcel and is already dense with not just people, but also history, character, and architecture. The Borough of Manhattan is also an island, making land supply even more dramatically inelastic. Moreover, the value of land in New York is mostly determined by its locational proximity to historic architecture and to the quality of the immediately available public infrastructure of parks, schools, business districts, and subways.

Faced with this geographic reality, Glaeser decides that it is the air and sky above NYC that should be transformed into a new, infinitely elastic variable of production, to be the new empty hinterland that Las Vegas once had. Planners think of it as the "skydome," and it is a public, common property asset (see Figure 4.5 in Chapter 4). But to Glaeser, the sky is a limitless frontier, a free resource to be ruthlessly mined, much like the once seemingly infinite gold deposits in the Alaskan Yukon. Developers see it that way too, explicitly thinking of air rights as "found money" (Finn 2013). Glaeser never considers that that resource, too, might be limited and owned by the public and merely in need of better management rather than privatized and auctioned off to the world's wealthy as views onto Central Park.

Problem: Why Ignore That Zoning Has a Public Purpose?

Zoning in New York City originated in outrage in 1913 over the Equitable Building's unfair seizure of light and air. New Yorkers saw the Equitable Building, at only forty stories, as monstrously tall, taking away a public asset—sunlight—from neighborhood office buildings. The City Council justified the original 1916 zoning resolution with a clearly stated legal intent written into the law itself: to assure that sunlight, air, and density were distributed to assure the public welfare. These public purposes have withstood Supreme Court challenges.

That might provoke the reader to wonder: Might zoning regulations about building heights be "socially desirable" even within economic theory? Of course, that is the case. Glaeser admits it when he notes in a brief aside, "If new construction generates negative externalities, then the optimal Regulatory Tax is positive" (Glaeser, Gyourko, and Saks 2003, 8), while he cautions that "welfare analysis of building restrictions are notoriously difficult to implement" (Glaeser, Gyourko, and Saks 2003, 12). He also admits that social cost analyses "are inherently difficult to perform," and that his own attempt to account for those costs is merely an "educated guess."[6]

Problem: The City Is Assumed to Have Infinite Carrying Capacity and Have Infinitely Elastic Public Resources for Hyper-dense Urban Life

Carrying capacity is a measure of how many people a given geographic place can sustain with a certain amount of existing natural resources under fixed technology. In the fundamentalist world, there is an infinitely expandable capacity to absorb more people on the sidewalks, streets, subways, parks, and schools.[7] Advocates of infinite growth think carrying capacity is meaningless and can be ignored, as technology will come to the rescue if things get overcrowded. But isn't that pre–global warming thinking? If the resources were infinite, it would mean there would be no gas moratoriums such as that which now exist throughout the outer boroughs of New York (St. John 2019).[8] What about sewage treatment capacity? The Newtown Creek Sewage Treatment Plant in Queens accepts most of the sewage on both sides of the East River, from the Two Bridges area of Manhattan to the East 50s. The plant cannot handle the volume of sewage and dumps the overflow into the East River "on average, once every 3 days in 2018" (Levine 2019). Sewage treatment just cannot keep pace with the existing city, let alone the massive volume of new construction.

The assumption of infinite carrying capacity and infinitely elastic resources also means that there must exist an infinitely expandable clean air supply. As of 2016, twelve NYC neighborhoods exceeded the World Health Organization's standard for deadly small particulate matter (PM 2.5), two of them in Manhattan's overly dense, overly crowded midtown business district (Hinsdale 2016), which was upzoned in 2013 for even greater density.

Looking at other public infrastructure, we can easily see that there are other kinds of resource limits that fundamentalists are ignoring. Take the research linking better student performance to smaller class sizes. Can we just fill up the schools with more kids without limit? If so, consider the underreported research finding that in overcrowded schoolrooms, high concentrations of carbon dioxide (over 945 ppm) result in compromised cognitive functioning (Allen et al. 2016). Pair that disturbing fact with the reality that already 30 percent of NYC classrooms already have more than thirty students (Haimson and Carrazana 2019) and the fact that dozens of schools cannot provide a mere three feet of personal space to each student (Gould and WNYC 2021).

Streets and sidewalks also face real constraints in how wide they are. The Department of Transportation already narrowed the sidewalks years ago to accommodate cars. Sidewalks and roadways are not infinitely malleable. And of course, the subways have limits too. The subways were at full capacity as far back as 1992 (Harris 1992, 137). An expert with the Metropolitan Transit Authority told the *New York Times* in pre-Covid 2012, "The system is at capacity all the time, except at night" (O'Leary 2012).

Problem: Fundamentalists Conjure a False NIMBY Bogeyman

The trope of the NIMBY bogeyman in New York City is endlessly presented in fundamentalist writings, with just anecdotal evidence, such as the case with Glaeser colleague Vicki Been's article titled "Supply Skepticism" or her paper "City NIMBYism" or City Planning staffer John Mangin's paper called "Exclusionary Zoning" in NYC (Been 2018; Been and Ellen 2018; Mangin 2014). But this is red herring rhetorical strategy. Leaving aside the patronizing insult that the word NIMBY is assumed to embody, the evidence in New York City contradicts the notion of NIMBY urban power. NIMBYs are not, as Glaeser alleges, mysteriously able to make unverifiable credible "threats" to developers with legal actions that stop tall buildings. In fact, opponents to over-scaled projects so rarely get their way in New York City that it is always newsworthy when they do, which may account for YIMBYs confirmation bias when they cite this or that anecdote. Community groups cannot afford to hire lawyers, and it is telling that in the Penn Station lawsuit, the major donor to the legal fight is another large property owner opposed to Vornado's ambitions, not rank-and-file New Yorkers. To those more familiar with the city's politics, it is laughter-inducing when Glaeser declares that the infamous "urban growth machine" (which refers to the economic and political lobby for unfettered, unregulated real estate growth discussed in future chapters [Molotch 1976]) has "weakened" so much in NYC that political power is now all in the hands of homeowners in New York City. More accurately, urbanist Susan Fainstein in a review of a twenty-year period concluded that "community groups have received only limited concessions to their demands" (Fainstein and Fainstein 1992, 317).

The recent years since 2020 provide many counterfactuals. For example, note that all the supertall skyscrapers now lining 57th Street were built without political fights. All were "as of right" projects that took place without any NIMBY battles that so irritate trickle-down housing supply fundamentalists. Indeed, the vocal objections of neighbors and nonprofits to these supertalls have been pointedly ignored for years. Most development is just as of right. During the De Blasio administration, there were 403 completed "Uniform Land Use Review" applications that took place between De Blasio's first swearing-in ceremony and October of 2019. New York's City Council only rejected 1 percent of those land use applications and only demanded improvements to them in 15 percent of cases. The council members' votes were not even aligned with prior negative votes by community boards. And of the six cases that the council rejected, developers resubmitted the projects, which all went flying through to approval.

It has long been the case that when it comes to real estate battles, City Council members do the mayor's bidding, not the bidding of their constituents, as shown in the rezoning cases of East Harlem, Inwood, Gowanus, East New York, Flushing, and East Midtown, all of which took place under Mayor de Blasio over substantial community opposition. More than 90 percent of community boards voted against the ZQA/MIH upzoning plans of Mayor de Blasio known as "Zoning for Quality and Affordability/Mandatory Inclusionary Housing," yet the plan passed without a hitch in the City Council and without significant modifications.

Community board votes and opinions on real estate matters also carry no legal weight. For that reason, their votes and resolutions are most often ignored at the level of City Council unless they overlap with the council member's personal views. Council and community board hearings have long ago become pure political theater and have no policy relevance.

Therefore, on an empirical basis, the NIMBY bogeyman in Manhattan is a red herring and does not represent a significant or even meaningful regulatory hurdle, although it may be a problem in the suburbs where homeowners control their own small-town governments. To press the point even further, note that during a recent panel discussion about planning and real estate in New York City, Zachary Bernstein, the chair of the Real Estate Board of New York's zoning committee, responded to a question that the editor of *City Limits* posed: Would the Real Estate Board of New York seek reform of the Uniform Land Use Review Procedure (known as ULURP)? Bernstein replied in the negative, stating that "we don't have a problem with ULURP" and "the process works pretty well" for big real estate (Bernstein 2019). The talk of reform died on the vine.

It is therefore deeply incorrect to suggest that NIMBYs somehow dominate land use in NYC. The exact opposite is true: Real estate power holds all the cards, and the "growth machine" has long been in full throttle, despite the 2019 rent reforms that have gained so much attention. In a similar red herring, Glaeser claims that "existing residents will also try to behave like monopolists and will try to reduce supply [of housing] to boost their own home values," an assertion that is contrary to the facts. In the zoning battles over Chinatown, Inwood, Williamsburg, the East Fifties, East Harlem, and SoHo, residents came up with superior plans to add housing to their neighborhoods that better balanced new construction with historic character and avoided displacement of residents and small businesses. All those community plans were ignored or, in the case of Chinatown, simply rejected by a city planning administration that is enthralled by fundamentalist theorizing and rhetoric.

WILL BUILDING NEW TOWERS LOWER HOUSING PRICES? WHAT DOES THE EMPIRICAL RESEARCH SAY?

Will new towers with 35 percent of units designated as "affordable" in the Mandatory Inclusionary Housing model in NYC lower housing prices, and if so, for whom? The answer is, no, it will not lower housing prices in a significant way that would matter to policymakers or to housing consumers. At present, advocates of the trickle-down effect merely insist that they are right by a general affirmation and an attempt at false consensus. This happened when New York Councilman Brad Lander pointed out at a *City Limits* public seminar that Vicki Been's paper "Supply Skepticism" (Been and Ellen 2018) constituted indisputable proof for the idea that towers with Mandatory Inclusionary Housing units is the only way to take the policy bus.[9] He said that "anyone who read it" would "understand." Yet, in that paper, Been points merely to an ambiguous paper by Mast, a simulation study that found that new towers *could* lower housing prices (Mast 2019). Since simulation studies are different from looking at painstakingly acquired real empirical data, we need to look elsewhere for some kind of "proof." Luckily, we don't have to look far. Mast did a second study with real world data where he continues to argue that new towers *do* lower housing prices (Asquith, Mast, and Reed 2019). But the results he points to are so weak as to be irrelevant (see below). Moreover, we need to balance that kind of weak finding of a negative price effect of a supply shock with other, significant studies, including those by Freeman, Angotti, and Rypkema which find the opposite: New towers raise housing prices and cause a displacement effect. Looking through this literature, I observe that there are papers saying the effect on housing prices is either negative or neutral on displacement in New York, but also papers showing that the new towers raise housing prices and do displace low-income people. How should policymakers react to this?

The problem is that both outcomes can happen, in the same city, in different neighborhoods, and at different times. This happens because of the unique economies, histories, zoning rules, and political economies of each place. That means it is impossible to predict a priori what will happen when a new tower gets dumped into a low-income neighborhood. The new tower might do nothing to prices. It might worsen housing price inflation and displacement. It might relieve or worsen the gentrification pressure in the rest of the neighborhood. None of these things can be predicted in advance with any theoretical or empirical certainty.

But even more disturbing is this: In those cases where there is a documented downward effect on housing prices or rents, *the size of the actual price effect ranges from non-existent to minimal, so it is policy irrelevant.* This means that even if you think the supply-side fundamentalists are right, you aren't going to get much of a price drop for poor and moderate-income people if you implement their policy. And "filtering" will not save the day. The price effects are just not significant enough to matter, especially to those at the bottom third of the housing hierarchy or even to the middle class of New York. New York City is just not Hiram, Georgia.

Let's get into a few of the details of some of the more-cited fundamentalist papers to show how complicated it is to make the claim that a "supply shock" will lower housing prices. Asquith, Mast, and Reed (2019) claim to prove that when "a supply shock" happens to a low-income neighborhood by way of a new, isolated tower of mostly market-rate housing, prices will fall. To show this, they looked at the price effects within one city block of the completion of an isolated market-rate rental tower in eleven cities, including one in Brooklyn. They found the following:

- Rents were "increasing generally" in most cities at the time of their study, but on the blocks where the new tower arose, rents ended up about 5–6% lower than the citywide trend—*but only within one block of the new building and only over the three-year period after the building was completed* (a time frame that would not account for secondary displacement). Moreover, that rent decrease was very small, amounting to a fall in rent of about $105 a month within that one-block radius.
- The effect on prices was zero once past the block.
- The authors did not mention that the beneficiaries of this modest rent reduction were the gentrifiers—in-migrants who moved to the new building—not the existing low-income, rent-burdened people of the neighborhood.
- The median rents within that 250-foot radius of the new tower were $1,790, but in the larger, surrounding census tract were much lower (at $1,165) lending credence to the accusation that the towers were providing housing for the gentry, not affordable housing for the bottom half of the income distribution. The researchers merely mumble that the data about migration were so "noisy" that it was hard to tell who was moving in or out. "Noisy" generally refers to a data set that contains a lot of meaningless data within it.
- When they studied the same policy shock of putting a similar high-rise tower into a wealthier neighborhood in the historic core of the city (a "hot" market), the tiny, extremely localized depressive price effect disappears altogether, or rather, in their words, they find *"noise estimates that are statistically indistinguishable from zero,"* which the authors explain this way: "This may occur because the demand elasticity for established high-income areas is much larger than for gentrifying low-income areas, leading a supply shock [meaning the opening of a new giant tower] to have a smaller [meaning *statistically insignificant*] effect on prices," a point made often by economic geographer Michael Storper discussed later in this chapter.

A similar study for New York City alone mapped hundreds of new high-rises built over a ten-year period, mostly in Manhattan, and found that prices only declined for condo units within 500 feet of the new high-rise, but only by a trivial 1.6 percent, and even that tiny decline took place only within that limited radius and only relative to the larger increasing price movement happening in the city. *Outside of the 500-foot radius, the price effect was nil or "statistically insignificant"* (Li 2019). Another study found a trivial rent decrease in San Francisco of 2 percent within a mere 100 meters of a new tower, but the effect quickly disappeared once past the block. However, the researcher did find a significant gentrification effect: The area within 100 meters of the new tower was 29 percent more likely to experience an influx of wealthy residents (Pennington 2021).

None of these studies valued the damage to the city of such excessive demolition of historic properties and their replacement by luxury high rises. As discussed in the following chapter, fundamentalists incorrectly value that social cost at zero.

The most important conclusion to take away from these "housing prices will fall" studies is that even if you believe in them, the effect they find is so small and so contained, that the only way to have a significant effect on prices citywide is to literally demolish everything and rebuild the entire city as giant towers as fast as possible (within three years) in order to make a tiny dent on prices. Wouldn't it be simpler to simply build housing for the lower third of the income distribution, rather than wait for the trickle-down effect to occur in the imagined long run?[10]

A compelling study of Greenpoint and Williamsburg in New York City, places where Mayor Bloomberg upzoned and unleashed massive amounts of new construction of luxury housing in the Glaeser manner, found three interesting things:

- There was a decrease of 15,000 Latino residents of Greenpoint and Williamsburg, even though the population grew by 20,000 in the same period.
- Five thousand Black and Latino residents left Park Slope between 2000 and 2013, even though Park Slope grew by 6,000 people overall in that period.
- Greenpoint and Williamsburg had a net loss of 942 rent-stabilized housing units, and Park Slope had a net loss of 1,470 rent-stabilized housing units (Cabello 2019).

The New Jersey waterfront is also a case in point. Jersey City and Hoboken have allowed developers to build massive residential towers along the waterfront at a relentless pace that has surpassed that in New York City and would surely have made Glaeser happy. Moreover, as of this writing, another 6,000 units are expected to come on the market over the next three years. Has this lowered housing prices? No. As the press has widely reported, rental prices in that area have only gone up and are the highest in the nation (Beyer 2022; Sparago 2022).

Village Preservation has done some fine recent research into the issue in New York City and their team reports that:

- The SoHo/NoHo (Manhattan) rezoning that De Blasio and Been imposed substantially increased the demolition incentives of historic properties throughout the area and into bordering Chinatown. If demolished and built out to the new zoning, there would be a net loss in affordable units in their study area.
- In neighborhoods elsewhere that have been subjected to upzonings and massive buildouts, housing prices have not fallen at all and in most cases have risen. Distressingly, they found cases in East New York and Ocean Hill (Brooklyn) where newly built "affordable" units in the MIH program rented *for higher prices* than market-rate units in the same neighborhood.
- Upzoned neighborhoods experienced higher apartment price increases than neighborhoods left to their contextual zoning (Berman 2023).

In sum, "the data" are too weak and contradictory to be used to justify a policy regime of massive tower building of market-rate housing (even with 35 percent of mandatory affordable units). It is a policy that will not help low- and moderate-income people.

NEW YORK'S AFFORDABLE HOUSING PROBLEM IS A SELF-CREATED POLICY CRISIS, NOT ONE CAUSED BY OVERREGULATION.

The shortage of affordable housing in New York City is not due to regulatory constraints on height but to forced gentrification and the policy-induced demolition of the existing stock of affordable housing. Let's do some accounting.

- During the long era of urban renewal (1935–1975) that featured the creation of massive tower-in-the-park housing projects, Robert Moses and Mayor La Guardia oversaw a huge net loss of affordable housing units. Between 1935 and 1942, the city built 17,048 large-scale "affordable" housing units in the form of public housing that was scattered among fourteen project sites (Schwartz 1993, 59). However, to build those, Mayor La Guardia told listeners in a 1938 radio broadcast that he ordered 15,000 tenement buildings (not units) to be demolished to make way for those projects (La Guardia 1938). If each of those buildings contained just twenty housing units—a low count as the typical number of units in most tenement buildings was twenty-four according to architectural historian Andrew Dolkart—(see Dolkart n.d.), it means that La Guardia and Moses demolished at least 300,000 housing units after that 1938 speech. With rebuilding, it was a net loss by 1942 of at least 273,000 affordable apartments. But the demolishing pair did not stop in 1942. "In the period 1949–1968, the city demolished 425,000 more units of low-income housing [the 'slums' under urban renewal] and only built 125,000 new units, more than half of which were luxury units (Angotti et al. 2016, 57), citing Gwendolyn Wright (1983), which implies an additional net loss of 300,000 units due to a second wave of urban renewal demolitions.

- During the policy-induced "burning" of the Bronx between 1970 and 1980, seven census tracts lost more than 97 percent of their buildings to fire and forty-four additional census tracts lost more than 50 percent of their buildings, most of them tenement-style buildings. Depending on how you calculate the math, a conservative estimate is a loss of 57,580 affordable housing units during that period (Flood 2010).[11] That does not even count the fires in Queens.
- In 1955, the city had more than 200,000 single-room occupancy (SRO) rooms. In the 1980s the Koch administration had a particularly aggressive policy to convert these buildings to other uses. By 1995, there were only 40,000 SRO rooms left in the city, a loss of 160,000 rooms as the buildings were converted to tourist hotels, co-ops, and condos.[12]
- Between 1981 and 1988, landlords converted 242,000 rental apartments into co-operatives (Peterson 1988), and untold numbers of rental tenants were forced out, unable to afford the "insider" prices that were offered during the initial wave of co-op and condo conversions of the 1980s. That process went on unabated, the annual figures dependent on wider economic conditions. For example, from 1998 to 2001, just 2,430 additional units were taken out of the rental market and converted to condos, hotels, or co-ops (Schill, Voicu, and Miller 2007), but in 2006, the *New York Times* reported that condo and co-ops conversion that year took 7,000 units out of the "affordable" rental market (Barbanel 2006).
- Between 1993 and 2012, 282,000 rent-stabilized apartments left the regulatory program: 152,000 of those were removed from the rent-stabilization program through rental hikes intended to convert them

to market-rate units, and 130,000 more were lost to the previously mentioned "co-op and condo conversions and expiring tax breaks" (Barker 2018).
- An audit of New York City's public housing stock found that whenever "a unit left the rent rolls for major renovations, it stayed unoccupied for an average of seven years," and at the time of the audit there were 2,342 such empty apartments in the public housing system (Durkin 2015). Managerial incompetence and corruption affected housing supply.
- The Mitchell-Lama housing program targeting the middle class produced 105,000 apartments for both renters and homeowners. The rental program was the largest component of the program. It required that the units remain "permanently" affordable, which did not happen. By 2014 as the program expired, "about half of city's Mitchell-Lama rentals—some 35,000 units—had been privatized, often delivering windfalls to the landlords and steep rent increases to tenants" (Kaysen 2014). That is a loss of 33 percent of the original stock of affordable housing of that type. Privatization of Mitchell-Lama buildings has continued apace since then. In mid-2018, there were only 45,000 Mitchell-Lama units left in the city, "two thirds of which were co-ops," not rental units, implying only 10,000 affordable Mitchell-Lama rental units remained out of the original 105,000 (Kamping-Carter 2018).

It is impossible to imagine that that regulations on height cause the city's affordability crisis when the city has a policy of destroying or converting affordable units to market-rate units. That is what has induced the housing shortage at the lower end of the market.

OTHER CRITICS OF GLAESER: ECONOMIC GEOGRAPHERS AND "MISSING MIDDLE" ADVOCATES

I am not alone in my dismay at Glaeser's theories. Other critics of Glaeser and trickle-down, supply-side housing theories fall into two groups. Foremost among them are prominent economic geographers who argue that excessive gentrification and displacement of low-income people is the most likely outcome of the fundamentalist policy agenda. There are also urban planners who advocate for the "missing middle" category of housing density rather than towerization. Let's review their ideas.

Economic geographers Michael Storper and Andrés Rodríguez-Pose have published a compelling critique of Glaeser's reasoning. Their argument is very pointed: The trickle-down theorists have an "insufficiently developed scientific case"; their arguments "are fundamentally flawed and lead to simplistic policy recommendations"; and "there is no clear and uncontroversial evidence that housing regulation is a principal source of differences in home availability or prices across cities" (Rodríguez-Pose and Storper 2019). Moreover, Storper and Scott point out in another paper that supply shocks via upzonings into wealthy cities would "increase gentrification . . . and not decrease income inequality" (Storper and Scott 2016). They accuse Glaeser and his allies of "diverting attention" away from the tasks necessary to address the problems of "lagging regions" and struggling cities like Detroit, places that Glaeser writes off as "losers." The geographers point out that housing markets are:

> Not like standard markets, so that aggregate increases in supply do not translate in any straightforward way to decreases in price, because the internal plumbing of housing markets—succession, migration, and occupation patterns—are full of frictions, sunk costs, barriers, and externalities . . . that create unintended or contradictory effects. (Rodríguez-Pose and Storper 2019)

They also dispute Glaeser's use of spatial equilibrium theory, "which holds that city size and population are the only important factors for economic growth," because once the conditions are in place for population growth, jobs and output growth will then follow (see Glaeser 2008). Storper points to U.S. data to suggest that "the link between initial city population size and economic growth during the same period is non-existent." Moreover, he notes, "since the turn of the century, there has been no connection between population and economic growth across U.S. cities." Storper's studies of urban growth point to unique combinations of serendipity, location, and innovation as the key drivers of economic growth. In his view, technical innovations arise in the making and selling of things, which in turn initiate a flood of demand for locations in response to unique forward and backward opportunities the innovation is creating (Storper 2013).

As for Glaeser's examples of low regulatory regimes in southern cities causing growth, Storper argues that these cases do not constitute anything approaching "proof" that deregulating housing creates growth. Storper and Scott's summary of the history of manufacturers seeking cheap labor in their move to the Sunbelt makes the point convincingly. In reviewing the data and evidence, Storper and Rodríguez-Pose argue that Glaeser and his allies have failed to show that zoning is behind housing supply and price changes, with the obvious conclusion that it would be inappropriate to base policy or a general theory based on the pattern of those variations, given how much they vary from place to place and over time.

Storper and Rodríguez-Pose point out once a city's land area gets filled in, "the structure of jobs and incomes" is what drives housing prices and affordability. They also point out that low-income workers' wages do not rise with density increases. Indeed, why should low-wage workers move to another city if they are just going to end up in another low-wage job? At the same time, college-educated workers are still concentrating in cities, at least at the early stages of their careers, regardless of high housing prices. This leads the geographers to conclude that "high-wage" industries are not affected by "spatial competition."

Storper and his colleagues argue it is high-wage worker preferences that are causing prices in the core areas of cities to rise, a demand-side variable. That means that if municipal governments unfetter developers with less zoning, all we are going to get is more gentry moving into the core, even with tepid Mandatory Inclusionary Housing requirements.

Moreover, they argue that poor and low-wage Rust Belt workers are not "kept out" of big cities but are more likely to be "trapped outside" in the towns and cities that lost manufacturing jobs. The "trap" consists of life-cycle conditions, family ties, local attachments, lack of training, and lack of better employment opportunities in dynamic areas. Nobel prize–winning economist Esther Duflo has recently seconded that view on that matter (Duflo and Banerjee 2019). Storper's conclusion is that the "housing as opportunity" school of thought, of which Glaeser is a core member, has an "insufficiently developed scientific case" for their theory and policy recommendations. Obviously, I concur.

Urban planner Pete Saunders also argues that Glaeser has it wrong. "There is no shortage of housing in most US metro areas," he writes, but "there is a shortage of housing in the areas most attractive to today's young and affluent urban planners," meaning a shortage of the "cool" places where young people out of college want to live, such as in the vibrant historic core of Greenwich Village, which are, alas, already filled with people. Saunders finds the Glaeser proposal—that the crowded, historic, already dense cores of Boston, Chicago, and San Francisco should copy the unregulated growth of Houston and Atlanta—to be silly indeed. Atlanta and Houston are new, young cities, he points out, with vast undeveloped hinterlands. Like Storper, he points out that the history of their expansion is so different that comparisons are pointless from a policy point of view. He would agree that deregulating the core would, as I have argued above, destroy it, transform it into Dubai, and is therefore a destructive strategy. Saunders argues that we need to start expanding at the periphery, and engaging in less drastic, but steady, densification outside the historic cores (Saunders 2017). That means taking on single-family home zoning and bringing efficient public transport network into transit deserts.

Proponents of the notion of the "missing middle" urban densities also disagree with the notion that we must towerize our historic urban cores. Architect Daniel Parolek (who does not practice in New York City) coined the term "missing middle." He is referring to that category of multifamily housing that is "in-between" the despised single-family home and the six-story "mid-rise" building we have in New York City: duplexes, bungalow courts, townhouses, and courtyard apartments. A Brookings paper similarly advocates for this "missing middle" scale of construction, pointing out that it is a roadmap to "gentle" densification of single-family home areas (Baca et al. 2019). Of course, in New York City, we have our own "middle density" already: the six-story post-1910 tenements in Harlem, Inwood, and Washington Heights.

Summary

I have shown in this long chapter how the theory of trickle-down housing fundamentalism comes apart when inserted into the reality of New York City. Fundamentalists are keenly interested in justifying a destructive, massive real estate demolition project for Manhattan (and downtown Brooklyn and other waterfront locations along the East River) as part of a program to re-create New York into Dubai-on-Hudson. The problem is that their economic theory is deeply flawed and should not be used to justify policy interventions in New York City.

In making the argument against the continued towerization of New York City and against trickle-down supply-side housing fundamentalism, the following conclusions emerge.

- Zoning is not the primary, or even the most significant, driver of high housing prices in NYC.
- NIMBYs are most certainly not in control of the city's land-use policy: Big Real Estate is unquestionably in the driver's seat.
- The trickle-down story about housing prices is a fairy tale. It does not happen and has never happened in any city like New York City. Every city has its own peculiar history and city-specific story about how its housing market works. In a place like New York, upzoning—even with the policy of "mandatory inclusionary housing"[13]—ends up flooding neighborhoods with luxury housing and does not result in lower housing prices for the bottom half or even the middle of the

housing market. Rental prices in New York do not fall and have not been falling as fundamentalists say they would even during periods of luxury oversupply.
- The housing crisis for those New Yorkers who are seriously rent-burdened springs from causes that fundamentalists ignore or obfuscate: foreign investment into New York real estate, the policy-induced destruction of affordable housing units, and the absence of purchasing power of the residents who are most rent-burdened. Therefore, the affordability problem cannot be solved by the fundamentalist policy agenda.
- New York City has carrying capacity limitations of its own when it comes to both natural resources and physical infrastructure. That, combined with the historic build-out that is already here, means that there are limits to how many new people the city can accommodate without destroying what is here. Therefore, housing policy must be incremental, following the thinking of the Jane Jacobs School of Urbanism, and oriented toward alleviating the shortage at the lower third of the housing market. I will discuss some options in the last chapter.
- The skydome has public purposes and therefore it is not acceptable policy to turn it into a new "limitless" frontier.

As onerous as this list seems, there are areas of agreement between trickle-down housing supply fundamentalists and their critics (like me) when it comes to policy in New York. We might agree on the following points:
- In New York City we are profoundly constrained about where we can build. We no longer have the "freedom" to just build anything, anywhere. People already live here—a lot of them!
- Single-family zoning on the periphery of New York City, within its municipal boundaries, is a problem. Cities are not suburbs, hence single-family home suburban zoning within the city limits prevents much of the city's land mass from housing more people. By creating a no-go zone, large areas of single-family zoning channels real estate capital into Manhattan and downtown Brooklyn and the waterfront where a free-for-all reigns to the detriment of the public good. The benefits and burdens of density must be more fairly distributed.

In the following chapter, I look at one more nail in the coffin of trickle-down housing supply theory: its trivialization of the social costs and negative externalities that its towerization agenda imposes on residents and the public at large.

Chapter 3

The Costs of Towerization and the Problem of Density

The skyscraper is still *ferae naturae* and it is highly desirable to bring it under the reign of law.
—*New York Times* Editors, "Tall Buildings," August 13, 1906

EVERY POLICY AND MARKET TRANSACTION has costs not directly embedded in the price of the product. Some of those costs are trivial and some are not. The individuals involved may bear some of the costs privately. For example, when a college student buys a keg of beer, he must privately take on the cost of gas to get to the store, plus the cost of his time to get the beer, and the cost of cleaning up the mess after the party. But there are other costs that society at large undertakes when we sell beer to college students: the cost to lost health and productivity due to alcoholism or the cost to those who are injured and die from drunk drivers. Society at large absorbs those costs, so they are called social costs.

Negative externalities are similar to the idea of social costs but refer specifically to unwanted by-products of a production process, by-products that the producers don't account for in their profit/loss spreadsheets. For example, nuclear power plants must release dangerous, cancer-causing radioactive substances into the air while producing power. The radioactive substances are negative "externalities" of nuclear power generation. There are also positive externalities. An example would be the way a honey producer's bees pollinate the plants of nearby farmers. In the case of real estate, a negative externality of towers is the shadowing of the street that inevitably takes place. The social costs of shadowing would be the loss of views and sunshine, and the resulting widely shared costs of a depressing, dystopic environment that drives people to drink or take antidepressants. The demolition and loss of the historic character of New York City is also a negative externality of towerization and a social cost borne by all.

One of the most significant flaws in trickle-down fundamentalism for housing is that it either ignores or just trivializes the social costs and negative externalities of the Glaeser agenda. As for an accounting of the social costs of what Edward Glaeser demands of cities, readers should be wary. Glaeser's "educated guess" about those costs cited in the preceding chapter was made under the pseudo-scientific flag of social welfare theorizing and is an exercise in omission, conservative biases, wishful thinking, and outright dissembling. Let's look closer.

According to Glaeser, there are only three possible social costs that might arise from his skyscraper agenda:

1. "Changes in density"
2. "The value of views destroyed" and
3. "Fiscal externalities"

Regarding the first, density, Glaeser gives the amusing rationalization that adding more skyscrapers to Manhattan wouldn't matter because "Manhattan is underpopulated" (Glaeser, Gyourko, and Saks 2003, 7). He believes people live in Manhattan "to be near other people"—not because they were born there or got a job there. Therefore, "adding a large number of housing units and people will not change the basic nature of the place" and that big increases in density "are unlikely to create large changes in the nature of the community" (Glaeser, Gyourko, and Saks 2003, 31).

That is false. Changes in density dramatically change the experience and nature of urban life that is nontrivial. Density changes the kinetic experience of walking through a neighborhood, modifies cortisol and stress levels, and alters the experience of a subway ride, a commute, classroom learning, emergency response times, and the use of a sidewalk. Changes in density can cause grass to stop growing in overused parks. Changes in density can create two-hour lines in the heat of summer to take a dip in a public swimming pool, as they do in Brooklyn. To be sure, humans can survive anywhere, but should New Yorkers be forced to adapt to the extreme densities that Glaeser wants them to live in? It is here that we see that Glaeser, a resident of a single-family home in the Cambridge, MA suburbs, makes the ethical mistake of imposing his own ideas of what makes for a good urban life upon New Yorker residents, pretending that it is all for the greater good of "affordable housing."

THE COSTS OF TOWERIZATION AND THE PROBLEM OF DENSITY · 69

Figure 3.1a. Hong Kong resident in front of his coffin home bunk. The term refers to homes that consist of bedspaces that are so small as to resemble coffins.

Figure 3.1b. The skydome above coffin-home buildings in Hong Kong. Images from *The Atlantic*, 2017.

Fundamentalists trivialize the social costs of views destroyed and the shadowing of the public realm. The assumption of homogeneous housing consumers and "perfect" housing markets makes Glaeser confident that the value of lost views and light will equal whatever price the real estate market assigns those views, not the value the residents assign. Blocking views and light doesn't matter to fundamentalists because housing consumers who "value their view more than the market does" can simply "move apartments and acquire a new (identical) apartment with an [identical] view, paying the market cost" for it (Glaeser, Gyourko, and Saks 2003, 30).

Figure 3.2. The shadow fan that Vornado's proposed towers around Penn Station would produce. They would stretch all the way to New Jersey. Image from Community Board 5.

That is silly. A New York resident can't move to another identical apartment with the same views at a similar price point. In theory, similar apartments may be found somewhere in the big city, but not true, not on that block, not with that view, not on that floor, not that close to family, friends, and work. The markets that we live in are real: They are not economic models where inconvenient realities can be assumed away. One thing is sure: Those who lose their view are never compensated for their loss, nor does anyone even try to compensate them. Nor is there is a way to accurately assign a price to their loss. Manhattan artist Gwyneth Leach put the issue succinctly in the documentary *The Monolith*. In it, she described the loss of the view outside her painting studio due to the construction of a giant tower that covered up her windows and entombed her workplace. She found the experience of the tower rising next to her like death: "Death is like a monolith that can't be shifted. . . . It's not going to go away" (Walunas 2017).

The shadow effect of skyscrapers is also deeply problematic. Take for example, the case of Penn Station (also called Pennsylvania Station) where the city's largest real estate investment trust, Vornado, proposes to build ten new supertall towers around Pennsylvania Station and Madison Square Garden, right next door to the new Hudson Yards towers. As part of the impact analysis, Community Board 5 hired a consultant to produce a "shadow fan" to illustrate how much shadow the ten towers would produce. It is shown in Figure 3.3. The shadows reach all the way to Central Park and New Jersey.

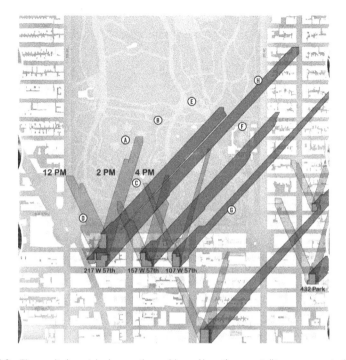

Figure 3.3a. The media has picked up on the problem of how the supertall towers excessively shadow Central Park. Image from the Municipal Art Society's report *Accidental Skyline*.

Figure 3.3b. William Carson Jr. photo of shadows over Central Park from the supertalls.

72 · THE COSTS OF TOWERIZATION AND THE PROBLEM OF DENSITY

Figure 3.4. The Twin Towers shadowing the low-rise neighborhood of Tribeca. Photo courtesy of Laurie Siegel.

Shadows make Central Park colder and stop the grass from thriving in certain parks. Shadows deprive us of a "Sunny Side of the Street" as the famous song goes. In fact, in overbuilt parts of Manhattan and Brooklyn, there no longer is a sunny side of the street at any time of the year (Kwartler 2015; Kwartler and Masters 1984). Or consider Washington Market Park in Tribeca where despite intensive pasture management, grass cannot grow anymore due to overcrowding and shadowing. Most of the children playing there live in the new residential towers surrounding the park to the south, none of which were there when the park was built. Grass there grows in one-third the area it used to grow in 2004.

Let's take a closer look at what Glaeser thinks about the third item on his list, the "fiscal" externalities. In his mind, these could arise in the following scenario. Imagine developers succeed in delivering a "supply shock" of new towers, but the new housing draws the "wrong" kind of new residents into Manhattan, poor ones. He worries that the new people might be so poor that they "require far more in local government expenditures than they pay in taxes" (Glaeser, Gyourko, and Saks 2003, 14). If this came to pass, the city could end up with far less property tax revenue, and that is the negative "fiscal" externality in Glaeser's theorizing.

Not to worry, says Glaeser; he offers up a luxury city idea as the solution to this risk. Why not build towers for young people with college degrees who stand a shot at getting good jobs in banking, finance, or tech? In that case, the new people "will tend to be far richer than the average New Yorker" (Glaeser, Gyourko, and Saks 2003, 15). Moreover, these young newcomers, almost certainly white, college-educated guys chasing high-paying Wall Street jobs will, when married, "enroll their children in private school," thereby showing a willingness to "pay taxes for the use of schools and not use them, to the benefit of the government's budget." Glaeser concludes that this new gentry class "would be an unqualified improvement" to the city's demographic mix and "a fiscal boon" to city government (Glaeser, Gyourko, and Saks 2003, 15).

Pause at that phrase: "an unqualified improvement." The sentiment is clear: Get rid of the poor, who are usually Black and Brown, and replace them with the (most likely white) gentry who, planners hope, will pay more in taxes than they take out. This is the very idea that animated Dan Doctoroff and Michael Bloomberg's proposal to remake NYC as a "luxury city" and "a city for the rich." To be fair to Doctoroff and Glaeser, New York City elites have always been worried that poor people represent a fiscal drain. Glaeser is just providing more theoretical cover for a policy of displacement of the unwanted.

Indeed, the policy of building for the lucky urban gentry has come to be the norm in New York City. One of the larger real estate investment trusts that builds and invests in high-rise luxury rental buildings brags to potential investors that "their" Manhattan renters have far "higher than average incomes ($278,000)" than the rest of the city's population (Equity Residential 2017).

Glaeser just ignores the negative externalities and social cost involved in the displacement that takes place with his towerization agenda. That is not good. Donovan Rypkema, studying Upper East Side census tracts over a ten-year period, noted that when eighteen new skyscrapers were built in the study area, the population of poor and working-class white and Black families declined—by a lot. Ominously, this happened alongside a marked uptick in people self-described in the census as "other," an indicator of foreign investors buying in (Rypkema 2016, 23). A study of Bloomberg's rezoning of Williamsburg under Bloomberg—a perfect policy example of the implementation of Glaeser's ideas—found that "in the area that was rezoned, residential and commercial property values increased nearly 250% between 2002 and 2013, and median monthly gross rents swelled from $949 to $1,603" (Angotti, 2018 citing Goldberg 2015, 51) and that as of 2013, at the end of Bloomberg's reign, "only 19 of the promised affordable units in Williamsburg had been built." Let that number sink in. Moreover, "the white population of Williamsburg increased by 44% and the Latino population decreased by 27% by 2013" (Angotti, 2018). Is that not enough to persuade? Economist Yonah Freemark also found, using real data rather than a simulation study, that upzoning in Chicago resulted in both displacement and increased prices, not a fall in housing prices (Freemark 2019). There is accumulating evidence of this type. One study found that more than 80 percent of the new rental housing that has been built in this country's overpriced housing market is "high end" and that filtering failed to supply housing to those most in need or lower prices beyond temporary dips here and there (Balint 2018).

The erudite, late architectural critic, Ada Louise Huxtable (who to her dying day thought that skyscrapers could in theory be art) came to rail against skyscrapers for the destruction they wrought on New York City. She described the social costs and negative externalities in words anyone can understand:

> In New York, the impact of these concentrated super skyscrapers on street scale and sunlight, on the city's antiquated support systems, circulation, and infrastructure, on its already tenuous livability, overrides any aesthetic. As bulk and density increase, avenues darken and close in; shadows lengthen and downdrafts multiply, winter sun becomes a fleeting penetration of cold canyons at midday, leaving neither warmth nor cheer. The city's oppressive impersonality increases, while services suffer, and civility diminishes; amenities disappear.... These structures make architecture unimportant and meaningless.... Art becomes worthless in a city brutalized by overdevelopment. (Huxtable 1984)

Huxtable did not use Le Corbusier's term of "pitiless" in her famous essay on skyscrapers, but she did use the following words: "crushing," "painful," "abrasive," and "relentlessly brutal." Skyscrapers are just not art. Rem Koolhaas, borrowing architectural language as old as the nineteenth century, describes skyscrapers as mere non-architectural "extrusions" upon an architectural base (Koolhaas 1994). Huxtable was right. In a dense city like New York, regardless of their architectural interest (or blandness), when skyscrapers start to dominate the context, they block too much light and views from those who had them before. They create immense visual rupture. Of course, a few skyscrapers here and there do no harm, as in the days when they amounted to isolated landmarks like the Chrysler Building, the Empire State Building, and the Woolworth Building. But as they proliferated, a tipping point was reached. At that point, they do immense harm, usually after they have overwhelmed or destroyed the historic context outside their agreed-upon zones. Let's review the social costs and negative externalities that we have not mentioned yet.

Skyscrapers Are Environmentally Toxic

The evidence has long been piling up: Skyscrapers pose a problem for the environment. One study found:

> Electricity use, per square metre of floor area, is two and a half times greater in high-rise office buildings of 20 or more storeys than in low-rise buildings of 6 storeys or less. Gas use also increases with height, by around 40%. As a result, total carbon emissions from gas and electricity from high-rise buildings are twice as high as in low-rise. (University College of London 2017)

Another study found that "on average, buildings completed in the late 1960s have primary energy requirements more than double those of buildings constructed in the early 1950s, less than twenty years previously" (Oldfield, Trabucco, and Wood 2009, 599). Another found that for skyscrapers, "total embodied carbon and material weight increase exponentially with building height" (Gan et al. 2017, 671). It turns out this issue also works at the scale of the city and that mid-rise cities like Paris emit less carbon than high-rise skyscraper cities (Berg 2021).

The energy and carbon critique makes a lot of sense. Even supposedly environmentally-green-built buildings with feeble "LEED" (a green building rating system of the U.S. Green Building Council) certifications emit huge amounts of carbon. For example, Citibank's LEED Platinum office building at 388 Greenwich emits 11,400 metric tons of carbon a year. A nearby glass building that is the New York Law School, famous for lighting up the entire neighborhood with night lighting, emits 80,000 tons of carbon a year. The 821-foot tall Jenga tower on Leonard Street, by Starchitects Herzog & de Meuron, a textbook example of Glaeser housing policy, emits a whopping 442,000 metric tons of carbon a year and gets an energy rating of just 1 out of 100 (City of New York 2021).

The other problem with towers, especially glass ones, is that steel, concrete, and glass—the staple content of modernist towers with glass curtain walls—are the largest contributors to embodied carbon in many a skyscraper. Glass facades also present a problem because they must be replaced every twenty to thirty years (Epstein 2019). Add to that all the carbon-filled aluminum in the curtain walls and the toxic foam insulations now common to tower construction and you have a real environmental problem on your hands (Melton 2018).

Most towers also lack operable windows, thus exposing workers inside the building to toxic air. One of many studies of office buildings around the country without operable windows found excessive levels of benzene, ethanol, and CO_2 indoors. The last at high levels reduces cognitive functioning (Salonen et al. 2009). This leaves engineers scratching their heads on how to retrofit these buildings to give them decent air and ventilation, a problem all the trickier in a tall skyscraper (Heffelmire 2014).

Skyscrapers Make Cities Hotter in Summer and Colder in Winter

The canyons that skyscrapers create make for dismally dark and frozen streets in winter, as anyone who has wandered New York's Financial District or Midtown blocks in January can attest. Just as bad, during the summer, skyscrapers absorb so much solar radiation during the day and release it during the night that they raise the temperature of their neighborhoods in the summer. This worsens the well-known "heat island" effect of asphalt-ridden cities. You can touch New York's tall buildings at night in summer and feel their heat. The NASA image of Manhattan in Figure 3.5 shows in dark shadows the heat of Manhattan's high-rise Midtown and Financial District in summer. High-rise city neighborhoods, says the Environmental Protection Agency, can be six degrees hotter than the surrounding area (Walker 2014).

Skyscrapers Create, Sustain, and Celebrate Oligarchy and Corporatism

Manhattan's skyscrapers have become a world symbol of the corporate domination of our society and the decreasing relevance of democracy. Municipal elites bend over backwards to hand corporations tax incentives to come to or stay in the city inside one of these towers. It is an ineffective tax-giveaway game that academics have said repeatedly is a beggar-thy-neighbor strategy that does not influence where corporations land or "create" jobs (Bartik 2018). Urban planning technocrats nonetheless continue to brag foolishly about how many corporations headquarter in their city. We will see in later chapters how big corporations are whimsical and unreliable overlords. In one period, they build headquarters in the city, like Western Union did, and then a very short time later they move to suburban campuses, just like Western Union. Building an economic development strategy around them is a fool's game.

Towers are also aggressively marketed to the world's wealthy for the views, which are part of the asset the wealthy are buying. To drive the point home, allowing the "free" real estate market to determine the allocation of our commons, the skydome, is both inequitable and undemocratic.

Figure 3.5. NASA image of solar heat in high-rise Manhattan. The heat is indicated by all the dark black spots, except for the lake in Central Park. Image by NASA.

Figure 3.6. Who gets the views in the race to the top? Here an interior designer enjoys the views from the terrace of his client's deck in the Jenga Building of Manhattan. Photo by Thomas Loof from an *Elle Décor* article on the building, November 19, 2019. The building has a 75-foot lap swimming pool, a fitness room, a sauna, a steam room, a movie theater, a parking garage, a children's playground, a private dining room, a catering kitchen, and a library lounge. The larger and higher units sell for over $20 million and have a tax abatement paid for by the larger public.

In Smaller Cities, Skyscrapers Damage the Downtowns with "Holes"

We've all been to places like Sarasota, Wilmington, Cleveland, Oklahoma City, or Richmond, where very few people live in the central business districts, where the original Black neighborhoods that once gave those downtowns life have all been demolished. You see there scattered glass towers and lots of "holes"—one-story buildings and empty lots used for parking. There is little street life to speak of outside the lunch hour. Urban planner Charles Marohn explains this by pointing out there isn't enough office demand to towerize all the buildable sites in these second-city downtowns. A single tower in such a city can drain demand into one building and leave other sites empty and without a market. He advocates instead for a more incremental zoning approach that puts in tight height restrictions, so that one tower cannot dominate, permitting the other sites to fill in with slightly smaller buildings. It is a "share the wealth" strategy among property owners instead of a winner-take-all free market approach (Marohn 2014).

Residential Tall Buildings Drain the Street of Urbanity and If You Aren't Rich, They Aren't Good for You or Your Kids

Entire neighborhoods of residential towers, like that in the East 50s of Manhattan, have been built mostly for speculative investors. The apartments are empty much of the year, thus having a deadening effect on the city. Sociologists have not coincidentally found that tower life increases the sense of loneliness and inhibits neighborliness, a problem particularly severe for the elderly on high floors (Coleman 1985; Wright 2015). Tower residents also use street services less because of the higher "transaction cost" of getting to the ground floor in elevators. For that reason, high-rise residents minimize trips to the street compared to residents in lower-rise buildings, further draining a block area of vitality (Anderson 1967). Readers can witness these effects in many places in Manhattan and Brooklyn, from Hudson Yards to the anti-urban street wall at the Two Bridges Tower in Lower Manhattan to the vast newly dystopic stretches of towerized downtown Brooklyn and Long Island City. Obviously, not all residents dislike high-rise life or miss living at human scale, but on average, the problems remain.

The luxury version of this "draining the street of vitality" problem found all over Manhattan and Brooklyn comes with a twist. It is the trend for new luxury towers to have dozens of amenities reserved for wealthy residents. These include gyms, social lounges, party rooms, golf simulators, children's playrooms, teen game rooms, libraries, yoga rooms, co-working spaces, tennis courts, cinema rooms, parks, parking lots, swimming pools, package rooms to store Amazon and food deliveries, concierge services, and even bowling alleys. They have become a gated resort for the residents who never interact with the actual city lying outside their front doors, further draining the city of vitality. They are anti-urban enclaves.

Robert Gifford has summarized a vast amount of the research about resident experiences of high-rise living. He evaluated the quality of that research and found that that the richer you are, the better your neighborhood and fancier your building, the more satisfied you are likely to be with high-rise housing. For everyone else, including those forced by circumstance to live in high-rise public housing, it is not so pretty. Public housing in tower form has been shown to be particularly problematic in this regard because the corridors, stairwells, and elevators became the redoubts of gangs of misbehaving teenagers and drug dealers. In Gifford's findings, children across all income levels were unequivocally worse off in high-rise housing due to lack of exercise and exposure to the outdoors. Neighborliness and social interaction were also significantly diminished in high-rise housing. Gifford concluded:

> Children are better off in low-rise housing; high-rises either restrict their outdoor activity or leave them relatively unsupervised outdoors, which may be why children who live in high-rises have, on average, more behavior problems. Residents of high-rises probably have fewer friendships in the buildings, and certainly help each other less. Crime and fear of crime probably are greater in high-rise buildings. A small proportion of suicides may be attributable to living in high rises. (Gifford 2007, 13)

The conclusion is that the negative externalities of excessive towerization should not be trivialized, nor should urban residents accept the fundamentalist accounting of them. To be sure, not building at all has social costs and negative externalities as well, but as we shall see in a future chapter, accounting for all this on a balance sheet is impossible without siding with either the winners or the losers of the game.

One-Sided Drumbeating to Bamboozle New Yorkers

Glaeser's influence in the Bloomberg years had some odd permutations, including the conjuring of a demographic "crisis" to justify the elite's enthrallment to Glaeser's program of towerization. Here is that story.

In the waning years of the Bloomberg administration politicians and planners began telling residents that one million "new" New Yorkers were going to swarm into our city over the next thirty years. Technocrats, planners, and allies of the real estate industry informed everyone that these future newcomers required new high-rise tower housing immediately, not incrementally, and that the housing needed to be in the historic core or in the floodplain of the East River in Brooklyn and Queens. It was a DEFCON 1 alert with an implication that anyone skeptical of tower building was a dog in the manger, hoarding New York for themselves. Every city council hearing featured borough presidents and council members declaiming that the city would need to make room for these new people who weren't here yet.

The figure of "one million 'new' New Yorkers" that came to be so endlessly repeated among the politicians and the New York press might well have started with a report written by real estate industry insiders of the hyper-density persuasion. The report was titled "NYC 2040: Housing the Next One Million New Yorkers" (Keenan and Chakrabarti 2013). It came out in mid-2013 and bore the logos of the Center for Urban Real Estate and Columbia University, despite the buried disclaimer that those institutions did not share the views of the authors. The demographic section of the report was a pitiful four paragraphs long. The authors had no training in econometrics or demography; indeed, neither had advanced training in social science research methodology or statistics at all. One was an architect who had worked as a vice president for one of the largest skyscraper developers in the city (Related) and was instrumental in getting Hudson Yards built, before going on to serve as the head of the Manhattan desk at the Department of City Planning under Mayor Bloomberg. That man's name was Vishaan Chakrabarti, whom we met in the preceding chapter. His co-author was Jesse Keenan, a lawyer with a master's degree in real estate.

The authors were faced with a conundrum in 2013: The data from the Bureau of the Census did not corroborate the narrative that New York's population was going to grow like crazy. In fact, it looked like the opposite was true, that the surrounding suburbs in the wider metro area were doing most of the growing. The city was entering a phase of slow, incremental growth, with much of the incremental growth going to the wider suburban metropolitan area rather than the historic core. The authors noted: "NYC's population is growing at a slower pace than many public and private analysts had projected" and that *"based on current growth patterns, it is unlikely that NYC will reach an additional one million new residents"* (Keenan and Chakrabarti 2013, 4; italics mine)—as if the one million figure was a special goal that civic leaders ought to be striving for. So where to get an additional one million people?

Buried in footnote 7 of the report, the authors tell us: "It should be noted that the start of the one million additional residents mark was the year 2000, whereas for the purposes of this report the year has been updated to the year 2010" (Keenan and Chakrabarti 2013, 6). The authors found that they had to fudge the growth rates of the city to meet the goal of one million new bodies. The authors point out that if you just took the growth rate of the population using birth and death data during the ten years between 2000 and 2010 and project it forward, you don't get to a million new people, you only get to 700,000 new people. The authors lament that the 700,000 could in principle be easily accommodated within the existing buildable envelope of the city. "Analyzing properties that can be redeveloped," they wrote, "about 70% of the anticipated one million NYC New Yorkers *can be accommodated within the existing fabric*" (Keenan and Chakrabarti 2013, 4; emphasis mine).

Since the actual growth rate was too small to justify a massive building spree, the authors mention helpfully: "If the population growth [is bumped up] to just 3.89%, then the city will reach the one million mark by 2040" (Keenan and Chakrabarti 2013, 2). Were they making up the 3.89 percent growth rate to get their magic number of one million? It sure looks like it.

The authors of the *NYC 2040* report concluded that to get the extra 300,000 people (above the 700,000 predicted from then-current growth rates), the city would need to encourage a special kind of in-migration. New citizens of the city needed to be found, but they should not be poor people from Central America, but high-wage college graduates who would shore up the property tax base, just as in Glaeser's writings on Manhattan. The authors warned that the city would have to aggressively compete with other cities along the Eastern Seaboard to get those additional college graduates to come to the city. Why? Because "this projected population could instead go either to our suburbs or to other regions with which the city competes." One way to compete for this fickle group of potential newcomers, according to the authors, is to build "hyper-dense" all along the East River waterfront. To be precise:

> Despite the impact of climate change, NYC can and must build resilient high-density waterfront development. (Keenan and Chakrabarti 2013, 3)

They argued for "hyper-dense" and "hyper-urban" solutions to their self-created problem of attracting an extra 300,000 prosperous residents to make the one million mark (Keenan and Chakrabarti 2013, 6). They said this kind of building must be done to prevent a "flight of people and capital." And if you don't do it, the authors threatened, it will "result in a significant loss of the municipal tax base." The "flight" they are talking about is not of current residents, but of "potential" residents who might choose to live in the suburbs of the city or start their careers in another metro area altogether.

It is "critical," the authors said, to "capture population growth in an urban environment," even if it is in a floodplain a few inches from the East River. And why, you might ask, did they urge development along the floodplain of the East River where the sewage treatment plants are overflowing on average every three days? Their answer: Other places in the city where "hyper-dense" development seemed feasible were just too far from the historic core and didn't already have mass transit, and nobody wanted to build more transit out there. Those areas were also already built out in single-family homes in Queens and Brooklyn, and the authors assumed that young new college grads would not want to live there anyway because those neighborhoods were more suburban than urban.

Their report, funded generously by the Carnegie Foundation, became gospel in NYC planning and political circles. There was incessant drumbeating under the brand of "*NYC 2040*." Vishaan Chakrabarti ran the Manhattan desk of the Department of City Planning, where he did a fair share of that drumbeating himself. That included a breathless panel discussion at the urbanist Van Allen Institute, news articles, videos, and exhibitions, one of which featured Chakrabarti's idea of connecting Governors Island to Manhattan with landfill and then packing it with towers that could potentially (in the eyes of the promoters) bring in $16 billion in new property tax revenue for the city (Finch 2011).

The same "new" New Yorkers argument was repeated in the Regional Plan Association's (RPA) 2016 "Charting a New Course" advocacy paper (Regional Plan Association 2016). In it, we read a story that the city is dangerously sclerotic because "the number of older adults will swell" and that "our infrastructure is old" (12). The RPA report then indulges in some unscientific back-of-the-envelope projections about job growth, happily concluding that by 2040 we'll have millions of new jobs, even though not even the RPA has any way to accurately predict the future. And like the Keenan and Chakrabarti report, the RPA report laments that "natural growth in the population . . . won't be enough to maintain growth in the labor force" and therefore "most new workers will need to be attracted into the region from elsewhere" (18). The RPA authors play the same game of building fanciful future migration figures into their model "to yield a population large enough to provide enough workers to fill the projected number of jobs in the 31-county region" (18). This is also called "fudging the numbers." Would that science, let alone the RPA, knew how to accurately predict in-migration over a thirty-year period!

Once the RPA came up with the familiar prediction about a million "new" people knocking on our doors, it used that prediction to justify a policy position of eliminating height caps in Manhattan, on the idea that all the new workers should be able to walk to work in either Midtown or Lower Manhattan from new high-rise skyscrapers. And of course, like the Keenan and Chakrabarti report, the RPA dangled before politicians the thrilling promise that the new high-rises they advocate for would result in "increased tax revenue" (19).

The problem is that this is all speculation. It is unscientific to make long-term predictions about in-migration, which is just an unknowable data point. It is also just a guess as to what college graduate housing preferences are or will be. For every young YIMBY person arriving in the big city who is content with a simulacrum of urban life in a SHoP-designed glass, gated community packed with suburban "amenities," there is another young person who wants the great urbanity of yore and is disappointed that New York's human-scale neighborhoods are being transformed by excessive towerization.

And of course, the population boom never materialized. Even before Covid, New York City was experiencing a net out-migration. The Census Bureau found that it had overcounted the city's population in 2020 by 695,000 people (Brown 2023). The city has also been part of the nationwide trend for middle-class Black families to migrate to the suburbs instead of raising their children in the city. There is no demographic crisis of "new" people that justifies a massive demolish-and-rebuild program, and none of the reports that attempted to justify a building spree of towers mentioned any of the social costs or negative externalities of a towerization policy.

"Density" without Adjectives Means Nothing

A *New York Times* journalist went to a bar to chat with NYC planners at the end of the day after a planners' convention. She asked if there was a natural limit to density. The planners just laughed. One of them replied, "That's a subject we don't really think about much" (O'Leary 2012). And that is the problem.

New York's urban planners, real estate industry lobbyists, libertarian market urbanists, and those who make a living off the real estate industrial complex have grabbed the persuasive rhetoric of the legitimate, environmentalist, anti-car planning war against suburban low-density sprawl. They are applying it inappropriately to our own already dense historic cities. They want "more density" but don't specify how much density, even though there is such a thing as too much density, and such a thing as not enough density. Therefore generic, sloppy, and unqualified usage of the word for New York City (Manhattan in particular, a place that is already the densest city in the country) fogs up public discussion. What Big Real Estate and its courtiers are really doing with such vagueness is engaging in sneaky advocacy of extremist hyper-density. Hiding behind the sunshine and lollipop blandness of the anti-suburban generic word "density," they seek to justify the squeezing in of yet more supertalls and towers. When famed urbanist and architect Michael Sorkin remarked to me in an email: *"Must squelch the Density Absolutists!"*[1] he was making the obvious point: Density without specific qualifiers is a useless word.

Hyper-density absolutists wrongly equate high-rise buildings with "density." Their theory, as we have seen elsewhere, is that nebulously defined "growth" is something that ought to take place infinitely, and that the measure of that growth is ever-taller buildings and ever more people crammed into the historic core of the city. These people have become hyper-density absolutists in a way that makes no sense whatsoever for New York City. Their position makes a mockery of the more meaningful Density Wars taking place in the suburban and small-city universe of the country, where some degree of densification is obviously necessary to break us of our automobile dependence. Density absolutists ask how many people can we physically squish into Manhattan? More reasonable people ask: How many people should we squish into Manhattan and at what point is this already dense island overstuffed? The policy nuance that these questions should generate is missing.

There are many measures of density. None is "the best," as each measure has its uses. The most common definition is the number of people living in or working in a specific unit of area, such as an acre or mile. That measure is useful when comparing places. That is not the only way to measure density. A commonly used indirect measure of density is "dwelling units" per unit of area, which is not a satisfying measure because we don't know how big the households are that live in a dwelling unit. Nor do we know how big the apartments or houses are that make up the dwelling units. Another density measure is "habitable square feet per person." That tells us about overcrowding. For example, a wealthy family of three people occupying a 10,000-square-foot apartment in a supertall skyscraper on 57th Street composed of just forty apartments creates a different experience of density than does a six-story human-scale tenement building in Jackson Heights, Queens, converted into illegal worker dorms, where every 200-square-foot room contains six or more mattresses rented out in shifts to newly arrived immigrants.

There is an even more indirect, and even less satisfying, indicator of density: the ratio of the gross floor area of a building to the gross floor area the property sits on. This is known as "FAR." FAR is unsatisfying on multiple levels because it is not even the measure of a building's actual volume. Because of this fatal flaw, building sites with the same FAR can produce vastly different shaped buildings since ceiling height is not part of the FAR calculation. Nonetheless, planners who like FAR sometimes use it to indirectly deduce population density by guessing at the number of people who occupy the habitable space that FAR uses. But it is not an accurate measure. For more variations on density definitions, see Forsyth's handout for planning students (Forsyth 2003).

It is also important to ask (even though one may not necessarily be able to find the answer) what is included in the area denominator when making a density calculation. That's because local streets, backyards, side yards, courtyards, sidewalks, parks, ponds, and natural areas are often deliberately left out of the physical area measurement, and sometimes all those important realities are left in. When such important parts of a city are left out, the density measure is referred to as "net density." When the public and natural spaces are left in, we are talking about "gross density," which obviously will come out to be a lower figure than that of net density. Most of the time, gross density gives us a better understanding of city neighborhoods than net density does, as public spaces really do matter to how we experience a city. That said, sometimes it is better to look at both measures since they convey different information. A lot depends on the specifics of the case. For example, the tony neighborhood in the 16th Arrondissement of Paris ("Passy") abuts a large, forested park, the Bois de Boulogne. With the forest included, Passy has only 23,747 people per square mile, but if we exclude the neighboring forest from the calculation, it packs in 49,349 people per square mile.[2]

"Net density" is usually of great interest to real estate developers because they want to know how many housing units they can pack into a given buildable site: They aren't interested in the parts of the site they cannot build on. But for the rest of us, concerned as we are with sidewalks, street trees, roadways, public libraries, churches, graveyards, schools, and

Figure 3.7. Hyper-density in the East 30s of Manhattan. Author's photo.

parks with swimming pools, gross density may be of greater importance for planning the public realm.

Density also changes during the day when workers commute into a city: Usually it goes up. Thankfully, Professor Mitchell Moss of New York University latched onto this concern in 2012, at least for the case of pre-Covid

Manhattan. He and a colleague figured that before the pandemic in Manhattan, an additional 3.9 million nonresident people poured into the city each day, mostly via public transportation, and mostly in order to work (Moss and Qing 2012). That adds a lot of additional density from 7 a.m. to 7 p.m. It is impossible to predict how that will change over time in any consistent way, including the changes inflicted by Covid.

With all these different measurements explained, the best way to understand density is visually and through comparisons of real-life cases. To that end, I have provided some density figures from sources between 2015 and 2020 that the reader can use to compare places in the world with New York City. They show how very dense New York City is, how that density is so unequally distributed among New York's neighborhoods and boroughs, and how New York City compares to other places in the United States and the wider world, including places that have great urbanity, such as Paris or Barcelona.[3]

- New York City overall has 26,402 people per square mile. This makes it by far the densest city in the United States. There are denser places, such as the oddity of Guttenberg, New Jersey, with 56,000 people per square mile, but Guttenberg is merely a high-rise, four-block skyscraper development on the banks of the Hudson River that happens to be incorporated as city. Guttenberg is an oddity and an agglomeration, not a city.
- The island of Manhattan has 69,467 people per square mile (Wikipedia).[4]
- Dharvi, the infamous slum of Mumbai, India, has about 717,000 people per square mile, while Manhattan's Lower East Side in the heyday of immigration in the 1920s had about 400,000 people per square mile before it got demolished and urban-renewed. (When one sees large figures like that for population per square mile, the data are usually signaling the presence of intense overcrowding, a common feature of poverty that is as old as time.)
- Within Manhattan, the densest neighborhoods are on the prosperous Upper East Side. The neighborhood of the far East 70s (zip code 10162) is the densest zip code in the city with a whopping 151,834 people per square mile.
- The comparatively bucolic, working-class, single-family home neighborhood of zip code 10210 in Staten Island has a mere 12,829 people per square mile, about the same people per square mile as found in Daly City, California. (Recall that Daly City was the object of the

famous Malvina Reynolds song "Little Boxes," with the lines "They're all made out of ticky tacky/And they all look just the same.")
- Tribeca, SoHo, and the western part of Chinatown in Manhattan are three historic neighborhoods that are mostly human-scaled, characterized by many blocks of mostly four- to seven-story buildings. They share the zip code 10013, which has an average density of 45,458 people per square mile, remarkably close to the density of the historic cores of Paris and Barcelona, cities that most urbanists concede embody many aspects of great urbanity.
- Consider Inwood and Jackson Heights, two famously human-scaled, working-class neighborhoods of New York City. Inwood has a Paris-like 47,051 people per square mile while Jackson Heights is nearly twice as loaded, with 97,325 per square mile.[5]
- Greenwich Village has an overall density of 79,000 people per square mile, but it is a sprawling neighborhood, so within it there is quite a bit of variation. For example, the wealthy far-west Village (around Hudson Street) has a robust, but much smaller density of 38,744 people per square mile while another tract adjoining it (closer to Fifth Avenue) has a whopping 85,000 people per square mile.
- It is important to note that back in 1960, the unspecified "fashionable" sections of Greenwich Village had, according to Jane Jacobs, a net density per acre that ranged from 124 to 174 people per net acre, figures that are not that far removed from the current average gross density for the Village of 114 people per gross acre.[6]
- Brooklyn Heights, a successful neighborhood by any measure, has a current gross density of 63,000 people per square mile. Jane Jacobs noted that in her day, the successful heart of Brooklyn Heights had a density that ranged from 125 to 174 people per net acre, whereas the current figure is about 98 people per gross acre, not an immense difference when taking into consideration the difference between gross and net density measurements.[7] The reason for the decline in density is easy to determine. In Jacobs's day, many brownstone neighborhoods had been converted to boarding houses and SROs and were much denser than they are now when so many houses have been reconverted back to one- or two-family homes.
- Paris, despite intense gentrification and the exodus of the working class from the heart of the city to the outer ring neighborhoods and suburbs, has an overall average net density of 52,240 people per square mile (or gross density of 66,000 people per square mile if the two great forests of Bois de Boulogne and Bois de Vincennes are

excluded). That makes Paris about twice as dense as New York City and five times as dense as Washington, D.C.
- The densest residential district within the historic core of Paris is the 11th Arrondissement with 41,598 people per square mile. Compare that to the empty 1st Arrondissement with about 9,000 people per square mile. But recall that the 1st Arrondissement has many non-residential administrative buildings, the sprawling Louvre Museum, and a good chunk of the immense Tuileries Garden, so a net density might be more appropriate measure for the 1st Arrondissement.[8]
- Barcelona has an average density of 41,248 people per square mile, with considerable variation within the historic core. There are some immense, tightly packed neighborhoods such as the historic La Sagrada Familia, which has a density of about 130,000 people per square mile, still not as dense as the Upper East Side of Manhattan.[9]
- The walkable, lively small "city" of West Hollywood North has a density of about 18,500–24,000 people per square mile depending on which tract you look at.[10]
- Suburban densities vary greatly. Geneva, Illinois, a charming small town on the banks of the Fox River has a density of 2,197 people per square mile, a density that triples to about 6,000 people per square mile in the core census tract around the walkable historic downtown.[11] The suburb of Levittown on Long Island, the heart of the crabgrass frontier, has 7,567 people per square mile.[12]
- Cupertino, California, the home of Apple, Inc. in the heart of suburban and small-town Silicon Valley, has a suburban density of just over 5,000 people per square mile (Wikipedia), less than Levittown's.
- Phoenix, Arizona, considered the epitome of disastrous American sprawl, has a rustic density of 2,797 people per square mile, barely above the small-town density of the above-mentioned Geneva, Illinois.

In her great book, *The Death and Life of Great American Cities*, Jane Jacobs argued that neighborhoods, and by extension cities, should be judged not by density numbers but by their overall "performance": a vague term she used to describe how well density served its intended purpose. Extremely low densities, she thought, served their intended purpose of creating "dull and gray" monotonous suburbs for those who wanted to live in them. Jacobs was also a die-hard empiricist. Unspecified, imprecise "density" was to her merely a "necessary," but not a sufficient condition for great urbanity. She preferred case studies to numbers when it came to density.

Although New York City, in her day, had an overall density of 55 dwelling units per net residential acre, Jacobs was insistent that it was dangerous to come up with an "ideal" level of density. She never said a particular density was the ideal one. Nonetheless, she thought certain neighborhoods were more successful in her terms than others. She frequently cited the great urban neighborhoods of Brooklyn Heights, Greenwich Village, an unspecified stretch of the "fashionable Upper East Side" in New York City, the Rittenhouse Square area of Philadelphia, the "slum" of the North End of Boston, and Telegraph and Nob Hills in San Francisco. These places, to her, embodied the great urbanity and were filled with vitality, diversity, convenience, and safety. Each of those neighborhoods, she noted, had a considerable range of dwelling units per net acre within their bounds, from a low of 80 dwelling units per net acre in some parts of Telegraph and Nob Hills to highs of 174 dwelling units per net acre in certain blocks of the Upper East Side and Brooklyn Heights. They did not have uniform densities throughout. She did not think much of the homogeneity and excessive scale of West End Avenue and Park Avenue, places that have a certain formal architectural elegance but lack diversity, interest, and small-scale street commerce.

One of her favorite neighborhoods, Boston's North End, was an Italian and Jewish working-class neighborhood that planners considered a "slum" and, as Jacobs knew, was targeted for urban renewal. It was composed of mostly four-story buildings. The North End, Jacobs observed, was extremely dense, the exact figure of which she was unsure. On page 463 of her book, she claims the North End had 963 people per residential acre (referring to its overcrowded new immigrant heyday) while a few pages later she says it had 275 people per net residential acre. But never mind the numbers, the low-rise North End neighborhood generated a wonderful, lively street life that charmed her: "The streets were alive with children playing, people shopping, people strolling, people talking" (Jacobs 1961, reprinted 1992, 29). Pressing herself to answer the question as to what a maximum density (not an ideal density) might be, she wrote that perhaps that maximum figure could be 200 dwelling units per net acre, depending of course on everything else:

> I doubt that it is possible, without drastic standardization, to go higher than the North End's density of 275 dwellings per net acre. For most districts—lacking the North End's peculiar and long heritage of different building types—the ultimate danger mark imposing standardization must be considerably lower; I should guess, roughly,

that it is apt to hover at about 200 dwellings to the net acre. (Jacobs 1992, 482)

Note that in gross density terms, the current density of Boston's North End is smaller than Jacobs's net measurements in 1960 when she was doing her research for her book. According to Wikipedia, the North End still has a respectable 27,680 people per square mile, about 43 persons per gross acre. But a lot has changed for the worse since Jacobs's day. Her defense of its great urbanity was to no avail: Big chunks of the North End got demolished and replaced with Le Corbusian, high-rise housing in the public housing style. And, as happened in so many cities, highways came through, and small businesses died off as chain stores and Amazon came to rule. The North End we see today is nothing like the North End Jacobs experienced and delighted in.

Jacobs disliked what she called "in-between densities." In her view, they risked generating dull, "gray" neighborhoods that just weren't dense enough to generate a lively street life. She wrote:

> The tremendous gray belts of relatively low density that ring our cities, decaying and being deserted, or decaying and being overcrowded, are significant signals of the typical failure of low densities in big cities. (Jacobs 1992, 375)

She also did not agree with the Garden City notion that "little cities" and "small towns" could possibly prosper in the shadow of ever-expanding metropolitan areas that in her day were growing at the rate of "3000 acres a year" (Jacobs 1992, 400). She criticized the great writer, urbanist, and advocate of Garden Cities, Lewis Mumford, no doubt provoking his scathing and patronizing review of her book in the *New Yorker* (Mumford 1962). She dismissed his advocacy of "in-between" densities of 125 people per acre and was contemptuous of his dislike of very dense urban neighborhoods that packed in 500 people per acre (Jacobs 1992, 400).

In imagining an alternative urbanism to replace the so-called crimes of the too-dense Lower East Side of Manhattan, Garden City fans argued for a new urban vision intended to guarantee access to nature in the form of either individual gardens or views to greenery from every window. It is still not a bad planning consideration, but that path toward nature (rather than just scattering parks around), Jacobs thought, led straight to demolition of the great immigrant neighborhoods whose only real crime was being a bit too overcrowded for the refined sensibilities of the intelligentsia and the upper-middle-class urban planners. She was right about the war she was fighting against the demolition of the successful historic city, but in my view, wrong about the specific density crimes of Garden Cities.

She was right to object to statements of some Garden City advocates who favored extremely low, suburban densities of 12 dwelling units per acre, which is shockingly low and anti-urban. Yet things did not turn out that way. For example, Sunnyside Gardens Historic District in Queens, a hugely successful neighborhood in New York built on the Garden City idea, and successful on all of Jane Jacobs's terms, was built to twice that density at a mere 21 housing units per acre (1,200 dwelling units on 26 acres). It now houses a dense urbanity of 74,000 people per square mile or 115 people per gross acre, making it extremely far from a McMansion suburb or a miserable "in-between" density place. It is also just short of Mumford's proposed "maximum" density (Jacobs 1992; Talen 2018; Zipatlas.com).

Jane Jacobs was most interested in a different empirical point, one that was not about an "ideal" density, but about a "turning point" density. She asked herself: Is there a magic inflection point of people per acre at which the dull gray neighborhoods she disliked would suddenly become lively and convenient? She guessed, from her empirical work describing successful neighborhoods such as Brooklyn Heights, Rittenhouse Square, and Telegraph Hill, that the density turning point of "dull and gray" to "lively" might take place at 100 dwelling units per net acre, but much actually depended on other factors unique to a place (uses, location, the wider economy), so that a safer guess might be a higher density figure, but how much higher she was clearly loath to specify. As she was reasoning this idea through, she cautioned: "It will not do to jump to the conclusion that all areas of high dwelling density in cities do well. They do not, and to assume that this is 'the' answer would be to oversimplify outrageously" (368). To that caution she added:

> No concentration of residents, however high it may be, is "sufficient" if diversity is suppressed or thwarted by other insufficiencies. As an extreme example, no concentration of residents, however high, is "sufficient" to generate diversity in regimented projects, because diversity has been regimented out in any case. (Jacobs 1992, 369)

Note that "regimented projects" and diversity suppressors are Jane Jacobs code for high-rise towers and other massive single-use buildings, especially those in the style favored by her archenemy, Robert Moses, with his insistence on Le Corbusian "towers-in-the-park."

In a recent exhibition of density, the curators of the Skyscraper Museum in Manhattan took Jacobs's guesstimate figure of a possible maximum density of 200 dwelling units per net acre as the turning point for urban vitality. They multiplied that figure by 2.5 persons per household to get 500 persons per net acre and then claim to have found Jane Jacobs's "ideal density" (Skyscraper Museum 2019). Their notion is not just incorrect, but absurd. If we developed Manhattan at that density, we'd have to squeeze 7 million people onto the island.

When talking—and arguing—about density, it is also important to understand that the issue is less simple than it first appears because architects, developers, and planners can use design to play around with density in interesting ways. They can manipulate the form of the buildings on the lot, the size of the housing units in the building, and how much of a site of a building is left for gardens, courtyards, balconies, stairways, stoops, driveways, parking lots, and sidewalks. An excellent book for appreciating this point about density is the fascinating work, *Visualizing Density*, by Julie Campoli and Alex MacLean. The virtues of the book are twofold. First, the authors successfully illustrate that great densities can be achieved at low- and mid-rise, as anyone who has spent time in the Haussmannian buildings of Paris and Barcelona can tell you. Therefore, if anyone tells you that skyscrapers are the only way to get high densities, you can tell them they are wrong and point them to *Visualizing Density*. Second, the diversity of physical forms of buildings that is possible at any given level of density is worth pondering: Smart design really does matter. These points need to be more widely understood among those who talk about "densification of cities," which is too often a dog-whistle phrase in New York City for more skyscrapers and luxury condos that mostly benefit real estate developers and investors.

And last, one aspect of density that we must all understand and accept is that density in great historic cities had declined in the twentieth century, often for good reason. The historic core of these cities had shocking, overcrowded densities that reached their highs in the heyday of urban industrialization. The fact that Paris and Manhattan are less dense now than they were is not something that is to be lamented from a quality-of-life point of view. We do not need planners trying to densify us back to the Lower East Side of the 1920s. Instead, we need to find ways to keep the beautiful historic cores of our cities affordable to a wide range of income classes. This can be done through rent regulation, legal protections against eviction, and zoning rules that prevent de-densification of individual buildings, such as when hedge funders buy row houses and loft buildings, kick out the tenants, and convert the building to single-family use.

"More density is always good" advocates do not talk much about the serious issue of the distribution of density, but they should. In New York City, density is astonishingly concentrated in Manhattan and a few sections of historic Queens and Brooklyn. Council member Ben Kallos pointed out in 2019 that "nearly half of New York City's residential area (44%) is zoned at the lowest possible density of 0.5 FAR—covering 1.9 billion square feet and spanning 67 square miles—amounting to only 659 million square feet of buildable space" (*Kallos Testimony at Hearing on Affordable Housing Development* 2019). The real question, therefore, is why so much of New York City is zoned for single-family homes with yards and garages and why politicians do not attempt to gently densify those neighborhoods. I suggest the goal should be to spread density like thick peanut butter on a slice of bread rather than pile it up in the middle. At the heart of the matter is the need for a fairer distribution of the benefits and burdens of urban densities within the boundaries of New York City. Right now, Manhattan and historic core areas of Brooklyn and Queens are assumed to be capable of absorbing infinite densities, while single-family home areas are sacred cows, never to be mentioned in polite urban planning company.

Let's summarize:

- Despite Jacobs's equivocating about ideal densities, it is clear from the density comparisons that her favorite neighborhoods—used repeatedly as examples—are close to the densities of the great historic cities of Paris and Barcelona. To a great many urbanists, these cities epitomize great urbanity and share similar overall densities. These range from 25,000 to 70,000 persons per square mile, with the average about 40,000 people per square mile. We should take this lesson to heart and stop destroying those places that *are already* within that range of livable densities. Stop trying to densify already dense places that exceed these Goldilocks levels and realize that there is an upper limit to density at which point the beauty and livability of a city is forever compromised by overdevelopment. Moreover, we need to turn our attention to the distribution of density.
- Manhattan, and much of Brooklyn, is overbuilt and more than dense enough. It is in fact, far too dense in some neighborhoods. Moreover, nowhere in Manhattan are there suburban densities. Therefore, it is reasonable to conclude that the historic core of NYC has been filled

up. We cannot fit any more people in without demolishing significant historic fabric and making our collective sardine can unlivable.

Urban planners and economists have tried to expand Jane Jacobs's 1961 analysis about the benefits of density. To Jane Jacobs, the virtues of density were variables like vitality, convenience, diversity, and safety. But academics and planners have long wanted to find a way to "prove" the superiority of cities over suburbs. Alas, much of the work they produced in this vein is just bad science. Hundreds of studies have been done around the world to make the argument that willy-nilly adding more density will increase prosperity and creativity and happiness. In fact, so many studies have been done that a team at the Organisation for Economic Co-operation and Development (OECD) in 2018 finally did the world a service and conducted a meta-analysis covering some 400 such studies (Ahfeldt et al. 2018). On the one hand, their review provides a great summary of how poorly academics, especially economists, theorize about density; on the other hand, their review falls into a serious trap of bad science. The problem is that the OECD team tried to compute unscientifically how much more money municipal authorities would get from a policy of generically "increasing density." Specifically, they tried to estimate the monetary value that policymakers could get for every 1 percent increase in imposed density (this is also known in econ-speak as an "elasticity").

There are many problems with this kind of analysis that should make policymakers run for the hills and hide, but the most important is that the chain of causality between density and a given "good variable" like innovation (or safety and diversity) is not clear at all, especially when the studies, including the OECD meta-analysis, blithely ignore specific city policies, histories, and architectural morphologies that explain more about cities and the good things that density is supposed to create than does the density variable of "population per square mile."

Nonetheless, the study is an excellent guide to the reason "density" as an abstraction is useless in understanding cities—unless specific ranges of density are being discussed. One learns in the study that the researchers believe that "compact urban forms" (aka cities) are "associated" with more good things than sliced bread: greater productivity, patents, real estate prices, access to services and "amenities" (another word without clear definition), social equity, efficiency of public services, energy efficiency, pollution reduction, traffic flow, health, and general "well-being." Can the data that the researchers reviewed explain how much of all those good things are justified, or caused, specifically, by "density"? Alas, when compiling the four hundred studies, the OECD team ran smack into what they call an "interesting heterogeneity" of results. That means there is no clear pattern in the studies for many of the variables they looked at. For example: For 56 percent of the studies the authors deemed credible, greater density seemed to be associated with better job accessibility, but 33 percent of studies found the opposite. There was more consistency in studies that looked at productivity and patent applications: Ninety-six percent of the studies found an increase in productivity positively associated with greater density, and 80 percent found that "innovation" (defined as patent applications) was positively associated with greater density. Yet they stretch this observation into absurdity when they claim that a 10 percent increase in population per square mile will result in $793,000 worth of new patents, as if patent production wasn't dependent on a host of other obvious variables they neglected to look at, such as education and the presence of universities and research institutes, neither of which require hyper-density, let alone high levels of urban density. To show just how ridiculous this conclusion is, compare the patent applications coming from the suburban densities of Silicon Valley in California to the number of patent applications coming from the hyper-dense slums around Mumbai, India.

The problem with this kind of work is that it stretches the data beyond what it can justify in terms of policymaking. "Population per square mile" is not the only thing that explains great cities and neighborhoods: It is not the "God" variable that defines everything. As Jacobs said, it is a necessary but not a sufficient condition. So, what are the other variables? They are the unique policies; the unique political, economic, and institutional city histories; and the local geographies of specific places. These all interact with each other and give rise to the success of cities and their specific morphological forms (compare, for example Hong Kong to the city of Fez, in Morocco). The other variable is human agency: policies and the history of decisions about urban spaces that have taken place over several hundred years.

Chapter 4

Economics of the Urban Commons

IN 2019, SHAUN DONOVAN, a former Secretary of Housing and Urban Development under President Obama, ran for mayor of New York City. One of his more curious policy planks was a vow to pass a law about the Landmarks Preservation Commission (LPC). He wanted the City Council to oblige the LPC to calculate the monetary value of unbuilt airspace atop every potential landmark or historic district before the LPC could designate it. The idea was to impose a crude, Reaganite, cost-benefit analysis to shame the commission into reducing the number of properties it designated as historic and thereby not "waste" unbuilt airspace on historic preservation and saving the skydome. It was odd to see a liberal Democrat, a secretary of housing under Obama no less, espouse such a libertarian, Chicago School ideology, but it illustrates how far Edward Glaeser's ideas have traveled. But as we have seen, unleashing the developers in the historic core of the city in the name of affordable housing is a vast demolition project. Even the ancient Romans were more circumspect: in 43 A.D., the Roman Senate passed a law that said "buildings might not be destroyed for the purpose of speculation in land" (Craver 2010).

When making these financial cost-benefit proposals, fundamentalists reveal that they value the city's skydome only in terms of the dollar value world investors are willing to pay for buildable space into the skydome. They cloak this valuation in public interest language, insisting that their only concern is the supply of affordable housing. In the preceding chapter, I explained how that theory of trickle-down housing supply is wrong,

Figure 4.1. Widely circulated image of 111 West 57th Street supertall, seizing the views to Central Park. Image was used to market the building to buyers. Rendering attributed to Hayes Davidson.

especially in New York City. This chapter focuses on a related issue: how the approach to valuing the city in terms of whatever can be immediately monetized is also wrong, both in economic theory and in terms of ethics. I lay out an alternative economic framework in which the assets of a city make up a public "urban commons." This framework confounds traditional price theory, which holds that supply and demand seamlessly determine market prices and that the resulting market prices are the only meaningful and accurate measure of the value of a thing.

The things that make up the urban commons are a mix of public goods and common-pool assets. These include the public face of architecture that buildings present to the street, the streets and sidewalks, the bridges, tunnels, the skydome and the distribution of unfettered sunlight and clean air, historic districts, public parks, the public mass transit system, and all the buildings that serve the public such as libraries, hospitals, railway stations, bus stations, and schools. Jeremiah Moss, the author of *Vanishing New York* (Moss 2018), has made a strong case that many unique small Mom and Pop businesses occupying small storefronts are another asset in our collectively owned urban commons. I agree with him.

To understand the problem of pricing the urban commons, it is important to understand the difference between a commons and other forms of property and to dig into words and phrases like "skydome," "value," economic efficiency, and Potential Pareto Improvements (and its real estate grandchild, "highest and best use"). Understanding these concepts shows how the current policies of the city are stacked against assigning proper value to the urban commons. Finally, this chapter analyzes two assets within our commons: the skydome and historic districts. Fundamentalists have accused one of these assets, historic districts, of multiple crimes. These accusations have filtered into the mainstream press where we too often read (wrongly) that historic districts are "too white" and "too elite" and are the cause of gentrification and the affordable housing crisis. This chapter pushes back, showing how those accusations are unfounded.

What Is a Commons?

From time to time, shifting views about the scarcity of something cause societies to change the rules of the game for how we use or exploit the newly scarce thing. A famous example is fisheries. Back in the day, we imagined there were unlimited fish in the ocean. Unregulated fishing drove a few species extinct with giant nets that scraped the ocean bottom of all life. Society woke up and changed the rules. Now, in some parts of the world, fishermen have quotas for the catch of certain fish. Some nets have been outlawed. Someone monitors the fish and the catch. It's not perfect, but many of the oceans off our coasts are now a managed, regulated public commons. Today, most people consider these rule changes about how we manage fish to be normal, but at the time of the change, it seemed outrageous, and many fishermen hotly contested the new rules.

Here in the big city, we have a similar problem, but the disappearing catch is not fish. Instead, what we are losing is sunlight, sky, socioeconomic diversity, viewscapes, historic districts, small businesses, sidewalks, and streets, as well as the experience of successful urbanity (Sassen 2001). To preserve these assets, we must assert society's collective ownership of them and experiment with new ways to manage them better.

Our urban commons resources are crucial to successful urbanity. They consist of a mix of public goods and what economists call common-pool resources (Poteete, Janssen, and Ostrom 2010). Common-pool resources are resources that are difficult to privatize, enclose, limit access to, and trade in markets. Since nobody owns them outright, people think of them as unlimited and free for the taking, but the reality is they can be rendered scarce through overuse since the resource is not in unlimited supply. The unfenced, grazing lands of yore out west are a classic example of a common-pool resource, often simply called "the commons" (after shared, non-privatized pasture and forest land in feudal villages). Old-school academics used to say such grazing lands should be fenced and privatized entirely to avoid what Hardin called "the tragedy of the commons" (Hardin 1968). That's a situation where if there are no rules, everybody who owns cattle is tempted to put just one more cow onto the common grazing land. Bit by bit a tipping point is reached as each extra cow begins to erode the grass and the soil until a dust bowl ensues and then everybody's cows starve. We now know that the tragedy of the commons is not inevitable and that many common-pool resources can be and are well managed in the public interest. Indeed, Elinor Ostrom got a Nobel Prize in Economics for making just that point (Ostrom 2012).

Common-pool resources, like the ocean, are a bit different from public goods, although sometimes there is a fuzzy boundary between them. Public goods are those things that government provides, like policies to deal with global warming, public schools, streets, sidewalks, fire-fighting services, and national defense: things that everyone can use without diminishing the ability of others to do so as well. Like common-pool resources, they are goods for which it is difficult to exclude people from gaining access. Private property is different from both a commons and a public good: You can exclude people from using private property, and when you use it, there is less of it for someone else.

Types of Value

Some economists tie themselves up in knots over how to value public goods and common-pool resources. These are not objects like pencils that get traded in thick, busy markets full of buyers and sellers, and so these assets don't have a market price. There aren't even markets where suppliers can meet up with buyers. The consequent knots economists tie themselves into to assign prices to these goods include the use of "shadow prices" (a fancy phrase for making up a price) or a procedure I discuss below called "contingent valuation." The problem is that value is just not the same thing as market price. Value is the relative desirability we assign to something. It reflects our flawed, fraught, confused, and ever-changing miscalculations about the benefit something brings to us. It's even more fraught when we realize that the total value of anything can be divided into three kinds of values. These are:

1. Values in the object we know exist and that can be accurately measured by the amount of money someone will pay for it. In the case of city sunlight, we might look at the price of energy and calculate how

much electricity solar panels can produce. That tells of one tiny part of the actual value of sunlight.
2. Values in the object that we know exist, but we don't know how to measure accurately using money. In the case of sunlight, think about how sunlight is known to affect psychological well-being. We can pretend to figure out a price for that, by guesstimating the value of psychological counseling forgone per unit of sunlight gained. But really it is a guess at just one part of the value of sunlight. The real value is just unknowable.
3. Values in the object we don't know about yet, including the value future generations assign to it. For example, many years ago we assigned no "ecosystem" value to forests because we didn't have the scientific understanding about what ecosystem services forests provided to humanity.

This categorization of values sounds easy enough, right? In practice it is complicated. Let's examine a couple of cases to illustrate the dilemmas that arise. First, consider a particular forest in Canada, not too far from Montreal, one that houses a cemetery belonging to the Mohawk First Nation. The Mohawk have resided in the area for millennia. What's the value of their forest? Our first thought might be that its value is the money we could make by clear-cutting all the trees, killing all the beasts, and then toting up the sales of wood, fur, meat, and feathers. Or we could also assume a sustainable timber business in the forest, stop ourselves from a wholesale clear-cut, and instead add in the money people pay to hunt, ski, hike, camp, and swim in the remaining forest while we sustainably harvest timber now and then. Another possibility is to calculate the amount of money we could get if we not only clear-cut and sold the trees to the paper companies but then subdivided the land and built a housing development with a golf course next to it, as was proposed for this Mohawk land in a famous land dispute. Those are the values we easily calculate with money, even if they are speculative.

The second type of value for the Mohawk Forest, the one that can't be measured, is more complicated. There is, for example, an "existence" value to the forest to the Mohawk. They may consider the forest to be their fundamental place in the world. The loss of their place in the world cannot be measured on any yardstick known. City dwellers in Montreal might also assign an unmeasurable existence value to the forest. They may dream of one day knowing the pleasure of walking through an old-growth forest that

Figure 4.2. During the 1990 Oka Crisis in Canada, Mohawks asserted their rights to their forest when a local mayor proposed to build a golf course and housing development on the site. Photo from *Montreal News*.

is connected to the history of a First Nation. They value a world in which such places exist, in which the Mohawk have a home.

The third type of value is also tricky. It might be the value of the ecosystem services that the forest provides to society, such as carbon sequestration or water filtering, or the value of unknown mushroom species in that forest that might save the planet from oil slicks, depression, and posttraumatic stress syndrome. We know about some of those kinds of values only recently in world history, but a hundred years ago we could not even imagine them. They were values we came to understand only after scientific knowledge about the forest and mushrooms grew. The prices of all those things are not known with any precision.

To make it even crazier, different people weigh all these three values very differently. For example, the real Canadian mayor of the small town next to this Mohawk Forest dreamed of increasing property tax revenues—if only he could turn that forest into a suburban housing subdivision and a golf course. On the other end of the spectrum, the Mohawk there might assign a negative price to the housing subdivision because the forest is part of their home. They don't want to move. And then a timber company would be interested in the value contained in the market price of paper made from trees. Whose valuation is more important, the Mohawks' or the small-town mayor's? In this example, the battle over what the forest would be and who it would serve and whose valuation of what aspect of the forest's total possible value would triumph led to armed confrontations. The 1990 battle to determine the outcome was an ugly one, known as the Oka Crisis. The Canadian government used military tanks to assert its will against the Mohawk. The Mohawks took up hunting rifles and stones. But there was no economically "best" or "optimal" solution, no cost-benefit that made any sense unless you took the side of the mayor or the side of the Mohawks. Economists have nothing relevant to say in that situation. There was only a political or a military solution.

In a second example, consider how the great urbanist, writer and West Village resident Jane Jacobs might assign value to her place in the world, the human-scale historic neighborhood of Greenwich Village and Hudson Street where she lived in New York in the 1950s. Although years later, her

Photo 4.3. The Canadian Army, with armored cars, comes for Mohawk Forest. Photo by Tom Hansen of *Canadian Press*.

neighborhood was designated a historic district, it was not protected in the 1950s and 1960s. The powerful urban planner Robert Moses wanted to demolish Jacobs's neighborhood and build a highway over it to stimulate all kinds of new tower housing river to river. Jacobs and her neighbors managed to stop him.

Because Jane Jacobs was passionately attached to her neighborhood, let's assume she chose to value her neighborhood at "infinity." Now imagine a hard-core suburbanite who dislikes cities and might never visit Greenwich Village. To that person, maybe Jane's neighborhood has zero value. And to highway builder Robert Moses, the value of the West Village was also zero: He imagined huge sums might accrue to the city if he replaced the neighborhood with a highway and new towers all around it.

Whose value wins out? Will it be Jane's value of infinity or Robert Moses's valuation? Whose valuation is even considered? And more important, who wins? The answer is whoever has the political power to make their personal valuation trump everyone else's. Although Jane Jacobs saved her Greenwich Village neighborhood and that of SoHo and much of Lower Manhattan in a unique moment in New York City history, it was a rare victory, which is why it is so legendary. Most of the time, in New York City, the powerful win, and the non-financial, non-monetizable values of places are simply lost to history. The key point that I explore in the following pages is that when you decide to pay attention to only the monetizable money values of a place and ignore the non-monetizable values, you are explicitly choosing sides in these battles and *that is a political choice, not one dictated by economic theory*. There are ethics involved when picking sides as well. For example, is it okay to just ignore the Mohawk First Nation and do what's good for the winners of the game?

Ethics arise because there is simply no unbiased, value-free, nonpolitical way to claim that one type of value inherently trumps another, *without at some point deciding to value one person's well-being as more important than that of another person's*. There is certainly no technocratic or scientific way to pick sides. What's a policymaker or politician to do in such situations? I suggest that the only valid way forward is greater use of deliberative, lengthy, direct democracy. That's a high standard. And democracy is a scary way to do things. What if voters choose something that the real estate developer, urban planner, economist, or architect doesn't like? What if they choose a course of action that an "expert" panel disagrees with? In such a situation, fundamentalists tsk-tsk and murmur that uneducated NIMBY yahoos are taking power. Nevertheless, and without a clear alternative, I see no choice but to propose a more democratic way of making

Figure 4.4a (*above*). Jane Jacobs with her family on Hudson Street in the Village. Photo cropped from the Burns Library photo collage of family photographs, oversized folder 46, Jane Jacobs papers, MS-1995-029. John J. Burns Library.

Figure 4.4b (*right*). Architect Paul Rudolf's Ford Foundation–sponsored rendering of the glories of the Lower Manhattan Expressway that Robert Moses wanted to build to replace Jane's neighborhood (and SoHo) river to river. Image from the Library of Congress.

the judgment call about how to value non-monetizable public goods and common-pool goods. It is undemocratic for the powerful and wealthy few to impose their will upon the many, and nonsense for them to claim it is just Econ 101 or "just economics."

The main point is to understand that social science cannot compare values that can be measured against values that have no price—without choosing to weigh the benefits to one group of people as more important than the benefits a different group would get under a different solution to the problem. Such rankings or comparisons can only be done—and should only be done—through direct democracy.

But Wait, Can't We Use "Contingent Valuation" to Assign Monetary Values to These Hard-to-Value Things?

Environmental economists have tried in vain to work around the problem of how to assign value to non-traded things that have no markets by using a controversial methodology called "contingent valuation." Sounds fancy, but it is not. To conduct a contingent valuation study, the economist corners willing citizens off the street, describes a long, hypothetical scenario that gives all kinds of details about the public or common-pool resource in question. Then she asks the citizen to choose a price that they would be "willing to pay" for the thing just described. The problem is that people respond to these questions with various levels of incredulity at the inanity of the question. Some things have no price. They often humor the economist with an off-the-cuff answer, instead of saying, "How the hell can I answer such a dumb question?"

If contingent valuation sounds fishy and unscientific to you, that's because it is. Back in 1991, two well-regarded economists surveyed contingent valuation (and another method called travel-cost method) and concluded in high academic-speak:

> Neither method can be legitimized in a theoretical or applicable sense from a neoclassical, psychometric or general systems point of view.... [The] approaches lack methodological, theoretical and empirical grounding. (Eberle and Hayden 1991, 682)

The use of contingent valuation methodology was so controversial that in 1993 the National Oceanic and Atmospheric Administration convened a panel of *éminences grises* of the economics profession to opine on the method. The panel included Nobel Laureates Kenneth Arrow and Robert Solow. While the pair pronounced it acceptable under exacting methodological conditions and best practices, controversy continued to boil. One of the problems, as a judge pointed in plain language during a court case in which these issues were argued, "from the bald eagle to the blue whale and snail darter, natural resources have values that are not fully captured by the market system" (Loum 2013). Another problem, as eminent economist Jerry Hausman noted in one of two serious surveys on the methodology:

> I believe that respondents to contingent valuation surveys are often not responding out of stable or well-defined preferences, *but are essentially inventing their answers on the fly, in a way which makes the resulting data useless for serious analysis.* (Hausman 2012, 43; emphasis mine)

Hausman is a noted specialist in econometrics at MIT and an academic similar in stature to Arrow and Solow. He concluded that contingent valuation was a "hopeless" methodology without any actual science in it. He pointed out that many of the method's supporters were beltway consultants making money off federal contracts doing legally required cost-benefit analyses. Recall that cost-benefit analyses were a requirement that Ronald Reagan put into the regulatory system after his election in 1981. And yet, despite Hausman's damning conclusions, thousands of consultants still labor under federal contracts producing such pseudo-science and "hopeless" analyses to this day.

The Uselessness of Efficiency and Pareto Optimality as a Standard of Value

Could we get away from these valuation difficulties if we compared not money but efficiency gains? What if we compare the incremental "output" to Gross Domestic Product that a policy might generate and compare it to GDP without the policy? Is that a more neutral standard to decide things by? The answer is no. As we saw in the Mohawk Forest case and the Jane Jacobs West Village case, different people want different "outputs" from the same resource. And we are still left with a profound ethical dilemma: How can anyone compare the "benefit" Jane Jacob and her neighbors got out of saving their neighborhood versus how much utility Robert Moses and his followers would have gotten by destroying it? If we make increases to "output" as the unit of measure to make that value comparison, it just rigs the entire game to only valuing the "output" of monetizable GDP gains and nothing else. We end up with the same conundrum that we started with. Alas, the choice of measuring unit determines the value game, be it money as the measuring unit or incremental quantities of output. Either way it dooms us to circular reasoning, dubbed the "numeraire illusion" (Ellerman 2009).

What this means is that economists have nothing "scientific" to say about what should be done when different people want a different "output" from a resource. It is a political and thus ethical decision, not an economic one. Whose values, whose goals, whose desired uses for the resources of the Mohawk Forest or Greenwich Village win?

Some economists ignore this problem of comparing people's competing ways of valuing an outcome and turn to the "gold standard" of economic efficiency among traditional neoclassically trained economists, something called "Pareto Efficiency." It is an idea named after an Italian sociologist, Vilfredo Pareto. Pareto argued that a state of the world is the "best" of all states of the world *if you can't reallocate the goods of the world to make someone better off without making someone else worse off*. Economists call this state of affairs "Pareto Optimality" and teach the idea to everyone who takes Econ 101 in college. The use of the word "optimal" is a bit misleading, as economist Amartya Sen has pointed out: "A society can be Pareto Optimal and still be perfectly disgusting" (Sen 2017, 22).

To understand what Sen meant, imagine a society of slaves and slave owners. The slaves long for freedom. The slave owners don't like freedom, but slavery is legal. In this society, it is impossible to make the slaves better off without making the slave owners worse off in a purely financial sense. That slave society, according to Pareto, is "optimal," and as Sen said, "perfectly disgusting."

Economists tend to brush over that problem in a kind of professional cognitive dissonance. Lots of economics papers have been written to explain how, under the extremely strict conditions of a "perfect" market, people making deals in a market economy will bring society to a Pareto Optimal place through the Econ 101 miracle of supply meeting demand to create stable equilibria. The only problem, as we saw earlier, is that the conditions of a perfect market are hardly ever found in the real world; hence, Pareto Optimality is a bit of a theoretical idea, useless for real-world policy where slavery and all kinds of horrific injustices remain.

Economist Lionel Robbins, to his credit, argued that economists should not be in the business of unscientifically comparing the welfare of different groups of people such as slaves and slave owners, or First Nation People versus small-town mayors. That, Robbins said, could never be a scientific exercise; it was really something that belonged to the realms of justice and politics. And he was right. But economists just could not leave it alone. Enter the historical discussion of this problem by two British economists, Nicholas Kaldor and Nobel Laureate John Hicks. They published papers in 1939 arguing that economists could get around the sticky ethical conundrum of differently valuing the welfare of different people under various policy regimes by concerning themselves only with *improvements to the sheer quantity of potential extra output* that could—in theory—be produced by a proposed policy. They defined a "Potential Pareto Improvement" (abbreviated PPI) to be the increased value of national output that might take place—regardless of how the benefits of the new bigger pie got distributed after the new policy was implemented. (Note that "output" often gets measured by Gross Domestic Product, which is the market value of goods and services an economy produces.) If the new policy increases output or GDP, Kaldor and Hicks called it "Pareto Efficient" after our guy, Vilfredo Pareto.

Kaldor and Hicks said economists could stand proud as unbiased social scientists if they concerned themselves only with the following ethical standard: If the winners of the policy that increased output could *potentially* compensate those who lost out in the implementation of the policy, it's a go and a win. *The actual compensation does not have to take place*:

> A potential Pareto improvement . . . [is] in all cases [when] it is *possible* [through government taxes and transfers] to make everybody better off. . . . There is no need for the economist to prove—as indeed he never could prove—that as a result of the adoption of a certain measure that nobody in the community is going to suffer. (Hicks 1939)

That is an awfully weak ethical standard and pretty much a fig-leaf justification for capitalism, which is why it is beloved by libertarian types. Here's an illustration of the ethics and political choices that the Kaldor and Hicks efficiency concept imposes. Take the long period of industrialization in eighteenth- and nineteenth-century England. The period saw massive dislocation of people, untold suffering from colonization, slavery, Satanic mills, child labor, and the brutalized lives of countless people whose very bodies, early deaths, and miserable lives fed the industrialization process that increased output by fantastic amounts. By Kaldor-Hicks standards of efficiency, it was all a glorious success. The pain of those who fed the machine was worth it to the winners of industrialization. After all, the winners could, in theory, compensate the losers, even though they did not. Libertarian economist Deirdre McCloskey from the University of Chicago explains it this way: "The gain since 1800 from economic change has massively outweighed in monetary and ethical terms [sic] the loss to English woodmen disemployed by Swedish timber, or American blacksmiths disemployed by automobiles" (McCloskey 2009, 22). She is of course directly comparing the "utilities" of the present-day winners and past losers, and ignoring vast categories of people whose lives were made miserable or sacrificed during the industrialization period.

Despite sustained controversy over the years over the ethical dubiousness of Hicks's statement, economists started applying the Kaldor-Hicks efficiency test for public policy. Some call it the KH test for short. Others came to call it the PPI test. It was used, as the distinguished economist Marc Blaug pointed out, to justify the very virtue and superiority of capitalism itself. The PPI efficiency test is ubiquitous in the economics literature and came to be embedded in the foundations of Reagan-required federal cost-benefit analyses. It is, as we shall see, also at the core of the real estate notion of "highest and best use" of a plot of land. The PPI test chooses the side of the monetizable values or the output-increasing values that accrue to capitalism's winners in an ugly eternal battle over what gets valued and how it gets valued. As economist Lionel Robbins insisted some years after Kaldor and Hicks published:

> I contended that the aggregation or comparison of the different satisfactions of different individuals involves judgments of value rather than judgments of fact, and that such judgments are beyond the scope of positive science. Nothing that has been said by any of my critics has persuaded me that this contention is false. (Robbins 1945, vii)

To be fair, because of the ugly and the questionable ethics behind it, many economists sided with Robbins in this discussion and disavowed use of the Kaldor-Hicks efficiency test. Economists are not all libertarians. For example, economist David Ellerman pulled no punches in agreeing with Robbins: "MPKH [Marshall-Pigou-Kaldor-Hicks] is fatally flawed . . . incoherent, and 'rather pointless' . . . and as a shortcut to efficiency a 'dead end'" and "recommendations based on KH efficiency reasoning are baseless" (Ellerman 2009, 3). Another economist joined the chorus:

> KH is an unusable standard. To implement KH efficient policies, government would require wisdom beyond its grasp. Prices only provide evidence of past willingness to pay and cannot be used for formulating future polices. (Stringham 2001, 48)

Another economist pointed out, "The Kaldor-Hicks approach has long been recognized to be riddled with logical inconsistencies and ethical failures" (Glick and Lozada 2021, 1). Economist David Ellerman entered the fray again and dealt the concept a definitive deathblow, pointing out that if we start the analysis by valuing everything in, say, the money value of increases to Gross Domestic Product (or any other unit of measure) we may fantasize that we are being scientific, but that is just an illusion, we are in reality biasing the whole enterprise from the get-go—merely by our initial choice of unit with which to measure value. To wit:

> Policy recommendations based only on the use of one numeraire [the units in which benefits and costs are stated] are groundless. The critique applies to all uses of the Kaldor-Hicks (KH) principle. Hence it is not just another nail in the coffin, but the last nail and final demise of the KH principle. (Ellerman 2009, 6)

The upshot? The temptation to assign money prices to everything will always be there, and our captains of industry will want it that way because they always win if we play that game, but it is a meaningless way to compare values. It is not "scientific." It is only efficient in terms of your choice of numeraire. The attempt to assign prices to many things is simply shot through with built-in bias for the winners in a certain extreme version of capitalism.

The alternative is to insist—as a society—in our courts and laws and regulatory agencies that many things are indeed priceless and require non-market means to decide their use and management (Ackerman and Heinzerling 2005).

If the Kaldor-Hicks Test Is Dead, Then So Is "Highest and Best Use"

Vicki Been is a professor at New York University who teaches land use and zoning. Mayor Bill de Blasio appointed her as his affordable housing commissioner, so her ideas matter. A clue to how she thinks might be found in the textbook she assigns in her zoning course. It is a famous "anti-zoning" textbook by Ellickson and Tarlock called *Land Use Controls: Case and Materials*. The authors tell the reader upfront:

> Our approach is revisionist in that the premises underlying public land-use controls *are rigorously questioned at every opportunity.* (Ellickson and Tarlock 1981, 62; emphasis mine)

Subsequent chapters are devoted to giving strategic guidance to attorneys who might want to go to court to challenge public-land-use controls (aka, regulation) on the side of property owners rather than the public at large. Been took charge of revising the book and is now a co-author for the updated edition, but the orientation remains.

Ellickson and Tarlock rely on what turns out to be a tragically flawed and outdated nugget of economic theory: the same Kaldor-Hicks efficiency test we have been talking about above. They urge lawyers who wish to challenge a land-use restriction to use three arguments. Their first is an extremist and incorrect assertion that a land-use restriction or regulation is "inefficient from a social perspective" (Ellickson and Tarlock 1981, 63). Then they proceed to define inefficiency in the strangest of terms: "when the burdens on the restricted landowner are greater than the benefits of the restrictions to the landowner's neighbor and other outsiders." At this point, the reader might join me in asking Ellickson, Tarlock, and Been: How on earth can you compare those different benefits in two columns without taking the side of either the neighbor or the landowner? How are you measuring benefits and costs? This is a classic trap of the Pareto Optimality concept. To their credit, the textbook writers recognize this, but then merely reassert a hopeless mangle of the PPI concept:

> Economists prefer to define efficiency as Pareto-superiority, but usually recognize that the policymaker must rest on the Kaldor-Hicks test, which calls a policy efficient if those who gain from the policy value their gains in an amount greater than the amount the losers from the policy value their losses. (Ellickson and Tarlock 1981, 64)

Clearly, the authors don't see how the KH test is ethically compromised and unscientific. But how do courts look at this issue when it comes to land-use fights? Sadly, many judges turn to professional real estate appraisers for guidance out of this swamp. Yet appraisers are typically just MBA graduates whose job in land-use battles is to provide an opinion during routine dogfights over competing proposals for a plot of land. For training on how to do their job, appraisers rely on their own professional body, the Appraisal Institute of the United States. The institute instructs them on best practice when applying a test called the "highest and best use" (HBU) to value the competing uses of a property. The institute tells appraisers that a new proposed use of a property (usually the demolition of a building and its replacement by a new building) must fulfill the following conditions:

1. The proposed new building must be a physical possibility given the nature of the site.

2. It must be legally permissible under the current zoning.
3. It must be financially feasible.
4. It must produce maximum productivity [to measurable, monetizable GDP] (Wilson and Hungerford 1995a). For example, if the Mohawk Forest was clear-cut and turned into a housing subdivision and thus might generate a speculative 20 percent profit, and a sustainable forest enterprise that kept the forest generates only a realistic 5 percent profit, then the appraiser must say that the housing project fits "highest and best use," and the small-town mayor wins, and the Mohawks lose.

Notice immediately that the Institute's Criterion Four is just a version of the discredited Kaldor-Hicks test. It explicitly ignores all the values of the site that cannot be monetized and pretends that some values can be accurately assigned, guesstimated with pretend shadow prices or through a bogus contingent valuation exercise. This kind of hopelessly biased, non-economic, purely financial reasoning happens all the time. A New York judge confessed to me in an interview that he would rank as more valuable to the world the wealth that AT&T produces over the health and well-being of thousands of residents near the building where AT&T produced nuisance noise, even though the noise affected five square blocks of a residential area. A lawsuit against AT&T would be pointless in his courtroom, he explained. To the judge, the GDP wealth produced by a powerful actor in the economy (AT&T) is valued more highly than the well-being of thousands of residents in a five-squareblock area around the building AT&T was renting.

"Highest and best use" remains controversial in some real estate circles, but only a few. For example, one of the most eminent of real estate economists, James Graaskamp of the University of Wisconsin, complained long ago that highest and best use (HBU) was being wrongly defined as "that use which would maximize the owner's wealth." Graaskamp accurately pointed out that

> highest and best use is an anachronism from laissez-faire attitudes of the nineteenth century.... It implies certainty of one man's judgment.... Highest and best use is theoretically and pragmatically untenable as presently defined. (Graaskamp 1972, 519, cited in Vandell and Carter 2000, 308)

Environmentalists also attacked HBU and the Appraisal Institute for neglecting values that could not be monetized. The issue was especially important under Ronald Reagan when his administration made the decision to sell off government-owned forests to private developers. The administration needed a price at which to sell national forests. It hired a firm to appraise the value of the forest as a public good. A conference was held, the Interagency Land Acquisitions Conference, in 1995. It reached an unethical and unscientific verdict:

> Non-economic highest and best use is not a proper basis for the estimate of market value, and accordingly, that a highest and best use of conservation, preservation, or other use that requires that property to be withheld from economic production in perpetuity is not a valid use upon which to estimate market value. Such an estimate is, therefore, not in conformance with the uniform Appraisal Standards for Federal Land Acquisitions. (Cited in Roberson 1997; Dotzour, Grissom, Liu, and Pearson 1990)

Although it has been attacked repeatedly, that political standard has been undemocratically imposed on our society ever since. A debate about its rightness raged for years in the pages of the Appraisal Institute's magazine, *Right of Way* (Wilson and Hungerford 1995b; Lusvardi 1996). Many of the criticisms focused on the issue of how the decision was made (in a committee) and on the fact that the writers of the verdict never defined what the public interest value of the lands might be. The conclusion? It is time to mount a serious legal challenge to the use of HBU that imposes market-determined standards of output efficiency as the standard for anything.

To sum up so far: The problem we have surveyed is that economics as a discipline does not have an acceptable, unbiased way to assign monetary values to public goods or common-pool resources. That means we can't turn to economists (or real estate appraisers) for answers about the trade-offs between the values that the Mohawk First Nation assigns to its old-growth forest and the competing use of that forest as a monetizable housing suburb that generates property-tax revenue. Neither can economists ethically weigh in on competing uses of the land that makes up Greenwich Village. These decisions cannot be made by social scientist "experts" but must instead be made in the very flawed political realm of democracy, so we might want to improve the way our democracy functions as a top priority.

Let's now look more closely at two assets in our urban commons that are always under the threat of being valued solely for their value to the real estate industry alone: the skydome and historic districts.

The Skydome as an Element of Our Urban Commons

It is easy to imagine the sky above the city as a dome that covers us. Designers of video games call it a skydome, and we saw its use in the film *The

Figure 4.5. Rendering of a skydome, illustrating regulated airspace around a city. Image by Daria Boryensova.

Hunger Games. Figure 4.5 shows a portrayal of the skydome. The skydome above our cities is a common-pool resource and a public asset of our urban commons. It is not a private asset. It belongs to everyone. Overuse of it can result in a tragedy of the commons as in the case of Midtown Manhattan, where, as we learned earlier, we have overbuilt into the skydome such that certain streets no longer have any direct sunlight at any time of the year.

In New York, the City Planning Commission regulates the skydome. Height restrictions and buildable space allotments (called floor area ratios, or FAR) determine how high one can build into the skydome. Very tall buildings reduce access to the skydome for those down below who walk the streets and privatize it for those who can afford to buy or rent the higher floors. Views into the skydome and the visual accessibility of the sky from the street vary by how high the buildings are. Inwood in Upper Manhattan is a neighborhood of six-story buildings on wide streets, so the skydome there is vivid and accessible to all. Contrast that to the skydome from street level in the towerized Financial District: The sky is hardly visible from the street (Figure 4.6a and 4.6b).

Some property owners want to claim that if they buy a plot of land, they own the skydome "to the heavens," in what jurists call an incorrect, extremist, "Blackstonian" interpretation of property rights. William Blackstone was the eighteenth-century author of a series of books called *Commentaries on the Laws of England*. He favored a biblical interpretation of property ownership, referring to a God-granted "despotic dominion"

Figure 4.6a and 4.6b. Disappearing Skydome. Left: the sky from low-rise Tribeca on West Broadway at Thomas, next to the Odeon restaurant. Right, the skydome from the middle of Park Row between Church and Broadway next to the Silverstein tower that is a Four Seasons. Photos by author.

of "man over beast." The quote that inspired Blackstone about property rights is Genesis 1:28:

> God said unto them, Be fruitful, and multiply, and replenish the earth, and subdue it: and have dominion over the fish of the sea, and over the fowl of the air, and over every living thing that moveth upon the earth. (Genesis 1:28)

Blackstone particularly liked the words "subdue" and "dominion." He wrote:

> There is nothing which so generally strikes the imagination, and engages the affections of mankind, as the right of property; or that *sole and despotic dominion* [my emphasis] which one man claims and exercises over the external things of the world, in total exclusion of the right of any other individual in the universe. (Blackstone, *Commentaries*, chap. 1)

"Despotic dominion" was always a nonsense idea beloved by the lordly class, even in Blackstone's days. It never really applied in England and is more a myth, a fantasy of those with property. The reality is that all property comes with caveats and limitations. More typical was the English law of "ancient light" (Campbell-Dollaghan 2013; Buckley 2013; Gevurtz 1977; Zielinska-Dabkowska and Xavia 2019; Pereira 2018; Gray 2012; Hu 2017). The ancient light rule said: If you could prove that you had sunlight coming in through a window for twenty years, nobody could block that window with new construction. Here in our country, we don't have England's ancient light law, indeed, our legal system does not recognize light as a scarce resource. But it must start.

With the arrival of airplanes, Congress legislated that the sky above 500 feet is public domain (Banner 2008). Later, the Supreme Court decided that a country chicken farmer could only own the sky up to 83 feet because airplanes needed to fly down to 83 feet to land on an airstrip next to the farm. That figure of 83 feet is about the height of an eight-story building. But that ruling leaves a question: What about the sky between 83 and 500 feet? Is it a no-man's-land? It is not. There is no such thing as no-man's-land. It belongs to us as a public common, an asset for us all. And clearly, the judge in the chicken farm case seemed unaware that zoning court cases prior to 1926 already regulated the space between the earth and 83 feet into the skydome.

The amount of visible sky has the effect of determining how much sunlight flows onto the street and into the windows of our buildings. Public health authorities in New York in the 1930s understood this. They sought to calculate the minimum amount of light city residents needed to have inside their apartment in order to stay healthy and happy, a figure that kept shrinking in New York until the topic was dropped as politically unpalatable, given that nobody but the wealthy had enough light to be healthy and happy.[1] But scientists now tell us—and our common sense agrees—people need sky, sunlight, and the sight of grass or trees to thrive. When we have sunlight, our blood pressure lowers, we laugh more, and we are kinder to others. People who work in natural sunlight are more productive than those who work in artificial light (Buckley 2013). The challenge is therefore how to share the skydome equitably instead of auctioning it off to the highest bidder.

But in New York we are in a battle over competing use of the skydome. Real estate developers seek ever more buildable space to sell to investors. They continually want to pierce the skydome ever higher, as the "supertall" skyscraper phenomenon illustrates. To get their way, developers bypass the democratic process and seek to control the regulatory body that allocates buildable rights into the skydome. We'll see more about that in the following chapters.

Clearly, the solution to the mismanagement of New York's skydome is not full-scale privatization of the skydome, but better management in the public interest so we don't shadow parks or entomb people's existing windows. We want to ensure that we share the skydome equitably, so all have access to its benefits instead of letting developers mine it like a gold field for their gain alone.

Former City Planning Commissioner and real estate developer Joe Rose understood all this. He called the unregulated way builders have been grabbing the skydome "a race to the top." The result, he said, was "violence to the urban fabric" (Rose 1999) or in economists' lingo, a "social cost" and a "negative externality." Rose was right. Look around New York City: Out-of-context, ludicrously tall, luxury condos are popping up everywhere, many of them built "as of right," which means without public oversight, mostly through New York's weakly regulated procedures for air rights transfers.

Recognizing that the skydome and the sunlight and iconic views it grants are scarce resources that need to be husbanded in the public interest is hardly a revolutionary concept in economics. But the legal and regulatory worlds seem not to have gotten the memo. It's not hopeless, for we can be creative about laws that address the issue. San Francisco has a shadow law. London protects view corridors to Saint Paul's. Boston and Washington,

Figure 4.7. Supertalls lining up to seize the views of Central Park. Rendering by Municipal Art Society.

D.C., have tough height limits. Santa Barbara has a rule that regulates construction for 100 feet around landmarks. Bhutan measures happiness as a national goal. All it takes is recognition that the skydome needs better management.

Historic Districts as Assets in Our Urban Commons

Historic districts are areas of the city that connect us visually to some part of our past. These places exist in all parts of New York City. They range from a half-block row of spectacular brick row houses on Henderson Place on the Upper East Side, to Black-owned row houses in Bed-Stuy, to the tall prewar apartment corridors of West End Avenue. Some official historic districts are very small, like Pomander Walk on the Upper West Side. Some are very large, like that of Park Slope in Brooklyn. Together, they occupy a tiny percentage of the city's land mass and property lots.

The unique character of a historic district is defined by a combination of scale, architectural language, aesthetics, building materials, void ratios, treatment of street walls, sense of place, and cultural and historical significance. These combine to create a unique sense of place. "Official" historic districts come into being when the Landmarks Preservation Commission declares an area historic and issues a map. Building owners inside the boundaries of an officially designated district must submit to not-very-burdensome regulatory oversight so that the physical integrity and the distinctiveness of each building is maintained and the value of the larger asset that is the historic district is not compromised. When the commission does this, we as a society are declaring a district's distinctiveness to be a gift that we wish to bequeath to future generations (Semes 2009). There are unofficial historic districts as well. These are neighborhoods that also connect us to our past and have great visual integrity but are ignored by the political process involved in official designation.

These districts—official or not—are full of public spaces: facades, sidewalks, roadways, parks, libraries, and civic buildings. They have stores, hotels, and restaurants open to all. They are public spaces. When made official, historic districts are government-created public goods and a public commons at the same time. Of course, all real estate has some elements of a public good. As two economists put it:

> Real estate consists of a bundle of characteristics and amenities. Certain of these, such as structural amenities (rooms, shelter, windows, etc.) are private goods in the sense of being excludable and

depletable in terms of consumption (others can be excluded from consuming their services, and their services per individual decline as additional individuals consume their benefits). However, other characteristics, such as exterior aesthetics, density, externalities stemming from type of use, and so on are more properly defined as public goods in that they are, for good or ill, also consumed by the public which is not able to be excluded and are not depletable in the sense that their impact is as great on 20 individuals as it is on one. (Vandell and Carter 2000, 315)

Historic districts in cities are part of Vandell and Carter's "and so on" characteristics. They are better examples of the public good characteristics than generic "real estate" because they are examples of *successful* urbanism as opposed to just any old streetscape.

We know as well that we can create the opposite of a desirable public good: Cities are full of areas that are visually alienating, ugly, filthy, and experienced as painful and even dangerous. People ignore the pain of walking through such areas or, often, just flee them. Historic districts, by way of contrast, have that Goldilocks "just right" quality: a fragile mix of uses, types of businesses, density, storefronts, parks, plazas, block length, street widths, sunlight, and architectural beauty that combine to create the quality of great urbanity that we all long for. We realize, as we walk through them, that we are in a great and wonderful place that is unique in the world.

Historic districts exist on that fuzzy boundary between a pure public good and a common-pool resource. The visual integrity of a district is, contrary to Vandell and Carter's statement above, most certainly depletable through mismanagement. Badly drawn boundaries can destroy a district in a few years during a real estate boom, allowing a proliferation of towers to overshadow the entire district, drowning it in glass and steel. Ugly modernist buildings can come up in the middle of a historic district on a poorly regulated vacant lot, thus destroying the collective asset's visual integrity. Bizarre additions, add-ons, and hack-job renovations can also destroy the visual character of an entire block.

Trying to assign a dollar value to historic districts is an impossible task. Not only do we have the usual issue of *what-values-are-we-leaving-out-or-unable-to-measure* problem, we also have the problem that since there are no markets to buy and sell historic districts, we can't figure out a price for them. And because they are greater than the sum of their parts, we can't just add up the current value of the buildings or apartments. They are also unique and not tradable. In fact, the only way to increase the supply of historic districts is to designate another or to build another neighborhood anew that has its own distinctive sense of place and the qualities that embody successful urbanity. Historic districts are consumable via new real estate development, although you can't hog one all to yourself. The facades and the neighborhood are open to all. Of course, it is possible to live inside a historic district, but that is different from consuming the historic district; it is merely paying a price to be immersed in it 24/7 if one so chooses and has the means. Other people can come and go in the public streets of it, as they were intended to do.

In the case of historic districts, what might be the values that we don't know how to measure? A professor at University of Pennsylvania, Randall Mason, tried to categorize some of the values that might be related to historic districts. He came up with a two-columned list which obviously ignores the values we haven't become aware of yet (such as the value of one's place in the world). I've meddled with his table a bit. See Table 4.1.

Can we even figure how future generations might assign value to historic districts using contingent valuation? Not really. For those who insist

Table 4.1. Provisional Typology of Values Relevant in "Heritage Analysis," adapted and expanded from Randall Mason (Mason 1999; 2002)

Non-measurable Values	Measurable Values
The value of being connected to history	
Pleasure in beauty	Market value of the units
Cultural/Symbolic	
Social	
Spiritual/religious	Tourist revenue
Existence (benefit from knowing a thing exists)	
Option Value (private willingness to pay for a thing even it one doesn't plan to use it)	Value of the Rehab Economy
Bequest Value (value attached to passing something on to future generations)	
Value attached to having a stable place in the world to conduct one's life and raise one's children	

Adapted and expanded from Randall Mason (Mason 1999; 2002)

on coming up with a speculative price tag, the best we can say is that even at tiny levels of willingness to pay for public goods using the fraudulent contingent valuation method (along with some ad hoc shadow pricing), we can easily say that the intergenerational value of such places goes into the trillions of dollars and outstrips what Big Real Estate claims it is going to get out of the next big site it feels it wants to develop.

Housing fundamentalists, haters of historic districts, have launched a fusillade of critiques against historic districts: They cause high housing prices; they are "too white"; and "only rich people care about them." They are accused of being the cause of gentrification, displacement of poor and Brown people, and they are criticized for being the cause of a city's high housing prices. None of these things turns out to be true.

As we've seen in the preceding chapter, even Edward Glaeser has been unable to prove his idea that historic districts (or regulation, broadly speaking) cause high housing prices. In a 2005 review of such literature, two economists from this anti-regulatory school admitted:

> The literature fails, however, to establish a strong, direct, causal effect [of regulation on housing prices], if only because variations in both observed regulation and methodological precision frustrate sweeping generalizations. A substantial number of land use and growth control studies show little or no effect on price, implying that sometimes, local regulation is symbolic, ineffective, or only weakly enforced. The literature fails to address empirical challenges. First, most studies ignore the "endogeneity" of regulation and price. . . . Second, research tends not to recognize the complexity of local policy-making and regulatory behavior. (Quigley and Rosenthal 2005, 67)

Despite these warnings, there is also a literature on localized housing prices and historic districts. It asks the question: Does designating a district historic raise the prices of housing inside the district? This literature has been surveyed multiple times in multiple places, notably by Randall Mason of the University of Pennsylvania (Mason 1999; 2002). The answer is ambiguous. It seems that for every study that finds a negative correlation between local housing prices inside the historic district and historic district designation, there is one that finds a positive correlation. And when correlations are found (either positive or negative), they vary widely in significance. Causality remains unestablished. Studies on either side of the fence are riddled with methodological problems (Powell 2014; Allison 2005; Passell 2016; Pierce O'Brien 2013; Gravel and Michelangeli 2006). My conclusion is this: Housing values inside a historic district will go up or down after historic district designation depending on highly specific local market and political conditions that vary too much for economists to make accurate a priori price predictions. There is just too much local variability. That said, there are some takeaways:

- Not a single researcher, Glaeser included, has been able to show that historic districts inevitably drive housing prices higher overall in a city.
- When real estate prices are rising overall in a city, historic district designation often (but not always) generates a price premium for housing inside the district.
- This "price premium" that historic districts sometimes command can be significant or just modest, so it is not clear that there is any policy relevance to what happens. Moreover, when real estate prices fall overall in a city, historic district prices tend to fall too, suggesting that housing prices within historic districts are driven by wider trends in a city more than by historic district designation.
- The occasional price premium historic districts sometimes command is an interesting phenomenon and needs more nuanced interpretation than the standard interpretation of "regulation = higher prices." Historic districts have ever-rarer characteristics that embody successful urbanity. People want more of those characteristics. That means we should designate more historic districts or build approximate substitutes: more neighborhoods that resemble historic districts in terms of scale, density, stability, predictability, beauty, access to the skydome, distinctiveness, livability, and connection to history.

One report on this topic was specific to New York City. The authors made some observations worth summarizing (Zahirovic-Herbert and Gibler 2012):

- "Between 1970 and 2010 [limit of available data] historic district designation had relatively little bearing on rental prices and the number of rent-burdened households" inside the historic districts.
- Historic district designation "did not prevent government-subsidized housing from developing in specific neighborhoods, nor did it prevent subsidized units in historically designated areas from remaining affordable and maintaining subsidies at similar rates compared to subsidized units overall in NYC."
- "Subsidized units remain affordable whether the units were developed before or after historic district designation."

The general conclusion, as we found in the preceding chapter, is that historic districts are not a hindrance to affordability.

What about the gentrification problem? Do historic districts cause it? The basic narrative is this:

Artists, bohemians, and gay couples come first. They move into run-down—but charming and historic—homes and loft spaces close to the urban core. Houses are restored. Funky coffee shops appear. Public safety improves. Then rents and home prices start to go up. The open-minded, diversity-loving creative types who were the first wave of gentrifiers give way to lawyers, bankers, and techies. As rents and home prices continue to rise, the earliest residents—often lower-income people of color—are forced out. (Buntin 2015)

The case of Harlem might fit this classic storyline, with Black households slowly and incrementally priced out by richer white households over a thirty-year period. But into this narrative come all kinds of questions: Does the described pattern hold everywhere? To what extent is gentrification both a market phenomenon and something policy-induced? How much gentrification is too much, or, put another way, when does it become a negative externality? What does "forced out" mean? Who gets forced out as opposed to "bought out"? Is getting bought out okay and different from "forced" out? Is the policy implication that we should demolish all those "charming and historic places" that the gentrifiers are attracted to and replace them with high-rise glass towers? Last, what should be done about market-induced gentrification (if anything)?

Into the explosive gentrification narrative people have introduced a lot of plotlines. For example, places like the Furman Center at New York University accuse historic districts of being something that only wealthy white people, aka, "the gentry," want. Even Paul Krugman, a Nobel Prize–winning macroeconomist specializing in policy advice on stimulus packages, has jumped into the argument insisting that there are too many rich white people in Manhattan (Krugman 2015). The housing fundamentalists and real estate industry and politicians such as Shaun Donovan want an explicit end to designation of any more historic districts in Manhattan.

All this is troubling because as we saw in the preceding chapter, there is no evidence that dumping more market rate or high rises with inclusionary "affordable" units into Manhattan will make it more racially integrated. There is plenty of opposite evidence that this type of housing only makes such gentrification worse. It is also against the law to impose racial quotas on new housing, so it is not clear how to use housing policy to impose policies concerning racial integration. Second, there is plenty of evidence that people who are not white want their neighborhoods protected from real estate demolition as well, evidence that poor and Black people like beautiful places, and that people who do not identify as white or middle-class appreciate good historic architecture and want historic districts as much as anyone. Third, there is a confounding factor to the gentrification narrative from the quote above: the huge movement of Black people to the suburbs that the Census Bureau has found—something that is happening decades after white families made the move in the 1950s and 1960s. And it is not poor Black households who are leaving for the suburbs, it's the middle-class households. A Brookings study notes:

> Leading black movement to the suburbs are the young, those with higher education, and married couples with children—attributes that characterized white suburbanization for almost a century. While delayed for decades, a full-scale suburbanization of blacks is finally underway. (Frey 2015)

Are those people being pushed out by white gentrifiers or are they moving to have a better quality of life and an easier place to raise their children?

It is the case that what we are seeing in successful cities like London, Paris, and New York is that wealthy people, many of whom are white, show a strong preference for living in areas of great historic character and architectural distinction. At the same time in New York City, we are seeing a massive loss of rent-stabilized units in these same desirable areas, as developers seek to buy up properties, rid themselves of rent-stabilized tenants, and turn the properties over to a higher-paying residents. The policy solution here is not to tear up the historic districts to punish the wealthy for their preferences, but to better protect the low-income people already there, and to regulate away the rampant speculation so that these areas don't end up mere targets for global investors.

It is also important to understand that each gentrifying historic neighborhood has its own data and its own drama and history that require a 10- to 15-year time horizon to understand. The real story of each neighborhood usually defies the simplistic narrative told above. Take the case of Tribeca's historic districts: It was a nonresidential neighborhood of warehouses and manufacturing buildings, most of which were emptying out because of the toxic effects of a poorly thought-out urban renewal policy that left the neighborhood desolate. That policy demolished the successful and prospering Washington Market, and created blight and an urban vacuum throughout the Lower West Side during the 1960s and 1970s. Then, slowly, in search of cheap rents, mostly white artists moved into the half-empty buildings, creating an artistic Bohemia of which much has been written. Tribeca's gentrification did not happen until financial industry employers opened new skyscraper workplaces nearby in the 1990s (Shearson Lehman, now Citibank, and American Express), an event that took place at the same time as the opening of a new public elementary school (ostensibly to educate the children living in the brand-new towers of a Mitchell-Lama middle-class housing project that replaced the demolished Washington Street that was home to the famed produce men of the food market). This confluence of changes caused rich, white, financial industry families to seek out walk-to-work housing rather than commute from New Jersey. Incrementally, these families took over the historic housing stock in the loft buildings. However, not all white artists were victims of this process. Many were "bought out" with generous voluntary cash deals. Others got a lifetime of unbelievably cheap rents as their warehouse units became rent stabilized under the new "loft law." Others were real estate microentrepreneurs who owned the buildings they occupied, renting space to other artists. Such artist-owners made huge sums cashing out as the financial industry families moved in. Some became real estate brokers. This is not a gentrification story with a clear category of winners and victims, which is usually the case with gentrification narratives. Tribeca's historic districts were designated only midway in this process (1989–91), in reaction to the real estate industry's move to demolish magnificent historic properties and replace them with towers. Historic district designation in this case did not drive gentrification.

That is a quite different gentrification scenario than the history of Bed-Stuy in Brooklyn. Bed-Stuy row houses and apartment buildings were built out between 1890 and 1920 for a solidly white, middle-class population (largely Irish and German) adjacent to a free Black community dating from 1838. The second generation of residents of the newly built row houses ran smack into hard times when the Great Depression hit. Owners responded to the problem by turning thousands of row houses into small apartments and boarding houses. The same happened in other row house neighborhoods all over the city, from Turtle Bay to Sugar Hill. Ann Petry described it for Harlem in 1949:

> Many of the old brownstones were long ago turned into rooming houses. The landlord or the lessee found that he could double, triple, quadruple his income if he partitioned the big rooms into cubicles just big enough to hold a bed, a bureau and a broken chair or two. These were offered for rent. (Petry 2019, 770)

In 1938, Bed-Stuy was officially redlined, but note that five years *after* the redlining, Bed-Stuy still had 100,000 white people (28,000 of whom were foreign born), *twice as many* as the 48,000 Black residents (MCNY 2020).[2] Who was redlined, Black people or just "poor" people? After World War II, the situation in Bed-Stuy changed again. The federal government initiated a national policy to move white families to new single-family-home suburbs. White families left, and middle-class Black families began buying the deteriorating, divided-up row houses, turning themselves into new homeowners, and yes, landlords. In the late 1950s real estate speculators began to swoop in and buy up the remaining Bed-Stuy row houses and to get cheaper prices by engaging in aggressive "blockbusting" with inflammatory racial rhetoric intended to scare the remaining white sellers who had thus far ignored federal policy to move to the suburbs. In this way, by the 1960s, Bed-Stuy was a majority Black neighborhood. It is also worth noting that Bed-Stuy community groups leading the twenty-year fight for Bed-Stuy's designation as a historic district were composed of Black middle-class rowhouse homeowners. Then, in the hyper-gentrification years of Bloomberg and De Blasio (2000–2019), there was a reversal of this process: Richer white people began to move into Bed-Stuy, offering shockingly high sums for the ever-scarcer row houses. Over ten years white people become the neighborhood's majority (NYU Furman Center 2020). What happened? It appeared that older Black homeowners voluntarily cashed out, likely joining a larger middle-class exodus to the suburbs, which is not exactly a story of victimhood. Perhaps we should consider the actual victims to be the earlier generation of low-income people who lived in in the divided-up row houses created during the Great Depression. They were the ones forced out in the long run. Those "boarding houses" and homemade "single-room occupancy hotels" were an affordable housing stock that was lost to a thoughtless, unregulated market-led gentrification process.

Or take the case of St. Albans in Queens where there is a large historic district. Prosperous Black families have long thrived there—and continue to do so. It was once a majority white neighborhood. It is composed mostly of single-family homes with big yards. Many of the homes in the Addisleigh Park section of St. Albans are particularly large and mansion-like. Starting in the 1930s, a *Who's Who* list of wealthy, successful, Black artists and celebrities such as Count Basie, Lena Horne, Fats Waller, Billie Holiday, Ella Fitzgerald, and John Coltrane bought homes in the area, first in a trickle started by Fats Waller and then in larger numbers once the racial covenant (rules forbidding sales to Black people) was finally struck down by the Supreme Court in 1948. Whites incrementally moved even farther out to single-family home suburbs as per national policy, so by 1964 St. Albans was mostly Black and often referred to as a "Gold Coast" for a wealthy Black elite. Was this a kind of gentrification? I think the answer is yes. Is all gentrification bad? No. Black residents of St. Albans have lobbied hard and successfully to make the neighborhood an official historic district of New York City. Did historic district designation "cause" Black celebrities to move there? No. Should their neighborhood be torn down and replaced with high-rise market-rate housing with a few Mandatory Inclusionary Housing (MIH) units? I think not. Is St. Albans causing the affordable housing crisis in New York City. The answer, I believe, is no, although the outer third of New York's land mass is largely suburban and not sharing fairly the burdens of urban density.

My conclusion is that there are just no credible data for the claim that historic district designation causes gentrification or that historic districts are things that only rich white people want, or that historic preservation or historic districts are inherently racist, as many on the left have claimed on social media.

What to Do about Preferences?

What is a policymaker to do when richer people (Black or white) decide they want to live in low-rise and mid-rise historic districts of beautiful architecture with tree-lined streets that are protected from the effects of massive real estate overdevelopment? Count Basie lived in a Tudor house with a yard in St. Albans in Queens. Mayor Bloomberg lived in a particularly palatial single-family row house in an Upper East Side historic district, as did mega-developer Bruce Ratner. Mayor De Blasio lived in a low-rise row house in Brooklyn. When Supreme Demolisher of New York Mayor La Guardia retired, he bought a single-family home in the Bronx, in what is now a historic district.

Because they are richer, the rich can outbid everyone else to assert their preferences. If we don't like the rich, should we demolish the neighborhoods they want to live in and replace them with glass towers that have 30 percent of the apartments reserved as vaguely defined "affordable" units? Should we blow up the things the tax-paying gentry hankers for? Much as I would love to replace former Mayor Bloomberg's landmarked town houses with a single 100 percent affordable glass tower, destroying the Upper East Side Historic District will not make New York City a better place nor will doing so solve the affordability problem. Neither do I think that strategy would integrate the neighborhoods that were once much more diverse prior to the Koch, Giuliani, and Bloomberg years. Fixing the problems we face is not as simple as replacing the historic districts of the Upper East Side or Greenwich Village and SoHo with more glass towers.

Middle-class and low-income people also like trees and sunshine and are perfectly capable of noticing great architectural beauty, even though Edward Glaeser suggests otherwise. They just don't have the means to make their preferences felt.

So, what are the policy options other than blowing up historic districts and replacing them? We could dismantle the market system of capitalism that allows wealthier people to make their preferences known. Sometimes I am quite sympathetic to that view, but it is not going to happen. Or maybe we could regulate capitalism to prevent desirable neighborhoods from turning into empty, wealthy enclaves like Mayfair in London, a place that has been emptied of residents and street life and is intensely favored by embassies and nonresident world investors. I think that is the path forward. When developing a better policy regime to avoid an urban monoculture, the goal needs to be what Rachel Brahinsky describes as a policy of "eviction-free development" (Brahinsky 2014). That is at least the beginning of a plausible regulatory agenda. But just as important, we must learn how to build more great neighborhoods that share the qualities that make historic districts so desirable so that more people of all income levels have access to great urbanity.

Other Assets in Our Urban Commons Also Need Better Regulation

When common-pool assets have unclear rules of access or weak regulation, people will always try to seize the asset for themselves. For example, in New York during Covid, the restaurant industry lobbied for greater access to the sidewalks and roadbeds of New York for their private businesses. The city granted them their wish, and restaurateurs often doubled the square footage of restaurants through expansion into the public roadway. The owners built large, enclosed dining sheds, complete with air conditioners, heating units, fans, and televisions, a classic "enclosure of the commons." The policy originally had public support as a temporary way to help an industry suffering under the Covid lockdown rules. But post-Covid, public support eroded as the city made the giveaway permanent and ham-fistedly handed over regulatory oversight to an ill-equipped Department of Transportation (DOT). DOT had no viable regulatory plan and could not keep up with the complaints of eyesore sheds, trash, rats, and homeless encampments in the sheds and abandoned sheds. In certain streets, it became impossible for fire trucks to get through or for handicapped people to pass on the sidewalk.

Street parking, be it free or cheap, is a flawed giveaway of a common-pool asset to a minority of private car owners in a city where the majority do

Figure 4.8. "Outdoor" dining New York style, in a poorly constructed air-conditioned shed with plastic plants seized from the public roadway. Photo from the author's collection.

not own cars. Indeed, handing the roadway over to the exclusive use of cars is an abuse of the asset. Early movies of street life in Manhattan at the 1910s before the car ruled, show our roadways packed with pedestrians, streetcars, horses, buggies, horse-pulled buses, newsboys, peddlers, and dawdlers, all crisscrossing the roadbed as if it belonged to them, which it did. Then we gave the roadway over exclusively to motorized vehicles and people got moved to sidewalks, which then got reduced in size throughout Manhattan as the roadbeds got expanded to allow for ever more cars. Obviously, it is time to reconsider how we regulate this asset and for whom we do so.

Another example of a mismanaged asset in our urban commons is that of the bizarre space called a "public private plaza" or "POPS." These are small parks around skyscrapers. They are publicly owned, but privately built. The Department of City Planning creates them in negotiations with a developer who wants to build a skyscraper that pierces the skydome beyond what is allowed. The developer gets approval for his plans in exchange for creating a public asset, a plaza. Many of these plazas are miserable, inadequate public spaces of no significance or possible use, so the Department of City Planning began insisting on better deals with developers that included a specified number of chairs, tables, benches, trees, plantings, water fountains, and opening hours for the public. So far so good, but the department assigns no regulatory authority to anyone or to any agency to monitor the plazas and ensure the agreed-upon opening hours and amenities. Property owners soon attempt to privatize the plazas, enclosing them, to great public outcry that so far has rarely stopped the privatization.

Another asset that is poorly regulated are views onto parks, waterfronts, and the borders of low-rise and mid-rise historic districts—any view that the real estate market deems "desirable."

Many tower builders, for example, sell their clients a fantasy that they are becoming part of charming historic, human-scale neighborhoods like Tribeca or Brownstone Brooklyn, eliding the reality that the tower is shadowing the district, disrupting its visual integrity, and eating away at the very "charming" locational qualities the developer is using to sell the property. It is a classic "free rider" problem: Someone seizes the benefits of a situation without contributing to it. The demand for views and the premium developers get for selling views onto historic districts or water and park views is so high that the pressure to overbuild to capture those views is relentless. Some have proposed regulating this by taxing windows or "glass voids" in buildings over the floors that rise above the average cornice line on a block, but that policy proposal never got any traction (Frankel 2015). Figure 4.1 illustrates the problem for Central Park, while Figure 4.9 illustrates it for a tower that has come up in the middle of Tribeca's historic districts.

Figure 4.9. Herzog & de Meuron's "Jenga" tower tries to dominate Tribeca's historic district and destroy the historic context. Author's photo.

Conclusion

The public goods and common-pool assets we have in the city make up an urban commons that requires creative regulation to protect it from overuse and privatization. It is impossible to assign monetary values to these assets, rendering cost-benefit analysis impossible. These assets must be valued in the public realm, through direct democratic means, not market mechanisms or pseudo-scientific and unethical theorizing about how much they are worth.

Historic districts are not the cause of gentrification. They do not axiomatically raise housing prices. Instead, they are a valuable part of the urban commons that embodies aspects of successful urbanity. We need these historic districts and an equitably shared skydome so that cities are places we want to live in and pass on to our children rather than tolerate while we build careers and then flee for the suburbs. The policy challenge is how to create more of these resources over time so that beauty, sunlight, history, architecture, views, human-scale places, great schools, libraries, and street trees are not so rare that only the wealthy can have them. The real estate industry's attempt to reduce these historic districts and the skydome to the speculative value of the possible air rights above them, based on the scenario that these assets should be demolished and replaced with skyscrapers, is an attempt to impose their own value system and their own self-interests on the entire society.

Chapter 5

The Curse of New York

The Real Estate Lobby as the Demolition Machine

> Real estate on many levels has been more powerful than local government or state government.
> —State Senator Liz Kruger, cited by John Leland, in "Real Estate Thought It Was Invincible in New York. It Wasn't," *New York Times*, December 2, 2019

> They've been the most powerful industry in New York State for decades because of their wealth.
> —Ellen Dobson, Legal Aid Society, cited by Elizabeth Kim, in "Powerful NYC Landlords Secretly Met with Affordable Housing Advocates to Seek Rent Reform Compromise," *Gothamist* (blog), May 29, 2019

> It is the developers, not the city planners, who are making the decision about how buildings get built in NYC.
> —Paul Goldberger, "When Developers Change the Rules during the Game," *New York Times*, March 19, 1989

BIG REAL ESTATE'S WEALTH[1] has given it immense power in New York City, exercised through its principal lobby, the Real Estate Board of New York, known as REBNY. Earlier chapters described how Big Real Estate shaped the city's choice of economic development strategy via the "luxury city" model that inflates property tax revenue through real estate gentrification. Implementation of that model is ruinous of the city's beauty, visible history, socioeconomic diversity, and livability.

This chapter looks at the institutional landscape of real estate power in New York. It describes the network of real estate organizations and dependent groups who support Big Real Estate's agenda. It summarizes the history and organization of the sector's official lobby, REBNY, and explains what REBNY wants. Finally, this chapter lays out additional examples of how the sector has exercised excessive influence in public policy to the detriment of the wider public good.[2]

The Growth Machine as a Demolition Machine

Sociologist Harvey Molotch characterized the real estate industrial complex using the imagery of an urban "Growth Machine." In his eponymous article, he defined a growth machine as a coalition of city entrepreneurs "who make money from land and building" and who "make more if rents and real estate prices rise" and who capture local government so that it serves the machine rather than the larger public good (Molotch 1976). The growth machine confounds physical growth with economic growth, limiting the term to mean a "constantly rising urban population, . . . increasingly intensive land development, and higher population density" (Jonas and Wilson 1999, 310). Growth in the machine ideology is not about widely shared economic prosperity or a rising quality of life; it's just more people and buildings. Molotch concluded that the machine's relentlessness in adding ever more people and buildings "takes a toll on . . . how well people live" and "undermines local people's standard of living" (Logan and Molotch 2007, xi).

One of Molotch's key insights is that the insistence on the infinite growth of buildings and people will come to "pervade virtually all aspects of local life, including the political system, the agenda of economic development and even cultural organizations" (Logan and Molotch 2007, 300). Although I wholeheartedly agree with Molotch, New York's special circumstance suggests a variant of the idea: Big Real Estate as the city's Demolition Machine. The Demolition Machine operates on the Robert Moses premise, "When you operate in an overbuilt metropolis, you have to hack your way through with a meat axe" (Robert Moses cited in Caro 1975, 849).

When a city is "overbuilt" as early as 1955, it means there are few empty, buildable sites to expand into and to build anew. To build, people must be evicted first. To be sure, in a built-out city there is the odd bit of open land in public parks, underneath libraries and public schools, and in dangerous, hard-to-build spots like flood plains, waterfronts, river landfill, platforms over rail yards, and scattered parking lots around the remaining manufacturing zones. But their number is small. Construction in those spots is of dubious environmental sustainability. The Regional Plan Association recognized that New York was fully built out as far back as 1919, and developer-planner Robert Moses lamented the fact again in the 1950s. So when former Chair of City Planning Joe Rose said in 1999 that "we change ... as a result of reuse and redevelopment of individual properties" (Rose 1999), he was diplomatically explaining that the only way for New York City to "change" at this point in its history is *by demolishing individual properties and rebuilding on top of what was there.*

That observation raises the million-dollar question: Who gets the wrecking ball? The real estate industry's answer has been to reject the low-rise suburban outer borough neighborhoods and demolish instead in Manhattan and Brooklyn. Their reasoning may have political roots in a fear of provoking homeowners in the outer boroughs, but their preference has solid market logic. The historic core is where the existing subway lines converge. It has no "transit deserts." The core is also where locational demand for real estate from the worldwide pool of investors is greatest, creating pre-Covid rates of return for luxury condos in Manhattan as high as 95 percent (BAE Urban Economics Inc. 2015). Hence the pressure to demolish and rebuild the core is intense.

As pointed out in earlier chapters, the pace of demolition has been extraordinary. The real estate industry demolished 4.5 buildings a day every day for thirty-two years, mostly in Manhattan. The reality is that eviction, then demolition, then new construction has been Big Real Estate's game plan for a long time. Former REBNY president Rexford Tompkins even

Figure 5.1a and 5.1b. The fine building at the left, 519 Fifth, was demolished along with two adjacent prewar buildings. They were filled with Class B and C office spaces. Aby Rosen sold the properties to Thor Equities who proposed the glass tower with public subsidies. Thor sold out to another firm seeking a billion in condo sales, but the deal fell through. The fate of the demolished site is still uncertain as of this writing. Historic image from Municipal Archives. Rendering from CityRealty.

Figure 5.2. Demolitions in Community Board 5 (Midtown) during the Bloomberg era. Image from Community Board 5.

advised the City Council in 1970 that "easier eviction is our only hope for reviving the sagging construction industry" (Newfield and Du Brul 1981, 82). A map from Midtown's Community Board 5 also illustrates the Demolition Machine's success. The sites in black were demolished between 2000 and 2016, a process accelerated under Mayor Bloomberg's reign (Community Board 5 Planning Fellows 2017).

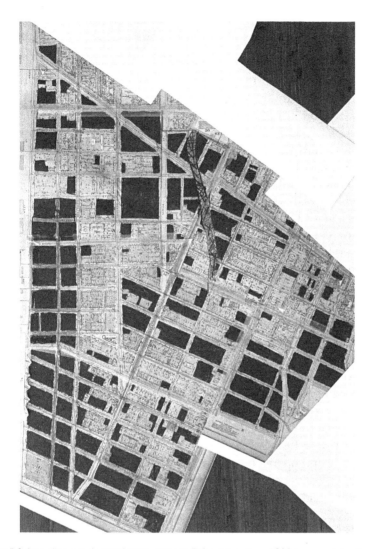

Figure 5.3. Demolitions in the Washington Market–Tribeca area from 1930 to present day. Image from author. The sites in black were demolished.

Other neighborhoods have seen similar fates. Consider Tribeca, a historic neighborhood much smaller in area than Midtown where the scale of demolition has been even more breathtaking. It lost thirty-three historic buildings during the seven years of the De Blasio administration alone. Going further back, the image in Figure 5.3 shows demolition below Canal Street since 1929. Blacked out are the buildings and blocks that were demolished between 1930 and 2019. In all, the Tribeca-Washington Market neighborhood lost about half its historic assets to the Demolition Machine over that time.

Origins of the Real Estate Lobby

The origin of the Demolition Machine goes all the way back to the launch of the street grid in the 1820s when the Common Council imposed a rectilinear grid of roadways upon the city north of Houston Street. At first it might seem odd that the City Fathers did not plan for more natural, curving street lines, as found in many old cities in Europe. According to grid historian Gerard Koeppel, the reason was the Common Council's profit-seeking motive. It justified the grid by noting, "straight-sided and right-angled houses are the cheapest to build." Koeppel added: "The plan led to decades of real estate speculation throughout the grid" (Koeppel 2015, chaps. 8 and 9). The grid was the first Demolition Machine, for it flattened hills, seized property for roads, evicted residents, and destroyed neighborhoods and homes that didn't fit the scheme. Rem Koolhaas said of it: "150 years after its superimposition on the island, [it is] still a negative symbol of the shortsightedness of commercial interests" (Koolhaas 1994, 18).

The grid wasn't the only nineteenth-century project to evict people and demolish neighborhoods. Elizabeth Blackmar, a historian of the early real estate and property market, described slum clearance projects as early as 1829, pointing out that, "City officials and real estate developers recast the rule of property in the first third of the 19th century by mobilizing public authority to support private proprietors' pursuit of profit in real estate" (Blackmar 1991, 167).

Real estate power in New York eventually crystallized in the form of the Real Estate Board of New York in the late nineteenth century. Real estate "brokers" operated out of rented halls in Lower Manhattan called "exchanges." They trucked in a bit of everything: horse carriages, church pews, tenement buildings, row houses, and plots of land. Some brokers were jack-of-all-trades businessmen, combining roles of developer, speculator, and trader. In the early 1890s, there were about eight hundred of them in the city. Dirty deals and scandals frequently rocked their exchanges, undermining the brokers' credibility with the public.

In 1896, a new "Board of Brokers" arose to reassure the public that the exchanges were not corrupt places of business. The founding group limited membership to 250 people (RERG 1896; 1897). In 1913, they renamed themselves the Real Estate Board of New York and expanded their membership to "any owner of real estate or other person, corporation or company who may be interested in the welfare and advancement of real estate interests." It took another ten years for the new organization to herd most of the real estate interests and organizations in the city under a single flag. Before then, there were competing entities like the United Real Estate Owners and their subgroup, the Allied Realty Interests. All of them strenuously opposed attempts in the new 1916 Zoning Resolution to regulate height (Makielski 1966).

In 1917, just after the first Zoning Amendment passed, adolescent REBNY was advocating for City Charter reforms, complaining of "over-restrictive building laws" and bragging that they represented the owners of "at least half the assessed valuation of real property in the City of New York" (RERG 1917, 13). By 1920, REBNY fretted how to prevent politicians from treating real estate as a regulated public utility. Early REBNY also opposed an excess profits tax and lobbied in Washington for a mortgage interest tax exemption (RERG 1920).

REBNY claims 17,000 members, most drawn from the corpus of more than 50,000 licensed real estate brokers that REBNY licenses. But REBNY's board of governors has 121 members and only two of them are brokerage firms (Corcoran and Douglass Elliman). The reality is that brokers are powerless, and developers now rule REBNY. There are 99 different real estate firms on REBNY's governing board. Of those, 35 are development firms of immense wealth, the majority family dynasties. The rest of the board of governors consists of big landlords (many are family dynasties as well), real estate investment trusts, private equity firms specializing in real estate investment and speculation, lenders, real estate advisory services, a parking lot empire (Edison), and big banks who grant loans to speculators and developers. All these firms (including brokerage firms) dabble in ground-up demolition and reconstruction of new buildings from time to time. Many participate in speculative investing, partnering with various sources of money like the Ugandan Sovereign Fund.

Serving as well as "governors" of REBNY are four lobbyist law firms also representing Big Real Estate when it goes on the legal offensive: Kramer Levin and Naftalis; Fried, Frank, Harris, and Shriver; Roberts and Holland; and Stroock and Stroock. Fifty REBNY members compose the smaller executive committee of REBNY, with the largest developer firms and landlords dominating that committee.

The most active Manhattan developers as of 2018 were Related, Brookfield, Tishman Speyer, Extell, GID, SL Greene, Two Trees, and TF Cornerstone, all members of the board of governors of REBNY. This group overlaps with lists of the ten largest property owners in the city, who collectively own 546 million square feet of property earning an estimated $7.5 billion a year of net operating income. The intergenerational family dynasties that are long-term members of the board of governors include the clans of Brodsky, Durst, Le Frak, Silverstein, Rudin, Tishman, Rose, Rockefeller, Cohen, Fisher, Fetner, Resnick, Elghanayan (of Rockrose and TF Cornerstone), and Zucker (Manrodt 2020; Rebong 2020; TRD Staff 2019a; TRD Staff 2020b).

Also active inside REBNY are developers who work in the subsidized affordable housing market segment such as The Hudson Companies and L + M Partners. Smaller nonprofit affordable housing developers work this segment as well, as do quasi-public economic development corporations that dabble in construction. But these are not a significant part of REBNY's inner-circle governing apparatus, although their interests and policy preferences often overlap.

At the time of this writing, developer Bill Rudin is chair of the REBNY board. Long-time REBNY staffer James Whelan is the current president. Whelan took over from a former real estate lobbyist and City Council staffer, John Banks, who had taken over from Steven Spinola. REBNY has a big budget and a large staff of professionals who lobby in support of REBNY's agenda, most of them former staffers for city politicians or former technocrats from city agencies that regulate real estate concerns. The REBNY annual gala raises millions—the cheapest individual tickets go for about $1,400 and "presenting sponsor" tickets go for $100,000. Politicians, large and small, be they city, state, or federal, make it a point to show up to the gala to show that their office doors and phone lines are open to REBNY.

REBNY's website, newsletters, press releases, and testimonies to City Hall yield no surprises about its policy agenda. REBNY wants no height limits, unlimited buildable space in the "hot" markets, an end to regulation, an end to historic districts, severe limitations or an outright end to landmarking, and no green building rules. REBNY does not want public oversight and does not want members of the City Council naysaying their projects. They want to be free to demolish anything and for their buildings to go up "as of right." They want to hire non-union construction workers. The members would like an end to building permit fees, property taxes, and inspection fees. They would like as many public subsidies as possible. They want the state to give them public waterfronts, piers, libraries, parks, and public housing, so they can build whatever they want anywhere. They want all rules interpreted in their favor. REBNY frames these wants in public relations sound bites about "a business-friendly climate" and the endlessly repeated claim that their buildings "create jobs." Hey, claims REBNY staff in radio interviews, "we pay the salaries of teachers, firemen, and the police," as if the taxpaying public has no part in paying those salaries.

Figure 5.4a–e. Collage of politicians mugging it up with REBNY officials or giving keynote speeches at one of REBNY's annual galas: Mayor Adams (5.4a), ex-Mayor de Blasio (5.4b), Governor Hochul (5.4c), Senator Schumer (5.4d), ex-Borough President Gale Brewer (5.4e).

Above all, developers don't like paying taxes, even though as one researcher found, real estate is so favored by the tax code that "the average effective tax rate for real estate development is just over 1%. Across all industries, the average is roughly 11%" (Ehrenfreund 2016).

Other Branches of the Real Estate Industrial Complex

Allied to REBNY, with overlap in membership, is the landlord lobby known as the Rent Stabilization Association (RSA). There is also the Community Housing Improvement Program (CHIP) representing 4,000 building owners in the medium-to-large category. CHIP and RSA joined REBNY to oppose the 2019 rent reforms. There is also the much smaller, volunteer-based Small Property Owners of New York (SPONY). It represents property owners of a couple of rental units or a single building. Their interests do not routinely overlap with REBNY.

The money side of the business is huge. Consider that the top fifteen commercial loan brokers in NYC lent the industry $45 billion in 2017. Meridian Capital dominated the niche, lending 34 percent of that money over 1,657 deals while employing just three hundred people nationally (Putzier 2018). Investors and speculators also are part of the scene. Nearly $45 billion worth of buildings categorized as investment property have been traded every year in NYC since 2010 (TRD Staff 2019a). It is a telling indicator of the city's built-out character that the amount spent on the speculative churn of buying, holding, selling in NYC is seven times larger than the money spent on actual construction. In 2018, the top twenty big construction firms were working on building 16 million square feet in contracts worth $6 billion, while the top firms doing interior construction and renovation work held $3.75 billion worth of contracts that same year (TRD Staff 2019a).

It would be lovely to think the urbanist-oriented nonprofits of New York City are independent of the Demolition Machine's influence, but that is wishful thinking. Many have boards of directors dominated by Big Real Estate and are dependent on Big Real Estate for most of their budgets. As anyone who attended public hearings on the many zoning battles in New York during the Bloomberg, De Blasio, and Adams administrations can witness, these nonprofits reliably deliver testimony and op-eds in support of the REBNY position on whatever land use battle is at hand (e.g., SoHo/NoHo, Midtown, and Gowanus upzonings; Zoning for Quality and Affordability; anti-Landmarks legislation; opposition to rent reforms; the Zoning Amendment on Voids).

Here are some of the organizations, both public and private, with close ties to REBNY. They share REBNY's vision for the hyper-dense, vertical city of towers.

- The Empire State Development Corporation (ESD) is a state entity originally known as the Urban Development Corporation. Ex-Governor Nelson Rockefeller created it in the late 1960s. The governor wanted a real estate development vehicle that could evade local zoning controls and oversight and conduct eminent domain proceedings to seize private property. The ESD can do all that, plus it has the power to issue bonds without taxpayer or legislative approval. The governor appoints seven of its nine directors, as well as the executive director. The Institute for Justice (a D.C. think tank) reviewed the ESD's eminent domain projects and concluded it acts as "Robin Hood in reverse, stealing from the poor and giving to the rich" (Carpenter and Ross 2015). Controversial urban renewal projects that the ESD has responsibility for include Atlantic Yards, the East Harlem Urban Renewal Area, the Jamaica Gateway Urban Renewal Plan, the Javits Convention Center, and Columbia University's project to seize property in Harlem to expand its campus.
- Not to be confused with the ESD is NYC's Economic Development Corporation (EDC), a "self-sustaining" nonprofit managing 660 million square feet of publicly owned real estate. It creates real estate deals with the private sector, leveraging public real estate assets. The EDC board is filled with real estate players, like Margaret Anadu, former partner at Goldman Sachs and chair of its Urban Investment Group, or a past president of real estate investment trust and mortgage banker Longview Capital Advisors, or permanent government technocrat Andrew Kimball. Kimball was the ex-CEO of the controversial "Industry City" project to rezone the waterfront at Sunset Park and director of the private effort to bring the 2012 Olympic Games to New York, a special project of Dan Doctoroff during the Bloomberg Administration. Also, on the EDC board (at the time of this writing) is the president and CEO of the Partnership for New York City, a director of Blackrock (an investment company big on real estate), a VP of the controversial landlord-developer Phipps Houses, several REBNY-affiliated attorneys who advise real estate firms, and finally, public relations specialists who massage the reputations of those involved in controversial real estate projects. According to the EDC's by-laws, the mayor appoints twenty-six of the EDC's

twenty-seven board members (sixteen directly, five with approval by each of the borough presidents). The last member, the twenty-seventh, who serves as chair, must be appointed with consultation of the Partnership for New York City. Appointees must be "prominent in the financial, commercial, industrial, professional or labor community." There is no required reporting to the public and no City Council oversight.

- Citizens Housing and Planning Council (CHPC). While this organization has the inoffensive mission "to develop and advance practical public policies that support the housing stock of the city," in practice it acts as a lobby to promote Big Real Estate's hyper-dense view of housing. There are no "citizens" on its board, which is instead dominated by Big Real Estate players. Everyone from Red Stone Equity to Slate Group to Durst is there, along with the usual bankers to real estate like JP Morgan, plus the real estate industry's favorite lobbyist, Capalino & Co., and the REBNY member law firm Kramer Levin. Predictably, CHPC's 2022 op-eds favor REBNY positions, such as with the upzoning in SoHo.
- The Furman Center at New York University is a real estate think tank that churns out excellent datasets, well-written white papers, and copious analyses, while also orchestrating that output for favorable play in the local press. Though it purports to advance research and "debate" on housing, neighborhoods, and urban policy, almost all the published titles convey a one-sided tilt toward infinite growth and a hostility to historic preservation. To understand why, note that of the Furman's Center's sixty-two-member board of advisors, 84 percent are REBNY members. The remaining 16 percent are a scattershot group representing New York City's housing agencies, the Empire State Development Corporation, Phipps (the largest nonprofit affordable housing developer in the city and known in the press as a "bad apple" landlord), a lobbyist for big real estate at the firm of Nixon Peabody, a couple of smaller affordable housing nonprofits active in the boroughs, the big business lobby calling itself the "Association for a Better New York," and Goldman Sachs Investment Bank.
- The Center for an Urban Future bills itself as an independent, nonprofit think tank that is a "catalyst for smart and sustainable policies that reduce inequality, increase economic mobility and grow the economy." Yet the word "independent" is not appropriate when most of its funding comes from a board dominated by real estate (HR & A Advisors, L & M Partners, Cushman and Wakefield, global

finance giants who lend money to real estate such as Citigroup, JP Morgan, and Goldman Sachs, and public relations lobby firms for real estate (Miller Strategies, Edelman, Zimmerman & Edelson) as well as an entity known as the "Global Gateway Alliance," whose chair is Joseph Stitt of Thor Equities. Also on that board is Kyle Kimball of Con-Ed, whose previous job was running the Economic Development Corporation (EDC) under Bloomberg. The center's main activity is granting fellowships to journalists who support their worldview.

- The Skyscraper Museum in Lower Manhattan might have been merely the scrappy project of an architectural historian who loved skyscrapers, but big real estate elevated the project to another function, the ideological legitimation of the skyscraper as the best future for New York City. The museum is housed in the ground floor space of a skyscraper in Battery Park City. The developer of that skyscraper (Millennium Partners) donated the space. Millennium's CEO served on the organization's founding board. The museum lists on its website its major donors. Without exception they represent Big Real Estate, including many members of REBNY's board of governors (Fishers, Rudins, Dursts, and Silversteins). REBNY is itself a major patron of the museum. Only three board members of the current thirty-two might be considered not part of the real estate industrial complex. The museum's programming is worshipful of skyscrapers and tends to be biased in favor of hyper-density.
- The Regional Plan Association (RPA) is a nonprofit dating from the 1920s. The RPA represents that segment of the real estate complex that wants substantive planning to take place *in their own interest* (Fitch 1996). The RPA steadfastly supports REBNY's position that we need no height limits in Manhattan. Big Real Estate dominates the governing board of the RPA. The board chair is from RXR Realty. The RPA has been vociferous in support of the Vornado plan to build supertall skyscrapers around Pennsylvania Station. One vice-chair of the RPA is from the Durst real estate family, and at this writing another runs the Jamaica (Queens) Community Development Corporation and sits on the City Planning Commission. The RPA's chief counsel is from one of the largest law firms in the city that advises big real estate as its bread and butter. Of the co-chairs of the New York City Committee of the RPA, one is a Goldman Sachs alum, and the other is a retired professor of real estate who also sits on the Skyscraper Museum Board. The rest of the RPA board is littered with

the marquee names of the REBNY oligarchy, from Vornado Realty Trust to SL Greene to Blackstone. Real estate investing companies figure prominently on the RPA board. We also find (at the time of this writing) that ubiquitous advocate of hyper-density, architect Vishaan Chakrabarti, along with a smattering of the larger lobbyists and advisors to Big Real Estate like Capalino and HR & A.
- Association for a Better New York is growth machine central: "dedicated to the constant growth and renewal of New York City's people." Big real estate firms of Rudin, Tishman Speyer, Related, and Lodestone sit on the board. It also has the famed private equity investor of Two Sigma Investments plus the head of a major financial planning firm. Another member is the private equity investor and ex-owner of the Mets, and last, a person representing the interests of Con-Ed.
- Partnership for New York City is a nonprofit organization that seeks to "build partnerships between business and government" and wishes to "advance NYC's standing as a global center of commerce, innovation, and economic opportunity." Although it claims to be an outgrowth of the more ancient Chamber of Commerce, banker-oligarch David Rockefeller founded it in 1979 for big corporations to do "hands-on" work with government, mostly through housing programs and efforts to halt crime. The Partnership predictably contends that we need "more flexibility in building and zoning codes" (meaning less regulation). The Partnership is also of the view that the city should not raise taxes on the wealthy (Partnership for New York City 2020). Wrapped up in the Partnership membership and board are many large real estate firms that are also members of REBNY. The Partnership does not champion the interests of small businesses, representing instead the interests, attitudes, beliefs, and biases of the large corporate sector.
- New York Bar Association committees that deal with real estate are part of this real estate industrial complex. In 2019 the property law committee of the Bar Association testified loudly against the Small Business Jobs Survival Act, a piece of legislation that REBNY had sought to kill off in the strongest possible terms since it was first introduced to the City Council committee twenty years earlier. It is odd that the Bar Association would bother to testify on legislation that had nothing to do with the Bar Association's mission and purpose. The lawyer who wrote the testimony was Steven Kirkpatrick, a former property manager in Upper Manhattan. After becoming an attorney, he specialized (in his own words from his bio on the Bar Association's site) in representing "property owners, management

companies, financial institutions, retailers, hotels and commercial office tenants in a wide variety of matters" but never small business. The physical presenter of Kirkpatrick's testimony during the hearing was another lawyer, Jason Polevoy, who at the time worked for Paterson Belknap, known for its roster of big real estate clients. Polevoy's bio states that he "has represented owners, investors, and developers of office, hotel, and multi-family residential properties" (Polevoy n.d.), but never small businesses. Similarly, in 2018, several real estate–related committees of the Bar Association jointly lobbied Governor Cuomo in favor of the real estate tax break known as "421a." The chair of the Bar Association's land use committee, who co-signed the lobbying letter to Cuomo on the 421a tax break, was Ross Moskowitz of Stroock & Stroock, one of four law firms sitting on the board of governors of REBNY.

- New York State Association for Affordable Housing has a seventy-nine-member board of directors. On it are companies that invest in or finance real estate, construction companies, and real estate title and insurance companies. While it does have credible affordable housing builders on the board (e.g., B & B Urban) there is significant overlap with REBNY membership, such as Slate Property Group (of the Rivington House scandal that ended affordable housing for that historic site in Manhattan), Douglaston Development, Jonathan Rose, Bluestone Group (who has a senior staffer appointed to the Department of City Planning), Monadnock Construction (who lobbied heavily for the Inwood and Gowanus upzonings during the De Blasio years). There is a smattering of community-based, nonprofit affordable housing groups on the board, but such small-fry affordable housing nonprofits are outnumbered by bigger guns. The press has pointed out that even small "affordable housing landlords are among the city's most active evictors" (Pincus 2019).
- Citizens Budget Commission is a nonprofit founded during the fiscal crisis of the 1970s. While it claims to be looking out for the "citizenry at large," its 121 board members include the president of REBNY and 29 big real estate firms and not a single person who might be construed as "the citizenry at large." The rest of the membership is equally divided between major banks, private equity, investment firms, and large corporations.
- Manhattan Institute is a far-right libertarian think tank funded not by real estate moguls, but by conservative hedge-funders and billionaire money managers. It is a different network than the real estate world.

The Institute has taken millions from the ultra-conservative Koch brothers. It finances a fellowship program, paying people to write books that fit its libertarian, anti-regulatory agenda, one that overlaps with REBNY's when it comes to the deregulation of real estate (thus explaining the Institute's support for the diffusion of Edward Glaeser's ideas [Peck 2016]).

Builders, engineering firms, and large architectural practices are dependent on big real estate for their bread and butter. For that reason, they make a natural set of tentacles for the real estate industrial complex. The architect lobby is the American Institute of Architects, known as "the AIA." To be fair, the AIA doesn't just lobby: Its New York branch runs continuing education classes and professional certifications. It has thematic committees, among them the Historic Buildings Committee, whose main purpose is to advocate for the preservation of modernist architecture—not buildings built prior to 1920. The biggest donors to the AIA's New York education center are the large architectural firms that often truck with big-developer projects in the city, such as SHoP and Robert Stern, but on that list of donors one also finds Capalino & Co (one of the largest lobbying firms in the city) and a long list of big real estate clients including L & L Holdings and the Tisch Family (AIA-NY 2020).

The AIA-NY 2019 president, Kim Yao, stated that "we as architects can influence and chart a path forward for the city." Yao informed all of AIA-NY's ambition to make "a clear policy platform that we will use in communication with public officials" (Yao 2020). AIA-NY even formed a political action fund. Clutches of architects from AIA-NY testifying on urbanist issues at City Hall are a common sight at public hearings. Of sixty-seven testimonies the AIA posted on their website since 2014, 54 percent had to do with issues about urbanism broadly defined, such as rezonings, preservation, or housing. Three-quarters of policy testimonies were congruent with the REBNY line on the issue at hand. The AIA-NY testified in favor of REBNY's pet projects, such as the one to upzone neighborhoods called "Zoning for Quality and Affordability" and the bill to weaken the Landmarks Preservation Commission, known as "Intro 775." The AIA also testified in favor of real estate firm SL Green's desire to build a mega-skyscraper next to Grand Central called "One Vanderbilt." They claimed it was "sound planning to add density" and that New York needed "a future characterized by the design of the next generation of great buildings." Even when testifying in favor of the Park Avenue Historic District Extension, which REBNY did not do, the AIA-NY added that the "insertion of a taller structure into the street fabric of Park Avenue" would be important because "both market rate and affordable housing are critical for the future," thereby echoing REBNY's pro-MIH upzoning stance described in Chapter 2. The AIA-NY also testified in favor of REBNY proposals to adjust the zoning code for "voids and mechanicals," in favor of the height and scale of the SHoP-designed Domino Sugar Factory project in Brooklyn, in favor of a proposal to maim the Frick Museum with a modernist addition, and in favor of the modernist expansion of the landmarked American Museum of Natural History by Studio Gang Architects. They testified repeatedly in favor of the project to sell public-private plazas back to the owners of the buildings on Water Street in Lower Manhattan and in favor of building new tower-jails throughout the boroughs. They testified in favor of the plan to privatize the interior landmark spaces of the Clocktower building at 346 Broadway.

Minor but important additional players within the real estate industrial complex include business improvement districts (BIDs). BIDs are membership organizations of property owners—renters need not apply. By state charter and with the cooperation of the city's finance agency, BIDs levy new taxes on all property owners in their districts. The money gets spent on managerial salaries and a variety of often reasonable projects: street cleanup, street trees, cultural events, "gentrified" signage, and private security patrols. BIDs routinely get themselves appointed to community boards. Small BIDs with budgets under a million dollars in peripheral zones of the city have a membership composed of smaller property owners and arguably provide a useful public service. But the problem with the big BIDs is weak oversight and lack of democratic accountability in their governing structure. Only 51 percent of property owners in each BID zone need to agree to the creation of a BID. Many property owners never realize someone is organizing a new BID until it arrives as a fait accompli. Residents and renters have no say in BID management and spending. Dissident property owners must pay taxes to the BID even if they didn't want the BID to exist.

The BIDs take over from government the management of sidewalks, plazas, parks, and roadways in those sections of the city that are dominated by large property owners. This weakens democratic control over the public realm, ruling out renter and resident participation. Disturbingly, BIDs make property ownership a condition of suffrage in a BID organization, a condition that runs counter to the New York State Constitution. Large, real estate–backed BIDs whose board are dominated by REBNY members have accomplished the takeover of the public realm of vast stretches of

Manhattan. These include the Alliance for Downtown (the BID for the Financial District), the Grand Central Partnership (the BID for the Vanderbilt corridor), the Bryant Park Corporation, the BID for the 34th Street area near Macy's, the Vornado-dominated BID around Penn Station, and the BIDs for Downtown Brooklyn, Union Square, and Long Island City.

The Effect of Real Estate Power on New York City

Examples of Big Real Estate's excessive influence in public policy for the city are many. To these well-known cases discussed in other chapters, this chapter describes five additional stories of how a single lobby has come to determine policy for our built environment.

Example One: Subverting the Zoning Code to Favor the Real Estate Industry

The political origins of zoning in New York lay in an uneasy alliance between disparate groups who shared one thing: unhappiness with the real estate market's seizure of the skydome and the unregulated, "anything goes" manner of building. First there were the height limit advocates, who, for twenty years prior to the Zoning Resolution in 1916, raised the hue and cry about the need to regulate the height of the emerging skyscrapers proliferating in Lower Manhattan. Supporters of height limits kept getting beaten back by real estate men—for example, in 1902 the head of the Bureau of Buildings said to the *New York Times*:

> I will appear at a public hearing or at meeting of the Board of Aldermen and will oppose the change [height limits]. Many of the most powerful organizations that have the best building interests at heart have declared against this tampering with the code by the Board of Aldermen. (*New York Times* 1902)

In 1913, the height limits group persuaded the city to investigate their cause with the formation of an official "Heights of Building Commission." The commission's report noted the need "to arrest the seriously increasing evil of shutting off of light and air from other buildings and the public streets, to prevent unwholesome and dangerous congestion both in living conditions and in street transit traffic" (Board of Estimate of New York City 1913).

In the same period, ritzy Fifth Avenue building owners and shopkeepers were alarmed at the northward creep of working-class garment factories whose workers troubled the shopping habits of their wealthy customers.

Neither group's concerns went anywhere until the Equitable Building in Lower Manhattan rose to its full height of forty stories in 1915, casting in shadow the surrounding businesses still dependent on daylight to illuminate their offices. Outraged property owners in shadow joined the two pro-regulatory groups. Thus, an uneasy coalition was born to support regulating buildings in New York City. It resulted in the passage of the 1916 Zoning Resolution, or "code." This was a regulatory document that assigned height limits throughout the city as a multiple of street widths. It laid out districts where residential buildings were to be kept separate from manufacturing and commercial activity. It created setback rules for tall buildings, meaning once a building reached a certain height, it had to set back, creating a terrace. The setback rules created the "wedding cake" skyscraper so common in New York. The new code gave lip service to concern over sunlight, presenting obscure concepts like a "sky exposure plane" to regulate access to the sun. (It is an imaginary plane that measures the angle at which sunlight hits a building and the street once the setbacks began.) A building wasn't supposed to poke through the imaginary plane into the sky, organizing its setback terraces to accommodate the plane (although in practice they ended up doing so all the time). The setback and sky exposure plane rules did not solve the concerns of the Heights of Buildings Commission but gave the appearance of trying.

The new code was a poor political compromise between the interest groups that wanted regulation and those that did not. From the get-go, the rules failed to protect street sunlight as the reformers had hoped (Lubove 1963, 244). As for height limits, when you realize that the Equitable Building is now puny in height compared to what came after, it becomes obvious that the code's height limits were ineffective at limiting congestion in the Financial District, and later, in Midtown. In the years after the code became law, the Financial District became so congested and dark that it hastened the emergence of a rival business district in Midtown around Grand Central Station.

The city planners involved in the 1916 code soon disavowed it as a failure. One of the leading drafters of it, George Ford, admonished other cities not to copy NYC's model. Ford said that the city's attempt to limit height was too compromised by concessions to real estate. He noted, "[The zoning law] is full of unduly liberal provisions in the way of height and size that tend strongly to defeat the object of the law, but which were necessitated by the exceptional economic conditions of New York." Those "exceptional economic conditions" referred to "a number of leading real estate men on the Commission. . . . They insisted constantly that real estate values must not be jeopardized and wherever possible that they should be enhanced" (Ford 1916). Ford's collaborator in the zoning project of 1916, Edward Bassett, made a similar point in 1926:

New York City did not advance very far when it adopted the two and two and one-half times [street width] limit with setbacks and the 25 percent towers, and there are many who say that with this limit the skyscraper problem was hardly touched, that skyscrapers are being erected as high as they probably would have been without zoning . . . and that street congestion is as great as if buildings had been left unregulated. These criticisms are partly true. (Bassett, cited in M. Weiss 1992, 68)

After World War II, James Felt, a real estate developer turned city planner, got behind the creation of a "modernized" zoning code. He wanted new rules to encourage modernist, Corbusian tower-slabs rather than the wedding cake towers that had proliferated under the 1916 code. Politician Robert Wagner joined in the cry. The pair talked the city into hiring the skyscraper design firm of Voorhies & Co. to draft something new. After considerable tinkering by big real estate interests, the new 1961 code passed the City Council under Felt's leadership at the Department of City Planning. Some argue—thoughtfully—that the new code got City Council's blessing because it "dramatically reduced the amount of new housing that could be built in the boroughs outside Manhattan, in exchange for development-friendly changes in parts of Manhattan sought by the real-estate industry" (Kober 2020). In the words of Felt the new code was "designed for the convenience of the potential developer" (Voorhies et al. 1958, viii).

After the passage of the 1961 zoning code, Big Real Estate began to tinker with it, imposing on municipal government a multitude of modifications of a concessionary type: mapped carve-outs, discretionary approval rules, loopholes, Byzantine bonuses in exchange for height violations, Talmudic definitional changes of technical terms, arcane procedural pathways to special dispensations, and a long list of "no counts" (things that wouldn't count against the department's allocation of buildable space to a developer). The result was not good. By 1982 the city had granted so many special permits, discretionary approvals, and variances to Midtown developers that whole blocks failed to get direct sunlight at any time of the year (Kwartler and Masters 1984; Kwartler 2015). REBNY even killed off a 1982–83 attempt to improve the aforementioned light and air problem in Midtown (Goodwin 1982).

To give a feel for the scale of the changes and modifications, note that the original Voorhies/Felt proposal for the 1961 code was 376 pages long. By the late 1980s the code had been amended so many times that it was 835 pages long, not including appendices and the "Table of Restrictive Declarations" (Marcus 1992). It is now several thousand pages long.

The *New York Times* obituary of a famed real estate attorney, Samuel "Sandy" H. Lindenbaum (whose father had been on the City Planning Commission), laid out one of the ways these concessions and rule changes happen: lawyerly twisting of the meaning and intent of the code before challenges at the Board of Standards and Appeals, the courts, and the City Planning Commission. The obit noted that Lindenbaum "was able to bend the [Zoning] Resolution to his clients' will without breaking it and that his interpretations sometimes seemed to contradict the plain meaning of the resolution" (Dunlap 2012; 1996). A Lindenbaum obit in the *Commercial Observer* also noted:

> In the 1990s, [Lindenbaum] played a key role in helping Mr. Trump secure the rights to raise the Trump World Tower on the East Side, a building that Mr. Trump envisioned as the city's tallest residential tower and that drew heavy opposition from the powerful neighborhood residents. . . . Mr. Trump had used a controversial process to achieve the building's size, buying up air rights so that it could blossom beyond initial zoning limits. (Geiger 2012)

Fellow attorney for Big Real Estate Michael Sillerman said of Lindenbaum:

> Sandy was great at not just helping developers win approval for added development rights or a zoning change but finding creative ways to get more out of what they already had. (Geiger 2012)

Lindenbaum worked for the giant real estate firm of Vornado, getting approval for Vornado's mega-tower at Penn Station called "15 Penn Plaza," now a contentious problem in the planning for a new Penn Station.

By 1993, Professor Jerold Kayden of Harvard summed up all the incremental, real-estate-initiated tinkering with the code: "The net effect was that anyone can build anything anywhere" (Bressi 1993, 106). There was talk of reform among technocrats and specialists who said that there was a need again for a new code—but it was talk that went nowhere.

That is, until Joe Rose appeared on the scene with new ideas in 1999. Mayor Giuliani had appointed Rose, a "princeling" of one of New York's real estate clans, to the job of chair of the City Planning Commission (Bumiller 1999). To his credit Rose used his position, reputation, and influence to develop and promote significant reforms (Rose 1999). His criticisms of the existing code were devastating, backed up with a legion of expert opinions (Bressi 1993).[3] Technocrats attacked the 1961 code as having encouraged the anti-urban building form called "towers in the park" described in Chapter 1. It allowed tall buildings to arise where they should not be, usually by telling developers to build ugly plazas for scant public use in exchange for the extra height. The code let developers engage in "the overly aggressive harvesting of air rights," as Rose described it. Rose argued that the code's twisted rules incentivized an unregulated "race to the top" of the skyline, the purpose of which was to capture profitable views and sell them off to the wealthy, all while pretending not to shadow the public realm. Rose gave his reform proposals the unappealing name of "Unified Bulk" and argued that under his chairmanship, the City Planning Commission would fix the code's ills, while protecting and restoring the city's great streetscapes.

The content of Rose's reforms was not very radical: laughably modest height limits—360 feet in high-density residential neighborhoods and 720 feet in certain other zones (New York City Department of City Planning n.d.). Strangely, these not-very-strict height limits were intended *not* for the two existing central business districts of Midtown and the Financial District. Those business districts were to be covered by a "build any way you want and as tall as you want" rule, which was a major giveaway to the industry. But outside the two districts, the idea was to regulate height so as to retain the existing "contextual character" of residential neighborhoods, with "contextual" referring to the existing height and bulk of an area (L. Weiss 1999).

Rose nourished support for his plan among professional planners, community boards, journalists, and civic groups such as the Municipal Art Society and Civitas. He held workshops and pushed the concept for a year. The *New York Times* penned an editorial in favor of the reforms, calling Rose's proposal the "boldest change in zoning rules since 1961." The *Times* editors went to the unusual length of criticizing the real estate industry for opposing an "attempt to save residential neighborhoods from destruction by wanton development of towering skyscrapers" (*New York Times* Editorial Board 2000).

At public hearings, support for Rose's reforms came in at a 2:1 ratio in favor (Blair 2000). But when the Board of Governors of the Real Estate Board of New York studied the proposal, they dug in their heels: no reforms, not ever, no way, no how (H. Weiss 2010; L. Weiss 2019). They had two complaints. First, they did not want height restrictions imposed in neighborhoods outside the business districts, such as the Lower East Side, Brooklyn, East Harlem, the downtown area later known as Hudson Square in Manhattan, or Long Island City. REBNY members held "speculative" rights in those places and wanted to be free to towerize those neighborhoods when the time felt right. Second, there were already more than a few skyscrapers in the early stage of plans *outside* the two business districts. These had yet to break ground or gain regulatory approval. REBNY wanted those grandfathered in. REBNY began a "frenzied opposition" (Bagli 2000).

Things fell apart for Joe Rose and his allies after their year and half of labor. Mayor Giuliani turned his attention to an exploratory run for Senate. Journalists speculated that he didn't have the stomach for a fight at that moment, let alone one with the chair of REBNY, a man widely thought of as "a close friend of the Mayor" (Bagli 2000). The situation made Rose's job of persuasion difficult. So it was a grave setback for Rose when his ally, a deputy mayor with Giuliani's ear, left for another job. REBNY saw weakness and went in for the kill, making a phone call to the mayor. According to comments Rose made to a Congress for the New Urbanism gathering years later, the proposal died an immediate death after that call.[4] No reforms of similar substance have been proposed since.

REBNY of course, works full-time to make things go their way. In 2019, REBNY proposed bizarre changes to the zoning code that would legalize the use of immense stilts and vast empty spaces in the sky. Planners call these spaces "voids." REBNY did not want these immense empty spaces to count against their allotment of the buildable space City Planning doled out. Voids had become a secret way to jack up buildings into the skies, leapfrogging the darker lower reaches of the city so as to create more high-value views to sell to the world's speculators. The REBNY-sponsored "void amendment" passed the City Council without a squeak of protest from council members, although community groups spoke out against it. The result is that anything can be built using entire empty floors with no housing at all. In the illustration in Figure 5.5, prepared by George Janes, an urban planner, observe that voids in the building account for 390 feet—27 percent of the allotment of buildable space (FAR).

Example Two: Real Estate Power and the Landmarks Law

In 1966, as the city began to draft the Landmarks Law, the real estate lobby insisted on weakening the powers of the new regulatory agency the law would create, soon dubbed the Landmarks Preservation Commission.

217 W 57th Street is under construction

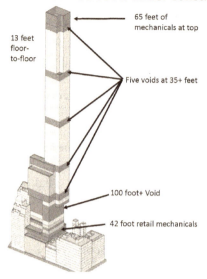

- Voids and mechanical floors account for about 390 feet (27%) of the building's height and volume

- One floor is 100 feet floor-to-floor

- Apartments are 13 feet floor-to-floor

- First 14 stories are 370 feet tall (26.5 feet average)

- Zoning lot is now enormous (91,000 SF!)

Figure 5.5. George Janes's illustration of voids eating up FAR at 217 West 57th. Image courtesy of George Janes, urban planner at georgejanes.com.

At issue was a proposal to allow the new commission to regulate the height and massing of buildings within 400 feet of an individually designated landmark. Such a rule was common in Europe. It protects the public interest by conserving the surrounding historical "context" of a landmark, which is just good urban design practice. REBNY refused it point-blank and caused the text to be purged from the proposed Landmarks Law (Wood 2008). REBNY also managed in the same year to force into the new law shockingly stringent limitations on when the new commission could operate: It could only designate landmarks during six months out of every three years (Pearson 2010; Wood 2008; Gratz 1973). The result was years of massive under-designation of properties that merited protection. The only sizable historic districts it created were in Brooklyn Heights and Greenwich Village, as those were the outcome of years of intense community lobbying prior to the law's emergence.

REBNY also managed to make sure that those appointed to the new Landmarks Commission would serve as volunteers, unlike commissioners appointed to City Planning. The commission was thus underfunded and understaffed from the beginning. That, combined with the constant threat of new lawsuits over imaginary "takings of speculative value" while the Penn Central case wound its way through the courts, succeeded in turning the

Landmarks Preservation Commission into a weak and ineffective institution. One spokesman explained it to investigative journalist Roberta Gratz:

> Opposition [by the industry to the LPC's work] diminished because the Commission turned out not to be as much a threat as expected. When people saw what was being preserved and understand the law, they were no longer worried. (J. Clarence Davies quoted in Gratz 1973)

It took eight years to rid the commission of the six-month rule, and it only happened after front-page work by Gratz.

The result was that despite the efforts of dozens of public-serving preservationists both within and outside the commission, there has been a relentless "death by a thousand cuts" to the historic city, the helter-skelter erosion of historic neighborhoods, and the burying of individual landmarks underneath mountains of glass, as anyone walking by Grand Central Station can observe. At this writing, fifty-five years after the law passed, the Landmarks Preservation Commission regulates only 27 percent of the property lots in Manhattan. Given how small most property lots are (most are 25 x 50 feet in size), that means that not much of Manhattan's land mass falls under the commission's purview. Other real estate industry attacks on the Landmarks Preservation Commission are described in the following chapter.

Example Three: Opposition to Small Business Rent Stabilization

The "Mom and Pop" retail landscape has been one of the great elements of New York's reputation as Wonder City. Even before the Amazon-induced small business apocalypse and the Covid crisis, small businesses faced decades of price gouging as landlords and real estate investors sought to replace low-rent Mom and Pop stores with higher-rent tenants, amply documented in books like *Vanishing New York* by Jeremiah Moss (2018). In boom times, landlords always squeeze short-term profits out of commercial spaces, usually ground-floor retail. After the low-interest rate policies of the Federal Reserve began to flood New York and "winner cities" with speculative real estate capital, the situation worsened. There was a constant churn of tenants as one set of investors sold out to another, each of them trying to profit from the exemption from capital gains, called a 1031 exchange (see Sidebar 5.1 of tax benefits in this chapter), each new owner in turn seeking higher-paying tenants.

Long before this, in 1986, the Small Business Congress, an alliance of mostly Korean shops in Queens, joined other small business lobbies to

Sidebar 5.1
Who Said Developers Weren't Socialists? An (Incomplete) Glossary of Tax Breaks and Giveaways to New York's Real Estate Developers and Landlords

- Developers can deduct the cost of buying a property from their incomes over a number of years (Sullivan 2019).
- A 1993 tax law allowed any "investor" in real estate to deduct losses from rental properties from their incomes. It was removed as a tax shelter in 1986 but reinstated in the first year of the Clinton presidency after intense lobbying by the real estate industry—including lobbying by Donald Trump (Miller 2016).
- Liberty Bonds are government issued tax-exempt bonds for the building of housing in Lower Manhattan after the 9/11 disaster. They were used to build much luxury, market-rate housing, including the Frank Gehry-designed 9 Spruce Street, but not affordable housing.
- 421a tax exemptions cut property taxes to incentivize the building of residential units and is widely seen as a policy failure (Community Board 5 Planning Fellows 2017).
- 421g tax breaks are twenty-year breaks from property taxes for owners who converted office buildings to residential use in Lower Manhattan—if the apartments stay rent-stabilized. Many landlords took the break but still rented at market rates, not stabilized rates. A 2016 lawsuit found justice in 2020 on behalf of one group of tenants who had been bilked (Rochabrun 2016).
- J-51 tax breaks reduced property taxes for twenty years for those renovating buildings into condos/co-ops.
- There are IRS rules that allow developers and landlords to write off operating expenses, repairs, lawyer fees, management fees, mortgage interest, and—see above—depreciation on appreciating property against tax liabilities.
- Opportunity Zones are designated areas, often in gentrifying real estate markets, mapped by government as places where investors pay zero capital gains tax if they hold their investments in the zone for ten years. (TRD Staff 2019b, 30).
- In the EB-5 green card program, the U.S. Government sells green cards to foreign investors who have at least $900,000 to invest. The money goes into "regional investment pools" and makes large sums of cheap money available to developers.

propose to the City Council a solution to the eternal problem of ever-escalating storefront rents: a piece of legislation called the "Small Business Jobs Survival Act." The idea was simple: When a business tenant's lease came up for renewal, the landlord could no longer impose a dramatically higher rent and evict the old tenant. The tenant would have the right to obtain the intervention of an independent arbitrator to come to terms. This was back in the day when arbitration was new and relatively cheap. REBNY dubbed the idea "rent control," and claimed without evidence that it was unconstitutional and threatened the city with a lawsuit. That

Sidebar 5.1 (continued)

- Developers of buildings converted to co-ops and condos in the 1970s and 1980s could retain for themselves the profitable retail ground leases in "sweetheart" arrangements for twenty years, short-changing the co-op owners of revenue to maintain their buildings (Poretz and Weiss 2000).
- In the 1031 exchange program, developers and real estate investors can sell one property and reinvest in another to defer capital gains taxes over an entire lifetime.
- The Empire State Development Corporation (an agency of government) makes a frequent practice of using eminent domain to favor private developers.
- The zoning code gives developers "height bonuses," meaning extra buildable space and height in exchange for the creation of minimalist public "plazas" or the provision of vaguely defined community facilities, which can include private clubs, churches, and synagogues.
- Zoning rules allow developers to harvest neighboring air rights and stack them on a site to gain extra height without limit.
- The buildable envelope that the city gives real estate developers is so generous that more than 80 percent of all development takes place "as of right," without any public oversight (2019 Charter Revision Commission Hearing Testimony of Marisa Lago, Chair of City Planning Commission 2019).
- The Board of Standards and Appeals is a regulatory agency (brought into existence in the 1930s as part of a state enabling law) that is charged with guaranteeing the real estate sector a 6 percent rate of return, a government gift that few industries can claim.
- Developers, landlords, and real estate investors can hide their investments in NYC buildings under untraceable limited liability corporations (LLCs).
- The state legislature put into place a variety of ineffective subsidies known as Commercial Rent Subsidies in Lower Manhattan after 9/11, and there they remain. One subsidy allows commercial tenants paying rents higher than $200,000 to be exempt from the commercial rent tax. Another subsidizes energy costs for building owners. A third exempts local businesses from sales taxes.

prevented a vote on the bill for twenty years. Small business advocates, after years of lobbying, finally got a new 2019 public hearing on the topic inside the City Council. There, REBNY mustered its forces and kicked the bill into oblivion once again using the threat of a lawsuit.

REBNY did the same with an alternative proposal for small business called the Commercial Rent Reform Act. That act proposed that the City Council set up a new regulatory body to set commercial rent increases, copying the rent-stabilization model. That legislation died on the vine in 2020. Both pieces of legislation were hardly perfect, but they were the only legislative attempts to level the playing field between small shop owners and Big Real Estate. One conclusion should be obvious: Big Real Estate is not a friend to the small business sector.

Example Four: The Case of Vornado and Pennsylvania Station

It has been a plan that the city has had for many years to try to really create Midtown as a river-to-river central business district and this [project to replace the Penn neighborhood with ten Class A office towers] is kind of the last piece in that puzzle.
—Empire State Development Corporation spokesperson Holly Leicht at a Community Board 4 Forum in 2020

The original Pennsylvania Station was demolished in 1963. It was an immense bit of eye candy: a neoclassical pile partially modeled on the Roman Baths of Caracalla. It covered an entire city block, replacing a working-class row-house and tenement district in the heart of the city (elements of which can still be seen on West 30th, West 29th, and West 31st Streets). That demolition may have been painful, but the old Penn Station was a spectacular public amenity, despite its private ownership. It had wide sidewalks and carriageways, vast public spaces, waiting rooms, newspaper boys, shoeshine boys, a plethora of shops, toilets, baby nursing rooms, and eating establishments at various price points. Commuters "entered the city like a God" in the words of Yale architecture Professor Vincent Scully (Scully Jr. 1969).

Scattered around the station were hotels for different classes of people, many with prewar charm. The Sloan House YMCA on 8th Avenue had 1,483 beds for soldiers and transients (and is now a private condo). The Governor Clinton Hotel (now the Stewart) on 30th Street is fifteen bays aside and thirty-one stories high with 2,000 rooms and two restaurants. Across the street from the station on the north side was a Greyhound Bus Station. The same architect who designed Penn Station also designed the massive Federal Post Office to the west (now known as the Moynihan Train Hall) and the magnificent, just-demolished 2,200-room Hotel Pennsylvania to the east. It was a brilliant, publicly accessible urban ensemble that contributed to the great urbanity of the Wonder City.

By 1960, with competition from the automobile, the railroad companies fell on hard times. So of course, someone took advantage. Irving Felt, the financier brother of James Felt (then chair of the City Planning Commission and the same person who had pushed for the modernist 1961 Zoning Code), bought the air rights to build over Penn Station site from the railroad company in 1960. Irving and James then orchestrated the demolition

Figure 5.6. The great, demolished Pennsylvania Station was an architect's gift of civic space to the people of New York. Image from Library of Congress.

of the old Penn station and the building of a sports arena on the site that we know today as Madison Square Garden, catapulting the Felts into the Robert Moses category of urban villains (see Irving Felt's obit in the *Times* [Salpukas 1994]).

The two Felts replaced the demolished, above-ground station with an underground rat's nest of a train station, its ugliness universally deplored. Low ceilings, artificial light, endless corridors, and junk food shops replaced the once great station, which is still the busiest in the country. New Jersey Transit trains, Long Island Railroad trains, Metro-North, Amtrak trains, and the city's subway system still all converge at the underground Penn. The construction of two bland, glass office skyscrapers on top of the footprint of the old station, known as One and Two Penn Plaza, made the ugliness even worse. The bus station moved inconveniently to the new, also ugly, Port Authority Bus Station to the north. Years later, to the immediate west, behind the Federal Post Office, rose the controversial modernist utopia of Hudson Yards, built on a platform above the train lines. Hudson Yards is composed of high-end skyscrapers filled with luxury housing, "Class A" office space, and a luxury shopping mall.

The area on top of the footprint of the old Penn Station is known as "Penn Plaza." It immediately became what urbanist Jane Jacobs calls a "border vacuum" in her book *The Death and Life of Great American Cities* (1992). Border vacuums are depressing, characterless, scary, boring, "nowhere places" in between more successful urban zones. They are places people scurry away from, the opposite of successful, great urbanity. That means the homeless, the mentally ill, the panhandlers, and the drug-addicted congregate there, a place no one else wants to be. Sports fans, office workers, and commuters, once their business is done, routinely flee across the street to the businesses on the periphery of the old station in the surrounding historic blocks. Scattered to the north, east, and south are tall brick Garment District buildings with setbacks on their upper reaches and the beautiful nineteenth-century Church of St. John the Baptist with its parish hall and rectory. Brown-robed Franciscan Friars of the Capuchin order, the ones who take a vow of poverty and serve the poor, have occupied the rectory and labored for the poor there since 1870. While the garment businesses have been officially zoned out by the City's Economic Development Corporation, many remain. These tall brick buildings now shelter rent-stabilized residential apartments and a platoon of small businesses whose owners seek what real estate agents delicately refer to as "Class B and C office space"—code for cheap rents. There we find rabbit warrens of theater companies, music studios, therapists, chiropractors, single-shingle law firms, and tech start-ups who don't have enough money to afford the Class A office space that hedge-funders and bankers prefer.

Enter into this world Vornado, the country's third largest real estate investment trust. Vornado is one of three commercial real estate companies in New York that collectively own 75 percent of all commercial square footage in Manhattan (the other two are Brookfield and SL Green). Vornado saw this neighborhood as ripe for hyper-gentrification. Vornado's idea: Get rid of the "obsolete" brick buildings and low-class, low-rent-paying tenants; replace them all with Class A office space with a richer class of tenant. This is the "luxury city" concept again.

Over a thirty-year period, Vornado bought up so many properties in the area that it bragged to its shareholders in 2019: "We are the largest owner in the Penn District, with over 9 million square feet" (Roth 2020). Vornado decided to create a rival to Hudson Yards, called the "Vornado Campus." The CEO, Steven Roth, proposed to demolish all the old buildings that ring Penn Station, including eight that are eligible for listing in the National Registry of Historic Places, such as the Hotel Pennsylvania and the Church of St. John the Baptist. He would replace them with ten brand-new glass skyscrapers, most of them supertalls, filled with Class A office space for tenants like Facebook. It would take at least sixteen years to build out

Vornado's fantasy. The towers would cast shadows as far as New Jersey and overshadow even Hudson Yards. And yes, the Capuchin Monks and their business of serving the poor would have to go. Their church and home would be replaced by a gentrified Vornado supertall. To make this happen, Vornado and the State agency doing Vornado's bidding propose to evict more than 2,200 households on the sites that Vornado wants for towers. While that drama plays out, Vornado has reclad its existing office towers that sit on top of Penn Station with new glass to make them look more like Hudson Yards. Vornado hired a landscape architect to redesign the toxic border vacuum of Penn Plaza with new outdoor seating that might appeal to Vornado's imaginary, new, high-end tenants. Roth, the CEO, bragged that he planned to pack his new towers with exclusive "amenities" such as swimming pools, private restaurants, private gardens, and dog-walking terraces. The only problem Roth faced was that the area only had tower zoning, not supertall zoning.

To make his plan a reality, Roth realized he would have to do two things: Get a hold of properties he didn't own and obtain a massive override to the city's current zoning so that it could break the height limit and erect the supertalls. To that end, Vornado made a big bet on the developer-friendly politician Governor Andrew Cuomo. Cuomo controlled the appointments to the aforementioned Empire State Development Corporation (ESD). ESD alone had the power to override the city's weak zoning on heights in the area. EDC's board appointments were all obedient Cuomo appointees. But to make sure Cuomo would not look askance at its ideas, Vornado shelled out over $350,000 in campaign donations to the former governor.

Cuomo ordered the ESD to initiate the bureaucratic process to approve the Vornado plan. All EDC had to do was declare the area "blighted," an awkward trick given that Vornado's CEO was publicly bragging to his shareholders how economically vibrant the Penn neighborhood was (and is). To deal with that problem, Cuomo, Vornado, and the EDC needed a public relations strategy.

So ESD came up with the following rationale for the giveaway to Vornado: Vornado would pay the city unspecified, to-be-determined "payments in lieu of taxes" after the sixteen-year construction period. With a nebulous "promise to pay" from Vornado, the ESD could issue a modest amount ($4 billion) of New York State bonds. The State would then recycle the money raised from the bonds into five other Penn Station improvement projects that were currently underway or under discussion between the many agencies, state and federal governments that care about Penn Station

Figure 5.7. Rendering by the Empire State Development Corporation of the proposed Vornado towers, most of them supertalls. Image from Empire State Development Corporation General Project Plan.

(Amtrak, the MTA, New Jersey Transit). Those station improvement projects were unsettled when Vornado entered the scene. Nobody knew what they would cost or how much money the federal government would contribute to them (a lot, it turned out later). Transit officials had not even settled on where the new federally financed "Gateway Tunnel" coming in under the Hudson River would land, nor had they settled internal debates about whether Penn Station's tracks should be converted to a more efficient "through-running" hub. There was still no transit plan for Penn Station. But this didn't matter. Vornado gloated to shareholders in 2021 about its monopolistic situation and how much money it would make:

> The Penn District is our moonshot, the highest growth opportunity in our portfolio . . . over time our Penn District Campus will almost certainly command premium pricing . . . we will provide our tenants with an unparalleled amenity package (of over 200,000 square feet). . . . Part of the deal here we will gain long-term control of an additional 22,000 square feet of retail on the south side, so we will now have all the retail along both sides of the heavily trafficked Long Island Railroad concourse. And we have all the retail in the adjacent Moynihan Train Hall and Farley. (Vornado's 2020 *Chairman's Letter to Shareholders*, in Roth 2020)

THE CURSE OF NEW YORK · 165

Vornado and EDC exchanged over a thousand emails in 2019 just to set up private Zoom meetings between EDC staff and Vornado executives. Vornado agreed to pay for the EDC's legal expenses and an accounting firm to figure out the project finances (Weinstock 2022). Vornado contributed to EDC's strategic planning in multiple meetings on the topic of how to manage widespread opposition to the project. Attorney Charles Weinstock found in his Freedom of Information Act requests to ESD that Vornado's senior vice president blithely noted in emails:

> Our team [referring to a joint Vornado/ESD group of staffers] is gathering intel this morning. The two Community Boards are planning a press conference for Tuesday. [State Senator Brad] Hoylman is planning to be there—but not [State Assembly Member Richard Gottfried]. Once our team has made the rounds, we should share all we've gathered, compare notes, and see how best to coordinate the plan. (Vornado executive cited in Weinstock 2022)

An executive vice president at Vornado, Barry Langer, told ESD—who was worried about a presentation EDC staffer Holly Leicht was planning in a public forum, "I will do the dancing for Holly's narrative." Weinstock also found an email from Ms. Leicht to the Vornado/ESD "team" with the plea, "We need to coordinate and script this meeting to ensure we're cohesive and have a good story to tell about why we landed on these densities" (Weinstock 2022). ("Densities" here is code for the height limits that Vornado wants the State to override without getting permission from the city.) In the words of good government think tank Reinvent Albany, the Cuomo-Vornado-ESD project is "a massive public subsidy in disguise to Vornado" (New York Senate 2022). Even former Mayor Bill de Blasio called it a "land grab" (Haag and Ferré-Sadurní 2021).

When Cuomo was forced to resign in disgrace over a MeToo scandal, Vornado gave similar campaign funds to his replacement, Governor Kathy Hochul (Meyer 2022). Hochul tweaked the ESD plan insignificantly, adding 800 "affordable" housing units into the supertalls and slightly diminishing the amount of buildable space another developer (not Vornado) would get. She decided to close off a roadway to traffic to make more "plaza" space. These were minor tweaks that did not alter the basic ten supertall tower plan. She ignored that 2,200 housing units would be destroyed and engender a net loss of housing units.

Roth admits to blighting areas to get more out of government. At a talk at Columbia University's architectural school, someone asked why Vornado kept the landmarked former Alexander's department store empty for so long. Roth responded:

My mother called me and said [of the site], "It's dirty. There are bums sleeping in the sidewalks of this now closed, decrepit building. They're urinating in the corners. It's terrible. You have to fix it."

And what did I do? Nothing.

Why did I do nothing? Because I was thinking in my own awkward way, that the more the building was a blight, the more the governments would want this to be redeveloped; the more help they would give us when the time came. . . . And they did.

Laughter followed. (Brown 2010)

City, state, and federal politicians closed ranks tightly under the Vornado plan. Senator Chuck Schumer approved it, as did Congressman Jerry Nadler. The only politicians to denounce the plan were Jumaane Williams (New York's public advocate) and State Senators Brad Hoylman-Sigal and Liz Krueger. The city council member affected, Erik Bottcher, was utterly silent and ignored his constituents' multiple pleas to stand against the plan. (Big Real Estate had backed his candidacy.)

Governor Hochul held a press conference just prior to a Public Authorities Control Board (PACB) vote on the project (the last bureaucratic hurdle). There, in July of 2022, she mustered the heads of the MTA and Amtrak, the governor of New Jersey, and the mayor of New York City. They stood behind the ten supertall tower plan and then all of them ran out of the room before questions could be asked. No opponents to the plan were allowed into the press conference room. Big Real Estate, in the form of Vornado, had won the day. Throughout this, the Empire State Development Corporation orchestrated a Potemkin "Community Advisory" working group to act as a focus group on the project. EDC tightly controlled the agenda, the membership, and access to the working group, filling it with a majority of Vornado plan supporters and only one person whose home would be demolished. EDC threatened legal action if any member of the advisory group shared information from the meetings or failed to accept nondisclosure rules.[5]

In late July 2022, the Public Authorities Control Board punted on the project, asking for more financial data, but did not oppose the project. Opponents in November 2022 organized a lawsuit opposing it, much of it financed by Garment District property owner, Arthur Gumowitz. The approvals for the zoning override are in place, and there is nothing to stop Vornado from doing the plan except Vornado's own internal decision-making. Roth hinted he might delay the project in a call to shareholders in

October 2022 during which he said that "headwinds" were making Vornado significantly slow down on the supertall project, although the demolition of the magnificent Hotel Pennsylvania was already half-completed (Vornado Realty Trust 2022). Despite this bizarre twist, Governor Hochul and the Empire State Development Corporation doubled down on the project in their statements to the press, but it is unclear how they will get money out of Vornado.

To add to the perversity of the situation, there was a better plan all along. The Empire Station Coalition's better plan had the following elements: moving Madison Square Garden to a parking lot site next to the Javits Convention Center (an idea that's been floating in the city for a long time); a new Penn Station rebuilt aboveground on the former site of the old station; the widening of the underground tracks at Penn following Rethink NYC's brilliant plan for track improvements; redevelopment of the existing "soft sites" in the historic east, north, and west in a contextual way to favor small businesses as Class B and C office space; and last, making Penn a "through-running" station (meaning trains go through to other destinations, rather than backing out and redirecting and creating havoc as they do now). With those elements in place, Penn Station could then serve as the hub of a regionally unified transit network called "RUN" (see the video material at www.rethinknyc.org). This would create massive transportation efficiencies and equitable economic growth opportunities throughout the Tri-State region. Nothing needs to be demolished under this alternative plan. It costs less money, causes less disruption and demolition of historic buildings and homes. It benefits more ordinary people—commuters from New Jersey and Westchester, Capuchin monks, and NY residents—rather than Vornado. And there is no need to displace 2,200 households. The new tunnel would just allow more space underground for the train station. So far, the better plan has been studiously ignored.

To let the planning of the country's biggest transport hub be dependent on the agenda, fantasies, whims, and campaign contributions of a single Big Real Estate company encapsulates the perversity of real estate power in New York City.

Example 5: The Case of Governors Island

Governors Island perches tantalizingly close to Lower Manhattan. It is accessible by ferry and water taxi. In the late nineteenth century, it housed a small army barracks. The army liked it so much that it added 103 acres of landfill to expand the island to the south. A small village arose with

Figure 5.8. View of Governors Island campground and bike path. Image under Creative Commons license.

Figure 5.9. Vishaan Chakrabarti's proposal to extend the tower world of the Financial District across the harbor and into Governors Island. Image from Columbia University's Center for Urban Real Estate circulated widely to the press, including the *New York Times*, *New York Magazine*, and the *New York Observer*.

two- and three-story houses called Officers' Row, showcasing vernacular American architectural styles. The larger brick barracks along the waterfront housed soldiers throughout two World Wars. There is a brick school, cafeteria, post office, library, community center, and even a swimming pool. At its residential high point, the island housed three thousand families.

THE CURSE OF NEW YORK · 169

Figure 5.10. Officers' Row on Governors Island, a National Historic District. Image from Creative Commons license.

Architecturally, it still is a fascinating experience of extreme contrast, a dialogue between the military's vision of American small-town life covered in greenery and trees within sight of the overbuilt Skyscraper Center of Wall Street.

In 1966 the army transferred the island to the Coast Guard. In 1996, the Coast Guard abandoned the island. In 2001, President Clinton designed 22 acres of the island as a National Monument. The New York City Landmarks Preservation Commission designated much of it a local historic district. Finally, in 2003, the National Trust for Historic Preservation gave the island to the people of the City and State of New York through a trust deed that stipulated that there was to be no housing built and that most of the island would be a park for the benefit of the public. Management was handed over to the Governors Island Preservation and Education Corporation. There was much hand-wringing in the press about what to do with the island, how to make it profitable, how to develop it so it could pay its way, like say, Central Park or Prospect Park. Architect Vishaan Chakrabarti even proposed solving the city's financial anxieties by filling in the harbor between the island and the Financial District and extending high-rises right into the island. But that idea didn't go anywhere, at least for a while.

The Governors Island Corporation did some clever work. It talked a high school into moving into one of the brick Coast Guard buildings. The corporation built a new park with a hill. It invited arts organizations to run seasonal music and arts events out of Officers' Row. Eventually, children of New York got to go to a summer camp there. The corporation let a beer garden move in and invited food kiosks to set up. It wisely demolished a few of the unfortunate modernist housing blocks built in the 1950s as the eyesores they were. Bike rentals arrived. Ferry service improved. Concerts and unique events brought New Yorkers from all over the city to the island. The events and concessions generated about $5 million in revenue, just enough to pay for the actual physical maintenance of the place, but not the ferry service.

This comfortable arrangement began to change—big time—when the real estate industrial complex got its tentacles into all aspects of planning for the island. The corporation became a new nonprofit called the Trust for Governors Island. The CEO of the trust was Michael Samuel, a former executive from Related Companies, one of the largest developers in the city. An additional Friends of Governors Island organization was formed, filled with marquee names of the REBNY oligarchy. The chair of the trust's board was an eminent advisor to Big Real Estate, Carl Weisbrod (formerly of H & A Advisors and former head of the City Planning Commission). Weisbrod brought his friend Alicia Glen on to the board. Glen is formerly of Goldman Sachs and was Mayor de Blasio's prime gentrifier-in-chief and is now a private real estate investor. Glen ousted her former colleague from Goldman and got herself named head of the trust (L. Weiss 1999). Glen got the trust's mission changed to be about "bold visions" and "full potential" and produced a real estate–driven development plan, opposed by the community board and a coalition of parks advocates. From the outside, it looks like a privatization-by-stealth program that skirts the edge of legality, given the strict conditions under which the island was given to the people of New York City.

The Glen/Weisbrod plan: Upzone thirty-three acres of the island; demolish the old brick buildings and replace them with towers; then rent the new buildings, or preferably, sell them as hotels and other businesses. The plan was presented to the public in 2018.

How would it all work? First, the trust creates a "red herring" to serve as bait to justify an upzoning, a nonprofit given the grandiose name of "Center for Climate Solutions." To make it all happen, the trust will upzone 33 acres, demolish the brick buildings, then get "someone" to build new glass buildings on the upzoned area under a trust contract, and then finally rent the new buildings to some undetermined third party who would oversee running one of the smaller buildings as a "climate solutions center." At the time of this writing, the organization that is playing along with this is a public organization living on the public dime, the State University at Stonybrook. Glen pitches to all that new tenants in the new glass buildings will somehow agree to pay the city as much as $120 million a year in rents. She says there could be splashy new faculty housing or dorms for the climate researchers, and a variety of hotels—as long as nothing is categorized as "permanent" housing (which the deed transferring the island to the City forbids). Buildings as high as 300 feet will be allowed.

The climate research center would be the smallest part of the plan and get the smallest of the new buildings, and its work could easily fit into an existing brick building. Stonybrook will get its rent money from the governor of New York State, who oversees the state university system's budget. Taxpayers will pay for the necessary demolitions and the unspecified cost of raising the height of the south part of the island to protect the infill part of the island from sea-level rise. Who wouldn't want to do all that to get a climate solutions center? The switch will come when the fiction of a nonprofit "climate solutions center" proves impossible to sustain financially, thus requiring a deed change to allow for the privatization of the speculative towers so that they might be turned into luxury condos and Class A office space. That, in the Glen/Weisbrod luxury city way of thinking, would bail everyone out. And wow, dangling $120 million in fantasy annual revenue! As E. B. White said, that's "some pig," astonishing Goldman Sachs voodoo using public money all the way. Of course, it is not hard to imagine that it will be a member of the REBNY-laden Friends of Governors Island who gets all the construction contracts.

The upshot is that New York's last open space, given to the people of New York as a public asset and park, will be incrementally privatized and turned instead into a real estate deal.

Figure 5.11. How the redevelopment of Governors Island could look under the new zoning pushed by Alicia Glen. Image courtesy of Metro Area Governors Island Coalition.

With that ends the tour of the history and wants of the real estate lobby in New York and an examination of how that power has informed public policy. REBNY and its Big Real Estate friends have kneecapped the Landmarks Law, undermined the public purpose of the zoning code, hounded out small businesses, turned a public park into Wall Street in the Harbor, and limited public policy options over how to modernize regional transit around Penn Station. The next chapter reviews the practical tools Big Real Estate uses to extend its influence into every part of city government.

Chapter 6

How Big Real Estate Stays on Top

> Logic tells you you're more likely to find bad stuff happening when the real estate industry is involved.
> —Preet Bharara, former U.S. District Attorney for the Southern District of New York, in an interview with journalist Brian Lehrer, "Preet Bharara's Take on the News | The Brian Lehrer Show," *WNYC*, October 25, 2017

> Mayor de Blasio has met with lobbyists 83 times.... His first meeting was in February 2014 with ex-Real Estate Board of New York President Steven Spinola.
> —Anna Sanders, "City Hall Finally Discloses Lobbyist Meetings—and the Results Are Eye-Opening," *New York Post*, August 11, 2018

TWO THINGS LIE AT THE HEART OF real estate power's longevity in New York. The first is its ability to persuade politicians to veto, stall, or bury legislation the industry dislikes and to introduce, sponsor, or vote for legislation it wants. The second is its ability to "capture" the agencies that are supposed to regulate real estate power. This chapter reviews these and other practical tools Big Real Estate uses to maintain and extend its control over city and state government. But first, we must understand the idea of "regulatory capture."

The General Problem of Regulatory Capture

When a regulated industry exerts so much influence over the regulators that the regulator serves the industry rather than the public good, we can say that "regulatory capture" took place. Capture can be overt, for example, when Donald Trump appointed an enemy of environmental regulation to run the Environmental Protection Agency (EPA). It can also be subtle, for example, when regulators adopt a group-think pro-industry philosophical approach to their work that favors the industry. Capture can happen through lobbying, revolving door appointments, bribery, and behind-the-scenes influence-mongering to ensure that the politicians appoint people friendly to the industry's public policy positions. Capture is challenging to prove with statistical data: One needs instead "gotcha" emails, internal memos, and phone call transcripts to figure out when lobbying and influence-mongering have gone too far. Therefore, we must infer capture from an accumulation of data that suggests a systematic pattern of decision-making. In Chapter 7, we will see how capture took place with the Landmarks Preservation Commission and here concentrate on the City Planning Commission.

Capture is a tough problem to deal with. First, finding civic-minded regulators immune to influence-mongering to serve as heads of regulatory agencies can be difficult. That's because crafting effective regulations does require someone who knows how the industry operates, thinks, and, especially, how it cheats. That can mean looking for an "insider" to run the agency. But what insider would be willing to be the equivalent of a turncoat and be tough on their industry friends, when they know they will need an industry job when they are done with their public duties? You can see the difficulty. Regulated industries also lobby hard against appointments of anyone they can characterize to politicians and the press as a "hardliner," a "crazy," a "crusader," an "extremist," or a "zealot." Instead, they want someone who talks to them, understands them, believes them, talks about "balance" and "compromise," and who the industry believes can read situations in the industry's favor about how much to regulate and how much to step back. Politicians who make these appointments also mostly want to avoid appointment fights—they want the public to see them as doing their job. For these reasons they tend to favor "balanced" regulators. New York City and the real estate industry are no different in this regard. The problem for the public arises when balance becomes "capture," which this chapter argues has happened in New York City, through the tools summarized in Sidebar 6.1.

In New York, the mayor makes all the top appointments to the agencies that regulate or interact with Big Real Estate: The Department of City Planning, the Board of Standards and Appeals (BSA), the Department of Buildings, the Economic Development Corporation, and the Landmarks

Sidebar 6.1
The Big Real Estate Toolbox to Stay on Top

- Use campaign contributions to "own" politicians and assure privileged access to them.
- Create revolving door appointments for senior staff and elected officials who rotate in and out of government and the Big Real Estate's network of allied organizations.
- Spend big on lobbyists of all kinds.
- Make use of bribery and ignore trivial fines.
- Threaten lawsuits that stop legislation from moving forward or challenge it once passed.
- Create a tight network of allied organizations that share overlapping boards of directors filled with Big Real Estate players.
- Pay for public relations drumbeating, which consists of the following endlessly repeated accusations: Landmarking "stifles growth" and imposes "excessive costs" on property owners and "freezes the city in amber" and that the Landmarks Commission is guilty of "overreach" and everything the Landmarks Commission does is a "taking" of private property and last, that the commission designates too many "ugly" and "insignificant" buildings. (I've personally been in meetings where uneducated land use staff tell City Council members that landmarking is a taking.)
- Get real estate lobbyists appointed to Community Boards to influence community resolutions that City Council members are sensitive to.
- Capture the regulatory bodies outright.
- Push legislation to weaken the powers and functioning of the industry's nemesis, the Landmarks Preservation Commission (LPC). This includes keeping the LPC underfunded and understaffed.
- Use fronts and surrogates to advance policy positions to the public, press, and to politicians.
- Advertise heavily in the mainstream press to shape what journalists and the public think of as legitimate policy options in zoning, "growth policies," housing, and historic preservation.
- Donate generously to cultural nonprofits and serve on those boards. This broadens the network of urban "influencers" loath to criticize Big Real Estate's vision for the city.
- Create your own splashy ecosystem of industry-friendly publications.
- Give influential people (judges, politicians, permanent government technocrats) leases to apartments carrying rationed, below-market rents.

Preservation Commission. Big Real Estate has an extensive toolbox to deal with its regulators.

Power Tool One: Campaign Contributions

Again and again, our investigations have uncovered evidence showing that access to elected officials comes at a price and that Albany is filled with "a pay-to-play" political culture driven by large checks.
—Moreland Commission to Investigate Public Corruption 2013

About 62% of all campaign contributions have some connection to some element of real estate.
—REBNY Board of Governors member and supermarket mogul John Catsimatidis, in "Owners Magazine 2019 Q&A. Talking with the Top Developers and Owners of NYC," *Commercial Observer* (blog). November 5, 2019

You can't do anything without the fucking money.
—NYC Councilman Daniel Halloran, cited in the Moreland Commission to Investigate Public Corruption 2013

The biggest inducement for a politician to vote the Big Real Estate Way is campaign cash. As of the writing of this chapter, an individual donor in New York State, along with each of his family members, may contribute $157,000 in cash to a gubernatorial campaign. The law also allows donations from secretive, limited liability corporations (LLCs) that do not reveal the individual names of the donors. Numerous academics have pointed out that weakly regulated, "dark money" campaign finance systems fundamentally undermine democracy by creating access for the rich and friendly relationships between the donors and the politicians.[1] It happens all the time. For example, a REBNY president, when making an appeal to his members to donate to politicians, assured his members of the effectiveness of their donations: "I can tell you that in private meetings with the Speaker, the Senate majority leader and the Governor, our past efforts to maintain a personal and supportive relationship were critical in shaping the outcome of legislation" (Craig, Rashbaum, and Kaplan 2014). The cash ends up in political campaigns, political action committees, or state political party committees.

Former Governor Andrew Cuomo was a major recipient of real estate money—so much so that the real estate industry's own press described Big Real Estate's relationship with the ex-governor as "cozy" (Parker and Brenzel 2018). That said, many politicians at all levels depend on real estate cash for their campaigns. The result is that New York politicians are no longer dependent on their own constituents for campaign money. Take the case of State Assembly Speaker Carl Heastie. The good government group Reinvent Albany noted that Heastie "collected donations from 430 contributors for his campaign committee, but just one of them was from a person living in his district." Reinvent also noted that only "16% of campaign donations that Assembly leadership receives are from people in their districts" (Reinvent Albany 2019).

What does the industry hope its cash will get for their donations? At the state level, up for grabs are tax breaks and subsidies, the rent laws, and the tantalizing possibility of eroding height and buildable space limits for residential buildings in Manhattan via changes to the State Multiple Dwelling Law. There is also the game of getting the state agency that has eminent domain powers—the Empire State Development Corporation—to wield its power in the industry's favor. In the arena of municipal government, the game is about assuring friendly acquiescence to Big Real Estate's constant demand for modifications to zoning regulations, the daily battle for variance rulings that allow ever more industry-favorable interpretations of the zoning and building codes, and the job of keeping as many buildings and neighborhoods as possible away from the regulatory control of the Landmarks Commission. Finally, there is the task of assuring the friendliness of appointees to all the agencies that deal with real estate every day, notably the Department of City Planning, the Board of Standards and Appeals, the Economic Development Corporation, the Department of Buildings, and the Landmarks Preservation Commission.

Below are three well-documented stories that illustrate how the campaign finance game works.

STORY 1: CONTROLLING RENT LAWS WITH A REPUBLICAN STATE SENATE

For years the real estate industry—developers and landlords alike have been the most reliable and generous political donors to State Senate Republicans.
—Bill Mahoney, "REBNY Members Gave a Tenth of All N.Y. Campaign Money." Politico PRO (blog), April 15, 2015

New York City first regulated rents in 1920 during a six year "housing emergency," defined now as the situation when rental vacancy rates fall below 5 percent. Later, during World War II, the federal government regulated rents nationally under a wartime price control act. In 1947, the Federal Housing and Rent Act changed federal-level wartime rent and price controls to exempt new construction built after 1947 from regulation.[2] Three years later, the federal government abandoned rent control, but New York State continued it for the vast stock of New York City housing built prior to 1947. Following federal precedent, the New York State exempted buildings constructed after 1947 from rent regulation of any kind. Rent control meant, among other details, that a landlord had to get state approval to raise rents and could not evict a tenant without substantive cause. Rent control covered millions of apartments in New York City since most of the city's apartment buildings were built prior to 1947 (as is normal for a city that got built out early). In 1969, New York City, over the objections of the Real Estate Board of New York, created a weaker form of rent regulation called "rent stabilization." Their intent was to let the stricter "rent control" system fade away over time. The city appointed a "Rent Guidelines Board" to regulate annual rent increases in stabilized apartments, which became an epic annual battle between landlord and tenant. In 1971, under Republican Governor Nelson Rockefeller, the State legislature passed the Urstadt Law (named after its author). The law took most of the regulatory power on rents away from the city and returned it to the State. It also passed a landlord-friendly law called the Vacancy Decontrol Law. This allowed vacated apartments to raise the rent at each turnover by 20 percent, providing an incentive for landlords to get rid of regulated tenants and to churn tenants until they reached the rent that allowed exit from rent stabilization. As all predicted at the time, harassment of tenants exploded. City and State passed a series of too-late measures to try to protect tenants. For example, the city created a housing court in 1973 (but did not supply legal representation to tenants harassed into eviction until 2018). The State also ended vacancy decontrol for apartments in buildings with more than six units that had been under their regulatory regime.

In 1993 the city was in another wave of gentrification. Big Real Estate resurrected "Vacancy Decontrol" and got it passed in the legislature: Now any unit that reached $2,000 in monthly rent would leave the regulated part of the market and pass into the free market where any rent was possible, whatever the market could bear. Landlords were also freed to make a variety of "improvements" (often bogus) to an apartment, which would allow them to jack up rents faster to the $2,000 level, thus deregulating a "renovated" apartment faster. Landlords could also claim multiple units for "personal use" as another way to evict regulated tenants and get the apartments out of regulation. There was massive abuse of these rules.

By 2017, less than half the apartments in the city were under any form of regulation. Landlords had deregulated hundreds of thousands of units through evictions, demolitions, and the systematic jacking-up of rents to surpass the $2,000 threshold. Every year brought a lobbying battle to the fore: Would politicians extend or renew the laws covering various aspects of rent regulation, such as the Emergency Tenant Protection Act? Would they weaken the rules or strengthen them? Would the law have a sunset clause? What would the all-important exceptions and carve-outs to the rules be? Whom would the politicians appoint to lead the regulatory agencies? Landlords ask: How do I get the apartments I own deregulated and into the unregulated free market? How do I get rid of low-rent tenants? Tenants ask: How do I get security of tenure? How do I assure the habitability of the apartment and get freedom from shocking rent increases? Getting your way on either side required politicians. The tools are lobbying and campaign cash so that politicians take your requests for meetings, return your calls, or, at a pathetic bare minimum, accept delivery of your petition if you happen to be on the tenant side. Landlords have long had the upper hand in this game because of their wealth and their control over a Republican State Senate that could veto anything the Democratic Assembly could produce. And, of course, Big Real Estate could throw an infinite number of lobbyists, lawyers, and cash at any issue. Tenants could not.

Housing court, once intended as a help for tenants, became another landlord tool for generating evictions when the tried-and-true tactics of buyouts, bullying, cutting off the heat, setting of hallway fires, and hiring thugs to intimidate tenants failed to get rid of rent-stabilized tenants.[3] The oversight system was not in the tenants' favor. State-appointed judges can be influenced by a State Advisory Council representing the real estate industry, tenant organizations, the Bar Association, the governor, the mayor, and the Public Housing Authority. As multiple *New York Times* investigations over the years showed, eviction by housing court became a strategic tool used to deregulate apartments so that by 1979, "housing courts had failed to crack down on bad landlords" and by 1986, it was also well known that housing court was "in chaos" (Barker 2018). Then, between 1994 and 2018, a flood of speculative, globalized real estate capital poured into New York City, giving a frenzied additional incentive to landlords to get rid of poorer tenants and replace them with richer ones capable of paying free market rents. The situation turned the housing court into a full-on "eviction machine" (Barker 2018).

The state legislature during all of this was for years a safe landscape for Big Real Estate: They had a Republican majority in the State Senate that routinely did real estate's bidding. Doing Big Real Estate's bidding meant renewing weakened rent laws and meticulously avoiding raising the "vacancy decontrol cap" (the level of rent at which a regulated apartment goes into the free open market). It meant killing off campaign finance reform bills that the Democratic Assembly kept sending to the Senate. It meant introducing bills every year to get rid of the height cap in Manhattan that lies buried in the State Multiple Dwelling Law.

But in 2008–9, there appeared a storm cloud over the real estate lobby's comfortable control of the Senate: Their majority was narrowing, and they faced a serious risk of losing the State Senate altogether. Playing defense, the first order of business was for Senate Republicans to gerrymander—redraw voting districts where Republicans were vulnerable (Parker and Putzer 2017). One of those gerrymandered districts was near Albany. The candidate who received help from it was George Amedore, a wealthy real estate developer who had previously served in the State Assembly. Who better to serve real estate interests in the State Senate than an actual Republican real estate developer locking up a heavily gerrymandered district? Amedore, heavily backed by real estate, won the seat.

REBNY and its ally in the big landlords of the Rent Stabilization Association had other assets in their favor besides newly elected Amedore. They had Dean Skelos, a Republican state senator from Long Island who was Republican Majority Leader. Skelos was tight with real estate and business interests and later convicted of corruption for taking "bribes" from Big Real Estate, although Mayor Bloomberg called him an "honest guy" at the time. Much of Skelos's campaign cash came from a firm owned by real estate mogul Leonard Litwin of the big real estate firm called Glenwood. Litwin's obit in the *Times* noted how much money Litwin spent trying to weaken rent laws:

> In both [corruption] trials, prosecutors showed that Glenwood had received favored treatment in Albany by giving $10 million to political campaigns since 2005, mainly through a maze of 26 limited liability companies. Under a no-prosecution agreement, Mr. Dorego, a senior executive of Glenwood, testified that payoffs to leaders and members of the State Legislature assured Glenwood of endless benefits in taxes, State financing, and rent laws. One program alone, he said, saved [Glenwood] up to $100 million. (McFadden 2017)

Big Real Estate also had in their camp Assemblyman Sheldon Silver, who led the Assembly. Silver had always played nice with REBNY, although a judge would soon convict him of corruption for doing so. REBNY also had a pro-big business, right-of-center Democratic senator named Jeff Klein who had decided to go rogue against his party. Klein had formed a four-person caucus of conservative Democrats in the State Senate, calling his rogue band the Independent Democratic Conference, or the IDC. Their first press release sounded as if Klein had lifted the text from REBNY's website: to "remove obstacles to business investment and business creation" and a set a "property tax cap." Both items were classic REBNY agenda items.

Another preemptive move REBNY adopted to assure control of the Senate was to take advantage of the 2010 Supreme Court's Citizens United ruling that allowed "independent" groups to spend unlimited money on candidates and causes. When combined with a 1994 law that allowed limited liability corporations (LLCs) to donate without showing the names of the owners behind an LLC, real estate cash was everywhere. What had been a steady river of money dedicated to keeping the Albany Senate Republican turned into a tsunami. Susan Lerner of Common Cause reported that between 2005 and 2014, "REBNY and 37 of its Board Members contributed $43.9 million to State and local candidates, committees, and PACS, while REBNY's contributions have increased in recent election cycles, with $17.1 million given since 2011 alone" (Lerner 2014).

But suddenly, things began to look less rosy for Big Real Estate. A pro-rent regulation upstate farmer and former Senate aide named Cecilia Tkaczyk (pronounced Ti-kay-sic) decided to run against developer Amedore in 2012.[4] This meant game on. REBNY President Steven Spinola wasted no time in marshaling his troops. Out went a memo to REBNY members that explicitly directed the real estate community to donate generously to Amedore. And the members answered his call! Campaign finance donations from the real estate community flooded into not just Amedore's campaign but also into multiple PACs who spent their own money to support Amedore. Developers even dumped money into the Republican "housekeeping accounts," a practice considered quite irregular. The *Daily News* reported that four developers alone gave $1.5 million to various campaigns, PACs, and housekeeping committees between 2008 and 2015 (G. B. Smith 2015; Blain 2013). On the other side of this, pro-democracy billionaire George Soros was so outraged by the spectacle of campaign cash during the Amedore challenge that he set up a counter-PAC to support the Democrat (Tkaczyk) in the race (Podkul, Parker, and Kravitz 2016). After donors poured more than $2 million into just this one race alone, Democrat Cecilia Tkaczyk was the winner . . . by a mere 110 votes. While the ballots were recounted, "State Senator Jeff Klein and four other Senate Democrats" held a press conference to explain that their rogue Democratic posse was going to "share power with [Republican] Dean Skelos," with Klein acting as "co-leader" of the Senate (Podkul, Kravitz, and Parker 2016).

The narrow victory of Tkaczyk, a pro-rent reform Democrat in the Senate, was an all-hands-on-deck emergency of the first order for the real estate crowd. The following year (2013), REBNY set up a PAC called "Jobs for New York" that dumped $2.5 million more into upstate races. The board of governors of REBNY was the major donor in that effort. Governor Cuomo got his share of all that money: His top four donors in the 2013 election were all giant real estate firms (Samtani 2014b). Citizen Action Network reported that overall, the real estate industry "gave the state Senate GOP $4.53 million" in that election cycle. That sum was equal to what the next fourteen industries combined contributed (Samtani 2014b).

REBNY's allies helped in the all-hands-on-deck emergency. The New York Association of Realtors dumped $400,000 into Amedore's campaign. Real estate LLCs also pumped $20 million into the weakly regulated state committee funds. A single real estate firm (Glenwood) shelled out $450,000, mostly in support of Amedore. Other NYC real estate developers donated heavily to rogue Democrat Jeff Klein ($320,000)—more than to any other senator. Klein won re-election and dutifully began to carry water for his real estate backers. He went to bat for them against their internal squabble with newcomer StreetEasy, an NYC online real estate search engine. REBNY reported contentedly in a newsletter that Klein also supported "landlord-friendly rental laws and lucrative tax breaks" and "extended a tax break for real estate known as the Industrial and Commercial Abatement Program (ICAP) as well as the Relocation and Employment Assistance Program" (Spinola 2014).[5] The real estate industry's glossy paper, the *Real Deal*, noted of Klein and his rogue IDC Democrats: "For real estate, the Independent Democratic Caucus has been a godsend" (Podkul, Parker, and Kravitz 2016). This cozy victory would later fall apart in 2018, but for a time, the industry was back in the driver's seat with a state legislature set to be agreeable to real estate's wants.

But in 2018, progressive Democrats famously defeated Klein and his rogue IDC Democrats, taking down several Republicans as well. That made an opening for the Housing Justice for All coalition of upstate and downstate tenant groups to swing into action after years of preparatory organizing to finally beat the real estate lobby. It was a historic win for tenants, known as the 2019 Housing Stability and Protection Act. The act (among other changes) got rid of the infamous threshold at which a unit could go onto the free market and eliminated the notorious "vacancy bonus" rule that said every time a tenant moved out, the landlord could automatically raise the rent by 20 percent (allowing landlords to keep harassing out tenants until they passed the decontrol rent threshold).

Yet REBNY has not given up the fight. It has openly vowed to weaken those 2019 rent reforms. It has filed amicus briefs to bring down the reforms in a suit that REBNY's best friend, the Rent Stabilization Association, initiated right after Albany passed the law. On a more practical note, given the Democratic majority, REBNY has had no choice but to start spending on making Democratic politicians friendlier to their cause. To that end, REBNY set out to find "weak links" in the Assembly and Senate, meaning finding friendly faces among conservative and centrist Democrats and among Democrats who had won by narrow margins in districts with sizable Republican voter bases. The *Real Deal* reported that REBNY had turned to donating $157,000 to Assembly Democrats and that individual "real estate players" (such as Blackstone and Related) gave $367,000 to the Democratic Assembly Campaign Committee and to individual campaign committees (TRD Staff 2017). In the 2022 race for governor, REBNY's board members poured money into both candidates' coffers, and both candidates were explicit in supporting REBNY positions. Campaign cash, without reform, never stops.

STORY 2: CAMPAIGN MONEY TO A MAYOR

In this story, we turn to Mayor Bill de Blasio's dependence on Big Real Estate to finance his election campaigns. In Humanscale NYC's research project, this author, with interns from Columbia University and Barnard College, coded De Blasio's donor base for the 2017 election cycle using data pulled from the Campaign Finance Board. The following facts appeared (see Figures 6.1 and 6.2):

- Donors giving more than $400 (the maximum amount you can give if doing business with the city) accounted for 83 percent of his total take.
- Of those large donors, 53 percent came from the real estate industrial complex composed of real estate developers, their financial backers, construction companies, and brokers.
- Billionaires, CEOs, and C-suite donations accounted for 12 percent of the pool of large donors.
- Sixteen developers and property owners lobbying for the East Midtown Rezoning (which was unresolved after the mayor's re-election) each gave the maximum allowed donation of $4,950. Most controlled

184 · HOW BIG REAL ESTATE STAYS ON TOP

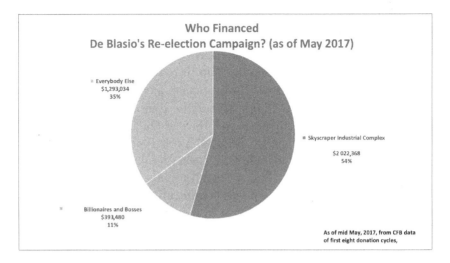

Figure 6.1. The real estate industrial complex funded 58 percent of De Blasio's re-election campaign as of the end of May prior to the election. Data from the author's research from the Campaign Finance Board's data.

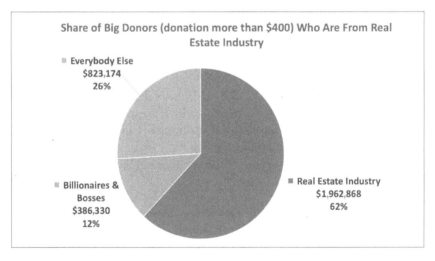

Figure 6.2. Large donations represented 83 percent of De Blasio's re-election campaign as of May before the election, and as the chart shows, the real estate industry represented 62 percent of those large donations. Author's research.

numerous blocks where the zoning was to take place. These included blocks owned by Rudin, Fisher Brothers, and Witkoff (see Table 6.1).
· De Blasio's small donor list appears to be artificially inflated. There are many cases of a single person, often not even a city resident, giving tiny amounts (less than $5) up to ten times.

Table 6.1. Donors to De Blasio 2017 Who Benefited from the East Midtown Rezoning

Date of Gift	Amount	Ref #	Donor	Organization/Business
	After Jan. 3, 2017				
01/09/2017	$500	R0054168	Herzka, Charles	Northend Equities
3/3/2017	$4,950	R0058643	Fisher, Steven	Fisher Brothers
01/10/2017	$4,950	R0054538	Gleser, Caroline	BD Hotels
	Before Jan. 3, 2017				
11/10/2016	$4,950	R0049612	Rosenberg, Samuel	Fisher Brothers
11/10/2016	$4,950	R0049609	Fisher, Kenneth	Fisher Brothers
11/15/2016	$4,950	R0049615	Fisher, Tammy A	(none—but wife of Kenneth Fisher)
11/10/2016	$4,950	R0049610	Fisher, Winston	Fisher Brothers
11/10/2016	$4,950	R0049613	Fisher, Jessica	(potentially ex-wife of Winston Fisher [Jessica Eckle Fisher])
01/11/2016	$500	R0044030	Aryeh, Michael	Heritage Realty LLC
01/11/2016	$500	R0044032	Shirazian, Edwin	Heritage Realty LLC
01/08/2016	$4,950	R0043838	Gupta Neil	Rudin Management Company
01/11/2016	$400	R0043952	Gilbert, John	Rudin Management Company
1/8/2016	$4,950	R0043840	Rudin, Ophelia	(homemaker—but is the wife of CEO Bill Rudin)
1/8/2016	$4,950	R0043783	Rudin, Susan	(homemaker—but is the wife of chairman Jack Rudin)
10/30/2015	$4,950	R0043158	Witkoff, Alexander	Witkoff
10/30/2015	$4,950	R0043275	Witkoff, Lois	(none—but grandmother of Alex of Witkoff)

In East Midtown Rezoning area:
Rudin owns: Block 1284, lot 21, Block 1287, lot 28, block 1295, lot 23, Block 1305, lot 13, Block 1306, lot 1, Block 1309, lot 23;
Fisher Brothers owns: Block 1288, lots 24 and 27, Block 1303, lot 1;
Witkoff owns: Block 1295, lot 58; Block 1301, lot 23, and Block 1307, lot 7501.

What did these donors get for their money? Nobody can say for sure, but it does give the appearance that they at least got the Midtown East rezoning, although there is no way to prove a direct quid pro quo. What we know for sure is that big donations buy frequent and regular access to the politician in question. Big donors get their phone calls, letters, and requests for meetings answered. Favors get done. One of the people who pleaded guilty to bribing Mayor de Blasio said in court, "Whenever we'd call him for access or a favor, we were getting the response and the results we expected" (Jona Rechnitz, citied in Nahmias 2016). That kind of access does not happen for ordinary citizens. Consider that in the year after De Blasio's election, two representatives of the Tribeca Trust, a preservation-oriented nonprofit, which this author co-founded, tried to deliver a petition directly to City Hall with a printout of the signatures of thousands of Tribeca taxpayers. Nobody at City Hall would take it, not even to drop it off to a staffer. The representatives of Tribeca Trust then tried to deliver the petition to the Office of Community Affairs across the street from City Hall where they were also turned away. They were not allowed to leave the document with the City Hall mailroom. They were told to go mail it at the post office. They did so. The city never sent an acknowledgment. Phone calls to the mayor's office went unanswered. By contrast, the names of 97 "elite" major donors to De Blasio were entered into a spreadsheet and offered appointments to various government agencies ranging from the Economic Development Corporation, the Civilian Complaint Review Board, Lincoln Center, and the Fund for Public Schools (Fermino and Smith 2016). In another example, a donor who ran an engineering and construction firm (HAKS) bundled some $48,250 to the mayor's first and second run at office. Not only did the man get appointed to the Workforce Development Board, but he also got a $15 million dollar deal with the Department of Design and Construction (Fanelli 2016). In another case of privileged access, the *Daily News* reported that the mayor held a meeting "with the city's biggest lobbyist and nine of his clients who had raised $100,000 for him in a period in which the mayor said there was 'no lobbying activity'" (G. Smith 2018).

Power Tool Two: The Revolving Door between Government and Real Estate

Offering cushy private sector jobs to politicians, senior political staffers, and to other government officials involved in real estate regulation is a time-honored tactic for the real estate industry to maintain power and influence (Newfield and Du Brul 1981). The examples are too many to count. Prior to serving REBNY, long-serving ex-president of REBNY Steven Spinola was president of the New York City Public Development Corporation (now called the Economic Development Corporation). Following him as president of REBNY was John Banks who was a former chief of staff for the New York City Council and who had worked for Mayor

Koch in his office of operations prior to joining REBNY. Banks's wife is the CEO of a big real estate firm working with the city, L & M Partners (Neuman 2019; Neuman and Goodman 2017). The current REBNY president, James Whelan, once worked as chief of staff to the Growth Machine Ideologue himself, Dan Doctoroff (a promoter of the luxury city idea discussed in Chapter 1), during the Bloomberg administration. None of these REBNY presidents even live in the Manhattan they seek to exploit for real estate wealth. Spinola lives on Long Island. Banks lives in Greenwich, Connecticut. Whelan lives in the remote single-family suburban enclave of Bellerose, Queens, an area of low-rise mansions with yards.

At REBNY, the revolving door turns in both directions. For example, Nicole Chin-Lyn was REBNY's vice president of communications from which she walked into a job as director of communications in Mayor de Blasio's Office of Immigrant Affairs. REBNY's chief of staff Ali Davis was able to walk into a job with trickle-down housing theorist Vicki Been, the mayor's former deputy mayor for housing. During the last three years of the De Blasio administration, Humanscale NYC collected a great many examples of the weakly regulated revolving door between 2017 and 2019. This was done with the help of journalist Jillian Jonas. The examples cited below are just the tip of a much larger iceberg that has gone on for many years and many administrations. They still make for troubling reading.[6]

- Chief of Staff for Mayor Eric Adams, Frank Carone, left the administration to found his own lobbying firm called Oaktree Solutions in 2023.
- A lobbyist and deal-maker for big real estate (Carlos Scissura) got appointed by incoming Mayor Eric Adams to run the controversial Economic Development Corporation (Honan 2022).
- One lobbyist and advisor to big real estate (Jeff Mulligan) works at the REBNY member firm of Kramer Levin Naftalis and puffs on his profile that he "has extensive experience in New York City government. As a former team leader with the Manhattan office of the Department of City Planning, Jeff supervised significant agency-sponsored rezonings, including Hudson Yards, West Chelsea/High Line, and the Far West Village." What is more, he "supervised major development projects that were subject to discretionary approvals." He was also the executive director of the Board of Standards and Appeals from 2006 to 2014.
- The director of community affairs (Basha Gerhards) for Manhattan President Gale Brewer walked directly into a lobbying job with

REBNY at the vice-presidential level and was soon testifying on REBNY's behalf in front of City Planning, literally opposite many of the community groups previously befriended.
- A long-time high-level policy advisor for government (Reggie Thomas) left a series of policy level jobs in the Bloomberg and De Blasio administrations to walk right into a lobbyist job for real estate at Cozen O'Connor, after which REBNY tapped him as their vice president of government affairs. Thomas got Manhattan Borough President Gale Brewer to appoint him to Community Board 1 that covers Lower Manhattan. There he served as co-chair of the land use committee until he was removed from that committee after residents complained. He did, however, stay on the community board despite his status as a professional lobbyist.
- Mayor Bloomberg appointed the city planner Meenakshi Srinivasan to the Board of Standards and Appeals, where she served for ten years. Mayor de Blasio then appointed her as chair of the Landmarks Preservation Commission, where she landmarked very little indeed. When she resigned from the commission in 2018, she went directly into a lobbyist position for the ubiquitous lobbyist firm of Kramer Levin Naftalis. A year later she lobbied for air rights transfer deals for an 800-floor glass skyscraper that would replace the demolished, historic Bancroft Building, one many considered worthy of landmark designation.
- Attorney Valerie Campbell came into the Landmarks Preservation Commission during an administration that was negative on the idea of landmarking (Pearson 2010). She replaced the existing, pro-preservation legal counsel to the commission. After service on the commission, Ms. Campbell then found her way to the real estate practice of the lobbying firm of Kramer Levin where she is a regular in front of the commission, testifying for her big real estate clients.
- In May of 2018, a staff attorney for the Department of City Planning for thirteen years (Emily Simmons) joined Davidoff, Hutcher and Citron, a lobbying firm, as "land use counsel." Davidoff, Hutcher and Citron's senior partner Howard Weiss pitches himself to developers in his *City and State* profile, saying that their firm helps developers "maximize every square foot as of right, through development rights transfers, zoning map and text amendments, special permits, and variances" (L. Weiss 2019).
- In April of 2018, De Blasio's senior advisor for strategic planning (Andrea Hagelgans) left City Hall to become executive vice president

Figure 6.3. The now demolished Bancroft Building (red brick facade), seen in context by the church, to be replaced by an 800-foot-tall glass skyscraper. Author's photo.

for global public relations firm of Edelman, a firm with many Big Real Estate clients. Ms. Hagelgans brought home the bacon for her new bosses, getting them an $80,000 contract from NYC's Economic Development Corporation (EDC) to do "reputational rescue" for the EDC, which was feeling worried about its reputation after Amazon withdrew from the headquarters deal (Goldensohn 2019).
- In January of 2018, Senator Chuck Schumer's director of policy (Nicholas Martin) joined Big Real Estate firm of Rudin Management Company as vice president for external and government affairs. Bill Rudin, the clan leader, is now chair of the REBNY board.
- The lobbying firm of Kasirer is an ace in the revolving door game. A former staffer for former Governor Mario Cuomo (Suri Kasirer) started the firm. She eventually married a former staffer to Mayor Koch (Bruce Teitelbaum). Mr. Teitelbaum has since turned up as a real estate developer at the Anabel Basin site in Long Island City and is active in Harlem real estate. Kasirer has grown into an immense lobbying firm that routinely hires people right out of the administration. The former district representative and legislative aide to Representative Nita Lower and State Senator David Carlucci (Cory Hasson), walked into a lobbying job at Kasirer. A former legislative staffer for Mayor de Blasio also walked into a job at Kasirer (Kara Hughes). The former director of land-use for Councilwoman Margaret Chin and for the City Council (Matthew Viggiano) also landed at Kasirer and

was seen by this author working in support of the city's plan to build a new decked city on top of the Sunnyside rail yards. In March of 2018, a former associate principal at SHoP Architects became an associate vice president of real estate at Kasirer (Omar Toro-Vaca). The former special advisor to the New York City mayoral chief of staff and deputy mayor for administration is now director of government relations for real estate at Kasirer LLC (Briana Peppers).
- A senior policy advisor to Mayor de Blasio moved over to big real estate developer Le Frak as a senior analyst for government and community affairs (Torrey Fishman).
- City Planner Sylvia Li, architect of the detested SoHo/NoHo upzoning, left the city agency to work for big real estate advisors HR & A Advisors in 2022.
- In 2024 former City Councilmember Marjorie Velázquez has landed a lobbyist job with industry group Tech:NYC as vice president of policy.
- A chief of staff and a legislative counsel to the New York City Council for over ten years (Robert Benfatto) mysteriously emerged as head of a group promoting Hudson Yards called the "Hudson Yards/Hells Kitchen Alliance" while also serving as the agenda-setting district manager of Manhattan Community Board 4, which covered the Hudson Yards area.
- A public servant appointed by the Mayor de Blasio to the Board of Standards and Appeals (the agency that grants rule exceptions to real estate developers) left that office in 2019, strolling into a lobbying job for Capalino and Company as a group leader for their "housing and real estate practice group" (Susan Hinkson-Carling). Capalino tells real estate companies on its website: "We'll help you thrive in New York's real estate market."
- The former chief of staff to New York City Councilman Robert Holden is now an associate consultant for RG Group's New York office (Gregory Mitchell). RG styles itself as "a leading NY Government Relations and Lobbying Firm" that represents Forest City Ratner among other Big Real Estate firms.
- A staffer for former Borough President Scott Stringer eventually landed at Edison Properties (Anthony Borelli), the real estate firm and REBNY board of governors member that imposed the SoHo and NoHo upzoning. It is not surprising that mayoral candidate Scott Stringer spoke out in favor of the proposal before the details were even known to the public.

HOW BIG REAL ESTATE STAYS ON TOP · 191

Many revolving door cases involve not just staffers but elected officials leaving office to become lobbyists. There is also a door to the financial industry. Here are some examples.

- Former City Council member Ken Fisher of Brooklyn Heights left public service to work for Big Real Estate at the lobbying firm of Cozen O'Connor. There he lobbied hard for deregulation of air rights transfers at the service of the big players of REBNY. The press routinely calls him up at his offices high in the sky in Midtown to get the Big Real Estate take on the controversy du jour. He told one of them, "I make my living trying to make as much growth in the city as possible" (Fisher 2017).
- In June 2018, City Council Speaker Corey Johnson appointed Jason Goldman, a former vice president at Kasirer, as his chief of staff. Corey Johnson himself once worked as a real estate lobbyist for GFI Development prior to serving in the council and told the *New York Post* that when term-limited out, he would immediately start his own lobbying firm (J. Levine 2021). He was true to his word and now has a contract with Vornado, which seeks to build towers in the councilman's former district.
- The head of Manhattan's Democratic Party (former assemblyman Keith Wright) became a lobbyist for the firm of Davidoff, Hutcher and Citron.
- A lobbyist for the firm of Constantinople and Vallone became a city councilman (Keith Powers) as did a lobbyist for Parkside Group (Barry Gordenchik).
- A Queens district attorney (Melinda Katz) has been a lobbyist for Greenberg Traurig (with many large real estate clients).
- A state assemblyman for Queens (Ron Kim) used to be a lobbyist for the Parkside Group.
- Former Governor David Patterson joined the lobbying firm of Kivvit, after leading a campaign against taxing wealthy New Yorkers.
- Former Deputy Mayor Alicia Glen, a Goldman Sachs alum, not only directs the Trust for Governors Island but started a private $150 million real estate investment fund that seeks to invest in newly upzoned Inwood. Glen was a major player in that upzoning battle.
- A member of the City Planning Commission (Joseph Douek) runs an "opportunity fund"—an investment vehicle targeting low-income neighborhoods of Brooklyn. Those are the same neighborhoods the planning commission has sought to upzone and gentrify.

Sadly, the Charter reforms of 2019 offered weak changes that do little to improve the situation. One small reform was approved by voters: Public servants who decamp to lobbying agencies must now wait two years instead of one before appearing before the agency they served. Members of the Charter reform commission told me they had pushed for a tougher "stand aside rule" of five years, but resistance from other Charter Commission members obliged them to accept the smaller gain of two years or nothing at all.

Power Tool Three: Influence Appointments to Regulatory Agencies

All the city regulatory agencies that act in the realm of real estate are strangely packed with appointees with deep experience inside the real estate industry. I refer to the City Planning Commission, the Board of Standards and Appeals, and the Economic Development Corporation. Although this has always been a problem, it took on new meaning under Bloomberg and De Blasio. Let's look at these a bit closer for the case of the De Blasio regime. As of November 2018, of the thirteen members of the City Planning Commission, we find that:

- One member is a real estate investor, a donor to the mayor and runs a $75 million real estate investing "opportunity fund" for Brooklyn (Joseph Douek).
- One is a former lobbyist for the real estate industry (Allen Cappelli).
- Five come from real estate development firms of various types (Michelle de la Uz, Kenneth Knuckles, Richard Eaddy, Hope Knight, and Orlando Marín), ranging from a senior employee of Bluestone Organization to CEOs of development corporations to the head of the Fifth Avenue Committee (a large "affordable" housing developer).
- The professional history of the chair (Marisa Lago) includes running the "let's demolish NY by eminent domain" agency known as the Empire State Development Corporation (ESD), a real estate development entity of the state with a large network of local development corporations doing its bidding. The corporation has so seriously abused eminent domain to the detriment of Black and low-income communities (Carpenter and Ross 2015).
- Only one member of the commission (Larisa Ortiz) has a degree in urban planning, but alas, runs a consulting firm advising city agencies and developers how to "optimize" their retail tenant mix so that it fits the "owner's goals."

- At least two have serious conflicts of interest with the rezoning project at Gowanus (Bluestone Organization and Fifth Avenue Committee). At least one (Kenneth Knuckles) had a clear conflict of interest with the East Harlem rezoning.
- Two are modernist architects with controversial high-rise projects under their belts, mostly glassy tower hotels in the Brooklyn waterfronts (David Burney and Raj Rampershad).
- One has long been a cheerleader for the Hudson Yards project and whose spouse, strangely, is a partner at the Big Law firm of David and Polk, the very same that advises Related Companies, the developers of Hudson Yards, as well as many other major real estate players in NY (Anna Levin).
- One is CEO of the real estate-controlled BID, the Grand Central Partnership, whose board of directors reads like the Who's Who of the Board of Governors of the Real Estate Board of New York and who has pushed for multiple upzonings in Midtown (Alfred Cerullo).

Is it any wonder that these commissioners, the majority of whom represent various parts of the real estate development community, reflect the attitudes and biases of the Demolition Machine overall? They consistently mistake upzoning, real estate profit-making, and high-rise projects for actual urban planning.

The Board of Standards and Appeals (known as the BSA) is charged with granting exceptions to the rules of the zoning code to developers who ask for them, all while guaranteeing them at least a 6 percent rate of return on their projects as a matter of established public policy (Stahl v. City of New York 2018). Citizens Union, a good government watchdog nonprofit, found that in 2011 and 2012, while under the leadership of Meenakshi Srinivasan during the Bloomberg administration, the BSA ruled 97 percent of the time in favor of the developer (Bubbins 2016). The BSA has a smaller board than the City Planning Commission, with only five members. All five are mayoral appointees. As of this writing, the supremely powerful chair of the BSA is Margery Perlmutter, a land-use and real estate lawyer who spent years (according to her firm's website) "shepherding clients through the city's zoning and land use processes, including the types of appeals she'll oversee" at the BSA. Perlmutter had briefly served at an appointee to the Landmarks Preservation Commission, much to the dismay of preservationists at the time. Another member (Shampa Chanda) is a quasi-permanent government employee who held a variety of jobs at the

Department of City Planning. The required engineer on the BSA is also a long-serving city employee at the Department of Environmental Protection and unlikely to second-guess the chair. Another member of the 2018 board, Susan Hinkson-Carling, has left the BSA and now works as a real estate lobbyist for the lobbying firm of Capalino and Company, the same firm that was involved in several "pay-to-play" real estate scandals during the De Blasio administration.

What happens when the real estate industry persuades a mayor to pack a regulatory agency with its own people? You get bizarre rule changes and procedural changes designed to undo regulatory power and give the industry more of what it wants. Attorney Alan Sugarman in 2010 summed that problem up when the BSA (under the chair of Meenakshi Srinivasan) posted new "instructions" for anyone wanting a variance. He protested that "the new instructions signify the intent of the BSA to ignore explicit law to make it easier for applicants to obtain variances" (Sugarman 2010). It is akin to when former president Donald Trump appointed anti-regulatory industry insiders to undo the Environmental Protection Agency.

The Landmarks Law requires that only one appointee be "a realtor," but in practice there is more than one representative of the growth machine on the commission. For example, at the time of this writing the commission has a realtor (Jeanne Lutfy) at Halstead Property Corporation who is a former staffer at the growth machine nexus, the Economic Development Corporation. Another current commissioner (Adi Sharir-Baron) is a fan of modernist architecture as long-serving executive director of the Van Alen Institute, an urban development organization that largely funded by a mix of the large modernist architecture firms who win big contracts from Big Real Estate. The Vice-Chair at the Van Alen Institute is the founder of the real estate development firm of Alloy, and another board member at the Van Alen Institute describes herself as a "global real estate development professional" (Jessica Healy), and yet another is a partner in the firm Holland and Knight, which is a member of REBNY's board of governors, and who (according it its website) "represents REBNY on matters related to Section 421a," one of the main tax breaks gives to developers. Just as troubling, the Landmarks Preservation Commission is often filled with several architects of a deep modernist ideological bent, adherents to an ideology that new buildings in old neighborhoods cannot and should not look anything like the old buildings. Rare, and often profoundly outnumbered, are members of the commission who might be categorized as actual preservationists, and even fewer are those with actual university training in historic preservation.

Finally in the landscape of city agencies packed with real estate appointees is the mysterious Economic Development Corporation (EDC), an agency with almost no public accountability and no public oversight. It is set up as a nonprofit organization charged with cooking up real estate development deals with city-owned property and public subsidies. As of this writing, it is headed by the former chief of staff of the Demolition Machine's top gun, former Deputy Mayor Alicia Glen, a Goldman Sachs alum. The EDC's executive vice president and chief strategy officer spent six years at Goldman Sachs, making this a tight group. The EDC's chief operating officer (Rachel Loeb) used to work for developer Avalon Bay. Of twenty-two people whose biographies were laid out on the EDC website, eight come from the world of real estate, not including Vicky Been herself, and five come from the world of real estate finance.

One also finds the real estate industry and its allies on community boards and other commissions. My own scan of all the membership of community boards in Manhattan in mid-2018 found professional lobbyists sprinkled all over, very often as chairs of committees in which they had an obvious vested interest. One community board member was a vice president of REBNY; one was the lawyer for the real estate–dominated Downtown Alliance; one was a senior vice president at Douglas Elliman Real Estate, which does development projects in historic districts; one ran a consulting/advisory firm for real estate (Insight Associates) and had negotiated the "gifting" of a public plaza to the ticket office for Lincoln Center; one was a lobbyist for the "outdoor café" industry; several were closely allied with the well-organized nightclub lobby; one managed an organization pushing for Hudson Yards development interests; one was a senior lobbyist for Capalino and Company on real estate matters, who orchestrated anti-landmarking votes on his community board concerning expansions at Friends Seminary; three were closely allied to powerful business improvement districts (BIDs) that were mostly composed of real estate companies such as the Grand Central Partnership and the Long Island City BID. One board member on the West Side commuter board represented the hotel lobby, one the bike lobby, and another the taxi and limo lobby. This is not to speak of the community board members who are senior members of political clubs or officers of the Manhattan Democratic Party, a situation that gives some community boards an unfortunate and delegitimizing Tammany Hall allure. I did not include the multiple cases of profoundly modernist, anti-historicist architects working for large firms (such as SHoP) who actively do business with the city on large projects while sitting on community landmarks committees, nor of the permanent government technocrats associated with agencies like the Empire State Development Corporation, the Javits Center (which is up for redevelopment, according to ex-Deputy Mayor Alicia Glen), or the Metropolitan Transit Authority, all of which have major development projects in the works, and who can be found serving on Manhattan's boards.

Power Tool Four: Spend Big on Lobbyists

Campaign money paired with the hiring of a lobbyist is a time-honored way to build close working relationships with elected officials, as emails between senior administration staff and the president of REBNY have revealed (Trangle 2016). Privileged access to politicians effectively "captures democracy" by making access a game for the rich. Journalists at the *Real Deal* found that "the real estate and construction industries spent $166.3 million on lobbying both the state and the city from 2007 through the first half of 2014." The *New York Post* reported in 2020 that all industries spent $113.19 million lobbying city government in 2019, 10 percent higher than the previous year, and that real estate represented a whopping 40 percent of that total (Campanile 2020). Although some big real estate firms employ their own in-house lobbyists, most hire law firms and more conventional lobbying firms to push their causes to legislators, to regulatory agency staff, and to journalists.

Lobbyists organize friendships and create collegiality. As one explained to a journalist, their success in winning clients "is the perception of your relationship with elected officials" (Samtani 2014a). And lobbyists do get results! For example, in the Gowanus neighborhood of Brooklyn, the original upzoning plan was human-scale with six- and seven-story buildings. Real estate interests decided the plan was too low-rise. They announced to the press that they were going to lobby to make the plan taller and more massive in scale. According to data on the city's lobbying database, they collectively spent about $800,000 on lobbyists who talked to City Planning staff and then Council member Brad Lander whose district covered Gowanus. The final, much-taller upzoning plan became the official city-sponsored plan that DCP shepherded through the multi-stage public review process for Gowanus. Humanscale NYC also found during the same research project that as of March 2019, real estate interests, many of them from Gowanus area investors, had collectively raised $199,604 for Brad Lander's race to become comptroller in 2021.

Lobbyists do other things for real estate and their financiers beyond talking nonstop to politicians behind the scenes. For example, Kramer Levin went on the public relations offensive for JP Morgan Chase to talk the city into forbidding public demonstrations or citizens assembling on the large "public private plaza" that is in front of the Equitable Building (where City Planning moved its headquarters during the De Blasio administration) in Lower Manhattan (Kramer Levin 2013). Regulating lobbying as a tool of corporate power has proven quite difficult. Although lobbying is legal free speech, reformers have made a bit of headway to at least make the information public. City Charter amendments created a publicly accessible database that reveals who is hiring what lobbyist to meet with what government official. This kind of information is a start but is not an adequate remedy to the broader problem of the capture of government by the regulated. A stronger remedy would be a legally binding non-compete contract for public servants that is a condition of public employ. The idea is that a public servant must agree not to work for anyone seeking advantage from city government for at least three years after leaving their government job or office. A rule to bar lobbyists from serving as appointees to city agencies or community boards seems an obvious additional fix. The city might also make lobbying meetings subject to open meetings laws and demand that community organizations get equal face time with public officials. The quote earlier in the chapter showed that former Mayor Bill de Blasio met with lobbyists eighty-three times. Not once did he meet with any community group I know in the 111-member coalition I participated in.

Power Tool Five: Provide Below-Market Housing for the Powerful

Do the politically powerfully get favorable rent deals from powerful landlords? This tactic sounds plausible but is hard to keep track of. Consider the famous case the *New York Times* brought to the public eye: the building on 2nd and 3rd Avenue at 68th Street, now 215 East 68th Street. In the 1960s the block was filled with low-rise brownstones that the owners had subdivided into boarding houses and small, affordable apartments. The row houses were filled with low-wage workers and just-starting-out journalists, such as Ada Louise Huxtable. The row house in Figure 6.4 had been the home of writer Stephen Vincent Benét and was filmed in the Dean Martin film *Bells Are Ringing* (Carlson 2014). The Rudin real estate family bought up the entire row house block in the late 1950s, demolished it all in the early 1960s, and replaced the row houses with a block-sized white brick apartment tower.

Figure 6.4 Photo from *Life Magazine* taken by Dmitri Kessel in the early 1960s shows the demolition of an entire block of row houses. The entire block was replaced by a single, white brick apartment building owned by the Rudin family at 215 East 68th.

The Rudins began to fill the building's cheaper, rent-stabilized apartments with political notables. Those who got leases from the Rudins included (Blumenthal 2008):

- Two former mayors (Lindsay and Dinkins)
- The New York County Clerk
- An administrative judge of the State Supreme Court in the Bronx
- A former presiding judge of the State Appellate Division
- A judge of the State Supreme Court in Manhattan
- A former police commissioner and a former fire commissioner
- A former anchor for Channel 5 news
- A deputy mayor
- A grandson of a former mayor (Beame)
- Former president of Off-Track Betting Corporation

In another case, the Olnick real estate family who built the Lenox Terrace houses in Harlem rented four stabilized apartments to Congressman Charles Rangel (Rizzo 2008). Rangel used one apartment for an office but gave it up after public outcry. In the same complex, former New York governor David Paterson keeps an affordable apartment as his "primary" residence (although he owns a mansion in New Jersey). His father, Basil

Paterson, also has an apartment in the same building, as does Percy Sutton, the former Manhattan borough president. The extent to which this practice continues to be in use across the city by other big landlords is unknown, but it is an effective tactic to maintain real estate political influence. Note that Charles Rangel was silent about tenant problems in the complex he lived in. He also did not speak out about Olnick's plan to create luxury towers on top of the complex in a controversial upzoning proposal for it. Future research on this tactic might expand the notion of political notables to include leaders of political clubs.

Power Tool Six: Use Fronts and Surrogates

Sometimes it pays to create fronts or support organizations to serve as surrogates for REBNY interests. The previously mentioned group called Partnership for New York City worked directly with REBNY in 2010 to form a front group—at REBNY's initiative—with the laughable name, the Committee to Save New York. The committee funded a $17 million lobbying campaign over 2010–2011 for passage of Governor Cuomo's "austerity budget" that had proposals for reform of taxation and the reduction of public sector pensions. In the partnership's eyes, the reforms would "put New York on a better course for economic growth and job creation." The committee declared victory on its wish list in 2013. Another example is the group that called itself Taxpayers for an Affordable New York. REBNY and the Rent Stabilization Association funded it to coordinate advertising against the rent reforms of 2018–2019. Another example is the Affordable Housing and Local Jobs Now Coalition. It paid for a television and radio campaign in support of tax subsidies for Big Real Estate. Oddly, the NAACP was part of that coalition. The money for the campaign came from REBNY through a lobbying group it set up called Putting New Yorkers to Work (Hutchins n.d.). REBNY even managed to line up Hazel Dukes of the NAACP to testify at public hearings to help defeat a bill that would have required construction sites to offer safety training to construction workers (W. Parker and Putzer 2017). Real estate mogul William Zeckendorf, a REBNY board of governors member and "among N.Y.'s most prolific condo developers," sought the support of the city's largest brokerage companies (Halstead and Corcoran) to create an "army of N.Y.C. homeowners" to lobby against a tax on broker fees. The brokerages hired Mercury Public Affairs to be their lobbyist. Zeckendorf put lobbyist Paul Jenkins on a $15,000-a-month retainer to lobby Albany legislators against that tax. According to the industry journal the *Real Deal* (Hudson 2020), a new organization to do all this coordinating is being born as of this writing.

Because REBNY has not been willing to pay union wages—unless forced to on public projects—the construction unions have been fickle allies to Big Real Estate. Never daunted by that kind of problem, REBNY has found in one non-construction union, the SEIU-32BJ, the union partner of its dreams. It is the union of office cleaners, doormen, airport workers, and building maintenance staff. It has about 170,000 members. Its founder, Héctor Figuera, died of a heart attack in 2019. The following year REBNY honored Figuera's life of close collaboration with REBNY with a posthumous humanitarian award at its annual gala in 2020. Sporting distinctive purple T-shirts, retired SEIU-32BJ union members have long been fixtures in large groups to testify in favor of every neighborhood rezoning favored by REBNY since De Blasio arrived in office. SEIU-32BJ famously went along with REBNY to support the controversial and much-opposed tax giveaways packaged to attract Amazon to set up a new headquarters in Queens. REBNY's current president often mentions REBNY's deep partnership with SEIU-32BJ in press releases.

Elements of the growth machine can even latch onto places as venerable as the Municipal Art Society, known as "M.A.S." Nonprofit M.A.S. has been around since the turn of the nineteenth century. During much of the research for this book, the M.A.S. board had Vishaan Chakrabarti on it (the architect-ideologue for hyper-density who advocates for skyscrapers; see Chapter 1). Chakrabarti moved on from M.A.S., but we also see (as of this writing) that M.A.S. has two fiercely modernist architects serving on board. One is the starchitect of the famed stegosaurus at the World Trade Center site, a building that is a financial black hole in the public treasury to the tune of $4 billion (Rosengaard 2015). For a while, controversial developer Joe McMillan was on the M.A.S. board as well. His firm, D.D.G., specializes in exploiting loopholes in the zoning code to build out-of-context buildings that harm historic districts, as in the cases of 51 White Street and at the corner of West Broadway and Broome Streets in SoHo. Current M.A.S. board members include Kent Swig, who owns Halstead Real Estate Brokerage and is a member of REBNY's board of governors; he is also founder of Realty Advisory Services, as well as a general developer and investor in luxury real estate. That said, M.A.S. is not a front for real estate but instead promotes a high-modernist aesthetic or "starchitecture" approach to the city and has on its board several people associated with developing large, high-profile contemporary architectural projects. For example, Elizabeth Diller serves on the M.A.S. board. She is the architect of Diller Island. Also present on the M.A.S. board is architect Richard Olcott, known for glassy insertions on older buildings. M.A.S. Board Chair Christy MacLear is an advocate for glassy modernism, having spent a good chunk of her career as director of the Philip Johnson Glass House. On balance, M.A.S looks like an intriguing alliance of private equity wealth, Big Real Estate, and advocates and designers of modernist starchitecture. I would not characterize the organization as a full-on member of the real estate complex.

Last, as a surrogate for real estate interests, there is the case of Open New York, which is not an offshoot of REBNY per se (I've seen no smoking gun). It is a just a group of amateur enthusiasts, many from within low levels of the real estate industry, who decided to turn themselves into a 501c4 lobby group for real estate. They are registered in Delaware and serve as a loud posse at hearings promoting Edward Glaeser's "build higher now" agenda. They meet in real estate offices to plan testimony in favor of upzoning and breaking the zoning of historic districts. The group is popular with politicians like Manhattan Borough President Mark Levine who has been appointing their members to community boards. The testimony they give is a rehash of what Edward Glaeser wrote in *Triumph of the City*. According to a Politico Pro article cited by Norman Oder, they have thirty members. But they are growing and raised enough money from a couple of Silicon Valley anti-zoning zealots in 2021 to hire two full-time staffers who function as lobbyists for them. One of their key organizers and founders is Ben Carlos Thypin, the head of a real estate investment firm called Progress Real Estate Partners and co-founder of a real estate investment software platform called Quantierra. The platform is popular with real estate firms. His family has two real estate investment companies of which he is a vice president. One is Bayard Street Properties, and another is Murray Hill L.L.C. Charles Dorseano, another key activist with the group, is a lawyer at the lobbying firm of Fox Rothschild, a favorite of REBNY members. He represents "developers, landowners, lenders, purchasers and other clients in all aspects of land use and zoning." Jake Smith, another Open New York activist often quoted in the press, is a managing partner of the real estate firm Alloy. One of their active members, lawyer Michael Lewyn, ran for Manhattan borough president as a libertarian candidate in 2021. As an effective surrogate for REBNY's growth ideology, Open New York is diligent.

Power Tool Seven: Brazenly Cheat and Pay a Trivial Fine if Caught

In 1989, Paul Goldberger, the architectural critic for the *New York Times*, described a problem: Developers were breaking the zoning rules blatantly and in significant ways and getting away with slap-on-the-wrist fines. The three examples were:

- Developer Harry Macklowe at West 44th Street illegally tore down a single-room occupancy hotel in Midtown, paid the consequent $2 million fine, and built a skyscraper hotel on the site "naming it after himself," after getting the law changed to allow him to do the build.
- Another developer built twelve stories higher than the zoning allowed at 108 East 96th Street. A judge ordered him to take down the extra stories two and half years later after a nonprofit group (Civitas) filed a lawsuit (Dunlap 1991)—the city did nothing to enforce the rules.
- A third developer, Ian Bruce Eichner, of the Cityspire building, built eleven feet higher than agreed but got to keep the extra height.

In a more recent case that hit the press, development firm Extell so abused the zoning code that it gained about 150 feet of illegal height for their glass tower at 50 West 66th Street. The judge ordered the extra height removed, but as of this writing, a higher court judge overturned the decision on the developer's appeal, with zero consequences for the developer (Parker 2019).

Power Tool Eight: Make "Side Payments" and Give Unethical Donations

In 2002, federal investigators said Mr. Litwin and dozens of other property owners had received illegal tax breaks arranged by a consultant who was charged with bribing tax assessors in a scheme that cost the city $160 million in revenue over four years.

He [real estate mogul Leonard Litwin] paid millions to Republican and Democratic leaders to ensure tax breaks, government financing, and favorable rent laws.

—Robert McFadden, "Leonard Litwin, New York Real Estate Mogul, Dies at 102," *New York Times*, April 3, 2017

There is another way for real estate to get what it wants: outright bribery (Teachout 2016). Preet Bharara, a former district attorney for the Southern District of New York, said to radio host Brian Lehrer in reference to the infamously shuttered Moreland Commission Against Corruption: "Logic tells you you're more likely to find (probably) bad stuff happening when the real estate industry is involved" (Lehrer 2017). Creative graft can astonish, such as in the case of a Department of Buildings official who "admitted to bribing several DOB officials and paying off a retired engineer to certify more than 100 buildings as safe" (Brenzel 2017). In a 1996 example, federal investigators discovered that property owners, Donald Trump among them, had paid "twenty-nine city workers to physically erase the records of their tax liabilities, defrauding the city of $20 million" (Richardson 1996).

Less creative cases illustrate how Big Real Estate uses money in a way that looks a lot like bribery. In 2012, at the end of his reign, Mayor Bloomberg decided that the city should sell two large, landmark buildings it owned. He decreed downsizing for the agencies and courts that had been using the two buildings as a place of work. The city employees moved to new rented locations. Their move and the cost of renting new city office space would eventually take place at the cost of $100 million, mostly to pay rent for new office space to other landlords. The city sold the buildings at low prices: $160 million for the Clocktower Building at 349 Broadway and $89 million for the former Emigrant Savings Bank Building on Chambers Street. These were strangely low prices for immense and architecturally spectacular buildings. Both buildings went to large real estate developers who promised to convert them into luxury condos without a single affordable housing unit.

The Economic Development Corporation (EDC) took charge of organizing the sale of these two landmark buildings. In late 2013 they published a notice asking developers for bids. Florida-based mega-developer Don Peebles sent the winning bid for the Clocktower Building. It was not the highest bid. The person at the EDC responsible for the bid process was a young MBA from Harvard, Tawan Davis. In March 2014, after Peebles had bought the building from the EDC, Mr. Davis left his city job at the EDC to become a vice president for Peebles. In filings for an unrelated lawsuit, the public learned that another Peebles employee accused Davis of having traded inside information to Peebles about the bidding process. Nobody investigated the accusation (Mathurin 2016; Hofmann 2015; Cullen 2015). Then Bill de Blasio became mayor.

Developer Peebles realized he needed to get his luxury renovation plan for the Clocktower Building through the Landmarks Preservation Commission with a new mayor with unknown sensibilities at the helm. It was not a slam dunk, as Peebles wanted to convert two interior landmarked spaces—one of which was the publicly accessible clocktower—into privatized apartments for his wealthy clientele. He also wanted to add a new glass story onto the roof—since, by his calculations, there was enough unbuilt FAR to squeeze in an extra story. Luckily, Peebles would make his case in front of the most developer-friendly LPC chair in history, Meenakshi Srinivasan. Simultaneously, Peebles was angling to win the bid for a separate, controversial high-rise project in a low-rise, landmarked stretch of Brownstone Brooklyn in Cobble Hill known as the Long Island Hospital site.

The developer began his campaign by making himself pleasant to the mayor's fundraiser and advisor. That advisor then set up a call to Peebles from the mayor himself. The mayor asked Peebles for a $20,000 donation to his nonprofit, Campaign for One New York. That organization was a lobbying front that raised money to convince the City Council to vote yes on the mayor's controversial "affordable" housing plans that required upzonings. Peebles paid the money. Months later, when his Brooklyn deal did not go according to plan, Peebles took the cash back but mysteriously got his way at the Landmarks Preservation Commission with the Broadway building at 349 Broadway. The mayor asked Peebles again for money for a different mayoral project, but Peebles declined to contribute a second time (Mays and Weiss 2016; Mays 2019).

Peebles would not have called his donation a bribe. But another real estate developer, investor, and all-around fundraiser for the mayor, Jona Rechnitz, would use the term "bribe" for similar contributions (Wang 2017). Rechnitz got close to the mayor by attending fundraisers, beginning with De Blasio's 2013 mayoral campaign. His money bought him access. Said Rechnitz under oath in court: "He took my calls. We were friends" (Wang 2017). To please the mayor, he gave $102,000 to Democratic committees trying to gain seats in the Albany State House. Rechnitz also bundled $41,000 in contributions to the mayor's 2013 campaign. He and his wife gave the campaign $10,000 more. Rechnitz later gave $50,000 to the mayor's favorite lobbying group, the Campaign for One New York. It was all in exchange for what the *New York Times* called "extraordinary access to the mayor and high-level city officials" (Ransom 2019). Rechnitz pleaded guilty to "bribery" and got a ten-month jail sentence (Wang 2017; Gartland 2019; Nahmias 2016).

Rechnitz was not the only case of a man with real estate on his mind pleading guilty to bribery and going to jail for it, but without charging the person bribed. Restaurant owner Harendra Singh steered about $80,000 to De Blasio's political campaigns in return for favorable treatment by the city in his restaurant lease negations. It turned out that the city owned the site of his restaurant (Keshner and Smith 2018). There is also the case of the Podolsky Brothers, known in the press as "slumlords." Among their holdings were seventeen dilapidated buildings that the city bought from them for a whopping $173 million, $30–$50 million higher than the appraised value of the buildings. Oddly, Podolsky's lawyer, Frank Carone, bundled about $23,000 of donations through his law firm to De Blasio's failed presidential bid. The mayor later obtained mortgages for his Park Slope properties from a bank that one of the Podolsky brothers had founded (Neuman 2019; Rice 2013). In the eyes of the law, this is only the "appearance" of corruption.

There is also the well-known case of a historic building on the Lower East Side known as Rivington House. It had begun life as a particularly beautiful public-school building. The city sold it off, and the building ended up as a hospice for people with HIV. It had over two hundred beds, owned by Village Care, a developer-manager of health care facilities. To its credit, the city had put a deed restriction on the building that specified that it could be used only as a public health facility. Investors called the Allure Group (operators of poorly run nursing homes) bought the building from Village Care for $28 million and then paid the city $16.15 million to lift the deed restriction, a move to dramatically increase the value of the building. They had executed a similar move on a building in Brooklyn. Getting rid of the deed restriction allowed them to flip the building to another investor, Slate Property Group, for $116 million just two years later. They made a quick profit of $72 million. Nonetheless, Slate was clear: It wanted to evict the HIV-positive residents and turn the building into luxury condos (despite Slate's membership in an affordable housing lobby known as NYSAHA). The city's Department of Investigation later reported that the city knew full well that the Allure Group was planning a condo conversion and of the plan to flip the property to Slate (New York City Department of Investigation 2016). Slate warned its employees to be quiet about the potential deal, not wanting negative publicity to interfere with the goldmine profit they were about to land. Investigators reported that city staff hid documents from them, needlessly redacted others, and were utterly uncooperative with the investigation. Because of that, the investigators could not find a smoking gun to prove who paid whom (G. B. Smith 2016).

Citizens United and a few other earlier Supreme court rulings raised the legal standard for what constitutes a smoking gun for bribery charges, making it difficult to pursue suspected cases of graft (Teachout 2016). The Acting U.S. Attorney for the Southern District, Joon Kim, wrote about the De Blasio case in this dry manner:

> In considering whether to charge individuals with serious public corruption crimes, we take into account, among other things, the high burden of proof, the clarity of existing law, any recent changes in the law, and the particular difficulty in proving criminal intent in

corruption schemes where there is no evidence of personal profit. (J. Kim 2017)

The Manhattan District Attorney summed up his separate investigation into the Rivington case:

> The transactions appear contrary to the intent and spirit of the laws that impose candidate contribution limits, rules which are meant to prevent corruption, and the appearance of corruption in the campaign financing process. (Rashbaum 2017)

Power Tool Nine: Threaten Lawsuits

REBNY can also get its way through threats of lawsuits. REBNY's deep pockets make this an effective tactic since those threatened with legal action know the threats are "credible" rather than mere posturing. REBNY filed a friend of the court brief in the lawsuit of its partner group, the Rent Stabilization Association, in what promises to be a multi-year fight against the 2019 rent reforms (Brenzel 2019). REBNY also dragged the city through three years of court fights, to overturn a weak law that tried to limit the conversions of hotels to condos pending an academic study (Appellate Division, First Judicial Department 2018). REBNY also sued the state for attempts to regulate rental property broker commissions (Spectrum News NY1 Staff 2020). Official fear of lawsuits made the Landmarks Preservation Commission tiptoe so quietly in the first ten years of its existence that it under-designated historic districts and individual landmarks. The first legal counsel to the commission even kept a sign on her desk to constantly remind all staff that there were still constitutional questions related to landmarking (Baccash 2010). (NB: the Penn Central case in the Supreme Court resolved those questions.) REBNY sued the City Council in 2007 over attempts to regulate homeless shelters (Real Estate Bd. of NY, Inc. v. City Council of City of New York 2007). Former City Planning chair under Mayor Giuliani, Joe Rose, informed members of an urbanist conference in 2017 that private threats of REBNY lawsuits finally killed his zoning reform proposals of 2000 (as reported to author by Anthony Wood). So it is no surprise that REBNY's public threats of lawsuits at public hearings at the New York City Council in 2019 over the Small Business Jobs Survival Act led to the abandonment of that legislation. REBNY's power here comes from wealth and resolve: vast sums of money to finance lawsuits and a readiness to walk its talk. With rare exceptions, ordinary citizens lack the means to use the courts similarly, even when banded together in small associations.

Power Tool Ten: Advertising to Keep the Overton Window Narrow

Given the scale and wealth of the New York real estate industry, there has been a proliferation in NYC of the pro–real estate, pro-demolition newspapers, broadsheets, and blogs that glorify the role of real estate and skyscrapers. Most live off the cold cash of real estate advertising. This refers to outlets like the *Real Deal*, the *Commercial Observer*, YIMBY.com, and *Crain's*. The real estate industry's self-promotion, boosterism, and nonstop flogging of the assumption that Nimbyism is rampant have filtered over to mainstream outlets. It means that the Overton window[7] (the list of what the *New York Times* and the *Wall Street Journal* consider legitimate topics for policy discussion on real estate) has become far too small. For example, throughout 2014–15, Chinatown community groups organized multiple rallies at City Hall. The coalition had long advocated adopting a locally produced zoning plan with professional planners' help. Several of those rallies had more than one thousand people in attendance. Yet neither the *Times* nor the *Wall Street Journal* covered a single rally. Over the entire De Blasio administration, the mainstream press failed to cover dozens of remarkably well-attended protests, rallies, and mobbed hearings concerning land use. The topic was demolishing public libraries, neighborhood-wide rezonings, demolitions of historic buildings, and spot rezonings in Manhattan, Queens, the Bronx, and Brooklyn. In contrast, the *Times* was careful to extensively cover a couple of very thinly attended protests in Crown Heights against a homeless shelter and a similar protest in the tony enclave of the East 50s, portraying those cases as pure "Nimbyism."

A search of the phrase "real estate" in the *New York Times* for 2019 generates 2,618 articles. Most of those articles cover real estate transactions, home decorating, sales, house hunts, what bathroom finishes developers prefer, plus architectural opinion op-eds, articles about charming suburban towns to buy into, and what views people like. A mere handful of the articles covered important news about the industry, most of them about the rent wars in Albany. By contrast, a search using the word "overdevelopment" (a term much used in public hearings that year and in town halls managed by council member Kallos) generated only twenty-seven articles for the same period, most of them irrelevant to the topic, except for a lone article about a fight against towerization of the Seaport area of Manhattan.

The coverage in mainstream newspapers rarely questions the assumptions of the growth machine. When it does, the articles are buried in the back pages with unthreatening headlines that are unclear about the content, such as "Everybody Inhale" or "Want to Relax in an NYC Park?" (Hu 2016; O'Leary 2012).

Summary and What's Next

This chapter has taken the reader through a review of the tactics real estate power uses to maintain and expand its power. Of course, the question is how to rein in such concentrated power and manage the problem of lobbying and a captured municipal government. That will be the subject of the last chapter. It is time to examine how REBNY and the housing supply fundamentalists went on the direct offensive against historic districts.

Chapter 7

Demonizing Historic Districts and the Capture of the Landmarks Preservation Commission

THIS CHAPTER DESCRIBES A TWO-FRONT WAR on historic preservation and outlines how the Real Estate Board of New York (REBNY) came to finally capture the Landmarks Preservation Commission. The first full-front contemporary attack on historic districts came in the form of Edward Glaeser's 2010 op-ed in *City Journal* called "Preservation Follies" (Glaeser 2010). It was a diatribe against preservation in New York. Glaeser suggested that historic districts should never have been designated. He argued that the protections on many buildings and historic areas should be removed. He complained about the very existence of the Landmarks Preservation Commission as a regulatory agency. He indulged in an odd bit of racial politics with the claim that in his opinion, too many of Manhattan's historic districts were filled with "white" residents and were "a refuge for the rich," never mind the irony that Glaeser himself had explicitly advocated for a hyper-gentrification strategy for New York to "improve" the demographic mix away from Black and Brown low-income people, as we saw in Chapter 2. In "Preservation Follies," he argues that historic districts are a luxury good desirable only to white rich people—an argument that denies the reality that people of all colors and income levels want to live in neighborhoods with historic character.

What the city should do, Glaeser argued, is stop "restricting construction in valuable areas" (Glaeser 2010). The "Preservation Follies" diatribe was followed quickly by the launch of Glaeser's popular book, *Triumph of the City*, which had the same agenda. Then his essay, "How Skyscrapers Will Save the City," came out in *The Atlantic* magazine that same year. Glaeser's bellicose posturing against preservationists—he demeans them as "villainous" and "white-haired"—generated him a flurry of publicity, including a series of interviews and radio appearances at the *New York Times*, *The Guardian*, and *WNYC-Radio*. His popular broadside against historic districts was soon accompanied by an academic paper, published in advance of his book, which was widely circulated. Glaeser co-authored it with Vicki Been, who at the time was at the real estate–funded think-tank called the Furman Center at New York University. The paper had a provocative title, "Preserving History or Hindering Growth?" The group floated a version of it at a 2011 conference and again in 2013 and finally got it online in 2014 as a working paper.

Glaeser and his colleagues argue that historic districts harm the city by preventing the demolition of low- and mid-rise buildings and the replacement of these historic buildings by skyscrapers. The title alone got the authors a lot of attention among free-marketeers and anti-regulatory "market urbanists." That crowd has widely cited the paper ever since. In a footnote we learn that Glaeser takes money as a speaker at big real estate gatherings. So what did he argue?

In the "Hindering Growth" paper (Been et al. 2014), Glaeser, Been, and their co-authors create a theoretical model to illustrate their ideas. They make five claims:

Claim 1: By preventing the demolition of historic properties and the replacement of them with skyscrapers, historic districts or landmarked buildings are "destroying value." Protecting a building from demolition takes away *the speculative profits* that a developer might get by demolishing an area and replacing it with towers.

Claim 2: Historic districts are "driving up the cost of housing beyond the reach of many" and "contributing to the larger crisis of affordability." The authors wrongly suppose that whatever might get built over a demolished historic neighborhood or landmark will offer the world more inexpensive housing or that the new housing will increase housing supply enough that lower prices will trickle down to the poor and middle classes.

Claim 3: Preserved neighborhoods "restrict the rights of property owners" and subject the poor owners of historic buildings to "extensive regulatory hurdles."

Claim 4: As the title provocatively suggests, historic districts can "hinder growth," where "growth" equals the building of new skyscrapers on top of historic areas, a claim not unlike the first one.

Claim 5: This absence of demolition of historic areas and their replacement with towers will prevent NYC from competing in the "increasingly global system of cities" (Been et al. 2014, 2, 3, 5).

The Big Picture

So, are historic districts and landmarks guilty of any of the crimes Glaeser and Been accuse them of? It turns out the answer is a resounding No. Let's look first at the bigger picture around these claims and then return to the specifics of the attack.

On Claim #1, we must ask: What kind of "value" might be "destroyed" by *not* demolishing a historic district and *not* replacing the area with skyscrapers? It is a nonsensical question if you pause to think about it. Simply by existing, a landmarked neighborhood destroys no value. The value lost that Glaeser and his colleagues refer to, is the *potential speculative* value of the unbuilt skydome above the historic districts. They are protesting height limits and air rights limits that never belonged to the owners, and we know that the Supreme Court has repeatedly said that nobody is entitled to *the speculative value* of their property (Wolf 2008).

But the speculative real estate values aren't the only values to consider. For example, we saw in earlier chapters that historic districts create a public asset that has a substantial public value that real estate prices do not embody, since no market trades the asset. We also know there is immense latent demand to live in and wander in such historic neighborhoods—to experience the sunny side of the street, the non-tangible, non-traded qualities of history, sunlight, beauty, and urbanity; to have a place in the world characterized by great urbanity. Why else do millions of tourists visit Paris and Barcelona? We must also weigh the pleasure of those who profit from the destruction of a neighborhood against the pain of those who are displaced and of those who mourn the loss of light, beauty, history, and great urbanity. That's a task that can only be done politically.

Claim #2 states that "historic districts drive up the cost of housing." One finds on close reading that Glaeser and his team in the "Hindering Growth" paper try—and *fail*—to provide evidence that historic districts are a factor in driving New York City's housing prices ever upward. Indeed, in "Hindering Growth," Glaeser and his co-authors are forced to conclude:

Our simple model *does not answer* the question whether the designation of districts reduced supply overall in New York City. (Been et al. 2014, 22; emphasis added)

and

Our results *do not capture* the external benefits that historic properties provide for society as a whole. (Been et al. 2014, 26; emphasis added)

Thus, the presumed guilt of historic districts implied by the paper's title, "Preserving History or Hindering Growth?" turns out to be salacious clickbait. The reality is nothing of the sort.

On Claim #3, regarding the regulatory hurdles of property owners, let's grant Glaeser and Been partial credit. Yes, historic district designation does limit a property owner's right to demolish a historic property offhandedly. But complaining about that is silly, for that is the exact policy intent of the Landmarks Law. Moreover, such a claim sounds even sillier when you realize that a property owner in a historic district can and does, despite designation, demolish a landmarked building in New York City. All a property owner must do is prove financial hardship to the Landmarks Preservation Commission. There's even a procedure for that.

Donovan Rypkema, economist and author of *The Economics of Historic Preservation* (1994), reports that over 95 percent of building alterations requested of the Landmarks Preservation Commission (LPC) are minor and that the LPC quickly manages them at staff level without bureaucratic delay. He found that less than 3/10ths of 1 percent of applications for modification and new construction inside historic districts are "ultimately denied" (Rypkema 2016, 1). Moreover, the staff at the LPC are extremely helpful to property owners who want to do large-scale alternations, advising them without cost on how to manage the alterations in a way that preserves or enhances the value of the property instead of diminishing that value through foolish alterations. Therefore, one can hardly claim that nothing is happening inside historic districts or that the economy of renovators is not in full swing.

On Claim #4, which charges historic districts with "hindering growth," we cannot grant the authors any quarter. There is no evidence that historic districts in New York City hinder job growth, real estate tax revenue growth, price growth, or the general prosperity of the city. They are instead substantial contributors to all those forms of economic growth, punching far above their weight. Rypkema gives multiple indicators of the contribution of historic districts to the city's dynamism. For example, 130,000 jobs are in the city's "heritage" tourism sector; more than $800 million each year is invested in historic buildings by homeowners; and about 9,000 New Yorkers work in the sector that renovates old buildings (Rypkema 2016, 1). Although historic districts represent only 3.4 percent of the city's property lots, nearly 11 percent of NYC jobs in "young" firms are in historic districts, 10 percent of jobs in start-ups are in historic districts (Rypkema 2016, 23), and 8 percent of all private sector jobs are in historic districts. Finally, consider that the districts contain 20 percent of all arts, entertainment, and recreation jobs in the city. The data suggest that we need more historic districts, not fewer.

Claim #5, regarding the competitiveness of New York City, borders on the nonsensical. This is a Chicken Little, "the Sky Is Falling," kind of rhetoric that is illogical and misleading. First, skyscrapers don't cause economic growth or job growth (beyond a temporary blip in construction jobs). Skyscrapers can be empty and wait for tenants. You can build whole cities of skyscrapers, and nobody will come unless force-marched out of their rural homes, as China has seen (Mallonee 2016). Second, the "competitiveness of cities" argument is overly focused on giant corporate headquarters and ignores the fact that the small business sector is the engine of economic growth in our economy, not giant corporations. Nearly half of all jobs created in 2016 come from small businesses (Sadeghi, Talan, and Clayton 2016).

And who says corporations always want to be in glass towers, in towers at all, or even in a city? Google, for example, chose an old warehouse in Chelsea for its New York headquarters. C-suite location decisions are also quixotic, unpredictable, and dependent on the whims of CEOs and the tax-avoidance strategies of CFOs. For example, Western Union built two different masonry headquarters in Lower Manhattan, then decamped in 1973 for a leafy green suburban campus. AT&T left New York City for Dallas years ago after using up two different NYC skyscrapers. More recently (2019), Fortune 500 corporations have been inexplicably flocking to the suburban wasteland of Plano, Texas (Jayson 2019).

The rhetoric about "competitiveness" also misses the point that it is the historic districts of New York that give the city its unique character. They are the places of great urbanity that cause corporate workers to want to live here in the first place. In Rypkema's survey, over half of respondents said they wanted to live in a historic neighborhood and over 30 percent said that if they had a choice they'd live in a brownstone (Rypkema 2016, 44). The upshot? Destroy the historic neighborhoods in the elusive quest of catering to the perverse whims of Fortune 500 CEOs and you will have foolishly destroyed the urban goose that is laying the golden egg of what makes New York unique.

A Closer Look at Anti-Historic District Theorizing

Let's look more closely at how Glaeser and his colleagues develop their economic theory in the "Hindering Growth" paper. They begin by ginning up a mathematical model to illustrate their notion that preventing the demolition of buildings "destroys" rather than creates value. (Be aware: You could just as easily develop a model to illustrate the opposite idea.) A two-dimensional table (Table 7.1) summarizes the unpredictable and multiple scenarios that Glaeser's model generates by considering the relationship between building height and aesthetic values. Unfortunately, Glaeser treats these variables as unrelated to each other, missing the reality that they are mutually interdependent. Thus, the model generates several possible indeterminate, inconclusive, unpredictable outcomes, or scenarios, which the authors dub grandly as "heterogeneous effects." It is worth pointing out that when the authors relax the highly restrictive model assumptions, the model doesn't even generate the various scenarios.

In Table 7.1, I summarize the scenarios and outcomes of Glaeser's model in a simplified manner. It illustrates four different situations that could arise in the model's imaginary universe. Which part of the matrix you land in depends on several variables: how tall and attractive the neighborhood's buildings are to start with; how much it costs a developer to provide aesthetically equivalent buildings to those in a demolished historic district; and how much additional height a new zoning regime would allow for.

One of the perplexing things about these predictions is that they are just rationalizations of a few different market scenarios. Moreover, once you realize that height and aesthetic values are mutually dependent variables, the theorizing seems pointless. So why build such a model? The answer is that the "Hindering Growth" paper is not a scientific exercise, but a rhetorical one. The purpose of such rhetoric is in the article's title, to persuade people that historic districts "hinder growth" even though they do no such thing.

Do the Data Back Up the Anti-Historic District Theorizing?

To prove their point—that historic districts destroy value and hinder growth—the authors turn to an econometric analysis of a large dataset

Table 7.1. The Two-by-Two Model of "Heterogeneous" Effects

This square of the matrix represents the situation in which developers would not be interested in demolishing even a few properties in a historic district, let alone the entire neighborhood. This could happen when the architecture is ugly and unpopular, and the area is far from either a booming real estate market or a transit hub.	This box represents the situation in which incremental demolition of a historic neighborhood takes place "at the margins," but total demolition of the neighborhood is unlikely—not even profitable. This arises when a historic neighborhood already has tall buildings and is already booming with high prices, making it costly for a developer to buy in, demolish, and rebuild.
This box represents the scenario when total demolition of a historic neighborhood is profitable and incremental demolition unlikely. This might happen when the historic neighborhood is very low-rise, and the city allows a large upzoning while the cost of rebuilding remains low. This, incidentally, is the policy regime Glaeser advocates for.	This box represents the confusing scenario when anything could happen—both partial demolition as well as total demolition of a neighborhood. Either might be profitable. This is most likely to take place when a few initial conditions converge: the initial height of buildings in the neighborhood is very low; the aesthetic qualities are very high (like Brownstone Brooklyn); a new upzoning is big enough so that developers want to get into the market; and when the costs of replacing the buildings of a similar aesthetic is also low.

of 35,000 property transactions from 1974 to 2009. The authors ask three questions of their data:

Question 1: Is there less construction in historic districts than in other districts (after an area's designation)?

Question 2: What is the impact of historic district designation on residential sales prices in the area and in the city overall?

Question 3: If there is a lot of unused or potential buildable space in play, is the effect of historic district designation negative? If it is negative, does that mean designation in those places is "destroying value"?

Question 1 is puzzling. Why even ask it? The public purpose of historic district designation is to prevent demolition and protect architectural integrity. Anyone on the streets of New York even vaguely conscious of historic districts could tell you there is going to be less new construction in a historic district than outside it, and more likely, a great deal of renovation work instead. No need for the Furman Center to labor over a dataset for that one. That said, the actual answer to the question turns out to be complicated by the unexpected discovery that "historic districts had less construction activity even before designation" (Been et al. 2014, 22), a finding the authors cannot explain.

For questions 2 and 3, the expansive data retrieved by Glaeser and his co-authors show that historic districts do *not* destroy value by lowering prices—despite the authors' efforts to claim that they do. There are a lot of reasons for this, some of this possibly just due to the nature of the situation. One is that historic districts in NYC are quite small relative to the landmass of the city. Also, each historic district emerged over the course of many different market conditions and thus they all have different demographics and different kinds of housing units for sale. They also have different shapes and vary significantly in amenities. Things like walking distance to work (such as is the case for Tribeca and SoHo, which are walking distance to the former financial center business district) can affect prices as much if not more than their historic district status. What the data do show, is that sometimes prices go up in historic districts after designation, and sometimes they go down. This is consistent with what researchers have found elsewhere in the country. As we saw in earlier chapters, historic district designation has no clear price effect one way or another (Rypkema 1994): It depends on what else is going on in a city.

To generate data for the price regressions in the "Hindering Growth" paper, the authors assign imaginary "shadow" prices to unbuilt floor area ratios (FAR) in historic districts. Alas, shadow prices are just made-up price data and are not worth our analytical attention. They should not be used for policy analysis or to claim any destruction of or gain in value. To make matters even more complicated, the paper neglects the problem that the buildable envelope (FAR) is "endogenous" to policy conditions. That means city administrators tinker with FAR constantly, depending on ever-changing lobbying situations, policy goals, market situations (including price), and political conditions. They give and take away FAR as they deem fit, and frequently. It is not an independent variable as "Hindering Growth" assumes.

Nonetheless, leaning into Glaeser's econometric exercise, we learn that in his dataset, prices rise modestly for housing inside historic districts *when housing prices are rising elsewhere in the city*. We also learn, interestingly, that this price premium includes the buffer areas immediately around a historic district. This is not as straightforward as it seems since the price premium for "historic district" is conflated in the data with the variable for the "pre-war character" of New York's older buildings, since prewar housing is of higher quality than new construction and therefore commands a price premium whether it is in a historic district or not. An even more peculiar finding is that the price premium is strongest for single-family homes in historic districts of remote Queens and Brooklyn rather than the dense row houses and apartment buildings of Manhattan's far older historic districts that are the objects of Glaeser and Been's ire.

When Glaeser tries his regressions for Manhattan's historic districts alone, we learn perplexingly that even though on a citywide level, historic districts appear to trade for 30 percent *higher prices* than non-historic districts, "designation appears to have a negative effect on property values" in Manhattan's historic districts, although *"the coefficient is not statistically significant"* (Been et al. 2014, 24). Translation: Designation has neither a negative effect on property values nor a positive effect—it is statistically insignificant in the dataset on Manhattan. Glaeser and Been have no result at all, so saying "designation appears to have a negative effect" is mere inaccurate rhetoric.

Instead of accepting their non-finding of zero statistical significance, the authors cherry-pick a couple of *unnamed* community districts in Manhattan, rerun the regressions, and conclude that, yes indeed, in those unnamed, smaller areas, designation has the hoped-for, statistically significant, negative effect on prices.

For the motivated reader, a look at page 41 of the appendix of the "Hindering Growth" paper shows why it is so hard to take any of this econometric data-massaging seriously. On page 41, readers can study a graph of the rise and fall of real estate prices across time for the entire city and for Manhattan. You can see the collapse in housing prices after the 9/11 catastrophe, and then further on you can see a second big collapse of prices after the 2007–8 fiscal crisis. But wait, shouldn't those price shocks affect Glaeser's analysis? The 9/11 shock, for example, tanked prices in the nearby historic districts of Tribeca, the Seaport, SoHo, and Greenwich Village, as well as in Brooklyn Heights and Carroll Gardens, for four years—far more than any other part of the city. That's because those districts were subjected to a year of the poisonous plume generated by the World Trade Center fires. All those historic districts had been designated well before the 9/11 tragedy. Are those price shocks even mentioned in the "Hindering Growth" analysis? No, they are not. The two shocks would account for a fall in prices, thus explaining a temporary "destruction" in value that has nothing to do with historic districts.

The more interesting finding buried within Glaeser's data is that historic district designation correlates with a price premium on the border areas just outside of the historic districts, not just inside them. Economically, this is fascinating. It explains the free-riding behavior of developers who circle in like pirates at the edges of Manhattan's historic districts, walling in the districts with high towers just outside the protected borders, trying to grab value for themselves out of the public beauty and livability of a designated historic neighborhood. These developers frequently (and laughably) market their glass towers as somehow part of a mid-rise, masonry-rich historic district. At the same time, their border-towers harm the original integrity of the neighborhood. It is an old-school "tragedy of the commons" outcome, a product of the weak regulation emanating from the Landmarks Preservation Commission.

The takeaways so far in the empirical section of the "Hindering Growth" paper are these: In the framework of Glaeser's model, he equates higher property values with higher social welfare, so lower property values mean lower social welfare and by implication, destroyed "value." But he finds that historic districts overall *are increasing* social welfare—the opposite of what Glaeser and his team hoped to find. The correct interpretation of their data is that the price premium historic districts sometimes command is a market signal *to build more neighborhoods with the qualities of great urbanity that historic districts embody.*

The Real Estate Lobby Starts Its Own War on Historic Districts

The second front of the war on historic districts came through the real estate lobby that we met earlier, REBNY. As discussed in earlier chapters, REBNY kneecapped the original Landmarks Law in the 1960s, eliminating the proposed 500-foot contextual development rule around individual landmarks, and imposed a rule for the new commission: It could only designate during six out of thirty-six months. In later years, REBNY also worked hard to ensure that mayors did not appoint commissioners of the LPC who were (in the real estate industry's eyes) too fierce in their advocacy and support for landmarking. Commissioners who advocated too ardently for preservation, such as Roberta Gratz and Anthony Tung, soon found themselves losing their appointments (Pogrebin 2010; Dunlap 1987). We've also seen, through the research of Marjorie Pearson, that chairs of the commission who turned out to be too zealous in favor of preservation were often followed by chairs who were more sympathetic to the desires of the real estate lobby (Pearson 2010). Since the mayor appoints all eleven of the commission's members, the real estate lobby also makes it a point—a serious, dedicated point—to gain intimate access to the mayor. Through lobbying and political contributions, they influence the mayor and ultimately the mayor's choice of the chair of the LPC, along with its other ten members. All this has long been business as usual in New York City.

But in 2013, REBNY went beyond its usual behind-the-scenes work. Emboldened by Glaeser's public relations campaign against historic districts, REBNY went on the offensive. It put up two white papers on its website attacking historic districts and landmarking in general. The papers accused the districts of causing the affordability "crisis" in NYC's housing market and of occupying too much physical space in the city (REBNY 2013b). The documents read as if they have been cribbed word-for-word from Glaeser's "Preservation Follies" op-ed (REBNY 2013a; 2013b). Here are their complaints.

- *REBNY Complaint #1:* Historic districts occupy "too much" of the physical space of NYC, especially in Manhattan.

In REBNY's eyes, preservation of a building inhibits the ability of "the city to grow." This language is code for limiting the ability of real estate developers to demolish historic buildings and replace them with skyscrapers. The reality is that REBNY has little to complain about. Only 3.4 percent of the lot area of the city is under the regulation of the Landmarks Preservation Commission and 20 percent in Manhattan's lot area. Read another way, in Manhattan, a whopping 80 percent of the lot area is *unprotected* (Rypkema 2016, 1). Moreover, more than 85 percent of construction in New York happens as-of-right, so why is REBNY complaining? As mentioned earlier, between 1985 and 2018, more than 44,000 buildings were demolished in the city, most in Manhattan, while over 300,000 building permits were issued in the same period. This is hardly a portrait of a real estate industry constrained.

These facts raise a question: What constitutes "too much" preservation anyway? Isn't that decision a judgment call that the citizenry of NYC ought to make, rather than a special interest lobby that gains from constant demolition and rebuilding? And wasn't the Landmarks Law itself supposed to set up a professional commission to make those judgment calls on behalf of the public good, at least according to the City Charter that covers the Landmarks Law?

- *REBNY Complaint #2:* Most new construction is not happening in historic districts or on top of individual landmarks. Moreover, REBNY adds, there are too many parking lots and vacant lots included in the boundaries of historic districts.

REBNY is correct: There is not much *new construction* happening in historic districts, because they are . . . historic districts. Again, this is simply a bizarre complaint. They are complaining about a desirable public policy. As for parking lots and vacant lots, they are included so that when they do get redeveloped, the new buildings are supposed to be designed in a way that is contextual to the surrounding historic district, also known as intelligent urban design policy.

- *REBNY Complaint #3:* Historic district designation imposes unspecified "costs" to property owners who are then subject to regulatory overreach by the Landmarks Preservation Commission.

These costs are not spelled out. The sole example REBNY brings up is a complaint that surfaced many years back in the *New York Times*: A Harlem brownstone owner complained that replacing historically accurate windows made of wood would cost him three times as much as buying aluminum frame windows (Powell 2005). Neither the *Times* nor REBNY pointed out that the commission routinely approves modern aluminum frame windows. To expand the complaint, REBNY states that alteration permits take too long and there are too many permits to process, given the size of the staff. Again, Rypkema gives the best answer to the latter accusation: "Of the 13,000 applications the LPC receives in a typical year, 95% are resolved at staff level and less than 3/10 of 1% are ultimately denied" (Rypkema 2016, 1). That is the very picture of efficient regulation.

- *REBNY Complaint #4:* Buildings made of glass curtain wall or certain kinds of 1920s masonry "were never intended to last forever" (REBNY 2013a).

Here, I must agree with a part of REBNY's complaint: Glass curtain wall and poured concrete modernist structures were never meant to last long, twenty years at most. In fact, one of the founding gurus of modernist architecture, Tommaso Marinetti, proclaimed in 1914 about modernist building techniques: "Houses will last less long than we! Each generation will have to build its own city" (cited in Conrads 1971, 38). But I am mystified as to why REBNY suggests that 1920s masonry buildings were not meant to last, when in fact they are extremely durable. More likely, REBNY's complaint is a strategic one, voiced to forestall preservationist efforts to designate landmarks among the historic masonry skyscrapers that were within the proposed Midtown East rezoning district. That upzoning was much talked about in New York at the same time as the publication of REBNY's White Papers under discussion (Kusisto and Brown 2012).

- *REBNY Complaint #5*: Historic Districts in Manhattan are "more likely to be white" and the residents are more likely to be "rich."

This complaint sounds just like Edward Glaeser's complaint in "Preservation Follies." There are four major points to make about it. First, the complaint reads as an unusual form of race-and-class baiting—it misappropriates widespread social concerns over racial injustice and weaponizes that concern into the service of Big Real Estate's agenda to get rid of historic districts. And how ironic for the complaint to come from REBNY and Edward Glaeser, both of whom have long advocated hyper-gentrification and the correlated "white-ification" of Manhattan for years. Their sudden concern about the issue just rings false. As we saw in Chapter 2, Glaeser has written that the "demographic mix" of the historic core of the city should be tilted to the wealthy, especially that segment of the rich who don't use public schools. REBNY's president in 1970 told the city council that "every wealthy person in the world should live on the island of Manhattan" (Newfield and Du Brul 1981, 82). Mayor Bloomberg, while pushing the "luxury city" model of economic development said, "Wouldn't it be great if every Russian billionaire moved here!" And the entire Penn neighborhood revamp proposed by the Empire State Development Corporation and REBNY board member Vornado is explicitly based on pushing out low-income people and replacing them with the 1 percent who are overwhelmingly white.

Second, the segregation of Manhattan by color and class has been going on for more than one hundred years and has no correlation to historic district designation. Tribeca was not a Black neighborhood when the LPC designated it a historic district, neither was Greenwich Village, Brooklyn Heights, the Upper East Side Historic District, or Ladies Mile. Indeed, the gentrification and whitification of Manhattan was a deliberate government policy that had nothing to do with landmarking and historic districts. As far back as the 1930s, Mayor La Guardia and Robert Moses specialized in demolishing diverse, low-income Manhattan neighborhoods on the Lower East Side, Lower West Side, Lincoln Center area, Upper West Side, and the area where Stuyvesant Town project now stands, neighborhoods filled with Black and Brown people, and building instead dystopic public housing projects. It was a process cynically—but correctly—named "negro removal." Then Mayor Koch got rid of as many poor people as he could who were still living in Manhattan SROs in the 1980s. And do not forget that REBNY has opposed rent stabilization for as long as it has been around, one of the very few affordable housing mechanisms we have. It is notable in that regard that historic districts are one of the last repositories of rent-stabilized apartments in the city (because new construction is exempt from rent stabilization). Last, even if REBNY were to get its way and replace Manhattan's historic districts with glass towers, the law does not allow developers to discriminate by race when deciding who should buy into or rent in the new glass towers. That means, of course, that developers will fill them with the wealthy, and by correlation, white people, while laughing all the way to bank about how Big Real Estate once again snookered those politicians in the City Council and mayor's office.

Third, we live under capitalism, which has an operating rule: People with more money get to buy more of what they want. We may not like the rule, but it is there. And yes, one of the things many rich people want is beautiful housing in beautiful neighborhoods with great historic architecture. Of course, non-rich people and non-white people also want beautiful housing in beautiful neighborhoods with great historic architecture, but richer people are willing to pay higher rents and higher purchase prices to get those things and have the means to do so. Does that mean we should forbid the rich access to what they hanker for, or perhaps demolish the neighborhoods that are the object of their desire? Maybe. But if we did that, wouldn't REBNY and Glaeser be advocating for a Soviet-style punishment of the wealthy, like when Stalin confiscated the land and draft animals of all the so-called rich peasants (the kulaks), sent them to Siberia to die, and then Russia had the worst famine of two hundred years?

We need to make a city that has a place in the world for everyone, and that means the city also needs to have something that the rich want, but we also need rules to prevent the poor and middle class from being displaced if the rich suddenly start eyeballing real estate in their neighborhoods, for example, on the Bronx's Grand Concourse. And, as Mayor Bloomberg did point out, the rich do pay a boatload of taxes, and the city needs the revenue, hence a housing policy that amounts to mere destruction is not helpful or desirable.

In the same vein, it is not true that being white—or rich—is a sufficient condition to get a district designated as historic. Rich white neighborhoods are able to mobilize a volunteer base of activists for years at a time to contend with the reality that the LPC is parsimonious in handing out historic districts to anyone, rich or poor. Being rich and white doesn't guarantee designation. A case in point is ritzy Park Avenue, in the very heart of one of the wealthiest neighborhoods of the city. The LPC did not designate it as a historic district until the mid-2010s and only after many long years of campaigning. Brooklyn Heights and Greenwich Village designations came about in the same way. Activism for preservation in those cases took place for twenty years before actual designation took place. Last, there is no evidence that landmark designations make a neighborhood whiter, but there is evidence discussed in Chapter 2 about how towerization on the non-designated part of the Upper East Side and Williamsburg rendered a neighborhood wealthier and less Black and Brown.

Fourth, the suggestion that people who are not white or rich don't care about historic buildings or historic districts does not fit the facts. Wing Lam, head of the Coalition to Save Chinatown and the Lower East Side, commented to this author about the lack of historic district designation on the Lower East Side: "Do they actually think Chinese people only want to live in glass towers?" Moreover, it is well known that for fifty years, the Landmarks Preservation Commission stonewalled or ignored the pleas of Black organizations for historic districts in Black Harlem who were furious at the tiny designations they did eventually get. The following section looks at that issue in detail.

Is It Only White People Who Want Historic Districts?

Harlem is where most Black Manhattanites have lived most of the twentieth century. Despite the advocacy work of multiple, Black-run organizations composed of residents advocating for historic preservation in Harlem, the Landmarks Preservation Commission mostly ignored Harlem. Whether this was due to racism, incompetence, or to a silent municipal alliance with the real estate industry is for the reader to judge.

By the time the Landmarks Commission came into existence in the mid-1960s, Robert Moses and Mayor La Guardia had already subjected Harlem residents to thirty years of the cruelties and demolition madness of urban renewal. That process demolished vast neighborhoods, destroyed more housing units than it created, evicted small businesses occupying ground-floor retail spaces, and herded the Black population into inferior quality, Le Corbusier-styled slab housing blocks. In Central and East Harlem, the city imposed twenty-five separate public housing projects on the Harlem population through the demolition of historic neighborhoods that the technocratic elite deemed "slums." In East Harlem, a third of the geographic area was demolished (Community Board 11 1999). The demolitions began in 1937 and only ended in 1977. A small number of public housing units also came into being in the early 1990s without demolition, using renovated, repurposed tenement buildings. The city also built in Harlem eleven large Mitchell-Lama middle-income housing complexes similar to public housing in the modernist style and physical mass. These ended up housing mostly Puerto Rican residents. The Mitchell-Lama housing used a different funding stream than public housing, but in many cases, it required similar neighborhood demolitions prior to construction.

In 1965, in the later years of all this demolition, Black Harlem residents advocated for the creation of a historic district around Mount Morris Park, now known as Marcus Garvey Park. The LPC held a hearing about it in 1966, but didn't vote on it, so nothing happened. In 1967, the LPC got around to designating as historic a tiny bit of the St. Nicholas area known as Striver's Row (*New Yorker* 1967). The calls for a more substantial Mount Morris historic district went nowhere. The city slow-walked the idea because some of the Mount Morris area was in fact scheduled for demolition via urban renewal for what would become the Milbank-Frawley project. Much negotiation ensued between the city and advocates. In 1971, a full six years after advocates had proposed a historic district, the Landmarks Commission finally designated a single block of just one side of Mount Morris Park. It would be another *forty-four* years before the commission finally agreed to extend this meager historic district with a tiny increment, but again less than a full block. Even in that extension, the commission left out all the corner buildings on Adam Clayton Powell Jr. Boulevard. By then, the commission was making it a practice to leave corner buildings out of historic districts so that they could be demolished for higher-rise buildings, a perplexing policy that defeats the original purpose of a historic district designation by undermining the area's architectural integrity over time (City of New York 1971; Landmarks Preservation Commission 2015). That tradition of leaving the speculative value of corner buildings in historic areas to the vagaries of future tower developers was also a bow to REBNY.

Between 1966 and 2020, volunteer Harlem preservation organizations came and went, from the original Mount Morris Committee to the present-day "Save Harlem Now." The LPC designated extraordinarily little.

Why was the Landmarks Preservation Commission so unwilling to designate historic buildings in an already heavily demolished neighborhood? One *New York Times* journalist observed that the city owned a third of the buildings in Central Harlem's community board district, much of it slated for urban renewal or conversion to public and Section 8 housing. The press intimated that the city housing authorities did not want those areas designated. Black preservationists also had to contend with the opposition to historic preservation of two Black real estate development organizations, the Abyssinian Development Corporation and the Upper

Manhattan Empowerment Zone. Both were influential Harlem-based nonprofits dependent on city and foundation funding. Both had multiple real estate deals in the works and were in the game of seeking funding for new housing projects. Both allied themselves with the city's real estate interests and growth machine and failed to advocate for historic preservation (Kennedy 1991). Nonetheless, Harlem community groups persisted, and in 1974, the LPC finally ceded to neighborhood activism and designated a ridiculously small part of Hamilton Heights. The agency later designated a much-merited extension to Hamilton Heights a full twenty-six years later, in 2000. That extension embraced part of the spectacular Sugar Hill area. The LPC then made small extensions to Hamilton Heights and Sugar Hill in 2001 and 2002.

Residents, angered by the meager scale of these districts, cried "too little, too late." For example, Carolyn Kent, on Community Board 9's landmarks committee, said she was frustrated with the commission's "intransigence and resistance." She claimed that the choice of historic district boundaries featured "too many public buildings and not enough residential buildings" (Fraser 1991). The head of the Emanuel Pieterson Historical Society commented: "Considering how long it takes for this community to be recognized, we don't think the commission has gone far enough. . . . Our historic districts are a minuscule portion of what is here. Part of the problem, I believe, is that the history of African Americans and the contributions we have made have not been of interest to the commission" (Kennedy 1991; Gonzalez 1998). East Harlem never got a historic district at all from the city, although white advocacy groups managed to get a small National Historic District declared in 2019. This was a mostly symbolic action of "too little, too late" because National Historic Districts have no regulatory teeth in New York City (Krisel 2019). Nonetheless, the national designation seemed a rebuke to the city, coming as it did on the heels of the 2017 massive upzoning Mayor de Blasio and Vicki Been imposed on East Harlem.

Articles appeared regularly in the *New York Times*, *New York Magazine*, the *New Yorker*, and the *Amsterdam News* lamenting the lack of action by the LPC for Harlem. Laurie Beckelman, one of the chairs of the commission, admitted, "African-American history has not been a priority of the Commission" (Fraser 1991). Another chair, Jennifer Raab, admitted to a reporter that "she tended to focus on neighborhoods where there was a strong outpouring of support for landmarks from residents" because she (patronizingly) wanted residents "to understand that landmark status was a responsibility as well as an honor" [*sic*]. But as Yuien Chin, of the

Hamilton Heights Sugar Hill Historic District Committee, told one reporter: "We are organized; it just may not be in the traditional way the commission is used to" (Gonzalez 1998; Kennedy 1991).

The biases implicit in Chair Raab's attitude infuriated Harlem author, historian, and preservationist Michael Henry Adams, who chained himself to the doors of the Municipal Building shouting, "Save Harlem Now!" Adams pointed out to the *Times* that "the law does not require neighborhood lobbying. . . . To contend that only if you have the leisure and the time to advocate on behalf of your community will you be able to get attention, then it is a foregone conclusion that people who live in poor neighborhoods will not get preservation" (Kennedy 1991). REBNY and Edward Glaeser seem unaware as well that it was Black preservationists who advocated for the Bed-Stuy and Addisleigh Park Historic Districts.

REBNY Captures the Landmarks Preservation Commission and Breaks Historic District "Zoning"

Obviously, the only force standing in the way of REBNY's desire to erase low-rise historic neighborhoods and replace them with skyscrapers is a fully empowered, fully operational Landmarks Preservation Commission. Therefore, it makes sense that REBNY would want to weaken, eliminate, or, at the very least, control the Landmarks Preservation Commission. In 1965 when New York's City Council passed the Landmarks Law over the fierce objections of the real estate industry, Big Real Estate had to face an entirely new regulatory power unlike the easily captured BSA and DCP: a regulatory agency that was the exact opposite of the Demolition Machine. The Landmarks Preservation Commission was supposed to preserve, not demolish. In one of the most important statements of public policy the City Council has ever made, it granted this new agency massive regulatory powers that have repeatedly held up in court:

> The council finds that many improvements ["any building, structure, place, work of art or other object constituting a physical betterment of real property"] and landscape features, having a special character or a special historical or aesthetic interest or value . . . have been uprooted . . . without adequate consideration of the irreplaceable loss to the people of the city of the aesthetic, cultural and historic values represented by such improvements and landscape features. In addition, distinct areas may be similarly uprooted or may have

their distinctiveness destroyed, although preservation may be both feasible and desirable. It is the sense of the council that the standing of this city as a worldwide tourist center and world capital of business, culture and government cannot be maintained or enhanced by disregarding the historical and architectural heritage of the city and by countenancing the destruction of such cultural assets. It is hereby declared as a matter of public policy that the protection, enhancement, perpetuation and use of these buildings, structures, places, works of art, and landscape features of special character or special historical or aesthetic interest or value *is a public necessity and is required in the interest of the health, prosperity, safety, and welfare of the people.* (Landmarks Law; emphasis mine)

The Landmarks Preservation Commission is an eleven-member group charged with the Landmarks Law. The mayor appoints everyone, including the chair and vice-chair. The law says that three commissioners must be architects, one must be a historian, one must be a planner, and one (pointlessly) must be "a realtor." Among the eleven, there must be someone from each borough. The Charter does not require any of its commissioners to have professional preservationist training. The chair is the only person on the commission who gets a salary (of course, staff and legal counsel get salaries as well).

Clearly, the City Council did not see the LPC as a quiet place where real estate interests would be "balanced," as recent chairs have suggested as a key role for the LPC. No, the council wanted the LPC to get out there and save the historic city. So what was the Demolition Machine of REBNY to do with this new power player that was meant to ignore "highest and best use" nonsense and instead preserve non-economic values for the benefit of the people? The industry is smart and decided to undermine and rein in the commission if they couldn't get rid of it altogether. There are plenty of ways for REBNY to do that. Here is a list:

- Kneecap the commission within the law itself (as we saw earlier), forcing the city to drop the 400-foot contextual rule around landmarks and impose a rule that only allows the agency to designate properties in three out of thirty-six months.
- Assure by statute that at least one appointee to the commission be a realtor.
- Keep the commission small and underfunded, so it does not have the means to conduct its mission.

- Influence who gets appointed, especially to the top jobs of chair and chief legal counsel, so that no "zealots," "crazies," or "goo-goos" (advocates of clean, uncorrupted government) run the commission.
- Intimidate the commission with constant threats of lawsuits.
- Tinker with its internal procedures and "rules" so that it makes it ever more difficult to function effectively.
- Introduce into the City Council legislation that weakens the LPC or limits its ability to function effectively.
- Flood the firms of the three commission architects that law requires to be on the commission with Big Real Estate design contracts. This forces the three architects to constantly recuse themselves to comply with conflict-of-interest rules. This brilliant flexibility of REBNY also creates some commissioners who are just unwilling to rock the boat of their current and potential clients.
- Infiltrate Community Boards with real estate advocates and lobbyists around areas with high real estate stakes (e.g., Hudson Yards area, or Lower Manhattan).
- Outright bribery, threats, and coercion of individual commissioners.

REBNY's attitude and pugnaciousness toward the commission have varied through time. In the early years (1966–73), the Penn Central law case (over the saving of Grand Central station) was winding its way through the courts with an accusation that the LPC was destroying the railroad's speculative value of its property, a kind of "takings." Although the LPC eventually won the case in 1978, a year into the Koch administration, the many years of legal uncertainty kept the commission cautious about what it would protect so as not to provoke more lawsuits. The city in those days was still in economic crisis, so there were fewer large buildings under development anyway. These considerations meant that Big Real Estate was content for a while to let the underfunded, part-time commission operate in peace since the stakes were low for them. Back then, borough presidents could also easily overturn LPC decisions. This was before Charter Reforms took that power away from borough presidents and gave it to the City Council as a whole.

That said, the early, weak commission still had to face down interference. Beverly Moss Spatt, a chair of the commission and a renowned advocate for the public good, explained in her memoirs how things worked. She served on both the City Planning Commission and then as the second chair of the Landmarks Commission in its early days. She reported the following undated exchange with the famous Roger Starr, the leader of the city's Housing and Urban Development agency and the author of the "let-the-Bronx-burn" idea of "planned shrinkage" of the city. In 1966, Starr had already served for ten years as executive director of the Citizens Housing and Planning Council, which researcher Deborah Wallace describes as "a bogus 'citizens' group' funded and governed by the real-estate industry" (Wallace and Wallace 2017).

The exchange between Spatt and Starr went like this:

SPATT: What are you doing here, Roger?
STARR: I'm trying to undo what you've done.(Moss Spatt 2011)

Spatt had the staff team of experts survey the entire city, producing fat reports for each borough on what was worthy of designation. Later administrations ignored these reports, which eventually got buried. During the subsequent Koch years under Kent Barwick as the third chair of the Landmarks Commission, the LPC had a burst of energy after their Supreme Court win in the Penn Central case. At that point, Big Real Estate's influence became more indirect. Barwick tellingly mentions the following in his memoirs:

In those days, it was understood that there was an absolute prohibition against the designation of any property in Lower Manhattan. . . . That was the Downtown Lower Manhattan Association [a Big Real Estate surrogate organization]. . . . There was a mental bat, this is—don't fuck around here. (Barwick 2011)

How that understanding to leave Lower Manhattan alone came to Barwick is a mystery, but it was not via telepathy. Oral interviews with him suggest that the primary means of communicating mayoral will to the LPC was through Barwick's frequent meetings and discussions with Koch's trusted deputy mayor, Robert Wagner Jr, a powerful politician in his own right. Indeed, Barwick mentioned that the deputy mayor did from time to time ask him "to slow down or moderate or to consider moderating something." Barwick noted that Koch did not personally intervene, but early on conveyed the attitude, "But if I don't agree [with your decisions as chair of the LPC], I'm going to get rid of you." That was a warning all chairs of the LPC would contend with and indicative of the behind-the-scenes control that would serve Big Real Estate well in the coming years.

During the political clubhouse-laden Koch years, the enormous stakes for real estate were the redevelopment and massive towerization of Times Square and the Theater District. In these two projects, in the end, the real estate lobby and theater owners (who did not want landmark designation and were inclined to just sell out) mostly got their way. Tragic demolitions happened, developers got their air rights transferred, and new towers went up, some right on top of old theaters in what is hardly a happy compromise with preservation interests. Later, as the city emerged from the fiscal crisis and boom times returned at the start of the Giuliani administration, the potential decisions of the commission became more of a risk factor for Big Real Estate, and its representatives did not hesitate. As long-serving commissioner Anthony Tung said in his book (written after Koch fired him):

> During my tenure, I was offered bribes, I received anonymous threatening phone calls, and I was coerced by the Mob. In later years, I was frequently cautioned to be more flexible when evaluating those construction projects politically blessed by City Hall. (Tung 2002)

As the city continued to heat up in a building boom, REBNY tried to influence the mayor's selection of both the commission's chair and the legal counsel. REBNY wanted a chair who had a degree in preservation or who was a credible advocate for the historic city, but did not really want a good government true-blue. What they wanted was someone who knew how to "compromise" and "balance interests" and be "flexible." REBNY seems to have gotten their wish with Barwick's successor, Gene Norman, who famously designated extraordinarily little. After that, REBNY may have been less thrilled with the subsequent chair, Laurie Beckelman, who had the nerve to designate (very lightly, with no corner buildings) inside Tribeca South, an area south of Chambers that was off-limits and known to be part of Big Real Estate's plans for what the *Times* called "Wall Street North."

Another problem for Big Real Estate was the original, long-serving legal counsel to the commission. A brilliant attorney, Dorothy Miner had played a key role in winning the Penn Central case on behalf of the city. That lawsuit has been an existential threat to the commission for years. Miner and her colleagues won the suit, making it clear to the entire country that developers did not have a constitutional right to the speculative value of their property. The commission was free to exercise its powers. Miner was renowned as an ardent preservationist and defender of the Landmarks Law. New chairs of the LPC depended on her counsel.

Then arrived Mayor Giuliani. He was utterly uninterested in the historic city as a value to the city. He appointed Jennifer Raab as chair of the LPC. She was a real estate attorney with experience at the South Bronx Development Corporation and cousin to Carl Weisbrod, one of the Big Real Estate's long-term advisors (and future chair of City Planning). During

Raab's reign, she got rid of Miner and brought in a real estate attorney as the LPC's legal counsel. This was Valerie Campbell, who did not stay long. Campbell left the commission to work full-time as an attorney for a REBNY-affiliated law firm and has ever since earned her living advocating for Big Real Estate. Insiders report that Raab and Campbell "sort of stopped doing historic districts" (interview with Simeon Bankoff). In oral interviews, Raab said that she is proudest not of any particular landmark or historic district designations, but of the two modernist insertions to individually Landmarked buildings that she navigated through the commission: the acontextual glass Hearst tower in Midtown and the equally questionable modernist addition of the Morgan Library (McEnaney interview with Raab 2011). See the photo in figure 7.1.

Raab's successor to the commission, Sherida Paulsen, also an ardent fan of modernism, noted this about Raab and the real estate community:

> Jennifer had been a member of the Giuliani inner circle.... Many land use attorneys said they felt very confident in what they were doing because they knew that Joe Rose [chair of the City Planning Commission] and Jennifer Raab talked to each other about things and that there would be no surprises down the road. (Paulsen 2011)

Paulsen explained in her memoirs that she was REBNY's favored appointee to the commission. She eventually became chair. Paulsen recalls how she got the job:

Figure 7.1. The Morgan Library addition. Author's photo.

I was at a meeting with the leaders of the Real Estate Board.... I said to them because I knew they were powerful people in city government, I said, "Look, if there are any opportunities for me to serve in the city government, I'd really love to do that.... So they put my name into the interview committee after Giuliani was elected. (Paulsen 2011)

She was chair during the 9/11 disaster. Her memory of that day illustrates another way Big Real Estate can influence the LPC: privileged access to the chair, access no community group or preservationist group can claim. She recalls getting a phone call on 9/11 from the infamous real estate attorney Sandy Lindenbaum, a man known for twisting the zoning code into developer-friendly knots (see earlier chapters). He wanted to reschedule a meeting with Paulsen (Paulsen 2011). Few, if any, community groups seeking designation for landmarks or historic districts can make that claim that they, like lobbyist Lindenbaum, have the home phone number of the chair in their back pocket.

In 2006, in the *New York Times*, the writer Tom Wolfe accused the commission of excessive timidity against the demolitionist tendencies of big real estate. He argued—correctly—that the LPC had been unwilling to stand up to Big Real Estate for the twenty years before his essay. Preservationist and former employee at the commission Marjorie Pearson also lamented in her book that several commissioners have mostly done the bidding of various mayors (Giuliani, Koch, Bloomberg), focused on the growth machine agenda rather than a preservationist agenda. Cases in point would be Gene Norman, Jennifer Raab, Sherida Paulsen, Robert Tierney, Meenakshi Srinivasan, and Sarah Carroll. For ten years under the Bloomberg administration, Tierney designated quite a few historic districts, but they were small ones, and mostly outside of Manhattan. Notably, he never touched historic district-worthy Williamsburg in Brooklyn, where Bloomberg's team was working on a major upzoning. Several observers joined Pearson in pointing out that the commission, over time, has also begun to defer excessively to the wishes of property owners (who rarely want designation) when deciding whether to designate (Pearson 2010). Ex-chair Laurie Beckelman concurs with this as a growing problem: "As I recall many of the chairmen after me, the designations were more hesitant if the owner didn't want the designation."

So, bit by bit the industry has tried to either undermine the commission, weaken the law, or put the fix in with a pliable chair they have privileged access to. Their final victory took place in the recent case of the Seaport Historic District.

When De Blasio became mayor, he met with the top brass of REBNY, agreed to their agenda, and appointed members of the real estate machine to his close cabinet. His cabinet included Alicia Glen, who had run housing investment funds at Goldman Sachs, and Vicki Been, co-author of anti–historic district academic papers with Ed Glaeser. She was one of the people leading the real estate–funded Furman Center at NYU. But who would chair the Landmarks Commission in a build-baby-build administration? Supporters of the Landmarks Law shuddered when Bill de Blasio, after interviewing many qualified candidates with experience in historic preservation, appointed Meenakshi Srinivasan to chair the Landmarks Commission. She had no interest or experience in historic preservation. Although an architect, she had made her career as chair of the BSA under Bloomberg, where she mostly let developers have their way (see the preceding chapter). And early in Bloomberg's administration, the deputy mayors assembled the many fresh appointees to various commissions for a general debrief on the new administration's priorities. A deputy told attendees to "stand down on historic preservation in the face of the affordable housing crisis." Srinivasan took that policy directive to heart and refrained from controversial or substantial designations in Manhattan, stalling and delaying requests for evaluation of new historic districts, and told staffers that it was time to "take off their preservation hats a little." She did not fight REBNY-sponsored legislation to weaken the Landmarks Commission in the bill known as "Intro 775." At public hearings, she described blithely to City Council how she made politicized and arbitrary judgment calls as to what she would designate, how she made decisions without minutes, without guidelines, and without any of the other commissioners present.

It turned out Srinivasan had eliminated the working committee composed of the other appointed commissioners who used to meet to review, analyze, and triage the 300 or so community and staff-initiated "Requests for Evaluation" (known as RFEs) that arrive in a steady stream at the commission's offices. This committee had long done the important job of looking over the requests and doing an informal triage, sorting them into three piles, "yes, no, and maybe." Landing in the "yes" pile meant that the staff would give the building or district the full research treatment and then send the case to the eleven-member commission for consideration. Landing in the" maybe" pile were those requests that seemed promising but lacked enough information to decide. A commissioner or a staff member might need to physically look at the building and take some pictures. "No" meant no, but applicants were free to try again with a new chair or new mayor or a new set of commissioners. These sorting decisions required the expertise of the appointed commissioners and were the very point of the Landmarks Law. Under Srinivasan, the chair eliminated this committee and made the decisions alone, without consulting any other commissioners, who now had no longer had any idea what the RFE pile looked like. It was like serving under a royal monarch. The RFE decisions became the sole province of the chair. The attorney for the LPC explained it all in a legal brief to a judge, claiming that the chair and the chair alone had "complete and unfettered discretion" to do whatever she wanted without consulting a single other member of the commission. Judges agreed with this farce, bowing to a legal doctrine that said courts should defer discretionary actions to an "expert" regulatory agency who was supposed to know what it was doing.

Srinivasan also came up with a new way to fulfill her anti-landmarking mandate from the administration. She had discovered 100 properties that had been languishing in the "maybe" pile for years, each for a unique set of reasons. Srinivasan decided that she would, in one fell swoop, all by herself, toss all those buildings to the "no" pile. Her idea was sold to the public as an efficiency move but nonetheless generated uproar. Critics of the decision argued that there were many reasons those properties had been languishing, ranging from bureaucratic ineptitude to advocates waiting out obstinate, real-estate beholden city council members who were about to term-limit out of office, thus breathing new life into various requests for landmark designation in their districts. After much pressure and a public campaign from a coalition of preservation organizations, Srinivasan finally agreed to let each of the 100 buildings have its day in court. The press called it the "backlog" controversy. Only twenty-seven buildings in this group of one hundred were eventually designated individual landmarks (Bindelglass 2016).

Srinivasan also routinely rejected historic district requests, without allowing those requests to come to the attention of the full commission (Hubert 2018b; 2018a), all of whom were unaware of the requests. Srinivasan handed out perfunctory rejections of historic district extension requests made for Tribeca, Chinatown, Crown Heights, and Lefferts Gardens. She greenlighted the shrinking of the proposed West End Avenue Historic District at the request of the real estate crowd, cutting out the lots that fronted Broadway. The shrinking allowed for greater real estate profit making in the higher-zoned Broadway corridor.

REBNY and its allies weaponized the backlog controversy to provide justification for a new law to change the rules of the game for designating landmarks. The backlog supposedly proved that the LPC was incompetent, inefficient, and overreaching. The Real Estate Board of New York first made the case for new legislation in its white papers of 2013 (REBNY 2013b). After publishing the papers, REBNY then convinced two key City Council members to write and sponsor the new legislation: David Greenfield and Peter Koo. Both were members of the powerful Committee on Land Use of the City Council. Greenfield was its chair. Both had received substantial real estate donations in their election campaigns, as had the co-sponsor of the bill, Melissa Mark-Viverito, then Speaker of the City Council. Greenfield described himself to the *Real Deal* as "as a diplomat, bridging the divide between the council's progressive wing and the real estate industry." Greenfield's then chief of staff, Matt Viggiano (who later went to work as a vice president for the lobbying firm Kasirer with many big real estate clients), authored a report for the council called "Landmarks for Future."[1] In it, he cited the REBNY white papers described above and Glaeser's "Hindering Growth" paper, outlining Glaeser's ideas as if they were fact, having clearly not worked through the details of the paper. He wrote:

> Designation has a more negative economic effect when the area's zoning would allow considerably more development than currently exists. Additionally, construction activity falls after designation. (New York City Council Land Use Committee 2016)

The bill in question imposed a draconian one-year deadline for the bureaucratic process of landmarking an individual building and a two-year deadline for the process involved in the designation of a historic district. The bill also created a controversial new rule: If the LPC did not designate a building or neighborhood within the allotted period, five years must pass before the LPC can reconsider the building or district.[2] The head of the Historic Districts Council pointed out that over half of the landmarks in the city had taken more than two years to designate. As described earlier, some districts in Harlem took forty-four years to get designated. None of them would have become historic districts under the new rules. Councilman Ben Kallos was among the few opponents. He argued: "In the name of streamlining the landmarking process, this bill will actually encourage delays and stalling tactics and result in sites that merit serious considering for landmarks designation being demolished" (Kallos 2015). His opposition—and those of many others—was to no avail. The bill, named "775," passed.

With Srinivasan at the helm and an anti-landmarking legislative victory under its belt, REBNY decided to push further and tinker with the internal rules of the Landmarks Commission. Under the innocuous rationale of simplifying bureaucracy (notably, nobody mentioned the better idea of simplifying the internal rules of the notoriously corrupt Department of Buildings), REBNY got its allied council members (like Greenfield or Margaret Chin who depended on real estate funding for their campaigns or who were sympathetic to the REBNY growth machine agenda) to agree on the important task of overhauling the internal rules and procedures of the Landmarks Preservation Commission. While nobody objects to making bureaucracies more efficient, there were several major red flags. Primarily, no preservation organizations were invited to the process of coming up with rule changes. Nobody, in fact, knew who was writing the new rules and who had authored the document with the proposed new rules. Studying them, I find it is not hard to imagine the guiding hand of REBNY. For example, one rule was a reduction of public input—meaning fewer opportunities for the public to testify and a physical limit on how much digital space the commission's website would offer the public who did want to submit testimony. Another proposed rule was to eliminate the public's right to physically view drawings of changes to buildings that the commission used to study applications for changes to a landmark. The public (including specialists on staff of the Historic Districts Council) had for years been able to come to the commission to study design posters called "architectural boards" that the LPC puts on display at the commission for its own staff and the public to study prior to preparing testimony for a hearing. REBNY did not want that.

The historian of New York City's Landmarks Law, Anthony Wood, objected to the rule changes, noting that "taking more actions out of the public process and moving them to behind the scenes for staff decision-making further restricts the public's ability to have input, an essential aspect of the Landmarks Law" (Hubert 2018a). No matter, said the president of REBNY at the time, the new rules "will make it easier for owners to maintain their landmarked properties and permit the commission to devote more time to evaluating which buildings warrant landmark designations moving forward" (Banks 2018). The parties agreed to some unhappy compromises. For example, board materials would henceforth be uploaded to digital space instead of being made available for in-person viewing (Landmark West! 2018).

Srinivasan's slow-walking of RFEs and sympathy for the real estate community finally so outraged preservationists that they finally united to call for her resignation (Corcoran 2018). Srinivasan denied that the call for her resignation had any effect, but a mere one week later she resigned from the commission to become a full-time lobbyist for Big Real Estate at the notorious firm of Kramer Levin, a lobbying firm that sits on the board of governors of REBNY. Replacing Srinivasan was someone that preservationists hoped would be their dream chair: a long-serving staffer who had an M.A. degree in historic preservation, Sarah Carroll. Alas, they were only dreaming, for Carroll ended up reigning over Big Real Estate's final capture of the commission. That took place under her watch over the Battle of the Seaport and is the story of the next section.

The Seaport Historic District is all that remains of a small, human-scale, small neighborhood of three- to seven-story buildings from the nineteenth century that front the former Fulton Fish Market. It sits cheek by jowl with the high-rise Financial District and a Mitchell-Lama housing complex. Much of it had been demolished under urban renewal plans. LPC Chair Beverly Moss Spatt designated the district in 1977 under Mayor Abe Beame, back when New York City was falling apart, Wall Street firms fled the city, and historic preservation revitalized the city's economy. The historic district includes a parking lot at 250 Water Street, a mercury-filled spot that once housed a thermometer factory. The Milstein real estate family bought the parking lot in 1979 and proposed a new tower. The LPC said no to that. Milstein tried again in 1983, 1984, 1986, and 1988, and the LPC always said no. In 1991, the Milsteins got lucky; the LPC finally approved an eleven-story building for the site, but the Milsteins rejected that as too small and tried again in 1997 to get approval for a thirty-two-story tower. The LPC said no yet again. Realizing that Milstein would never give up, Seaport community groups got together and proposed a rezoning of the area to put a modest height limit over the district. The City Council approved that zoning change in 2002. The *New York Times* reported on the community's zoning proposal as it approached the council:

> The Milsteins say their [32 story] project is a test of the mayor's resolve to rebuild downtown, increase housing and encourage risk-taking developers. . . . The Milsteins have enlisted the Real Estate Board of New York and hired a public relations specialist, George Arzt. . . . Many of the important principals know each other well.

Mr. Doctoroff [Bloomberg's deputy for economic development] was once a partner of Howard Milstein in their ownership of the Islanders Hockey team. . . . But the Milstein camp suspects that the Bloomberg administration will approve the [community] rezoning effort because it does not wish to tangle with Sheldon Silver [State Assembly Speaker and powerbroker later convicted of corruption]. (Bagli 2003)

Whatever Sheldon Silver did or whatever he promised Mayor Bloomberg and his team about a future deal elsewhere in exchange for letting the community have a height limit in the Seaport Historic District, we will never know, but Silver was at the height of his powers and gave the community a rare win: a height "limit" of 250 feet. Milstein sold the site in disgust, and a few years later it ended up in the hands of another developer, the Howard Hughes Corporation.

Hughes had been investing heavily in sites all around the Seaport, creating controversies along the way within their general idea to towerize the entire area and reinvent it as new hyper-gentrified "Seaport District," a version of Bloomberg's fantasy "Seaport City" that Bloomberg's team had floated a few years earlier as a way to infill the East River and build new towers. Part of the new scheme Hughes proposed was to transfer a pile of unused air rights from one corner of the historic Seaport to a different, far corner where they now owned their disputed parking lot, in violation of how air rights transfers are supposed to take place. The city's pro-demolition agency, the Economic Development Corporation (EDC), helped the transfer of leases of city-owned sites to Hughes to make this plan easier for Hughes. One academic wrote that "the EDC seemed to be handing over the Seaport to the HHC" (Lindgren 2014, 296). An EDC official who worked with Howard Hughes on these transfers, Ashley Denis, later left the EDC and took a job as a lobbyist for Kasirer, one of the firms Howard Hughes later hired to lobby the LPC for its interests.

The community organized in opposition to the taller-still tower that Hughes wanted. The city responded by creating a working group that met behind closed doors under the management of then Borough President Gale Brewer and then Council member Margaret Chin. The object of the task force was to find a way to silence the community and override the zoning, get the air rights transferred, and build the tower, which by this point had grown to a proposed 600 feet, well over the existing 250-foot height limit. Of course, the task force had no power or authority, but it duly sent various recommendations to Howard Hughes. Hughes dug in stubbornly for its 600 feet and decided to work behind the scenes with the Landmarks Commission to make the upzoning request happen. Hughes hired top-gun lobbyists who work for Big Real Estate and are deeply embedded in the REBNY ecosystem (Kasirer, de Milly, Kramer Levin, and Fried Frank). Throughout 2020, Hughes and the lobbyists held at least eleven (according to FOIL documents) secretive, behind-the-scenes meetings with the new LPC chair (Sarah Carroll), the commission's legal staff, and with various deputy mayors, including Deputy Mayor for Housing Vicki Been. None of the meetings with lobbyists and Hughes Corporation were open to the public. It is remarkable that the LPC did not hold a single meeting with the community coalition that had emerged. Rather, the LPC held the community at bay and ignored them.

The secretive team of lobbyists, the Hughes Corporation, and the LPC staff came up with a public relations strategy: Give an endowment to the Economic Development Corporation, which would agree to fund the yearly operating budget of the small, failing Seaport Museum, a sweet little museum known even among its supporters for how few visitors it had. The public relations line was, "If we give all this cash to the cute little museum, you must let us build the giant tower inside the historic district in defiance of the current zoning limits. If you oppose us, you oppose the cute little museum." This public relations sideshow, irrelevant in law and practice to the workings of the LPC, did split the community, which was ugly to see.

The culmination of all this behind the scenes lobbying and joint planning with the Landmarks Commission was an internal meeting called by the Landmarks Commission's legal counsel, Mark Silberman, to hold a "practice public hearing" ahead of the real public hearing on the matter (see image of the memo in Figure 7.2). The idea of a "practice hearing" was to ensure everyone got their scripts right about the need to save the cute little failing museum by the bizarre means of giving Hughes a giant tower in the middle of a historic district. On the distribution list for that "practice hearing" were:

- Five Landmarks Commission staff
- Landmarks Commission's legal counsel who authored the memo (Silberman)
- Member of and former chair of RENBY's Zoning Committee and lobbyist for Big Real Estate at the REBNY-member firm of Fried Frank (Karnovsky)

- Two lobbyists from Kasirer under contract to developer Howard Hughes, one of whom had been land-use advisor to Council member Margaret Chin, whose district includes the Seaport (Matt Viggiano)
- The founding partner of De Milly, a public relations and lobbying firm with big real estate clients, now under contract with Howard Hughes
- President of Tri-State at the Howard Hughes Corporation (Scherl)
- The CEO of the failing Seaport Museum (Boulware)
- Multiple people from Skidmore, Owens, and Merrill, the architectural firm that Hughes had hired
- An employee of the architectural firm owned by Landmarks Commissioner Michael Devonshire (Rouillard)
- A Hughes lobbyist from the REBNY-supported firm of Kramer Levin, one who just happened to be the former legal counsel for the Landmarks Commission (Campbell)

They all practiced their lines.

At the real public hearing a week later, the LPC voted in the tower and echoed the Hughes public relations line about financing forever the little, failing museum with few visitors.

With the writing of that memo and the holding of that practice hearing, REBNY had triumphed, finally realizing its fifty-five-year dream. It had attained the complete capture of its arch-nemesis, the Landmarks Preservation Commission. Who cares if the chair has an M.A. in historic preservation if under her watch REBNY takes over and runs the show behind the scenes? That is the very definition of regulatory capture.

The Attack on SoHo and NoHo Historic Districts

SoHo and NoHo are two world-renowned historic districts in Manhattan containing eye-popping cast-iron manufacturing and commercial architecture of the nineteenth century. They are unique neighborhoods, mostly six stories in height with a smattering of much taller historic buildings on the Broadway corridor. The neighborhoods are really all one unit and have a unique sense of place found nowhere else in the world. Despite REBNY's claim that such neighborhoods are frozen in amber, some sixty new buildings have come up in SoHo since 2000, most of them successful examples of infill architecture in parking lots that were part of the historic district. Notably, both SoHo and NoHo contain many charming examples

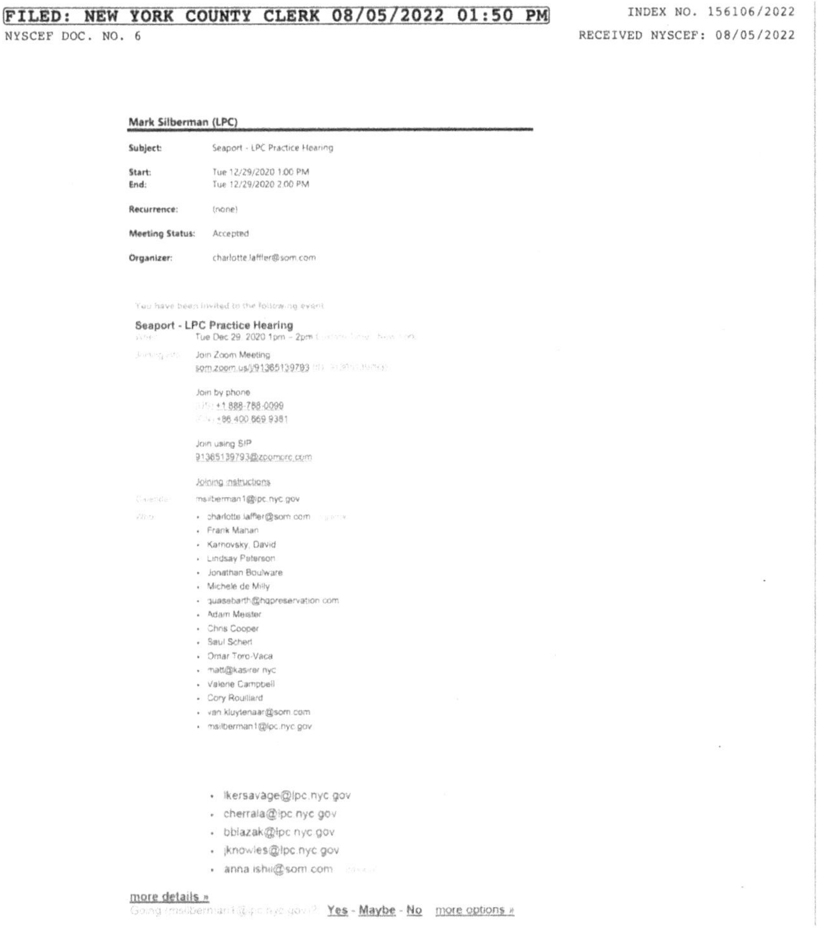

FILED: NEW YORK COUNTY CLERK 08/05/2022 01:50 PM
NYSCEF DOC. NO. 6

INDEX NO. 156106/2022
RECEIVED NYSCEF: 08/05/2022

Mark Silberman (LPC)

Subject: Seaport - LPC Practice Hearing

Start: Tue 12/29/2020 1:00 PM
End: Tue 12/29/2020 2:00 PM

Recurrence: (none)

Meeting Status: Accepted

Organizer: charlotte.laffler@som.com

You have been invited to the following event.

Seaport - LPC Practice Hearing

Tue Dec 29, 2020 1pm – 2pm

Join Zoom Meeting
som.zoom.us/j/91365139793

Join by phone
+1 888-788-0099
+86 400 669 9381

Join using SIP
91365139793@zoomcrc.com

Joining instructions

msilberman1@lpc.nyc.gov

- charlotte.laffler@som.com
- Frank Mahan
- Karnovsky, David
- Lindsay Peterson
- Jonathan Boulware
- Michele de Milly
- quasebarth@hqpreservation.com
- Adam Meister
- Chris Cooper
- Saul Scherl
- Omar Toro-Vaca
- matt@kasirer.nyc
- Valerie Campbell
- Cory Rouillard
- van.kluytenaar@som.com
- msilberman1@lpc.nyc.gov

- lkersavage@lpc.nyc.gov
- cherrala@lpc.nyc.gov
- bblazak@lpc.nyc.gov
- jknowles@lpc.nyc.gov
- anna.ishii@som.com

more details »

Yes - Maybe - No   more options »

Figure 7.2. Memo from the LPC Legal Counsel inviting lobbyists and Big Real Estate CEOs to a "practice hearing" before the public hearing. Copy provided by Joanne Gorman and Mark Kramer of the Seaport Coalition, who obtained this from a Freedom of Information Law request.

of one-story buildings tossed up in the 1930s during the Great Depression so that the owners could pay their property taxes. These have been converted to retail use, as have many of the indoor parking lots from the 1950s. They are among the most successful neighborhoods in the world, although they suffer from excessive, uncontrolled traffic in and out of the Holland Tunnel, the absence of grocery stores, and too much love by tourists and fashion fans from around the world who pack the neighborhood on the weekends to shop. Their beauty is great and success so obvious that it is hard to imagine that Robert Moses once tried to put a highway right through the area.

Due to special artist protections for live/work art space embedded in the zoning code for the neighborhood, the area is still home to many working artists. These are the same who provoked the renaissance of these neighborhoods into the successful urban places they became, even before Margot Gayle's campaign for their protection took place (Gayle and Gayle 1998). These protections have allowed artists to survive in SoHo and NoHo despite the transformation of the neighborhood into a stomping ground for the financial industry families who like the big loft spaces and want to walk to the Financial District for work. At Lafayette Street and along Canal Street, SoHo morphs into Chinatown to its east and into Tribeca historic district to the south. The northern and eastern borders of NoHo morph seamlessly into the East Village historic districts.

At three corners of the two neighborhoods (the northeast corner of NoHo, and the southeast and southwest corners of SoHo) lie a tangle of small buildings around three different parking lots of varying size. Two of these are owned by Edison Properties, the parking lot king of New York, who is a member of the board of governors of REBNY. Edison's business model is to buy cheap during recessionary periods, sit on the parking lots for a long as possible, then sell out in boom time to a tower developer. The Gutman family owns the business, and it is a second-generation business, meaning the kids want out of Daddy's boring business. And there we have a problem. Were Edison to develop the properties in the current "contextual" zoning of SoHo and NoHo historic districts, they'd be limited to six to eight stories just like the other sixty new buildings that had been built within the SoHo Cast Iron District. Darn it, thought Edison's C-suite, if the sites could only be up upzoned for towers, we'd get richer because upzoned properties would be worth much more in the speculative real estate market! So that is what they wanted to do. But how to change the restrictive zoning, in a historic district no less?

There is no proof that Edison went to the Manhattan borough president (Gale Brewer at the time) and the council member (Margaret Chin) to request a zoning change, but who else would have asked for one? Lost to history is why and at whose request Brewer and Chin agreed to launch a micromanaged, pretend "participatory" community planning process under the bogus pretext of "fixing" the "outdated" zoning of SoHo and NoHo, which as many pointed out in the public meetings, wasn't broken. To manage the inevitable community opposition to the fake-community process to upzone Edison's parking lots, Brewer paid for a professional facilitator whose job it would be to shut up, silence, or just isolate and micromanage community members during the meetings. Those meetings consisted of hand-picked, heavily curated advisory council members who would go through what Brewer dubbed a "Community Planning Process." The facilitator she hired was also charged with the task of writing a heavily edited report at the end, recommending changes that suited Edison and another property owner on the Chinatown border who owned the parking lot in the eastern end of SoHo.

The community meetings were a mess, but it didn't matter. Brewer and Chin launched the first one with an inconclusive workshop that was so poorly managed that infuriated marginalized residents shouted questions at the hapless facilitator and demanded to know who had asked for the rezoning. Residents got no answers. The meetings rolled on for months, even after residents withdrew and created their own advisory group. The facilitator wrote up the recommendations in a report called "Envision SoHo/NoHo" (Manhattan Borough President's Office 2019). The report contained vague recommendations to protect artist live/workspaces and to modify the current mixed-use zoning to allow for bigger footprint retail. It also called for further "community involvement and transparency . . . to allow time for residents and other stakeholders to contemplate the proposed recommendations." Hidden behind coded phrases were upzoning recommendations such as the goal to "ensure a balance of providing new housing with existing built landscape and historic character" and a goal to "identify opportunities for infill development." At a follow-up public meeting at the Community Board, Brewer's office confirmed: "There is no plan for a ULURP [meaning a Uniform Land Use Review Procedure for zoning changes] anytime in the near future." A city planner then abruptly grabbed the mic and stated there would be "no more questions." Mayor de Blasio later said to a journalist that there wasn't enough time left in his administration to get a complicated and time-consuming rezoning passed (Deffenbaugh 2020).

Was it over? Had Edison backed off? After nine months of silence, residents thought maybe the answer was Yes. So, it was shocking to the public when the mayor unexpectedly announced the start of the Uniform Land Use Review Procedure (ULURP) for a massive upzoning of SoHo/NoHo, one that indisputably benefited the owners of the three parking lots at the three corners of the neighborhoods since the upzoning gave the highest allotment of new building space in the whole plan to the three parking lot sites. It also threw in an inexplicable (and punishing) financial fine for anyone who was using an artist's live/workspace without official proof that they were artists. SoHo residents had not voted for Council member Chin and many saw fines as an attempted punishment for the community's activism against Chin. In any case, it was to be mayor's last big upzoning push before he left office. In a predictable move, a surrogate for Big Real Estate, the Citizens Housing and Planning Council (CHPC), came out in favor of the rezoning with an op-ed in the *City Limits* blog, a space that promotes affordable housing deals. An executive from Edison sat on CHPC's board at the time, which happens to be a board packed with REBNY notables, including the law and lobbying firm of Kramer Levin Naftalis. Kramer Levin even managed a print and TV media blitz in support of the upzoning. Connecting the dots, it is probably that the upzoning was suddenly resurrected during the global pandemic because time was running out for Edison Properties to develop their lots under a mayoral regime known to be sweet on big developers. It certainly did not happen because of "anti-police protests sparked by the killing of George Floyd" as Deputy Mayor Vicki Been claimed. The mayor told the *New York Post* that the city should upzone wealthy neighborhoods in Manhattan to make them more diverse. Been went even further to say that "the pandemic and the movement for racial justice make clear that all neighborhoods must pull their weight to provide safe, affordable housing options" (Marsh 2020a). This echoed her earlier report in which she said upzonings should take place in the already dense historic core of Manhattan and Brooklyn because that is where all the "amenity-rich neighborhoods" were. Given that you can't assign racial quotas to housing, it is forever unclear how Been and De Blasio would accomplish the envisaged racial diversity by flooding a historic district with market-rate luxury towers.

Community response to Been and De Blasio was quick. Sean Sweeney, director of the SoHo Alliance, told the *New York Post*, "He's playing his class card, his race card and that's despicable. They're trying to play this that we don't want affordable housing which is completely wrong. We want affordable housing, we want diversity, but it's really disgusting that they're introducing the race card and it's equally disingenuous to assume that more minorities will win a housing lottery that's totally random" (Marsh 2020b). The community also came up with a better, alternative zoning plan that the city simply ignored.

But Been and De Blasio's racial dog-whistling had its effect as the hearing process. The official review process for the rezoning ground on. Political clubs mustered testimonies. There were Twitter fights. Open New York, REBNY's grassroots posse of thuggishly behaving activists, got involved. They showed up in groups at the public hearings and accused SoHo and NoHo residents of being white and rich and racist for not wanting to towerize their neighborhoods. Vicki Been, Margaret Chin, and Gale Brewer justified their support for the plan on the basis that towerization would provide affordable housing. The press got involved, and the *New York Times* came out and said, yes, towerization was the only way to shoehorn in affordable housing in SoHo (Hughes 2021). Anyone who opposed it was deemed a rich white racist NIMBY. Open New York members bragged on Twitter that they had talked Vicki Been and the mayor into upzoning SoHo as a test case of "breaking" historic districts." That group's founder, real estate entrepreneur Ben Carlos Thypin, issued a bizarre call to action to his followers on Twitter on October 7, 2019, one that equated this fight with World War II:

> In the war to desegregate New York's exclusionary neighborhoods, today is D-Day and OPENNY is leading the charge to cobblestoned Omaha Beach. Join us and tell your electeds which side of history you are on. (Ben Carlos Thypin, October 7, 2019, Tweet)

Politicians Scott Stringer and Maya Wiley (both then running for mayor) then lined up to agree that SoHo needed to be upzoned. For the record, Stringer had long worked with a staffer who went on to work for Edison Properties. The coup de grace was a comment from mayoral candidate Eric Adams (now mayor) who was unabashed about taking real estate money for his campaign. In response to a question from Village Independent Democrats about his housing platform, Adams wrote this logic-defying paragraph.

> ADD HOUSING—FOR EVERYONE—IN WEALTHY NEIGHBORHOODS [caps original to response]: For years, our rezonings focused on adding apartments in lower-income areas—which often just led to higher-income people moving in, making communities less affordable and often forcing out longtime residents. Instead, we will build in wealthier areas with a high quality of life, allowing lower- and middle-income New Yorkers to move in by adding affordable housing and eliminating the community preference rule in those areas, which prevents many New Yorkers from living in desirable neighborhoods. (Adams 2020)

Village Preservation's board entered the fray with a slew of factual reports, trying to add some sanity to the discussion. They pointed out that many assumptions the City and Open New York made in the zoning proposal were literally "false premises." For example, they explained that not all residents of SoHo were white and rich, and that SoHo was socioeconomically diverse, that it had existing affordable housing, that the upzoning plan would not create a significant amount of affordable housing or have a trickle-down effect on housing prices in SoHo, and that the plan would fail to create a more racially diverse neighborhood. But facts and logic didn't matter; the upzoning team howled a public relations rhetoric derivative of Edward Glaeser, weaponized to ram the upzoning through. Nonetheless, some of the facts Village Preservation pushed out were:

- 28.4 percent of the population in the upzoned area is Asian. If the "community preference" for rehousing residents in the new buildings was abandoned—as proposed by the city—the neighborhood would get whiter, and the percentage of Asians and other minority groups would go down, not up.
- 12.5 percent of the current population in the rezoning area is below the poverty line; 39 percent have household incomes less than $75,000 and 65 percent (the majority) have incomes less than $150,000. Only 25 percent of the area's residents have incomes over $200,000, a percentage that would go up to 75 percent if the upzoned area gets redeveloped as the city wants. It is a hyper-gentrification plan, not a diversity plan.
- Only 23 percent of residents of SoHo and NoHo in the upzoned area own their own homes, with an average price of $1.5 million. Under the rezoning, the new developments would be 75 percent owner-occupied, carrying an average price of $6.437 million, making the city's claims of diversity goals absurd.
- 79.4 percent of the new tower developments will end up as commercial spaces (it is the choice of the developer to build commercial or residential in an upzoned space) without any housing whatsoever.
- The plan does not require any affordable housing at all. It is merely *an option* for whoever redevelops the parking lots.
- "Assuming that developers follow the zoning incentives in the City plan and build commercial . . . the number of affordable units that will be created will be only between 68–103, rather than the 330–498 units the city currently projects" (Village Preservation 2021a).
- The upzoning will create an incentive to demolish existing, historic, low-rise four- to six-story buildings with rent-stabilized apartments in them, to be replaced with tower buildings that have few, or even zero affordable units (Village Preservation 2021b).

The upzoning of SoHo and NoHo passed the City Council, although the punitive tax against people irregularly occupying artist live/workspaces was later reduced by Christopher Marte, the new council member who replaced Margaret Chin.

DEMONIZING HISTORIC DISTRICTS · 247

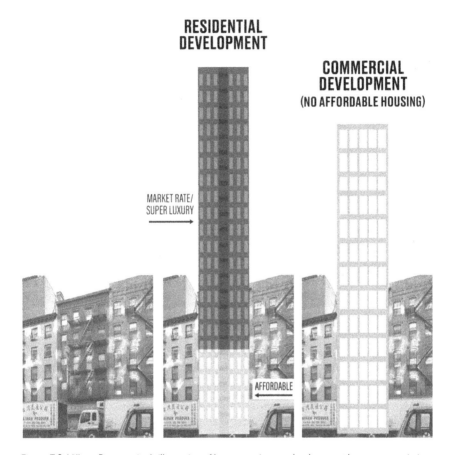

Figure 7.3. Village Preservation's illustration of how upzoning can lead to a net loss or zero gain in affordable units. Image provided by Village Preservation.

Hiding behind a flag filled with popular slogans like "tax the rich" and "the movement for racial justice," it looks like the zeal of New York City government for upzoning SoHo and NoHo has nothing to do with the disturbing facts that Village Preservation presented, facts that deeply challenge the city's Glaeser-style narrative. This suggests that the real agenda was to find a way to break the contextual zoning in a historic district using a new—and blatantly false—red herring as justification: racial equity. The irony is rich. Recall that in the Bloomberg years, Dan Doctoroff and Edward Glaeser argued that the city needed to upzone and create luxury towers to realize the vision of a "luxury city" with richer (whiter) people benefiting, which would be good for the city's tax revenue. Then, in the early De Blasio years, the only way to build affordable housing was also to upzone for the same demographic that Bloomberg wanted, but this time with a few affordable housing units that would come in through the modest Mandatory Inclusionary Housing requirement. Now, suddenly, the forces of Big Real Estate were offering up racial equity and justice as justification for the exact same policies.

Deputy Mayor Vicky Been argued that the city must build even taller in the historic core of the city for racial equity reasons. In her 2020 policy report called "Where We Live Now," Been describes wealthy neighborhoods in Manhattan as "well-resourced" and "high amenity" places and concludes that is where new construction ought to go, despite the reality that Manhattan is the densest county in the country. Note that both Been and REBNY define "well-resourced" neighborhoods as those closest to the best schools, to well-managed public parks like Central Park, to large grocery stores, and a short commute to office tower work in the Central Business Districts. In her report, Been advocates building more towers in Manhattan to allow low-income people to move to Manhattan and enjoy these same "amenities." Yet in the same report, low-income residents of Brooklyn and Queens told their focus group leaders that they had no desire to move, and by the way, why couldn't their current neighborhoods have good parks, good schools, decent grocery stores, and a convenient subway stop? (New York City Department of Housing Preservation and Development 2018). This is befuddling. Rather than create public goods that make all neighborhoods "well-resourced," Been claims the upzoning and towerization will result in more Black and Brown low-income people moving into hyper-dense Manhattan, starting with the upzoning of SoHo and NoHo. It will also, defying credibility, result in "racial equity." Mayor Adams echoes her logic.

Adding housing is fine if there is someplace to build it. In 2013, the entire technocracy of the city, including Vicki Been, was pointing out in tented workshops on Canal Street prior to De Blasio's swearing in, *that there was no place to build in Manhattan* and that it *was cheaper to get buildable space in the less dense outer boroughs*. And what happened to once common ideas about investing in low-income neighborhoods so that they become "high amenity" places?

This new policy approach of Been and Adams gives us a lot to think about: What is fair housing? Why is building housing in low-income neighborhoods considered a terrible thing and a nuisance by the residents themselves? Is it because it towerizes a neighborhood with mostly luxury units and creates immense displacement pressure? Why does Open New York conflate the idea of breaking historic districts with a fight against the Nazis? (Isn't this just extremism?) And which socioeconomic class in the city must pull how much weight, using Been's phrase? As every budget specialist has pointed out in the press, the gentry class is already pulling the weight of paying immense taxes into the city's budget every year. Moreover, the SoHo and NoHo narrative came with a separate ethical consideration: Should rich people be allowed to congregate through market self-selection in certain neighborhoods of New York City? And if they do, should municipal government engage in social engineering to break the party up, so to speak? Consider the idea turned upside down. If low-income Bangladeshis congregate in a neighborhood of New York like Jackson Heights, should we social engineer things to break up their party as well?

We need a bit of history to get a handle on this. In 1968, Congress passed the Fair Housing Act prohibiting discrimination concerning the sale, rental, and financing of housing based on race, religion, national origin, sex, (and as amended) handicap, and family status. Under Obama, a new rule about how to apply the act came into being: Anyone getting federal money for housing had to figure out local barriers to fair housing and present a plan to correct them. Many towns, including New York City, figured that the best way to comply with the Obama rule was to put some affordable housing into a "high amenity neighborhood." City managers can do this easily in the suburbs and in places like Chester County, Pennsylvania, or El Paso County in Colorado. There, one can still find space to build and get rid of exclusionary lot size zoning (like only 5-acre lots for McMansions), and there is also the possibility of eliminating small-town and suburban zoning restrictions on small houses, duplexes, and town houses. This is not the case for Manhattan. Manhattan was already built out in 1930, mostly with affordable tenement housing. When we export the suburban and small-town solution to the Fair Housing rule to New York City, we run into the befuddling problem that since 1929 at least, there is no place to build in the historic core of the city without demolishing something first. Last, why hyper-densify what is already excessively dense? Why not create high-amenity neighborhoods all over the city and enact rules that avoid hyper-gentrification and prevent displacement in the first place?

Summary and Moving Forward

What we have learned in this chapter is that the empirical economic data and model in Glaeser and Been's "Hindering Growth" paper do not tell the anti–historic district story that the authors long to tell. Nonetheless, the real estate industry weaponized their arguments to attack historic districts in New York. What everyone missed, however, is that even Glaeser's numbers suggest an alternative narrative that would get the trickle-down supply-siders' knickers in a twist: Historic districts are in hot demand, and the market is signaling that builders and planners are undersupplying great neighborhoods, not individual housing "units." This is a fascinating problem for urban planners. The signal says: Create the historic districts of the future; create neighborhoods that people want to live in, not merely endure. Alas, Big Real Estate no longer knows how to supply beautiful urban neighborhoods. That fact is itself a type of market failure.

Solving market failure of this type requires the opposite of unleashing developers to build hyper-density projects. It requires a different kind of zoning—form-based codes—that provide more predictability in the streetscape. We need policies that result in the incremental construction of new, beautiful neighborhoods at similar levels of beauty, scale, and density outside the already built-out historic core. This needs to happen both incrementally as modest sites become available as well as on the rare larger sites that the city can get hold of. Shock-and-awe upzoning will not get us there.

This argument is not a rejection of more construction of affordable housing. Rather, it is an argument about what we build and where, and where we need to stay our hand. Building great new neighborhoods will require incentives and direct funding streams to get developers away from the present, zoning-code-induced gold rush that makes developers salivate at more high-rise condo construction all over Manhattan, such as they did in SoHo. It requires more thoughtful policy and a revolution in city planning.

We've also seen in this chapter how there has been an intellectual and policy attack on historic districts. That attack has been successful, to New York City's ultimate loss. We have witnessed REBNY finally capturing the Landmarks Preservation Commission, defanging it and controlling it from within. And we have seen how irrational claims of racial equity were weaponized to "break" the contextual zoning of the NoHo and SoHo Historic Districts, a process that ignored the great urbanity that was already present in those neighborhoods. What we have witnessed is not Glaeser's much-hyped *Triumph of the City* but the Triumph of Big Real Estate.

Chapter 8

The Architecture of Rupture and Nihilism

Fuck context.
—Rem Koolhaas, *Small, Medium, Large, Extra-Large*

Contextualism is an opiate for the masses.
—Vishaan Chakrabarti, cited by Stephen Jacob Smith, in "Jed Walentas Plants a Tree (or Two) in Williamsburg," *The Observer* (blog), March 4, 2013

The role of art or architecture might be just to remind people that everything wasn't all right.
—Architect Peter Eisenman, in debate with Christopher Alexander, in *Katarxis*, 1982

The ideal of not pleasing is fundamental to modern art and modern criticism. . . . Contextualism . . . has led our architecture into the deadest of ends.
—Herbert Muschamp, ex-architecture critic for the *New York Times*, in "Measuring Buildings without a Yardstick," *New York Times*, July 22, 2001, and John Silber, *The Architecture of the Absurd: How Genius Disfigured a Practical Art*

If it doesn't make you feel desperately, crushingly alone, it's probably not a piece of prize-winning contemporary architecture.
—Nathan Robinson, editor of *Current Affairs*, in "Why You Hate Contemporary Architecture," by Adrian Rennix and Nathan J. Robinson, October 31, 2017

THE QUOTES ABOVE ILLUSTRATE THE PROBLEM: Modernist architecture is snobbishly hostile to non-architects and opposed to the existing context of a city. By modernist architecture I means all its variants: postmodernism,

252 · THE ARCHITECTURE OF RUPTURE AND NIHILISM

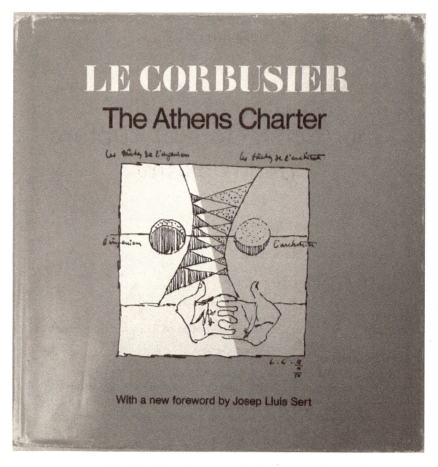

Figure 8.1. The cover of Le Corbusier's CIAM-sponsored book, *The Athens Charter* (1943), the founding bible of the modernist movement. Author's photo.

parametricism, brutalism, deconstructionism, and whatever Jean Nouvel calls himself. I understand that criticizing modernist architecture may be interpreted as quixotic. You're tilting at windmills, my friends say; modernist architects have taken over the world; nothing to be done but avert one's gaze to avoid the pain their buildings inflict on us. Yet I criticize anyway, as have many before me,[1] for the architectural crimes of modernist architecture against the city are too many to ignore. Of course, I admire many stand-alone sculptural buildings by members of team modernism, and I like modernist interior design, painting, and sculpture (of the size visible in museums and galleries). Yet rarely do I admire modernist architecture in urban settings where the goal is to impose a single person's view of the world on the rest of us, destroy and replace the city's pre-1920 context, and sow discord, chaos, disharmony, nihilism, incongruity, and anxiety. This destruction of context takes place under the architects' arrogant, misguided assumption that they are "genius artists" whose laughable self-imposed avant-garde duty is to lead us dumb peasants into their idea of the future.

Modernist architects share a bizarre quasi-religious belief that architectural styles other than their own are "dead." Also, as Chapter 1 pointed out with photos, adepts of modernism have dug themselves into a profoundly anti-urban, anti-street design philosophy that is ruinous for cities that have any historic fabric left (as opposed to places like Beijing, Houston, or Oklahoma City that decided to demolish their history completely). Modernist architects have also created a set of pompous, self-serving myths to justify their anti-contextual ideology: the myth of the genius artist engaged in art rather than craft; the myth that certain World Great Architectural Men embody a mystical "Spirit of the Epoch"; the myth that modernism is politically progressive rather than what it really is: a handmaiden to corporate capitalism. There is also the myth that nostalgia is evil, and the myth that height is glorious, inevitable, and without cost. Do you hate them yet?

Although they seem to have won the day, we don't have to be passive victims of their architectural hubris and mythmaking. We can fight back. Ayn Rand's arrogant modernist architect-hero of her novel *The Fountainhead* asks, "The point is, who will stop me?" The answer, I hope, will be those who read this chapter. First let's look at some definitions, do a critical review of what modernist architectural ideology is all about, and discuss critiques and myths of modernism.

The Fuck the Context Problem—and Some Definitions

The place to start is by understanding the words "context" and "integrity" and what it means when those words get combined into the phrase "integrity of context." This helps us understand the related and important idea of a "sense of place." "Context" in urban design is exactly what you think of instinctively: the visual character of how a place, a block, a neighborhood, and more broadly, a city, is woven together physically. The materials used in making the buildings are key elements in creating context. Building scale, materials, mix of uses, natural features, trees, street design, sidewalks, window size and shape, the architectural styles on display, and the small business environment (or its absence) on the ground floors—all combine to create the unique "context" of a neighborhood. Some contexts are stunning and widely acclaimed, such as Edwardian Marylebone in London, or the row house streets of Greenwich Village and Brownstone Brooklyn, Haussmannian Paris, the tenement districts of New York's Lower East Side or Harlem, or the art deco of Inwood in Manhattan. Each conveys a unique context. Using an ecosystem analogy, architect Michael Sorkin told me that some contexts are "apex" in the sense that they are just so pleasurable (or otherwise interesting) that there is no need to tear it all down and start over (personal communication).

"Integrity" of an individual building refers to the degree to which alterations to a building are visually compatible with the architect's original intent and not a cruel hack job. Integrity of a block or neighborhood refers to the larger setting, not just an individual building.

"Sense of place" is a phrase used to describe the visual and kinetic experience when all the things that create context come together for a unique and specific experience. It's a physical, whole body and brain experience as you walk through a place and realize you are in one specific place and not another. Urbanists have long decried the erosion of sense of place as our society slouches toward a world where all cities resemble each other, and uniqueness is lost.

When violent contrasts in style, materials, scale, and ratios of window glass to solid walls arise, the result is cacophony, disorder, anxiety, and physical discomfort. When there is frequent disruption of context, our experience of beauty and sense of place is disrupted. At some tipping point, sense of place and the experience of context are lost, integrity chucked out the window, and we get what writer and renowned urbanist James Kunstler calls "a clusterfuck." Modernist architectural philosophy is opposed to respecting context, saying "fuck it" or that context is an "opiate for the masses." Paul Goldberger, in his biography of skyscraper designer Frank Gehry, notes, "Frank's projects had worked best as one-of-a-kind designs *set off against* the urban context" (Goldberger 2015; emphasis mine).

Modernist architecture ideology dislikes the ideas of historic context, variety, and sense of place because it does not want to respect them. In modernism, each building is supposed to be judged on its sculptural qualities alone, as a unique freestanding work of art. Both modernists and the Demolition Machine want people to think that what is "exciting" about New York is the "dramatic" (aka harsh) ruptures in scale and style that have come to mark so much of New York. They want the violent rupture of context to be admired rather than loathed. They seek eventually for the rupture to become the context. Hence modernists (and REBNY) attack attempts to preserve or restore historic contexts and repeatedly claim that it would be foolish to "preserve the city in amber." Architects also want "disciplinary autonomy," which is another way of ignoring the context of a site and gaining an unwarranted "artistic freedom" to insert whatever they want into a building site. Architects believe they are due the romanticized freedom assigned to the category of humans known as genius "artists" (Daglioglu 2015).

The photo in Figure 8.2 illustrates aspects of the context problem. It shows the case of a humble nineteenth-century building typical of Tribeca West Historic District. It has been "modernized" by an architect of the modernist persuasion who was chair of New York's Historic Buildings Committee of the American Architectural Association (AIA), a committee that only concerns itself with modernist buildings constructed after 1920 (interview with committee chair). By way of background, that corner of Tribeca was left out of the historic district to accommodate the demolition proclivities of the New York Law School. The school owned much of the block and wanted to harvest air rights over the block and plant them over a parking lot to build a new glass tower (the "Jenga" tower by modernists Herzog & de Meuron), the profits of which would fund their new glass academic building (not shown). (We've seen that tower in Chapter 4.) The Law School said "no" to the inclusion of their property lots in the historic district; so this block was left out. Therefore, the property owner of the building shown was free to do anything he wanted. The renovating architect from the AIA pulled out the nineteenth-century storefront on the ground and second floors, put in as much plate glass as possible, and on the upper story, built an odd new glass window to honor the "new context" (in the architect's words) of the glass tower that arose behind the site. The result is a mangled mess and should bring shame to the AIA.

Some suggest we can conserve a sense of place and context by sticking with the existing, surrounding architectural language when we do infill development in a historic place.[2] I agree, but it is a controversial position, and yet no way to compromise. For example, "postmodernists" try to compromise and claim they can honor a streetscape's context by mixing up historical styles in ironic ways with Disneyesque pastiches and by mocking early architectural languages (Venturi 2011). Postmodernism failed in this endeavor, with most architects reverting to the original modernist position on the matter. The original modernist position on the matter, which opposed context utterly, is the dictatorial Commandment #70 of the modernist's bible, called *The Athens Charter*. Adherents to the charter call the traditional approach to conserving historical context in a city "an excuse for mediocrity, for a dumb servility to the familiar" (Wigley and Johnson, quoted in Daglioglu 2015). The modernist hatred of history and disregard

256 · THE ARCHITECTURE OF RUPTURE AND NIHILISM

Figure 8.2. The architecture of rupture, illustrated by Herzog's & de Meuron's "Jenga" behind a nineteenth-century building. This created a "new" context that the architect in charge of renovating the nineteenth-century building foreground tried to replicate with glass additions. Author's photos.

for historical context is best illustrated with Le Corbusier's proposal to replace the city of Algiers with a creation of his own mind.

A Brief Summary of Modernist Ideology

Coming out of World War I, revolted by Victorian-era dark, cluttered interiors, disdainful of the creative mashing together of architectural styles characteristic of the period 1880–1900, and awed by the intensity, financial power, and destructiveness of industrial capitalism, a tiny band of European architects began issuing manifestos about how to design buildings and how to remake cities. They weren't the majority, didn't all agree with each other, and other architectural trends and ideas abounded. But as a group, they were excellent polemicists and self-marketers. Over a thirty-year period, they managed to become darlings of an urban and corporate elite across two continents. The Nazi-sympathizer Philip Johnson (Saval

2018), whose inherited family wealth had gotten him a curator's job at the brand-new Museum of Modern Art in New York, organized an exhibit of these architects' work in New York in 1932. The elite of the city fell in line, and these architects became gurus of a destructive movement that took over the world. After World War II, they and their followers managed to win government and corporate contracts to build the office towers and public housing projects that we see across Europe, the UK, and the United States. They also got their way in promoting highway building right through cities—places they saw as dirty eyesores and disposable, as explained in Chapter 1.

The leading prophets were four. Most famous among them was a Vichy-collaborator and fascist-sympathizer, the architect Charles-Edouard Jeanneret-Gris, who renamed himself "Le Corbusier." Le Corbusier's manifestos we encountered in Chapter 1. He wasn't a competent architect (despite a couple of undeniably lovely buildings), but he was an astonishingly successful marketer of his ideas. The famous story of his architectural incompetence is about his most celebrated building, the Villa Savoye. The villa leaked and did not have heat and was so ludicrously uncomfortable that it was deemed uninhabitable by the person who commissioned it, Madame Savoye. Her oft-repeated quote in an outraged letter to Le Corbusier is this:

> After innumerable demands on my part, you have finally accepted that this house which you built in 1929 is uninhabitable. Your responsibility is at stake and I have no need to foot the bill. Please render it habitable immediately. I sincerely hope that I will not have to take recourse to legal action. (Cited in De Botton 2006, chap. 14)

A second modernist prophet was Walter Gropius, the man who founded the Bauhaus art school in Germany in 1919. He eventually ran the architecture school at Harvard just before World War II, a position that gave him immense influence in the American architectural world for an exceptionally long time. He was not well liked by the homegrown American architect, Frank Lloyd Wright, who called Gropius's buildings "faceless, characterless, god-awful rectangles of concrete and steel" (Miklovic 2016). New Yorkers should know that Gropius was opposed to preserving the historic Penn Station, calling it "pseudo-tradition," and was delighted that it was torn down (Curl 2018, 5:301). We also have Gropius to thank for the overbearing Pan Am tower that he partly designed. That's the building that squats nastily like a troll above the much greater Grand Central train station, a contrast that exemplifies the common "fuck the context" ethos of modernist skyscraper architecture.

258 · THE ARCHITECTURE OF RUPTURE AND NIHILISM

Figure 8.3. Modernist guru Walter Gropius was one of the architects of the Pan Am tower (now the MetLife building), which sits like a hostile troll on top of Grand Central. Photo from author's collection.

The third prophet of modernism was Ludwig Mies, who renamed himself "Ludwig Mies van der Rohe" (Curl 2018). He was the last director of Gropius's Bauhaus School of Art and Design in Germany and a famed designer of corporate glass towers. He believed his own buildings expressed the "spirit of the age." Among his many famous buildings is the boxy campus at the Illinois Institute of Technology, shown in Chapter 1.

The fourth modernist guru, one who was more of a theorizer than an architect, is the racist (his discussion of the aesthetics of "tribal" people is appalling) Austrian named Adolf Loos (Conrads 1971). Loos coined the quip "ornament is crime" and claimed pompously that abandoning all decoration was a sign of "spiritual strength." Subsequent architects, sheep-like, interpreted this as a commandment to eliminate ornament, decoration, and color on buildings. He was not a man to be admired: he was charged with pedophilia twice and eventually convicted of it (Craven 2019).

The manifestos these gurus wrote are mercifully short and make for fun reading if you have a cynical spirit and tolerance for gibberish. It is fascinating how they got their guru status despite being profoundly ill-educated in the liberal arts sense: Le Corbusier dropped out of grammar school at age thirteen; Mies went to vocational school; Gropius dropped out of technical school for architecture; and Loos never got a degree from a technical college. Nonetheless, the modernists imposed on themselves and their followers a host of enigmatic architectural rules, some of them written as bizarre edicts or commandments. Two of the most important sets of edicts were published just after World War II in two books: *The Athens Charter* and *Can Cities Survive?* An earlier manifesto, the *Futurist Manifesto*, published in 1914, included the mad scribbles of Antonio Sant'Elia (Sert 1947; Jeanneret-Gris 1943; Sant'Elia 1914). The modernist commandments, culled from the various manifestos, include the following:

- Build only flat roofs, and ground floors must be done with stilts and designed to ignore streets.
- Design only open room plans to allow for more light in the interior spaces.
- Windows must be done as horizontal ribbons.
- All buildings should be mass-manufactured, cheap, and with standardized, industrial techniques. Use only concrete, steel, and glass. No more wooden houses! No more wooden anything! The knowledgeable, skilled armies of house-building craftsmen all over Europe were to be abandoned. This one was hard for the Bauhaus school architects to do, but they did manage it (Curl 2018; Wolfe 1982).
- Office buildings, according to Mies, had to be steel, glass, and concrete, and consist of "skin and bones" which meant glass curtain walls hung between steel frames.
- There shall not be any color except white, nor decoration of any kind. That meant no sculpture, cornices, lintels, quoins, or moldings.
- Buildings had to be composed of abstract shapes, but not look like earlier, traditional buildings, and must be restricted to a palette of squares and rectangles. This edict was eventually modified so that the basic rule of thumb is that if it did not look like anything built prior to 1920, it was okay.

- There was also Sant'Elia's commandment: Build buildings with very short lifespans, so that each generation of architects would have the chance to build anew, in kind of a perpetual employment program for them. "Buildings," he said, "will last less time than we will. Each generation will have to build its own cities" (Sant'Elia 1914).
- Puritanical plainness must be celebrated in Orwellian terms with words like "honest," "elegant," "pure," and "clean." Glass is inevitably described by modernist architectural critics as "elegant" and "crystalline" instead of boring, ugly, and sterile (and corporate to its very bones, as nearly all of it was commissioned by those enthralled with modern capitalism) (Venturi 2011).

But the most important rule of all was Commandment #70 from Le Corbusier's *Athens Charter*, the cover of which graces this chapter's opening:

> The practice of using styles of the past on aesthetic pretexts for new structures erected in historic areas has harmful consequences. Neither the continuation of such practices nor the introduction of such initiatives will be tolerated in any form. (Jeanneret-Gris 1943, in 1973 ed., 89)

Vernacular architecture was also forbidden. In one of Mies's manifestos in a journal, he drew a big black X over a photo of a traditional German house with some classical elements to it (Neumeyer 1991). Don't do that, was the message to his students. To modernists, the whole point was to destroy the existing sense of place and impose their own idea of an alienated, hostile, uncomfortable modernity on the rest of us. They were—and are—on a mission.

To be fair, one of the greatest selling points of modernist design is a decluttered interior design. Nobody disagrees with them that it is pleasant to get more light into cluttered, dark Victorian living rooms. But great light is a virtue of many styles, such as can be found in many a Haussmannian building in Paris—so great interior light is not a virtue that modernism can claim for itself. Indeed, many Haussmannian apartments have better interior light than Le Corbusier's own apartment in Paris, in a building he designed for himself.

Still, for anyone who dislikes the excesses of Baroque, Rococo, and Mannerist styles, modernism's puritanical sensibility can bring visual relief—in limited doses. The problem arises when the style takes over cityscapes, demolishes all in its path, and we are forced to consume coldness, bitterness, and alienation at every turn. Just as bad, modernists add insult to injury by mocking our normal human need for a sense of place and belonging to history.

The core, anti-contextual modernist idea for cities is simple: Plunk a building down that ignores any reference to the surrounding context; ignore the street; attract attention to itself often through excessive scale; and metaphorically insult the surrounding architecture that is older than itself. The architect sadistically wants us to share his delight in the forced visual rupture with the past. For modernist architects, the historical context of a city is considered not just irrelevant, but (in an idea that has been given contemporary expression by Harvard Professor Jerold Kayden) constitutes "a tyranny" (Gewertz 2004). Not fitting into the surrounding context, be it historic or not, is literally the point of modernist architectural insertions into cities. As Rem Koolhaas said it:

> Together, all these breaks—with scale, with architectural composition, with tradition, with transparency, with ethics—imply the final, most radical break: Bigness is no longer part of any urban tissue. It exists; at most, it coexists. Its subtext is *fuck* context. (Koolhaas 1998)

How They Won, and What Happened to Our Cities

Several factors made for the success of the modernist architects and their followers. First, modernist architecture became part of an elitist, fashionable, "avant-garde" identity. Another factor is luck: The modernists won many post–World War II government contracts to design social housing—public housing—particularly in the United Kingdom. Their idea to build cheap was a major selling point to government contract officials. In the United States, modernist success also came from an extraordinary level of support from giant corporations. Many CEOs liked modernist towers and sought them out to glorify the new headquarters of the era. Suburban, modernist campuses also sprouted like mushrooms, such as IBM's modernist glass boxes in Rochester, MN (1956) or Bell Labs in Holmdel, NJ (1962). In New York, there were new modernist corporate buildings for the Lever Company (1951), Shell Oil (1957), the Seagram Company (1957), Chase Manhattan Bank (1957), Pan Am (1959), and General Motors (1964) (Stern, Mellins, and Fishman 1997). Chicago had its Prudential tower in 1955. As one researcher summarized: "Towering, glazed office blocks became fashionable as company headquarters.... Glass curtain walls became the status symbol of confident companies and the silhouette of glass towers the sign of a prosperous city" (Oldfield, Trabucco, and

Wood 2009). By the late 1950s, the destruction of our cities and the emergence of the glass box world was well underway (Kunstler 1994).

For General Motors (GM), admiration for the modernist architectural style may have had to do with a unique alignment between GM and the modernists about accommodating cars, something the modernists insisted upon. General Motors ran a traveling motorcade exhibition to promote modernist skyscrapers and an automobile-dependent version of the modern city to small-town Americans. The exhibition went all over the country in 1936, again in 1939 (even launching from the New York World's Fair site), and yet again in the 1950s, calling itself the "Parade of Progress." It consisted of a convoy of eye-catching, spaceship-like vans called "Futureliners." The vans had built-in exhibits that pulled out of the sides of the vans. The parade showcased modernist ideas for a car-dependent, towerized "City of Tomorrow": a city packed with concrete high-rises and embedded in a spaghetti-like highway system (N. R. Walker 2016).

Not everyone was thrilled with what the modernists were doing to cities and how modernist architecture was filling up cities with glass corporate towers or concrete slabs surrounded by grass, forms reproduced mindlessly everywhere, on the edges of town and in the centers. I don't refer only to the critique lobbed at this by New York's own activist-heroine and urban theorist Jane Jacobs, or the fury of Britain's Ian Nairn in his *Outrage* TV series. Even Ada Louise Huxtable, an aggressively pro-modernist critic and a fan of the notion that architects are artists, took a dim view. With the authority invested in her as the architecture critic at the *New York Times*, she lamented in 1961:

> For every glittering new giant that is going up, a substantial old structure has been reduced to dust and rubble and unceremoniously carted away. Behind each brittle glass façade is the ghost of an earlier, and often better building. . . . Each day more is uprooted in the name of "improvements." . . . The distinctive quality and appearance of a community, built up over many years of cultural development and architectural change are being eliminated in innumerable cities. Local flavor is being sacrificed to "look alike" efficiency. . . . The result is an increasingly bland, homogenous America. (Huxtable 1961)

Readers should recognize that "distinctive quality and appearance of a community" and "local flavor" are Huxtable's words to describe "context."

Eighteen years later, Huxtable's successor as architecture critic for the *Times*, Paul Goldberger, would note that Manhattan's Financial District—a world epicenter of real estate speculation—had been so demolished and rebuilt that it had ended up with "precious little soul" (Goldberger 1979, 4). He noted that "massive boxy buildings, parodies of the worst of commercial architecture of the postwar period, obliterated the old structures of Water and Front streets on the East River and the World Trade Center did the same with the Hudson Riverfront" (Goldberger 1979, 3–4).

Into this depressing visual mess in American and European cities, a new generation of modernist architectural gurus emerged in the '70s and '80s. Peter Eisenman, Rem Koolhaas, and Patrik Schumacher represent them. I classify them in the same school as the earlier modernists because they are united in a belief in their own gurudom, a lack of interest in the effect their buildings have on cities, and a deep conviction that all architectural styles prior to their own are "dead." Schumacher is an interesting offshoot of all this: He became enamored of parametric software to design buildings in shapes previously unseen and thus advocated for creating entirely new contexts, while continuing to disregard the existing cities. He explained himself in typical guru-like terms that obfuscate in the extreme:

> Parametricism differentiates fields. Space is empty. Fields are full, as if filled with a fluid medium. We might think of liquids in motion, structured by radiating waves, laminal flows, and spiraling eddies. Swarms have also served as paradigmatic analogues for the field-concept: swarms of buildings that drift across the landscape. There are no platonic, discrete figures or zones with sharp outlines. (Schumacher 2008)

Got that?

The tragedy is that none of this manifesto drivel is helpful to creating a sense of urbanity in a city. The deconstructivist modernists and the parametric modernists appear merely enthralled with new shapes of all kinds, the more shocking, the more bizarre, the better. It is the architecture of self-absorbed navel-gazers, lost in their own minds with the hopeless, nihilistic concerns of philosophers such as Foucault and Derrida, and resulting in nothing but angry, ugly spectacle, not the architecture of great urbanity.

The architect, professor, and prolific author Michael Sorkin commented on twenty years of this:

> When I gaze upon the ludicrous, hyper-energetic, size-queen skylines of Qatar or Pudong or 57th Street, I reach for the Pepto-Bismol. What victory is won? What are we really to make of those twisted dicks, riven shards and perforated signifiers of nothing in particular beyond the significance of signification? (Sorkin 2014)

Sorkin went on, in his usual compelling manner, to hit the nail on the head about how too many new buildings were toxic to the environment, many even built with brutalized semi-slave labor, as in the case of one of Zaha Hadid's infamous building projects in Qatar:

> Here's what I see. Oligarchy and BTUs. Construction-worker concentration camps filled with South Asian slaves. . . . Women not driving. Nobody walking. The Gini coefficient writ huge. Empty $100 million apartments in a city with 50,000 homeless. Too many Starbucks. Slums without end. The greatest minds of my generation diddling themselves on behalf of money and acting as if they have progressive politics. This is the architecture of neo-liberalism. (Sorkin 2014)

The reality is that most modernist buildings in their acontextual effrontery are deliberately ugly so as to discomfit us on purpose (Scruton 2013). They were designed with a philosophical contempt for beauty except in the limited sense of a play of light on geometric shapes. Yet these architects still declare that their buildings are "beautiful" and "harmonious," leaving the majority scratching their heads in puzzlement as to what dictionary they are using.

Anyone who disagrees with the modernist anti-contextual approach to design is accused of being an uneducated hayseed who somehow cannot understand the aesthetic of modernism. Such was the case when Ada Louise Huxtable made fun of her Boston cab driver who had commented to her of the brutalist Boston City Hall: "Whatever it is, it's not beautiful." He asked her if it was "gothic," a point she haughtily and metaphorically giggled at when relating the story to her New York readers. Huxtable went on to call the Boston City Hall building "magnificently monumental." Perversely, she wrote that it had a "sensuous impact" and trotted out textbook modernist dogma to justify her view in her review of the building in the *New York Times* (Huxtable 1969). See photos in Figures 8.4a and 8.4b.

I am not the only one to remark on the disconnect between the aesthetic preferences of what Huxtable self-importantly called "connoisseurs of the art of architecture" and the much wider urban population who more likely share the view of the Boston taxi driver about the Boston City Hall (Huxtable 1969). A Harris Poll found that Americans prefer traditional and classical architecture over modernist architecture 72 percent to 28 percent (Feider 2020). Others have summarized the strange divergence between what modernist architects prefer versus what the majority of non-architects find palatable (Mehaffy and Alterman 2019). One researcher found that

Figures 8.4a and 8.4b. Does the concrete of Boston City Hall have sensuous impact? Or is it "not beautiful"? Compare it to the civic architecture of Bruges in Belgium. Both images under license from Creative Commons.

the more architects got educated in their field, the less they shared the tastes of non-architects (Michl 2014; 2015). Adopting modernist aesthetic pretense has become part of their professional indoctrination, much like the way economists get indoctrinated to believe in the religion of free trade, no matter the evidence of the harms it can cause.

Part of the willingness of architects to accept this indoctrination is that there is widespread confusion about "beauty." Some say there is no such thing as beauty: It is just all in the eye of the beholder. Perhaps we cannot measure beauty, but we can measure confusion.

The 3M company created software that mimics the *pre-conscious* response of the human eye to visual stimuli. It tracks what the eye notices, what our brain is engaging with. It turns out that when we take a look at modernist buildings, the eye settles on nothing, sees only chaos and "rests" on nothing. Scan in a traditional building and the eye homes in on outlines and details, windows, doorways, and cornices and, pre-consciously, settles into the view, providing information for the brain to sort and categorize. This is damning research about the chaos that modernist stylistic tropes are inserting into cities and human life (Lavdas, Salingaros, and Sussman 2021): Modernist architecture is creating an urban environment that humans literally cannot engage with, creating visual chaos and cacophony.

It is important to state that not everyone who thinks that what modernist architectural philosophy has done to cities is ugly and depressing is a right-wing uneducated yahoo or a monarchist. Plenty of left-leaning people agree that there is a big problem, many of whom are more educated than the modernist theorists. Take Alain de Botton, for one. Who could dispute that he is a talented and prolific author with a left-of-center "let's reform capitalism" bent? He studied at Cambridge University and did a master's in philosophy with double honors. He is no rube and has serious elite educational creds. Yet his comment on modernist architecture is an eloquent expression of articulate pain:

> It is to prevent the possibility of permanent anguish that we can be led to shut our eyes to most of what is around us. (De Botton 2006)

De Botton started the philosophical School for Life as a public service. His team wrote that modernist architecture has produced urban environments that are "more dispiriting, chaotic, and distasteful than anything humanity has ever known" (School of Life 2020).

Or consider the late Nathan Glazer—a writer who sported a Ph.D. in sociology from Columbia University. He was a registered Democrat with an "open mind" whom the *New York Times* described as "intellectually formidable." Glazer described modernist architecture as "soulless, bureaucratic, and inhuman" (Glazer 2007; Gewen 2019). Or, consider the unequivocally left-leaning editor of the respected journal *Current Affairs*, Nathan Robinson. He has most architectural theorists beat in the elite credential department, with eye-popping bragging rights: a B.A. and M.A. from Brandeis, a J.D. from Yale, and a Ph.D. from Harvard. Robinson has written that modernist architecture makes people feel "confused, alienated, and afraid" and pointed out that it creates "dreary" buildings that look like the "headquarters of post-apocalyptic totalitarian dictatorship." My favorite quip of Robinson's: "If it doesn't make you feel desperately, crushingly alone, it's probably not a piece of prize-winning contemporary architecture" (Rennix and Robinson 2017).

Modernist architects may have had a post–World War II triumph for themselves, but it was not a victory for the cities that got demolished to make way for modernist design. I challenge anyone without a degree in architecture to walk up West Street from Chambers Street to 72nd Street in New York City or to drive up the FDR Drive on the East Side from Lower Manhattan to 96th Street and not be appalled by the ugliness and visual cacophony one sees. You would never know that a great city is hidden behind the wall of ugliness that lines the waterfronts. The race for river views and destruction of the once glorious and visually intact urbanity of brick warehouses and nineteenth-century architecture along the waterfront is an unforgivable crime committed by modernist architecture in league with the real estate industry. Even Paul Goldberger knows they went too far. He wrote back in 1985, still early in his career:

> It is the wretchedness of places like Third Avenue in New York and La Defense in Paris that made modern architecture seem not merely exhausted but worthless . . . exhausted as a vital force . . . the ultimate expression of the corporate state. (Goldberger 1985)

Sadly, I must add to Goldberger's list of miserable places the wretchedness of Midtown, Midtown East, Hudson Yards, the East 30s, Downtown Brooklyn, and the "new" Brooklyn waterfront.

Why is this happening? Beyond the real estate power that has so overrun New York City, Alain de Botton and his people at the School of Life in the UK argue that it has to do with the persistence of four "sacred" beliefs: the belief that beauty is unwelcome, unnecessary, and unknowable; the belief that car-induced sprawl and car-centric design is okay; the belief that it is okay, even desirable, to disdain the use of local building materials; and last, the belief that the mental health and pleasure of the citizens of the city and users of the buildings are irrelevant—all that matters is the idea of the architect (School of Life 2020).

Surely it is time to stop the insanity.

Myth: Historic Styles of Architecture Predating Le Corbusier Are "Dead"

An architect neighbor and friend strolled with me on our block on Duane Street, one filled entirely with brick, nineteenth-century loft buildings. It is one of the more remarkable places in the city. Even Paul Goldberger agrees in one of his early books that oddly enough, celebrates context:

> This is the sort of place cities around the country struggle to create; New York has had it all along. . . . It is surrounded—tightly—by superb buildings, all of which work together to create a coherent whole . . . almost everything is in masonry. (Goldberger 1979, 40)

My neighbor and I studied the scaffolding arising over a two-story building on the south side of Duane Park, the smallest building on the block. I lamented that the New York Landmarks Preservation Commission had given the owner permission to build a three-story glass box on top of the nineteenth-century structure. It would be the first non-contextual building on the block, an end to the "coherent whole" that Goldberger wrote about. The addition had been approved on the pretext that adding more stories was a mere "rooftop addition." "Too bad," said I, "about the glass. Why couldn't the LPC approve something in the style of the other buildings?" My architect friend looked stunned. "Because you can't!" he cried. "But why?" I probed.

"It just isn't done," my friend insisted. "It would be impossible. It would be kitsch."

I pressed him. "But what if you used real bricks? What if they used actual lintels and put up a real cornice? Surely that might be done?"

"No," he said, shaking his head firmly. "It just cannot happen. Can't be done. It would be a copy." He could not explain further.

The part of the modernist architectural ideology—that all architectural styles predating Le Corbusier must be considered as "dead" and somehow unavailable for contemporary use—is a poisonous aspect of modernist architectural discourse that needs to end. It misled critic Ada Louise Huxtable to rail against the perfectly fine brick Fraunces Tavern[3] building in New York City as a "dead copy" motivated by uneducated citizens experiencing an "artificial nostalgia" (Huxtable 1965). The tavern is in fact, an honorable and attractive part of Manhattan's downtown built environment. Nobody cares a wit that is an inaccurate reconstruction. And who is the *New York Times* critic to function as the emotion police, preventing us from enjoying some nostalgia? Manhattan is packed with imitations of Miesian skyscrapers and Corbusian slabs and nobody accuses the lovers of such buildings as people experiencing "artificial nostalgia." As William Duggan, author of *How Innovation Really Happens*, points out with endless examples from history and the arts, all innovation is usually a remix of existing things anyway; nothing is a pure invention out of nothing. Picasso even admitted, "All great artists steal" (Duggan 2004). So why can't architects steal from their forebears who predate Le Corbusier?

And what's the big deal about copying anyway? There are good copies and bad copies. The bad ones are usually made of shoddy materials, are poorly constructed, and leave out critically important details. Therefore, isn't the problem bad copying rather than worrying about something being "dead"? And if a copy is well made of good materials and doesn't look exactly like the original, isn't that okay? When copying, nobody is trying to "trick" or "fake out" the viewer into thinking they are in another epoch. A better way to think about it is that they are doing the public a service by restoring or maintaining the kinetic pleasure of an existing admirable streetscape, giving us a visual experience that our eyes can engage with.

This self-imposed limitation of architectural design derives from an archaic and discredited idea of history developed by the philosopher G. W. F. Hegel. Hegel and his followers (notably Karl Marx) saw history as an unfolding linear, evolutionary series of epochs, each inevitably better and more improved than the one preceding, all containing a mysterious pixie dust called "progress." That may sound laughable now, but architects took it seriously, and it means that the objects produced within each epoch quickly turn into "dead" artifacts of a "dead" age and cannot be used—are forbidden to be used—in subsequent epochs.

Yes, this is as ridiculous as it sounds, and yes, architects are imprisoning themselves in a jail of their own making with Le Corbusier's rule #70. An ideology that says we are forbidden to use older styles, that they are dead to us, is as ridiculous as saying we can't use elevators because they were invented in the nineteenth century, or we cannot use vaccines to save our society because vaccines were invented in a "dead" age. Architects, do you hear yourselves? Musicians, novelists, poets, sculptors, artists, engineers, and scientists all use knowledge, information, models, styles, and discoveries from long before they were born (Michl 2015). Why can't architects?

Styles don't die; they have no life force in them. And the modernist styles are not the end of history in some evolutionary process in which Le Corbusier's or Patrik Schumacher's buildings are the final apogee. The obsession with breaking with an evil "tradition" reads now as both silly and supremely arrogant. It would be laughable if it weren't a destructive idea with such a demonic grip on so much of the architectural world.

The adhesion to such a rule is doubly strange if one realizes that even in the heyday of Le Corbusier, Gropius, and Mies, there were different ideas about how we should experience our lives under capitalism and "modernity."

Not everyone feels alienation and the need to destroy continuity with the past. There were and are plenty of architects who practice the craft of architecture using lessons from vernacular, classical, neoclassical, and all the nineteenth-century styles. They don't think what they are doing is "non-modern" (Semes and Institute of Classical Architecture and Classical America 2009). And those architects had plenty of clients and still do. (Check out the work done by the group at CreateStreets.com in the UK) This is the nub of an excessively big problem. Jan Michl has explored it at length and brilliantly summarizes:

> In the eyes of the public, art of the past is perceived as a natural part of the present, while in the view of architects of the modernist persuasion—the absolute majority . . . the present is defined as the absence of the art of the past. . . . They view the aesthetic world of the past architecture as an impediment, standing in the way of their plans. There was to be no trace of it in the architecture of the present. (Michl 2015, 4)

That's a humdinger of a self-sabotaging belief and terrible restraint on creativity. The constraint needlessly leads modernists to falsely accuse and dismiss anyone who uses those styles as guilty of "pastiche" and "kitsch" and "historicism"—all words that have been shopworn into meaninglessness.

The Silliness behind the Zeitgeist and Self-Appointed "Historical Great Men"

The origins of Commandment #70 lie in architects' love affair with a concept called *zeitgeist*, a German word meaning "ghost or spirit of the time." Mies van der Rohe also used the term *zeitwille*, meaning "will of the age." Jean Nouvel expressed the belief in zeitgeist when he said to a journalist, "Architecture is the petrification of a cultural moment" (Escot 2017). Architects use the term to justify their own designs as somehow "inevitable" and as having the "force of history" behind them, which, as I will show here, is just nonsense.

The German philosopher Hegel popularized the idea of a zeitgeist in the early nineteenth century. He thought that history is driven forward in some linear evolutionary sense and that each epoch has a corresponding will of the age that determines history absolutely (Michl 2015). As a concept, zeitgeist is probably more useful to describe momentary, popular cultural memes among particular groups of people, but for historical analysis and science about how human agency shapes events, how mistakes influence history, zeitgeist theorizing ranks along with failed ideas like alchemy (Popper 1944).

As historians have long explained, zeitgeist is a thing that cannot be measured or detected by scientific means (Urbach 1985). It is a concept with no palpable reality, a bit like believing in magic. This is different from the way people use the term to talk about a trend or popular meme. Consider: Is the zeitgeist of the Covid era best represented by a smartphone or by vaccines, which were "invented" by Louis Pasteur in 1885 (or earlier, if we are thinking smallpox)?

The point is that in any given period, rival ideas contend for influence. Some ideas fade only to resurge later. There is no unique "will of the age." Besides, how can a period have a will, like a human? It is people who have agency. It is people who inflict their agency on the world, aided and abetted by specific policies and ideas created by other people with agency. And whose agency wins? Well, that is all about power, not zeitgeist or zeitwille.

Let's use Mies van der Rohe's own work to show how silly the idea is. In the image below we see a picture of a glass tower that Mies designed in Germany in 1923. Pause to note how Mies did not care about context—check out the remnant of smaller human-scale buildings barely visible next to the glass tower. Those are the buildings he wanted to stamp out, which is what his tower succeeds visually in doing. But look also at the more traditional house on the top left. It is the Mosler House that Mies himself designed a year later, in 1924. Houses like the Mosler house are all over Germany, and there are as many if not more of them than there are Miesian skyscrapers. Which represents the zeitgeist?

Consider the bottom left image in the collage in Figure 8.5. It is an American Craftsman bungalow, a style born in the 1910s that has remained immensely popular in the United States. Tens of thousands of them arose between 1910 and 1940, more than Miesian skyscrapers. At the same time the Sears mail-order catalogue sold over 100,000 kit homes in traditional American vernacular styles (Tudor, Cape, Federal, Four Square, Colonial, Craftsman). Sears called them "Modern Homes" and sold them between 1908 and 1940 (Sears Archives 2012). Which of these images represents the zeitgeist of that time? Hard to say, do you agree? Moreover, people of different cultures and socioeconomic characteristics may all have different and temporary zeitgeists that may not overlap much. Zeitgeist thinking erases all this complexity and robs us of human agency in affecting social change. It grants that agency only to self-appointed "Great Historical Men" who deliver their idea of the zeitgeist but have contempt for everyone else's agency.

Modernist architects, in common with Marxists and philosophers, thought that industrial-age modernity had created a universal sense of

Figures 8.5a–c. Which represents the zeitgeist? Top left, a traditional German house Mies designed. Right, a skyscraper Mies also designed. Bottom left, an American Craftsman bungalow from a Sears catalog of the same period. Images under license from Creative Commons.

displacement and alienation among "modern man." Navel-gazing, these men felt alienation from nature, from themselves, from the products of their labor, and from the imaginary "community" of the medieval manor house. Arrogantly, intellectuals of the period assumed alienation was "a spiritual condition common to everyone." They did not have evidence for this claim. It was just assumed to be true based on what was true for themselves. This blinkered way of looking at the world led them to want their alienation reflected in their architecture. They wanted to impose their alienated feelings on the civilian population, who, unless led by Great Historical Men, might seek out charm, beauty, comfort, old buildings, quaintness, livability, and picturesqueness, things which industrial capitalism (and its Great Historical Male architects) were not going to provide, at least if the modernists had their way.

Architects tended to think of themselves—in Hegel's words—as "the clear-sighted ones"—men with "an insight into the requirements of the time" that was "the very truth for their age" (Michl 2015, 9). Anyone who disagreed with the modernist ideology was cast out of the architect club as an irrational seeker of "dead" historic styles, a kitsch-lover, and an idiotic pursuer of "nostalgia." As the School of Life staff wrote, modernists deemed traditional styles of architecture to be playing the Marxist role of an "opiate of the masses"—meaning an emotional distraction that prevented people from feeling enough anxiety and misery, which if felt, might start The Revolution. The architects had contempt for the cozy and comforting Craftsman bungalow. To them, that desire for comfort was symptomatic of a delusional nostalgia that needed to be whipped out of humanity because it prevented radical acceptance of the (supposedly) universal condition of alienation. Once you feel alienation, you might revolt, or so went the thinking.

Their zeal to impose their personal notion of what constituted "modernity" on everyone turned these architects into authoritarian "fathers," insisting on cruel "truths. The childish masses were to be beaten out of their tendency to seek out a tree or some color or any visual relief from glass curtain walls (Venturi 2011).

Myth: Modernist Architecture is "Art" and Architects Are Genius-Artists Who Need Freedom from Design Oversight

Is architecture "Art" grandly speaking, or is it something else? There are three views to consider. First, architecture is indeed art (and architects are thus artists). Second, architecture is craft, hence architects are not artists, but craftsmen of an ancient tradition going back thousands of years. Third, as aesthetic theorist Roger Scruton proposed, architecture may be a *synthesis* of art and craft (Scruton 2013). I prefer Scruton's view: It corresponds better with my own empirical experience and has a compromising logic to it. It does seem that although each architect carries within a different combination of craftsperson and artist, realistically, most are largely craftspersons and just a wee bit artist. Yet even if the inner artist is large, the architect cannot do anything ex nihilo, no artist can. There are constraints everywhere to the imagination in architecture. Site, terrain, context, economics, budget, client, and the Commandment #70 of the modernists all put intense limits on an architects imagination, as does whatever the individual has put into their brain through their own education.

Moreover, consider that even of those few architects who claim artist status, only a few among them are going to be "good" artists, let alone genius artists. Furthermore, among the minuscule few who are indisputably talented artists, not all their buildings will succeed as durable works of art. And last, of those architects who claim to be more artist than craftsman, we should consider, are they artists of individual sculptural forms or are they artists of the urban environments? There is a huge and critically important difference.

The influential critic Paul Goldberger is an advocate of the "architecture as art" school of thought, as was his predecessor at the New York Times, Ada Louise Huxtable. They liked to consider each building as a potential individual sculpture, unrelated to its context. Both support the Hegelian notion that architecture is the "will of the epoch translated into space" and strongly disapprove of architects borrowing from or using styles "of the past" and approve of their adherence to Le Corbusier's Commandment #70. Goldberger claims that disobeying Commandment #70 will result in "comforting" buildings, which is supposed to be an insult. Instead, he is a fan of architecture that is "challenging and uncomfortable." He thinks that if we don't like starchitect Frank Gehry's buildings we are somehow "missing out" (Goldberger 2010). He wants our society and cities to grant massive freedoms for those he deems artist-architects. He also claims that vernacular architecture cannot be art—for unexplained reasons—and that only singular buildings might qualify as art; and, as the most famous critic of our time, he will let us know which buildings qualify as art. All this seems to fall under that strange category of thinking that says that if the artist and his friends say a urinal dumped into the gallery is art, it is.

I take the Goldberger view with a grain of salt, while still respecting his right to have it. Architectural critics have a job: attracting readers to the publication that hires them. The critic must therefore sell the business "proposition" of architecture as art. They succeed in this by engaging in artistic connoisseurship of new buildings. They must keep applauding the production of new buildings and stimulating discussion among readers about the new; otherwise, they would have nothing to write about. Notice that architectural critics in the newspapers and magazines rarely, if ever, write about buildings constructed in any period prior to the modernist movement.

But the duties of the salaried architectural critic aside, the truth is that 98 percent of all newly constructed buildings in New York, modernist or not, are obviously not art. Most are merely utilitarian, and many are outright ugly. To be fair, that may not be the fault of the architects. Their bosses, be they real estate developers or builders, hand them a scope of work—and most of the time the scope is to get the job done as cheaply as possible. Moreover, it has long been the case that much of the architectural design work nowadays gets done by the engineer and construction team (Tharpe 2017). It means the job of the architect is often just to help brand and market a building.

THE ARCHITECTURE OF RUPTURE AND NIHILISM · 275

Figures 8.6a–e. Collage of buildings deemed by modernists to be inferior "vernacular" architecture: a Swiss farmhouse; Indonesia's Pagaruyung Palace; Hōryūji, Japan's national treasure temple and pagoda; the Great Mosque of Djenné in Mali; and Russia's Church of the Transfiguration. Images under license from Creative Commons.

Even Frank Gehry, who fancies himself a great artist, recognizes this reality when he said, "98 per cent of what gets built and designed today is pure shit" (Rosenfeld 2014). Critic Ada Louise Huxtable said the same thing more gently in 1962 when she pointed out that "in general New York is producing few great—or even good—buildings" (Huxtable 1962). The conclusion is that most architects are not artists.

The romantic vision of artists as geniuses producing objects ex nihilo is in general at odds with reality. As Duggan has shown repeatedly, our brain is a bit like a warehouse storing everything we have seen, heard, read, or felt. Ideas don't come from nowhere: they come from a recombination of what we've allowed into our brains. For example, the idea of setbacks in the city's zoning code came from observing the effect of mansards, terraces, and dormers on light reaching a building. This reality about creativity makes it even more tragic that architects in the modernist paradigm refuse to allow pre-Corbusian architecture or plain old vernacular architecture into the warehouses of their brains. Why are those styles rejected as viable sources of data for the future or the present?

But even if you disagree and think architects are artist-geniuses, with plenty of Historical Great Men among them, it is not clear how to distinguish bad artists from the talented ones. That makes the public policy implications clear. If only a few architects are really artists, and not all their work is great, shouldn't we be setting up our planning and zoning systems for the reality that 98 percent of what gets built will be either "shit" or simply "ordinary" rather than a great artistic delight? That creates a new argument to adopt a different kind of zoning code, such as the "form-based" codes that produce more predictable streetscapes.

And who should do the judging among shit, ordinary, and great? Is that only a role for our aesthetic superiors, the critics? I think not. Since architecture is too public a craft and the damage to our cities has been so great, someone besides the architect and his fan base must judge the work. Who should that be? Perhaps it should be the users of the building and the residents who must see it every day. In his study of the politics of architecture of ancient Greece, historian Russell Meiggs explained the that in the heyday of democratic Athens, it was the assembly of people who decided who should build and design the Parthenon and a host of temples around it. In those laws, it is clear:

> It was the demos [body of citizens] in its assembly that should decide what public buildings were to be built, and who should build them. Commissioners elected by the people should supervise the progress of the work and its financing. Their account should be controlled by public auditors chosen by the people, and should be publicly summarized on stone and set up where all who wished could see them. (Meiggs 1963, 38)

It is difficult not to conclude that the olive-growing farmers of ancient Athens—hayseeds all—did a surprisingly good job of sponsoring civic architecture, did they not? So that, I suggest, is the way forward, to make citizens of the polis the ultimate arbiters as to what is good urban architecture and what is not, and to design for the reality that most architecture will be ordinary but nonetheless needs to fit into the surrounding context, and that we need standards for that ordinariness and contextual character.

Nostalgia Is Good and Useful, Not a Political Crime

An oddity of the modernist architectural movement is the way it weaponized the concept of "nostalgia." Modernists use it to dismiss anyone who wants to preserve an old building, or worse, design a new building in an older style that predates Le Corbusier. But why does the word have such negative connotations for architects? Why do they insist that nostalgia is something to be ignored, feared, and repressed, rather than respected as a normal and healthy human emotion? Why have modernists, in the words of one literature professor, "transformed nostalgia into a sort of political crime" (Natali 2004, 13)?

For the modernist architectural theorists, the emotion of nostalgia is thought of as toxic, "dangerous," and "reactionary," because, in their minds, it prevents people from accepting the inevitable death of their own epoch. Similarly, Marxists think nostalgia slows down the proletariat's ability to rise and fight for the coming Communist utopia. More cynically, you can imagine why architects and real estate developers love to cast nostalgia as a negative thing: They are the ones who benefit financially when old buildings get torn down and new ones are built in their places. Their self-interest requires them to demonize nostalgia. But the rest of us do not have to follow them.

In our favor, there has been a sustained and successful rebellion against the negative view of nostalgia, led first by psychologists and then by theorists of the Black experience. It turns out that nostalgia has unequivocally positive effects on our well-being (Layous, Kurtz, Wildschut, and Sedikides 2022). It increases social connectedness (Juhl et al. 2021). It can also increase "feelings of vitality" (Hutson 2016). Research also shows that the experience of nostalgia

> counteracts loneliness, boredom, and anxiety. It makes people more generous to strangers and more tolerant of outsiders. Couples feel closer and look happier when they're sharing nostalgic memories. On cold days, or in cold rooms, people use nostalgia to literally feel warmer. (Jarvis and Bonnett 2013)

Even more exciting, nostalgia can "make people become more optimistic and inspired about the future" (Tierney 2013). Black social theorists argue that nostalgia can induce a positive sense of political agency in the world (Ahad-Legardy 2021). It does that by generating good feelings in us—which in turn gives us the mental space and freedom to create a vision of what might be, what we might want, based on our idea of joyful elements of the past (Stewart 2021). Even "neurotic" individuals benefit from nostalgia, for it has been shown to strengthen "self-continuity through holistic thinking" (Hong, Sedikides, and Wildschut 2020).

Well . . . oops! Recall that modernist architects, exemplified by architect Peter Eisenman's deconstructionist philosophy, seek to make us feel uncomfortable and anxious. They don't want us to feel warm, connected, optimistic, or full of vitality. They want us to feel cold as steel, alienated, fractured, and anxious as hell. As Herbert Muschamp, the one-time architectural critic at the *New York Times*, said: "The ideal of *not pleasing* is fundamental to modern art and modern criticism" (Muschamp 2003; emphasis mine). It is perverse that they want to do this. Anxiety, doctors say, is a toxic emotion, causing not just weight gain and mental anguish but it also renders our bodies susceptible to disease. Could it be that modernist architects are trying to provoke us into revolution, or are they just sadists? Either way, they need to stop.

Who Knew Modernist Starchitects Live Like Historic Preservationists?

We've seen in the first chapter of this book how modernists have a profoundly anti-urban vision of cities. They dislike street life, love cars and highways, and argue for demolishing cities and rebuilding them in variations of the modernist style as the renderings in Chapter 1 so eloquently illustrate. In this chapter, we've also seen that they dislike historical context and do not want to be constrained by it in their designs. They want to oppose historical context and wipe it out, like Le Corbusier's wipeout of historic Algiers and central Paris. It's a philosophical position.

Yet despite these disturbing design beliefs, one of the stranger aspects of the modernist architectural worldview is how many of its proponents don't walk their talk in their personal lives. Instead of living in the dystopic glass towers and creations they push on other people, a great many prefer to live in single-family homes in the grassy lawn-filled suburbs or in low- or mid-rise historic buildings in historic districts of great cities. Here are just a few of the more notable examples, all of them a matter of public record. Many more might be cited.

- Starchitect Renzo Piano, designer of many glass towers such as the hated "Shard" in London and Columbia University's city-destroying uptown campus in Harlem, has long chosen to live blissfully in a

THE ARCHITECTURE OF RUPTURE AND NIHILISM · 279

Figures 8.7a–c. Starchitect Renzo Piano designed the widely despised "Shard" in London (shown) and Columbia University's failed Manhattanville campus in New York City (not shown). He lives in the idyllic and historically protected Place des Vosges in Paris. Author's photo of Place des Vosges. Other images under license from Creative Commons.

historically protected, seventeenth-century apartment on the magnificent and historically protected Place des Vosges in Paris. About that, he writes: "In Paris I retreat to a cocoon from the 1600s . . . detached and high above the noise. But in Paris, there is a feeling of belonging. When I look out at the other buildings ringing the square, they all have the exact same design and give me a feeling of community and anonymity" (Piano 2013).

- Rem Koolhaas, designer of indecipherable, acontextual glass tower-objects, lived for twenty years during his prime working life in an Edwardian apartment house in London. When he returned to Holland, he chose a 1924 brick house in the low-rise, wealthy, and historically preserved row-house neighborhood of "Old South" in Amsterdam (Loos 2020; *Financial Times* 2011).
- Walter Gropius, designer of high rises for the working classes and for the corporate world, lived in a low-rise, single-family home with a huge lawn in a grassy suburban lot, commuting distance to Cambridge, Massachusetts.

280 · THE ARCHITECTURE OF RUPTURE AND NIHILISM

Figures 8.8a–c. Skyscraper designer Frank Gehry has lived most of his working life in a single-family home (with a yard!) in ritzy Santa Monica, California, but designs skyscrapers such as the "Gehry" Building in Lower Manhattan. Images 8a and 8b under license from Creative Commons. Author's photo of Gehry Building.

- Peter Eisenman, designer of buildings that he hopes inspire anxiety in us, divides his time between a conventional, utilitarian, brick prewar NYC apartment in the West Village and an old New England farmhouse. When asked why, he said: "I am immersed in architecture all day, working in my office or teaching. Afterward, I want to go back to my home where it's cozy" (Salant 2011).
- Daniel Libeskind, skyscraper designer of the infamous "fuck the context" addition to the Royal Ontario Museum in Canada and a similar alteration to the military museum in Dresden, lives in a historic human-scale brick and stone former bank building in Tribeca dating from 1910, with spectacular unencumbered views of a low-rise brick Tribeca South Historic District from his windows (Hawthorne 2004).

Figures 8.9a-c. Architect Mies van der Rohe portrait by Hugo Erforth under Creative Common license. Mies's Seagram building (Creative Commons license), and the classically cozy low-rise, neo-classical style apartment building where Mies lived in Chicago for most of his life (Google Earth image).

Figures 8.10a–c. Rem Koolhaas spent much of his working life living in an Edwardian building in London, before decamping to a chic, residential historic district in Amsterdam. A typical streetscape view of that neighborhood is shown. Also shown is the CCTV building in China that Koolhaas designed. Images under license from Creative Commons.

282 · THE ARCHITECTURE OF RUPTURE AND NIHILISM

Figures 8.11a–c. Architect Jean Nouvel, his Torre Agbar in Barcelona, Spain, and the historically preserved village of St. Paul de Vence in the south of France where Nouvel has a home and holds staff retreats. Images under license from Creative Commons.

- Jean Nouvel, designer of glass towers and shapes worldwide, keeps his design offices in Paris in a low-rise block of a traditional, historic stretch of the 11th Arrondissement of Paris—the historic core of that city. He commutes frequently with his staff to do "brainstorming" in his medieval stone "country house" in the historically preserved and protected hill town of St. Paul de Vence in the south of France. He noted "wistfully" to one journalist, "It's calm there" (Isserman 2015). He told another journalist he does not decorate his own Paris apartment because "I live in a historic place" (Escot 2017).
- The late Zaha Hadid, architect of curvy parametric skyscrapers, lived in an apartment in a humble four-story building in low-rise Dallington Street in the historic Clerkenwell district of London. Her building was a "conventional, ordinary" building, according to a journalist interviewing her. When she was asked about it, she simply said, "It is not my project" (Arch20 n.d.).
- Herzog and de Meuron, architects of modernist glass towers imposed on various cities around the world, have their offices in a beautiful two-story, sixteenth-century historic building in the historic center of Basel, Switzerland, a magnificently preserved historic town that exiles glassy towers to the suburban outskirts. Their Paris offices

THE ARCHITECTURE OF RUPTURE AND NIHILISM · 283

Figures 8.12a–c. The Italian architect Carlo Scarpa, a revered modernist among modernists, celebrated for his work in concrete. He lived near Venice in an apartment above the historically protected neo-classical stables of a villa, both designed by the Renaissance architect Palladio. The stables are part of a UNESCO World Heritage Site. Images from Wikipedia's Creative Commons license.

are also in a historic "hotel particulier" in the chic, low-rise Marais neighborhood.
- Carlo Scarpa is an Italian architect and master of alienated concrete modernity, whose concrete walls in Verona are revered by modernists. He chose to live most of his working life in a stunning neoclassical sixteenth-century stable building within a Palladian villa complex outside Venice—smack within a World Heritage Site. His studio was on the ground floor, his apartment above. Palladian villas

Figures 8.13a–c. Famed architect Louis Kahn, his home in a nineteenth-century row house in Philadelphia, and a concrete work he is known for. Author's image of Kahn's Philadelphia row house. Other images under license from Creative Commons.

Figures 8.14a–c. Architects Herzog & de Meuron, their "Jenga" tower in New York, and a Google Earth photo of their office building in historically protected, low-rise Basel, Switzerland. Images under license from Creative Commons.

are classically inspired, for those who are unfamiliar (Villa Valmarana 2016).
- Louis Kahn, the master of concrete, chose to live in a charming, upper middle-class, context-ridden nineteenth-century brick row house on a tiny, historically preserved enclave and dead-end street of Philadelphia. His secret second family lived in the suburban outskirts in a lovely old vernacular house. Moreover, his offices were at 1501 Walnut Street, a five-story "classical" building that looks to be circa 1910 and is obviously "premodern" (Fiske 2013).

The lessons of such jaw-dropping hypocrisy are clear. One, ignore what these people have to say about cities, places, or context, look instead where they live. Second, build more neighborhoods that share the great, human-scale contextual qualities of the Place des Vosges, the beautiful Edwardian neighborhoods of London, the nineteenth-century row houses of Philadelphia or Old South in Amsterdam. It is equally obvious that we must never turn to any of these architects or to their ideology for the design imagination needed for great urbanism. They do not know how to design great places. They are not artists of urbanity. For that we must turn to the followers of the Jane Jacobs School of Urbanism.

Chapter 9

What Policies for a Human-Scale City?

THIS BOOK HAS TAKEN READERS on a critical tour of the conventional wisdom in many fields relating to urban life. We have seen where the battle lines are drawn about the fate of our Wonder City. Big Real Estate, along with its dependents, hired guns, allies, and courtiers, pushes upon us their goal of demolishing Wonder City and replacing it in hyper-dense form with ever-taller towers, usually of glass, the so-called "luxury" city remade for the pleasure of world corporations and their highest paid elites. Their allies in the architectural community are a second assault battalion with the same goal of destruction. They are intent on ridding Wonder City of its historic character and replacing it with a modernist dystopia, justifying their ideas using ideological nonsense borrowed from the manifesto madness of their founding gurus.

On the other side of the battle are the many residents all over the city who seek a completely different vision, one of great urbanity in the Jane Jacobs, Camillo Sitte, and Jan Gehl traditions of diversity, liveliness, and visual interest, anchored in the human scale. What do we want on this side of the battle? We want to protect what is left of our Wonder City, not to continually demolish and replace it. We want to pass on to our children a city that has more than a passing resemblance to the Wonder City we have loved. Our Wonder City is a place of thriving small businesses with a bustling civic life in our public realm. It is a livable city filled with connection to our history, where historic districts are great, many, valued, and expanded without bending the knee at every turn to the real estate industry.

We have also seen how the real estate industrial complex is constituted, how it works, how it maintains its power. We've seen the damage it has done, from twisting the zoning code to its ends, to attaching its vampiric tentacles onto the Leviathan of government where it makes our mayors its puppets and takes captive the regulatory agencies that deal in real estate (Hobbes, 1651). We have seen how their public relations playbook steals magic phrases like "affordable housing," "housing supply," "racial justice," "equity," "growth," and "regulatory overreach" to serve as Trojan Horses for what amounts to just another variation on their hyper-dense towerization program in which they are the ultimate winners. The original excuse for demolition was to get rid of slums; then it was to shrink the city to its core; then it was to remake the city as a white-collar paradise for the wealthy; and now the excuse is "affordable housing" or "competitiveness." It is all a form of gaslighting to shield us from seeing real estate's power, to maintain the charade of pretending to be acting in the public interest when it is not.

This chapter explores how to turn the ship around before it is too late. What policies would help restore Wonder City and protect what is left of it? How do we undo the damage Big Real Estate has done? How do we prosper? What is a better way to deal with affordable housing if we accept that the trickle-down housing supply theory will never work in a city of our scale, history, and geographic circumstances? What do we do about regulatory capture? It is a big program of change.

First, turning the ship around will mean stopping the bad things we do now, and then moving toward a vision of prosperity for an equitable, diverse, lively human-scaled city. I do not pretend to have all the answers. I suggest a framework for developing reforms plus a few immediate fixes. The latter involve ending one set of bad rules and goals and adopting positive new rules, procedures, and laws. The idea is to change the rules of the game. My intention is to not to offer silver bullets, but to instigate debate and experimentation and to legitimatize those people who have ideas on how to fix things, ideas that are outside the current limited "Overton window" of the possible.

Some framework principles to do this might be:

- Revolution may be needed, but it is unlikely to happen. That means we are stuck with the imperfect but necessary requirement to regulate. With that in mind, intelligent government needs to learn how to experiment with regulation to eliminate the negatives of what the market produces and cope with unintended consequences with greater agility. So yes, we must regulate. The clumsy, slow, ham-fisted

nature of Big Government and the existence of unintended consequences to a regulation are not sufficient arguments to avoid, gut, or just overturn regulation.
- In search of better policy in any domain—be it for landmark regulation or about government support for small business—there needs to be permanent investment in research and scanning around the world into "what works" and "what sorta works" and "what doesn't work" and "what we don't know and need to experiment with" to inform better policy and regulation. In many cases, there is no need to reinvent the wheel, and the solution can be found through combining things that worked elsewhere in new ways.
- We must screen policies and regulations for their effects on the small business sector and on working-class families who are not part of the corporate managerial and financial elite. This concern requires asking a simple question: Who wins in any given policy regime, Big Capital or Little Capital? I don't mean to say that we have to tax and hound the elite out of existence—we need them in our city too, but a great city cannot be a place that is habitable for them alone.
- When in doubt, more direct democracy is better than less democracy. Permanent government technocrats, academics, and our corporate lobbies very often just don't have the answers. Beware of those pretending they do. They are usually hiding the complexity of the problem or taking the side of capitalism's increasingly small band of winners.
- We must rein in the real estate industry, improve the way we regulate it, stop subsidizing the big players within it, and reverse the industry's excessive power and influence within government. We do this in the usual way: Implement reforms that democratize and regulate our public commons, beef up the way we regulate historic assets, discourage the negative externalities and social costs that an unfettered real estate industry imposes on residents by taxing what we don't like (like height over say, twenty stories), subsidizing what we do like (like small business), and impose new rules on campaign finance and public appointments.

In the doing of all these interrelated reforms under this framework, it is possible to flesh out an entirely new, equitable human-scale approach to economic development and to affordable housing that does not require shock-and-awe supply tactics that towerize and destroy historic neighborhoods. That said, a human-scale policy regime does imply a hard stop to the proliferation of skyscrapers. Instead, engage in an incremental build-out of environmentally nontoxic buildings between four and eight stories high, subsidized for affordability. New buildings must also incorporate design standards so that they are sustainable in the long run and encourage the emergence of great urbanity in the Jane Jacobs tradition: low- and mid-rise, mixed-use buildings that open to the street with lots of space for multiple small, non-chain business. Policies and reforms must also emerge out of a fierce anti-displacement philosophy so that the city does not turn into an upper-middle-class or office monoculture in which planners see gentrification as their only policy tool. Overall, new policies must be protective of sunlight, neighborhood residents, historic assets, small business, and the public realm—the elements that generate great urbanity. All these goals represent a mentality shift: Public assets should not be sold off to developers, and public-private partnerships must be scrutinized for hidden costs, greater accountability, and much greater public benefits. This means an end to the sale of parks, libraries, plazas, roadways, sidewalks, schools, and air rights over public resources. Our city must abandon the outdated Reagan-era mentality that government cannot do anything or pay for anything unless it trades away public resources to big corporations. Non-property tax revenue must be sought, notably from the corporate sector.

Two sets of questions ought to be guiding land-use policy and the expansion of the public realm in New York City.

- If a new building arises, is it better than what was there before? In what way is what a developer proposes measurably better for the public than what local neighborhood residents propose for the site? Who decides this question? How democratic is the process for deciding? How does a new building fit and serve a human-scale neighborhood rather than replace it, reinvent it, or overwhelm it? How does the building enhance the public realm rather than take away from it or feed off it parasitically?
- In what way is a zoning or land-use policy creating opportunities for smaller, independent players in the economy, "the little guy" (so to speak), as opposed to serving large corporate entities—be they Amazon, developers, investors, landlords, real estate investment trusts, or national chain stores? (Browning 2019).

An Economic Development Approach: Prosperity through Investment in the Public Realm

New York's technocratic elite has for too long mistakenly equated economic growth with big, private sector real estate projects whose developers get public subsidies (*Real Deal* 2020; Doctoroff 2017). That's what was behind the unpopular idea to give public subsidies to Amazon if it built a second headquarters in Queens. We see echoes of that real estate fantasy about economic growth in Vornado's justifications for building ten "Class A" office towers around Madison Square Garden. We see it in the upzoning of East Midtown, and in former Deputy Mayor Alicia Glen's proposal to build glassy towers on Governors Island, a place that was intended as a park. We see it in the East Harlem rezoning that sought to extend Yorkville's hated Avenue towers all the way up the island past 125th Street. We see it in the fantasy that criminal justice reform can only happen by closing the dozen or so buildings on Rikers Island and building sixty-story gentrified tower-jails near each borough courthouse.

One obvious problem with the reigning narrative is that building speculative towers doesn't "cause" economic growth. It is more likely the other way around. Economic growth is a tricky thing: Economists can measure it, track it, find a lot of things that correlate with it, but don't know what causes it. It doesn't come from demographic growth, because plenty of places have had population booms resulting in starvation (which is not the same thing as saying population growth inevitably causes starvation). It doesn't come by building towers either, as China built whole cities that nobody went to until they were forced to (Shelton, Zhou, and Ning 2018). The secret is not just "capital investment," as many of Nigeria's highways-to-nowhere illustrate. And it's not just a lack of business-friendly policies: Whole countries have revamped all their policies to be as business-friendly as possible, but then nobody came, and nothing happened. Moreover, even when economic growth does happen through trade, it can happen in a way that can impoverish the majority of the population (Bhagwati 1958).

The best stories we have about how economic development happens are place-specific tales of serendipity, geographic particularities, and unpredictable technological innovations that drove whole industries and their spin-offs to congregate in specific places, a story that geographer Michael Storper at UCLA tells well (Storper 2013). So what's a municipality to do in the face of this reality? Well, the best strategy might be to focus on a few of the more generally accepted correlates of equitable prosperity, while also adopting a policy of not chasing away any remaining manufacturing that you might still have, and above all, stop destroying the historic city you've already got. The increasingly rare historic city is an asset, not a liability. With that policy in place, turn to three things that usually correlate strongly with equitable economic prosperity: great regional transportation systems, a great public realm in general, and a highly educated population. Luckily, a municipal government can do a lot about those three things, and an economic development strategy should be anchored in all three of them.

However, I would add a fourth item to this economic development strategy: the old idea of nurturing into existence all kinds of small businesses and supporting them once they come into existence. Small businesses accounted for 65 percent of net new job growth nationwide since 2000 (Small Business and Entrepreneurship Council 2018; Kane 2010). Yet small businesses, especially retail, struggle because the rules of the game have become ever more stacked against them in favor of Amazon and the big box stores like Walmart and Target. A human-scale economic development strategy would reverse that trend by tilting the rules in the favor of smaller scale businesses at every level. For a tiny start in that direction, we could let pushcarts come back and stop harassing the Senegalese micro-entrepreneurs out of Canal Street. But a massive overhaul and rethink needs to happen about how government supports small business.

Building an economic development strategy around these ideas would mean junking the tower strategy, ending subsidies to Big Real Estate and the large corporate sector, and instead channeling capital to public education, transit, and public realm improvements and small business. Bring transit to the car dependent! Phonics for all! Create tree-filled parks, sidewalks, libraries, and even swimming pools. Yes, you heard that right, swimming pools. NYC's high schools used to have them, but they got built over in the bad old days of the '60s and '70s (Dwyer 2012). The high schools that restored their swimming pools in the 1990s discovered that immigrant teens who learned to swim in those high school pools found lifeguard jobs in the summer. Some earned more money than their parents during those months; so yes, trees and parks and swimming pools are important. Why not make our city a place people want to live in on the weekends rather than merely for careerist people who endure Monday through Friday before zooming off to Long Island in an SUV? This strategy of development relies on enhancement of the public realm broadly defined: public transit, schools, swimming pools, parks, trees, generous sidewalks, libraries, community health clinics, community centers, bowling alleys, and glorious walkable boulevards lined with thousands of small, non-chain businesses and trees.

City government must of course be intimately involved in the task of bringing public transportation to car-dependent areas. A city this dense must also be rewired to work with less traffic and less car commuting, so yes to bikes, and yes to congestion pricing, and yes to a much bigger use of pedestrianized streets for playgrounds, community meetings, pushcart markets, and even dog runs. On the transport part of this, it would be wise to invest in a regional unified transport system, one based on trains that run through Penn Station rather than stopping and backing out, a current reality at Penn Station that gums up the whole system. A new unified regional transit system would connect Long Island to New Jersey, and Queens to Boston in a new set of pathways. The idea has been amply explored by ReThinkNYC, a think tank set up by Jim Venturi. Amtrak engineers have pointed out that the idea is feasible. It is more cost-effective than any of the other plans on the table and even New York's "train Daddy," transit expert Andy Byford, supports the plan. Besides making commuting easier, cheaper, and more comfortable, a regional unified transport system equitably spreads economic opportunity around the region. Instead of 3.9 million people converging only on Midtown and the Financial District every day to benefit Vornado, offices (and factories too) would spread out and slowly find other places to go. Density would incrementally spread out and be more even, like thick peanut butter on a slice of bread, rather than forever piling up on two neighborhoods in Manhattan. People would be able to commute to all kinds of places, in all kinds of ways, in routes that are unthinkable today. This is a great vision: equitable, distributed prosperity and opportunity. This is not sprawl, but a multi-centered great city where every resident is a fifteen-minute walk to great schools, housing, offices, manufacturing, small businesses, a library, a fantastic park, and a transit point. Imagine the outcome: New York City's brilliantly educated kids and CUNY grads swimming every weekend, working as lifeguards in summers, jogging under trees in heavily planted boulevards lined with a new small business every ten feet, and graduating into work opportunities that are everywhere in the region and easy to get to, with many starting small businesses themselves with skills they got while in high school. How can we not want this?

Zoning Reform

Part One: A New Code

There is no doubt that New York's Zoning Resolution of 1961 is a hopeless mess, despite sporadic efforts to rectify some of its more obvious faults. By 1993 it had some 3,000 amendments and thousands more since then (Bressi 1993). On democratic grounds it is also bad: It was built for, modified by, and supported by Big Real Estate's lawyers, so in its present form it fails to defend the light, air, and health of citizens not working in the real estate sector. On bureaucratic grounds it is indefensible: It is arcane, written in baffling language intentionally meant to deceive and keep lawyers busy. It cannot function as a useful regulatory document. On urbanist grounds it also fails. It exists merely to allocate buildable space to developers and provide loopholes for those who don't like their allocation. It fails to generate predictable built forms on the street or to provide the framework for the emergence of great urbanity (for that, we need a different kind of zoning code altogether). It is a Potemkin code, providing the illusion that there are rules to protect the public interest, but the reality is that anything goes. Consider these quotes to inspire a revolutionary spirit in the reader—they come from the serious NYC zoning experts attending a zoning conference, with the papers and discussion compiled in a book edited by Todd Bressi (Bressi 1993):

> "The notion that zoning is a tool that can be used to achieve some greater purpose does not seem to have taken root in New York City." (Sigurd Grava)

> or

> "The idea zoning could solve problems is a myth. . . . It's a zoning system in which canny, savvy lawyers and their hired expediters work with the intricacies of special permits, restrictive covenants. . . . The zoning ordinance has almost always given real estate developers what they wanted." (Jerold Kayden)

> or

> "The notion that a person should pay for his or her zoning change in the form of a public amenity actually contradicts the very idea of zoning." (Norman Marcus)

> or

> "How long must it take before the city comes to the conclusion that [the 1961 Zoning Code] does not work? It was built to replicate the Seagram Building. Do we want whole cities to look like the Seagram Building? . . . The [1916] ordinance did not deal so well with the problems of small-scale development." (Robert Stern)

> or

> "Amending the resolution piecemeal would be like the game of croquet described in *Alice's Adventures in Wonderland*." (Norman Marcus)

Traditional zoning arose from a good idea: Regulate height and separate noxious uses (like factories generating smoke and stink) from residential areas. From that good idea arose a mess. In practice, the code quickly became about producing ever more gerrymandered maps illustrating how much buildable space each area within the map gets from the city, with endless rules about whether you could get more buildable space with a special permit or a variance or by going through an even more arcane special process. The City Planning agency became like a Mardi Gras float queen, tossing out candy (buildable space) to developers who scrabble after the candy while screaming "more, more." It's a parade intended as a performance of protecting the public good. Our current code is beyond dysfunctional—it encourages the demolition of the historic fabric of the city in a destructive race to the top that disfigures the historic skyline.

A new and better code would lengthen and democratize the land-use process, embrace clear "bright-line" height restrictions, eliminate the plaza bonus, protect and encourage a varied, human-scale street wall, encourage small-scale businesses, and define "contextual" and "neighborhood character" more rigorously in a way that goes beyond height and mass. It would embrace form-based coding; use simple language and illustrations; and eliminate the multiplicity of special interest carve-outs. Moreover, all buildings over six stories should be subject to environmental review that includes cumulative analysis of the impact of new density and height on all public assets, including water, sewage treatment facilities, skydome, sunlight, and view corridors. Negative environmental impacts should trigger not superficial mitigation public relations but require "back to the drawing board" action. And until the code is reformed and we get a handle on the perverse incentives that now exist to demolish historic fabric, a five-year moratorium on the destruction of all buildings built before 1946 and a demolition tax would be a good start.

What is to be done more generally once we stop doing bad things? First up is to start widespread public discussion about the "just right" range of optimal, Goldilocks densities for a city. How much density is too much? How much is too little? How should density be spread out? How do we densify places that are too low in density, and how do we stop densifying places that are already packed in like sardines? How should the benefits and burdens of density be shared among citizens *in all corners of the city*? How do we spread density out to get the benefits of a fifteen-minute city for all residents, not just those of Manhattan? Once that is debated, we can get on to other big issues.

The second thing to do is to change the rules about "as-of-right" construction permits. I suggest making the only buildings that can be built "as-of-right" (without public review) anywhere in the city those that are residential, between four and six stories, with ground floors that provide small business retail space for every 10 feet of frontage. Get rid of all parking requirements and forbid the construction of any new single-family home as well as the conversion of row houses to single-family use. Allow anywhere: boarding houses, dormitories, single-room occupancy hotels, old-school YMCA type buildings with dorm-style rooms, and auxiliary units in garages, attics, backyards, and waterproof, windowed basements. Outlaw supertalls and further shadowing of public parks. Impose a glass tax on the square footage of glass above 120 feet from the street for all buildings after 1946 that shadow existing parks and waterways. Impose a contextual height limit such that a new building cannot be more than 20 percent higher than the average height of all prewar buildings on both sides of the block. Eliminate FAR bonuses, plaza bonuses, special permit and waiver systems. Replace those waiver and special permit systems with Michael Kwartler's flexible points system, basically a performance-based system, where developers can trade among desirable building qualities (such as sunlight, roomy interiors, quality facades, big windows, street trees) (Goldberg 2015). Each quality gets a certain number of points. Allow developers to mix and match as they need to, if the final building earns enough total quality points. Make the default zoning of the entire city "contextual": anything non-contextual should go through the Uniform Land Use Review Procedure. Reform the land-use process to require City Planning to notify the public one full year prior to any local intended zoning change and extend the review process to two full years for neighborhood-wide rezonings. Regulate air rights transfers as described below.

Even better than all the above, scrap the current zoning code altogether and go for new form-based code with some limited, but neighborhood-specific, architectural, and streetscape standards. We need this because traditional zoning is entirely focused on two things in New York: regulating what buildings can be used for and allocating that scarce resource known as floor area ratio (FAR), what I have been calling "buildable space" throughout this book. With traditional zoning the game in New York has been thus: You tell developers how much buildable space they have on a lot, and what percentage of the lot they can build on, and what they can use the building for. But because the measure of buildable space is not a measurement of actual volume, the games begin, and one never knows what a building will look like on a given site.

Enter into the picture the alternative: form-based zoning codes, as promoted by the Form-Based Code Institute. What gets regulated in this type of zoning is the way a building meets the street, the void ratios, the rooflines, and the height of stories so that on any particular lot it becomes predictable what a proposed new building would end up looking like. Last, and though it is not a zoning reform per se, it needs to be said: We must modify the rules at the Department of Buildings so that all demolition permits are publicly available, searchable, and cumulatively tracked at all times. The various reforms De Blasio instituted at that department strangely missed the need to track that most important of all indicators: demolitions.

Part Two: Better Regulation of Transferable Air Rights

Our sky is shrinking. In some neighborhoods, sunlight is turning into a limited resource. Current rules ignore the fact that the sky is a public asset in need of better management. Heights must be respectful of the historic fabric in each neighborhood and include restrictions that prevent air rights from piling on top of each other, a game that results in supertalls and pop-up towers that arise mid-block. Figure 9.1 illustrates how this can happen. Since the real estate industry cannot police itself on this matter, it is the job of government to do it for them. This policy change would include new rules to eliminate the negative impacts of the current transfer of development rights, or "TDR," policy. It means changing the rules to prevent free-floating "mushroom clouds" of air rights from being dumped wherever the city feels like adding density. The guiding idea is that in a big city, the air and sky are scarce public resources that require thoughtful regulation to serve the public interest. That is not happening in New York City.

An air rights transfer takes place when the owner of the small, old building in the middle buys small amounts of unused buildable space (floor area ratio) from his neighbors to the right and left, and around the corner and down the block. Then the buyer stacks that space on top of his own building, allowing for a giant pop-up building to occur. When this happens, the city administration now looks away like a "see no evil" monkey that doesn't know something troubling is happening that violates the intent of the original zoning of that block. Recall that buildable space is a creation of government. Government can give FAR or take it away, a right of government that is not in question.

Developer Successfully Assembles Air Rights For Supertall Mixed-Use Tower At 80 South Street

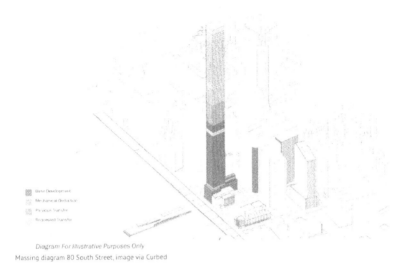

Figure 9.1. The figure illustrates how transferable air rights can create supertall towers. Image from Curbed.

New York City's rules for managing air rights are at present merely a set of bureaucratic *procedures* to encourage air rights transfers among property owners, not a *regulatory system* to minimize the social costs and negative externalities of overdevelopment. Worse, the current rules are smoke and mirrors that conceal the process of privatization of a public asset. They hide the city's failure to provide a well-considered plan for how density, light, and air should be distributed (Giordano 1988). Yet the game goes on and on. Carol Willis, the curator at the Skyscraper Museum commented: "The formula for FAR and the ability to purchase and pile up additional air rights has created an invisible Monopoly game in Manhattan real estate in which developers often work for years to acquire adjacent properties that could be collected into an 'as of right' tall tower" (Campbell-Dollaghan 2013). Attorney Robin Kramer dryly summed up the issue in a training document for real estate lawyers: The transfer of air rights is "often utilized by developers to facilitate the construction of a taller building than would otherwise have been possible had such rights not been transferred" (Kramer 2018).

There are multiple market failures here amid considerable social costs. First, weakly regulated air rights transfers provide real estate developers with perverse incentives to misallocate financial capital toward dramatically out-of-context luxury buildings that take capital away from more productive uses. Second, the resulting buildings rob the public realm of sunlight and air and sky. Third, the seizure of the skydome already happens in the most undemocratic way possible: The market substitutes for actual planning in a way that is contrary to the original public purpose of zoning as described in the state enabling law (Sorkin 2013). This dismal situation is made worse by the many proposals to free up and deregulate air rights transfers and create all kinds of new markets, such as what happened when the Catholic Diocese of New York got to sell the air rights to St. Patrick's Cathedral and then used the proceeds to fund payments to children abused by Catholic priests. Fourth, city residents are subject to an unpredictable and unplanned built environment that is helter-skelter in the extreme. Despite this, New York City's Department of City Planning under the Bloomberg and De Blasio administrations increasingly sought to meet the real estate industry's demand for *looser* regulations of air rights transfers (Been et al. 2014).

Modifications to the city's zoning code or the state Multiple Dwelling Law present unique opportunities to correct these market failures, reassert public command of the skydome, and model better regulation. Proposed revisions are laid out below.

1. Add a definition of where the law will apply, such as "The amendments apply only to cities with a population of greater than 5 million."
2. Add a new term with a definition, to wit: a "tax lot" is a parcel of land identified with a unique borough, block, and lot number for property tax purposes.
3. Add a phrase to limit lot mergers: "A lot resulting from a merger with any other tax lot for tax, zoning, or administrative purposes must not create any new non-compliance with the applicable, pre-existing zoning regulations."
4. Add three sentences about floor area transfers: Transfer of floor area from one tax lot to another may only take place subject to the following conditions:
    a. The transfer may not come from more than two adjacent tax lots, result in more than a 20 percent increase in floor area for the

receiving lot prior to a lot merger, or result in a lot with any new non-compliance with the existing zoning regulations.
b. The receiving lot of such transfers may not also be the recipient of floor area bonuses. (This limits the candy handed out to developers.)
5. Add wording to improve public records on the matter: "The relevant city agency shall maintain a publicly accessible database and map of tax lots that indicate that a floor area transfer has occurred, or lots have been merged, with a link to a scanned version of the legal documents known as Zoning Lot Development Agreements."

Democracy Reforms

Reform One: Elect Community Boards and Merge Them with the Business Improvement Districts

Civic engagement is not just about voting. It means stepping forward to spend time on local civic matters, from block associations to co-op board service, to raising funds for local schools to volunteering to tend a street tree. But when people feel that stepping forward is a waste of time, that their actions are irrelevant to the fates of their neighborhood, and when stepping forward embroils them only in trivial, pointless concerns (like participatory budgeting), they stop voting, and they stop engaging even with local concerns, and they just get on with their private lives. The solution to this disengagement? Give residents more power over local concerns, not less, so that stepping forward actually matters. That is where elected community boards could be part of the solution. The way forward is to create genuinely democratic community boards that take over the functions of BIDs. Call them Neighborhood Councils if you like, or Neighborhood Improvement Districts.

Unfortunately, Community Boards (CBs) were not set up as democratic entities. They were designed in the late 1960s merely as carefully controlled, curated town hall–style venues where a group of carefully selected, politically acceptable residents could meet with city agency staff and give feedback that could be ignored. The purpose was to encourage two-way chats on local matters concerning city service delivery such as trash collection. Over time the boards expanded in size and in the range of topics they talk about, but to this day they are powerless advisory councils. As the former chair of Community Board 2 told me, the boards exist "to provide political cover for local politicians."[1] That means the boards will dutifully craft resolutions that justify the politician's vote one way or another on controversial matters.

The City Charter states that each borough president must appoint fifty people (or slightly more depending on the population of the area) to each Community Board in his or her borough. Appointees serve staggered two-year terms, with a recent ten-year term limit (as of 2019). The borough president chooses half of the appointees from a list of potential board members that the relevant city council member gives the borough president, and the council member appoints the rest directly. Each board gets a full-time city employee to manage the board for them, called a "district manager," who often treats the borough president as the boss, not the chair of the Community Board. For example, the Manhattan borough president may believe in the virtues of negotiating deals with developers. He or she will appoint people with similar views, not those who believe in giving developers a hard no from time to time.

The borough presidents are free to appoint pretty much anybody. The official rules only say that an appointed person must live, work in, or have "an interest" in the geographic area covered by the board and that no more than 25 percent of the appointees can be city employees. Anyone—including civic groups—can submit nominations to the borough president. The need for the politicians to have political cover for some decisions means that many community boards are filled with "safe" appointees who do not rock any boats. Many appointees are outright lobbyists for some sector of the real estate industrial complex. Some appointees use the community boards as networking opportunities for architectural or real estate businesses. Last, many people serve on community boards in a quest to get a paid job in an administration, a problem as old as time but one that generates an unwillingness to rock boats.

Community boards are also, by nature, host to an endless parade of pitchfork mobs composed of residents who come to the meetings to vent against crimes to their neighborhoods, usually to no avail. This function of the community boards as a place to lodge mob complaints has a purpose. The boards function as a sandy beach for waves of community anger on land-use abuses to rise, unfurl, crash in fury, and then dissipate, without anything changing at all and a lot of people wasting time speechifying and writing intricate resolutions. It is a diabolically clever arrangement and a way to dissipate the energies of those opposed to overdevelopment.

Beyond that, the boards don't do much. According to the City Charter, the boards "review" and "consult with" city agencies and "conduct hearings" about plans for the area they cover. They can also make non-binding community plans (called 197 plans after a section of the charter), but few of them bother because the Department of City Planning almost always vetoes them. The boards are also allowed to "evaluate" the quality of services they are getting from the city and "to cooperate with, consult, assist, and advise" public agencies about the geographic area that the board covers. New York City's constitution says the intent of the boards is "to be used for the planning of community life within the city, the participation of citizens in City government within their communities, and the efficient and effective organization of agencies that deliver municipal services" (City of New York 2020).

It is time to rethink both community boards and business improvement districts. They have not lived up to their potential. Particularly troubling is widespread concern that the absence of substantive conflict-of-interest rules have rendered many community boards unrepresentative of their neighborhoods and ridden with bizarre conflicts-of-interest, cronyism, and Tammany Hall–type ambitions for jobs in city government. Whole self-serving lobbies, like pro–Big Real Estate Open New York, can take them over, like what famously happened to Community Board Five in Manhattan. Too many political club leaders, industry lobbyists, city employees, and self-serving people sit on the boards looking for professional advantage, such as real estate brokers, architects, lawyers specializing in sidewalk café permits, citizens hoping for a government job, etc. In many boards, these people have captured and held key committee positions, often for many years. In the words of one city council member, the boards have become "political cesspools" (Amato 2018). More and more, voters have come to understand that community boards do not represent residents. In short, the boards lack legitimacy.

There are other frustrations. Here are few of them.

- Board appointees become angry when they find out just how "advisory" their views are. In a recent case more than 95 percent of the boards voted against the mayor's Zoning for Quality and Affordability upzoning amendment, but the mayor and borough president pushed it through City Council anyway.
- Some board members legitimately fear being "purged" if they disagree with the borough president (Kallos 2014) on important land-use matters. Others report being politely "warned" by their borough president not to "pose a problem."[2]

- Bar owners wonder why they waste time getting community board opinion about a liquor license, when real control is in the hands of the State Liquor Authority.
- Historic district property owners resent paying architects twice: first to explain things to a community board committee, whose opinion is advisory, and then a second time to the actual Landmarks Preservation Commission, whose opinion is not advisory.

Reform is obviously needed, but none of the proposed reforms thus far—such as giving every board a city planner to work with or giving boards more training about what zoning means or giving them money to do community plans—will solve the underlying problems that create the political "cesspool" and lack of legitimacy. In fact, giving unelected boards more resources of any kind would only de-legitimize them more and further alienate the electorate.

What is needed is a comprehensive approach. Five separate reforms would re-legitimize the boards, insulate them from lobbying and old-school Tammany Hall influence, and provide them with effective purpose. The reforms are:

1. Term limits: The current ten-year maximum is a good start. To be sure, nobody currently serving on a community board liked the imposition of term limits, but then, politicians didn't like term limits imposed on them either. There is talk of losing them, which is unfortunate. Keep term limits.
2. Tougher conflicts-of-interest rules: Preclude appointment or election to a board for those who represent special interests or who have obvious divided loyalties over policy issues. Examples would be professional lobbyists of any kind or the senior management (executive members) of unions, political clubs, activist organizations, Open New York, and BIDs, who should of course be able to continue to use their influence as non-voting public members of the boards as the rules now allow.
3. Elect community boards to redrawn districts that make geographic sense. The reasons for this should be obvious but are expanded below.
4. Revamp the roles and powers of elected boards. Do this with one eye to the principle of subsidiarity in the regulation of public space and management of the public realm of sidewalks, trash, bike and car parking, streets, traffic, trees, parks, public seating, and liquor

licenses; and the other eye on checks that assure that the citywide public interest is accounted for.
5. Let elected boards hire, evaluate, and fire independent planners, land-use lawyers, and district managers; and not be beholden to the planners the administration imposes on them.
6. Allow the City Council to overturn a Department of City Planning veto on a community plan and require City Council to hold a public hearing on all vetoed plans prior to a vote.

WHY ELECT COMMUNITY BOARDS?

Doubtless borough presidents, council members, existing community board members, and political clubs will resist the idea of elected community boards or even a mix of elected, appointed, and "chosen by lottery" members. That's understandable: Reducing the number of appointed community board members is an erosion of the power of current members and a way to empower ordinary neighborhood residents instead. A better question is: Why not elect community boards, or tiptoe in that direction with a mix, say a majority of elected members with a few appointed members (if the appointees are not political hacks or lobbyists)? The advantages of having a citizen assembly legitimized by voting at the neighborhood level are well known and as old as the idea of democracy itself: greater civic engagement and a real sense among residents that they can be stewards of their neighborhood, not merely people passing through.

Those who dislike the idea of elected boards routinely give five arguments to explain their opposition to elections.

a. The first argument says: "Voters are so uneducated that they will be manipulated by moneyed interests." This is the same as the ancient argument that we should avoid direct elections, so that government is not influenced by "the passions of the people," as Alexander Hamilton would say. But consider that this is the very argument that led to the long life of the undemocratic Electoral College. It is the same argument that made Trump our unelected president. If you oppose the Electoral College, it makes no sense to oppose direct elections for community boards.

b. Some argue: "Good people won't get elected. There are useful, very shy people who serve on community boards who aren't charismatic or physically attractive and couldn't hold their own in an election against potentially 'bad' candidates such as expensively dressed,

articulate, and good-looking real estate brokers" (from a conversation with a friend serving on a board). This objection seems more to be an expression of generalized anxiety rather than a well-thought-out objection. First, just look around! It isn't Hollywood in the local political arena. And at the level of a neighborhood in NYC, it is far easier to flush out bad candidates for their ties to special interests and to successfully inform the locals about the problem: Anyone can hand out flyers at a subway station and stand a pretty good chance of reaching a lot of voters in a New York neighborhood. And how could the choice of local voters for representatives on community boards be any worse than the current, often bizarre choices of borough presidents in the matter? Anxious community board wannabe: Be brave! You can stand in a middle-school auditorium and make your case to your neighbors about how you might do right by them if they elect you to a community board. Besides, if you are too shy to run for office you can always be a non-voting public member.
c. "It's too expensive!" to elect community boards. This argument is weak. We are already paying for the nonprofit Democratic Party to put its own county committee members and district leaders on the printed ballots, at public expense, so why not add community board members to that same ballot? It is cheap to rent a public-school auditorium to host neighborhood debates or to use a tent in a closed street. Thus, the marginal cost of electing community boards is not a deterrent.
d. "Only NIMBY's who wouldn't build higher than three stories would get elected." This is a REBNY scare tactic, not verified by empirical evidence, and one that assumes elected community boards would have total control over land use, which is not what we are talking about. REBNY's scare tactics should not dominate public policy debate.
e. "When we had elected school boards, turnout at those elections was low and those boards were terrible!" The logic of this argument is not convincing. Should low turnout mean we should give people even fewer opportunities to vote in the future and give up on democracy altogether? I think not. Also, as the history of the old New York school boards shows, the cause of their failure was far more complicated than the fact that they were elected. It would be a mistake to trivialize or oversimplify that history.

Elected community boards should continue their function as a venue of two-way communication between city agencies and residents, but with some changes.

- They should be required to hold quarterly town halls for the wider community—and given the resources to rent auditoriums for that purpose or use the very streets.
- They should be required to use (and funded to do so) geographic-information-systems (GIS) enabled, democracy software that allows for debate and legitimate referenda on local matters with verifiable residents of the area.
- They should be free to develop community plans for the public realm and to lobby the city for approval of such plans, using their own hired staff, not those seconded to them by the city.
- They should not waste time duplicating technical regulatory functions (such as the ubiquitous Landmarks Committees).
- They should have more authority and regulatory power over many decisions concerning local public space, such as supervising and enforcing public-private plaza agreements, the auctioning of parking permits for street parking, location of bike racks, location of public art (and the right to tell DOT not to put art somewhere), the tending of street trees, the leasing of sidewalks and roadways, and of course, full control over the granting of liquor licenses, sidewalk café tables, parklets, street closures, and use of street space for restaurant space.

Broader and more stringent conflict of interest rules would restore confidence in the boards and diminish the public's perception that the boards are playthings of politicians and special interests. We also must have a broader, traditional definition of "conflict of interest" that rules out board participation in committees and discussion and voting by those who have axes to grind and institutionalized, divided loyalties. The importance of this cannot be overstated.

Reform Two: Strengthen Conflict of Interest Rules in the City Charter

Community boards are not the only places with a conflict-of-interest problem. The city regulatory agencies that oversee real estate, such as the Department of City Planning and the Board of Standards and Appeals, are packed with so many real estate developers, lobbyists, and real estate cheerleaders that we have a clear "fox guarding the henhouse" situation. A Charter Commission or special City Council legislation could easily repair the situation. The fix is simple: Create rules that forbid people who have worked as professional lobbyists or advisors to the regulated industry from serving either on community boards or as commissioners of our city agencies.

Reform Three: Fix Lax Campaign Finance Rules

Politicians must be owned by the broad electorate, not special lobbies like Big Real Estate. A first step in that direction is to revise both the state and the city's campaign finance laws to minimize the influence of donors who give big checks. But how do we define "a big check"? The city law on the matter now defines "big" as $1,000, and the state law says big is $15,000. But big to whom? I for one, cannot afford either "big" donation. The whole notion of what constitutes a "big" donation is a fantasy in the mind of the well-paid, upper-middle-class lawyer, technocrat, or lobbyist who drafted the current campaign finance law. This can be fixed, and must be. As Aristotle said, you cannot sustain a democracy unless the middle class is steering the ship in its broadest sense. Let's define "big check" here as something feasible for the average middle-class household. In New York City where the median household income for the region is as of this writing $56,000.

So how much should the average household earning $56,000 a year give away to political causes, given that they probably also have other charitable impulses like donating to food banks and children's charities? If we assume that the median household uses the concept of a traditional tithe to budget (a concept that spans cultures and time periods of history), that means we are talking about 10 percent of their income destined for charitable purposes. That means our median household thus has at most $5,600 to give away each year. How much of that should go to political "charities" as opposed to traditional charities? A reasonable answer would be 10 percent of that, so $560.

And there you have it. The maximum campaign contribution in New York State should be $560, adjusted annually for inflation. Instead of inventing a fantasy number in a smoke-filled back room that makes sense only to elite, upper-middle-class technocrats, I've proposed a number that makes political and cultural sense. It's anchored in the budget of the middle-class taxpayer, the very person we want steering the politicians in a democracy. Culturally, in that it fits in with a reasonable expectation about how households tithe. While we are at it, we should also be adding other reforms:

- Reduce the number of signatures required to get on any ballot as the current system requires too many and is meant to empower political clubs.
- Create a rule that bars anyone who is listed in any of the three years prior to the election in the "doing business with the city" database from contributing to the system at all.

- Cut out the infamous LLC loophole so that limited liability corporations are subject to the same maximum donation rules as individuals.

The upshot is that if the city and state campaign laws were rewritten in New York City and the state to permit a maximum campaign donation of $560, then we'd have gone very far indeed in limiting the influence of big real estate, and other big lobbies of course. It would remove the wealthy from the prominent place they now occupy in the brains of the politicians.

Of course, an even better solution is to chuck the system entirely and go for a publicly financed campaign system like Seattle's famous democracy voucher system. In Seattle, the Board of Elections sends every voter four certificates, each worth $25. Candidates then must chase after the voters and talk them into handing over one or more certificates. Candidates turn the certificates they have harvested over to the Board of Election and receive real money to finance a campaign. One could imagine all kinds of variants on this, but it works quite well. Imagine, every voter as important to the politicians as those who sit on the board of governors of the Real Estate Board of New York!

Reform Four: Charter Reforms to Reduce Lobbying and Revolving-Door Abuse

The Demolition Machine's slithery tentacles are impossible to eliminate, but there are plenty of ways to cut them back and reduce their reach. Here are some ideas to tidy up the language in the City Charter.

1. Insert language into the Charter such that nobody who has ever been a paid lobbyist or advisor to the real estate industry may serve on any regulatory commission.
2. Require at least half the members of the City Planning Commission to have degrees in city planning (architecture won't do) and half of the Landmarks Preservation Commissioners to have degrees in either history or historic preservation.
3. Require all requests for evaluation for historic districts or individual landmarks to be screened by the full, appointed commission or a sub-committee thereof, not the chair or staff.
4. Insert language in the charter such that no members of the Planning Commission or Landmarks Commission or BSA may be someone with a current job in senior management at a real estate development, investment, or advisory entity of any kind.

5. Require all senior staff in planning or land use agencies, and senior advisors in the City Council to sign "noncompete" contracts in which they cannot take up employment with anyone doing business with the city for three years after leaving city government employ. The private sector uses noncompete contracts, so should government.

Reform Five: Limit the Number of Apartments That a Single Owner Can Hold and Don't Let Real Estate Hide behind Limited Liability Corporations

We need a law that prevents excessive consolidation of property ownership. If we don't do that, we end up promoting a new version of medieval serfdom, in which thousands of renters pay homage to a single real estate lord who operates like a feudal aristocrat. It would be better to take a "small is beautiful" approach to property ownership. Imagine if no single landlord could own more than, say, one hundred apartments. Big players would be required to divest their excess units.

But to even get to that point where such a policy is feasible, we'd have to pass laws to have greater transparency about property ownership. At present, limited liability corporations can buy property and hide who owns the building if the building has more than four units. The current law only requires that owners of buildings with fewer than four units disclose the owners of the underlying corporation. Just as frustrating, ownership even of those smaller units is not publicly accessible information (E. Kim 2019a). This is just silly: I cannot think of a reason in a democracy to not modify the public disclosure law to apply to all apartments, unless of course, Big Real Estate wants to hide concentration of ownership in much of New York City.

Reforms for Small Businesses and Manufacturers

Small businesses are important elements of great urbanity. There are some good ideas floating around New York City about how to support them. The Small Business Jobs Survival Act proposes voluntary but binding commercial arbitration for lease renewals, with arbitration costs shared equally between landlord and tenant. However, arbitration costs have inflated massively since the bill was first written. One improvement to the bill would be to create a city-funded public arbitration unit with the Small Business Services Agency, one that charges modest fees compared to the commercial process. A related bill is the Commercial Rent Control bill, which imposes fixed rents for commercial spaces, basically frozen at their current settings. Given that fixed rents struggle against superior market forces, a better substitute for that bill might be passage of a small business version of the proposed "Good Cause Eviction Act" in the state legislature. That bill lays out legitimate causes for eviction and sets allowable rent increases for lease renewals that are based on a small percentage above inflation. And while we are at it, reverse the La Guardia-era discrimination against pushcarts. Allow them back into the city and allow for pedestrianized street markets—basically year-round versions of the holiday markets that pop up around Union Square and Columbus Circle. Also pass an anti-chain store law that limits chains to say, ten stores (Ingram and Rao 2004). The city could also make an effort to take ownership of abandoned storefronts and rent them at discounted rates.

Beyond this, we need to reject the view that manufacturing in New York City is a lost cause and stop zoning small manufacturing out of existence (Pratt Center for Community Development 2015). We might also start a new pro–small business regime by conducting a complete overhaul of the mission and purposes of the Small Business Services agency. At present, it mostly serves corporate business improvement districts rather than truly serving the small business sector in an imaginative, creative way. In such a reinvention, get rid of the structurally unaccountable Economic Development Corporation (EDC), which focuses on big corporate-style real estate deals anyway. Combine its functions into a new small business agency that refocuses government support onto ways to allow small businesses and manufacturers to thrive in NYC and to lead in job growth. Make it accountable to the City Council.

Another small business policy would be to use zoning to increase the availability of retail spaces for small businesses by requiring property owners to modify dead street walls around the city to provide small business space (or else allow for kiosks to operate in front of these dead street walls). Require all new construction to feature small business space. Combine that with education policies that produce a skilled, entrepreneurial population. Kick-start the latter with a new high school curriculum that requires all graduates to have had hands-on training and practical experience in setting up a business. Entrepreneurial experience should be a default high school experience of all New Yorkers, more important than requiring calculus for college-bound graduates. Create an army of gumshoed advisors walking the streets of the city talking to small business owners about what kind of help they need rather than endlessly theorizing about it. We might also give tax abatements to small co-ops and condos (not those owned by LLCs and giant corporations) if they renew small business leases on reasonable terms. Last, we urgently need to heavily tax cardboard, paper, and plastic packaging used in delivery services, targeting the rapid corporatized delivery services of the same-day and two-day variety. The point is to level the playing field for small Mom and Pop businesses that now cannot compete with Amazon's monopolistic power.

What to Do about the Landmarks Preservation Commission (LPC)?

The LPC is an institution charged with carrying out long-term goals for the city. It creates historic parts of the public commons, creating intergenerational economic value. It should not be concerned with bogus highest and best use fantasies. Therefore, the LPC should be insulated from the vagaries of short-sighted mayoral control. The institution also needs a bigger budget and new procedures and accountability mechanisms so that it remains a credible institution that is not visibly captured by the real estate industry (Kroessler 2018). To such ends, the following would be helpful:

- Distribute the power of appointing the eleven commissioners (including the chair) among the mayor, the City Council, the borough presidents, and the Public Advocate. I suggest three appointees from the mayor, which would include the chair; two from the council's Landmarks Committee; one each from the borough presidents, and one from the Public Advocate.
- Strengthen the professional qualifications of the commissioners, so that a majority of the eleven have graduate degrees in historic preservation, and none should be active in the real estate industry either as brokers, advisors, lobbyists, or developers. If architects are appointed, they must be architects who explicitly and on paper disavow the modernist philosophy of eliminating styles that predate Le Corbusier and disavow Commandment #70 of the modernist *The Athens Charter*. Such an ideology has no place on the Landmarks Preservation Commission.
- Modify the City Charter concerning the LPC so that all requests for evaluation (RFE) for potential historic districts or landmarks must be considered and voted upon by the full eleven-member commission or by a committee of commissioners and staff that the full commission appoints, not the chair. All staff recommendations regarding those requests must be publicly available, as well as minutes of all meetings regarding requests for evaluation.

- The criteria for making those RFE decisions must be publicly available and concern only the urbanist, architectural, cultural, and historic merits of each case, and not refer to the politics of the case or the speculative finances of potentially unbuilt floor area ratios of the designated area.
- The LPC must have the power to designate view corridors as historic districts and regulate development that interferes with those view corridors.

Other Tax Reforms

It should be a no-brainer to end the pointless 421-a tax abatements we give to developers and eliminate the other real estate tax breaks described in earlier chapters (Velsey 2015; New York City Independent Budget Office 2017; Independent Budget Office 2015). Other tax reforms that would help would be a pied-à-terre tax on unoccupied units and an end to the policy of granting beggar-thy-neighbor tax giveaways to the corporate sector in exchange for elusive, feeble, or poorly regulated public benefits.

Toward a Human-Scale Affordable Housing Policy

Here is a way to begin a new affordable housing policy in the broadest of strokes. Stop treating the problem as a DEFCON 1 crisis that requires an immediate shock-and-awe approach of gigantic solutions. Second, share the market opportunity that affordable housing construction represents with small-scale entrepreneurs, nonprofits, and "little guy" homeowners and builders instead. Third, rein in speculative real estate investment that is driving up prices. Cool down the overheated hot markets to reallocate real estate capital to where it can be more useful. Expand rent stabilization to all rental units, not just those officially stabilized. Last, aggressively beef up government direct investment in housing (including with land trusts) so that those units will be forever affordable rather than affordable for twenty years.

A new affordable policy regime for NYC might have many "planks." Here are eleven. Feel free to add more. The point here is to stimulate public debate. These are not presented in order of importance.

1. First, modify zoning in the entire city so that it is easy for owners of one- and two-family houses to add attic, basement, or garage apartments without facing a barrage of unnecessary restrictions. This is

not just about legalizing what is already common practice but about adding a serious number of more units: Census data tell us there are almost a million single- and two-family homes in New York City (Census Bureau 2015). If a mere 20 percent of those owners (at least those who haven't already done so) renovated a "granny unit," we'd have as many as 200,000 new units (compared with the 2,000 units the city built under ZQA/MIH after seven years of MIH policy as of December 2019). And those units would have the advantage of being at the lower end of the market instead of at the high end. Moreover, it would disperse the affordable apartments throughout the city precisely in the areas that need more density. To help that policy along, organize interest-free lines of credit so that small homeowners can renovate without impoverishing themselves.

2. Second, modify zoning and tax penalties to support "easy," but limited, densification. For example, allow boarding houses, "youth out of college" housing, and SROs to return as a housing category throughout the city. Do not fine or regulate this housing category out of existence but help these housing categories become livable places (L'Heureux 2015; Durning 2013). And in the doing, make it harder (and painful too, with tax penalties) to convert existing SROs to condos or multi-unit buildings to single-family homes or tourist hotels so we don't turn the West Village into a version of desolate Mayfair in London.

3. A third policy might be, as a Furman Center study suggested, to provide tax credits to the 57,000 owners of the city's nonluxury, non-stabilized units—provided they refrain from raising rents until we can get laws passed that put all units under rent stabilization (Furman Center 2015).

4. Fourth, modify zoning and tax incentives to encourage small developers to build mid-rise, human-scale six- to eight-story, high-density apartment buildings in the areas that need density, much like the six-story buildings one sees in Hasidic Williamsburg. The Romanian Hasids have built out this urban version of "missing middle" housing and done so largely for holders of Section 8 vouchers, which proves the idea is economically viable. To push the point further, such R6 contextual zoning should be the as-of-right standard for *all neighborhoods*, one from which developers must get special permission to deviate from. This idea is nothing new. Mid-rise and even low-rise public housing has been built plenty of times even in New York, but it is an option scorned by hyper-density fans (Bloom and Lasner 2016).

Again, this incremental, low- and mid-rise approach would add density to the very areas that need it at the periphery of the city where land is cheaper but instead got shrink-wrap zoning under Bloomberg (shrink-wrapped means zoning allowances that go no higher than the existing buildings). To cope with the so-called NIMBY factor such a policy might unleash, sympathize with neighborhood concerns instead of mocking them. How? Allow what has always been forbidden: community "aesthetic" design review to assure residents that they won't get stuck with ugly additions that stick out like sore thumbs. As a *Times* article about the "Monstrosity" in Queens demonstrates, residents often rebel against new construction for its refusal to blend in, not for who will move in (Semple and Singer 2015). And if you get pushback about access to transit for the new, dispersed renters, liberate rather than overregulate the "dollar van" entrepreneurs. They have already found a free market, small-scale way to transport people to work on time. Let them do it while we figure out how to bring public transport to transit deserts, a major function of intelligent government that NYC has abandoned.

5. A fifth policy plank has to do with regulating the game that international real estate capital is playing by combining new rules with new taxes. Why build affordable housing in Queens at a 4 percent profit margin when it is possible to do a cheap luxury tower in Tribeca with 96 percent gross profit margins? So change the game. What government gives it can also take away. Downzone the "hot" areas subject to overdevelopment by imposing height restrictions there, forcing real estate capital to move on. Impose a demolition moratorium for neighborhoods where speculation is rampant and where there are misguided zoning incentives that seek to demolish older, rent-stabilized buildings. Doing otherwise amounts to giving developers a free and unfettered market, which only results in the eviction of loft-law and rent-stabilized tenants as well as small businesses. Refusing to downzone in such markets is encouraging a kind of demented market failure: a developer's game to demolish and then replace everything with luxury condos (Cameron 2014). There are many other ways to tax, regulate, and channel foreign real estate investment capital and to regulate it. An essential fix would be to cap the use of as-of-right air rights transfers to 20 percent of the original allocation of buildable space (aka FAR) prior to any zoning lot mergers. This would solve much of the problem we see in working-class neighborhoods where bizarre towers filled with luxury condos pop up

mid-block to satisfy demand for real estate investors seeking a place to park capital.

6. Sixth, be more strategic about finding alternative sources of money for affordable housing of all kinds and build up public capacity for direct investment in city-owned affordable housing. If the political will is there, it would be possible to build a much bigger dedicated affordable housing fund, controlled by the city itself, with plenty of money for city-sponsored small-scale new construction. For example, what happened to the billions in fines that sat in a trust fund from bank payouts over the financial crisis? Re-engage with Albany on both a pied-à-terre tax and a flip tax. Take up Charles Urstadt's idea of capturing Battery Park City's $130 million yearly surplus and use it for bond financing for new affordable units in areas of lower density, as was the original intention for that pool of money. Although I usually disagree with Mr. Urstadt, he had a good idea in this case. None of this is rocket science. The annual "City Budget" reports issued by the Independent Budget Commission list dozens of ways to cut waste and reallocate funds in the city budget as well good ideas about how to find new tax revenue from former sacred cows like the giant nonprofit property owners in the city such as Madison Square Garden. We do not have to wait for federal government intervention to do this.

7. A seventh plank might be to do much more careful, community-supported and neighborhood-specific micro-zoning at a modest scale that uses rigorous notions of contextual and historic-district friendly design. For example, there is a stretch of 7th Avenue that has a considerable cluster of abused one-story brick "taxpayer" buildings that, despite their humble character, fit into surrounding Greenwich Village. They are not in a historic district. Why destroy them? Why not allow the owners to build up a couple of floors in the exact same architectural style? It used to be common for old federal houses to get built up an additional two or three stories. It was done so skillfully that only architectural historians notice the seam line. What if thousands of such blocks, incrementally around the city got that kind of historically sympathetic, form-based micro-zoning? Big developers would scorn this opportunity, but little developers and small homeowners would welcome it. Granted, the architectural elite would say such a design strategy risks being "kitsch," but why let them boss us around with vague aesthetic judgments that aren't even scientific? Low-rise historic districts could also be built up in

this small, incremental way, assuming of course that preservationists could agree on a way to do this without destroying the public architectural value that is there in the first place. (Preservationists are equally fretful of the accusation of "kitsch.")

8. An eighth plank: Expand rent-stabilization laws to cover all units in the city, market rate or not. Pass a Good Cause Eviction Act with a very tight inflation cap (note: California's 8 percent over inflation cap seems way too high). Even medieval serfs had protections from arbitrary and capricious lords. Now that historic rent reforms are in place in Albany, the next step is truly universal rent stabilization in the form of reforms that would apply to all rental units. Such stability should be for everyone in a city with such a large stock of rental units and would be a very powerful policy tool to restore affordability in the city.

9. Ninth, push back via regulation on the massive inflow of speculative real estate capital and the general financialization of housing. This is an expansion of plank 5 above. Was there any need for Gary Barnett of Extell to borrow $23 billion to build a supertall on 57th for the world's plutocrats? What a waste of capital. Such speculative insanity is what is largely responsible for the massive inflation in housing prices in NYC as well as the excessive profits that developers receive. Regulating this massive flow of capital would require a variety of policy measures: a pied-à-terre tax, beating back Airbnb, eliminating opportunity zones in NYC, imposing flip and speculation taxes, full disclosure of LLC ownership, a ban on REIT ownership of rental housing, and perhaps best of all, my favorite idea, an "anti-serfdom" law that limits the number of rental units a single human or company can own. Any city where a private equity firm like Blackstone or a real estate oligarch like LeFrak can control the lives of 30,000 tenants is a city that is returning to the feudal era.

10. Tenth, build up the public land bank, mostly with aggressive use of eminent domain on slumlords, "bad apples," and investors who warehouse either land or apartments or who leave retail spaces vacant (Blackstone, beware!). Once you have more land in the public domain, anchoring housing in community land trusts for human-scale housing becomes easy to scale up, rather than a quixotic search for buildings and land to buy. And be tougher about the use of existing public assets. Why, for example, is the publicly owned World Trade Center site 5 (the former site of the Deutsch Bank) to be sold for $300 million instead of handed over to the city for affordable

housing? And why did the city sell the massive 349 Broadway landmark (which had been city offices) to a luxury developer instead of keeping it for a land trust with 100 percent forever-affordable housing? The same could be said for the whopping 600 or so developable acres on Floyd Bennett Field (now part of the Gateway National Recreation Area). The point here is to make a land trust model the centerpiece of affordable housing rather than something the city gives lip service to.

11. Build 100 percent forever low-rise affordable housing on the vast open spaces that already exist in the large number of "tower in the park" housing estates scattered throughout the city. But don't do it the De Blasio way. Do it slowly and incrementally as the funds become available. Keep the infill low-rise and cheap and never more than six stories. Don't privatize the land or the apartments. Don't borrow for it or expect this tactic to also subsidize public housing renovations. Don't steal playgrounds. Use it also as a design opportunity to reconnect these estates to the urban street and have small businesses at ground floors. Above all, don't do it through any shock-and-awe plans. Incrementalism is the way to go here. See plank 6 for ideas on how to fund this. By the way, this idea comes from zoning guru Michael Kwartler.

All this of course must be done within a policy regime that defines a range of optimal densities that result in a beautiful, livable, human-scale city, using a variety of measures of "livable density" after public debate. For example, at the low end we might see sixty housing units per acre for the periphery of the city, and at the high end might be two hundred housing units per acre. We've already built some areas at densities far higher than that, and that is not the way to go.

These are suggestions for public debate. Once fair distribution of density is sorted out, use planning, not zoning, to get there. Plan transit to the transit-starved; plan for public parks and libraries and swimming pools; plan for Jane Jacobs streetscapes filled with small businesses spilling out into the street; plan for public access to the sky and sun. Plan for a human-scale city. If you do, all New Yorkers will get great neighborhoods that will become the historic districts of the future, places we want to raise our children and grow old in, not over-scaled dystopian enclaves of glass like Hudson Yards.

You may know of other thoughtful policy ideas that don't involve the current free-for-all designed to benefit an oligarchic real estate industry. It is time to share them. To be sure, hyper-density fans might sneer and say they have contempt for such incremental approaches. But incrementalism would get the job done while also creating a more human-scale city. It would do so without the displacement and destruction that is both cruel and short-sighted. Moreover, who would win under a human-scale alternative policy regime? The answer is obvious: the middle, composed of small homeowners, small builders, small contractors, small business, small developers, as well as the army of people seeking affordable housing. Another big winner would be residents of human-scale neighborhoods across the city. They would get a reprieve from the current plunder of the public realm that is taking place in the name of the scam known as "affordable" housing. We are also at a tipping point: If we don't act soon in finding politicians to champion a new housing policy, our city will be lost.

ACKNOWLEDGMENTS

THIS BOOK IS FOR MY DAUGHTER, that she may know what happened to the city she grew up in, the same Wonder City that gave me a home long before she was born. It is also dedicated to all those who have tried to save their Wonder City, wherever it may be, from demolition.

I am grateful to many people who have encouraged me and let me stand on their shoulders while talking, explaining, laughing, and arguing with me over the topics in this book and whose own writings have so deeply influenced how I think, but especially William Duggan, Steven Semes, Michael Sorkin, Anthony Tung, Tom Angotti, and the many brilliant minds—too many to mention individually here—working in the networks of the Historic Districts Council of New York, the Congress for the New Urbanism, and in the Alliance for a Human-Scale City. I am grateful to the editors at Fordham for supporting the book and to gimlet-eyed Teresa Jesionowski who copyedited my writing. Last, but not least, this book would not be if I had not been moved to action by the work and wisdom of Jane Jacobs.

NOTES

2. The Failure of Trickle-Down Housing Supply Theory

1. Those papers have titles such as "The Impact on Zoning on Housing Affordability" (Glaeser and Gyourko 2002), "Why Have Housing Prices Gone Up?" (Glaeser, Gyourko, and Saks 2005), and "Why Is Manhattan so Expensive?" (Glaeser, Gyourko, and Saks 2005). Some of Glaeser's papers are co-authored with a core group of intellectual collaborators such as Vicki Been at New York University's real estate–funded Furman Center and Joseph Gyorko, a professor of real estate at Wharton School of Business. For readability, I use "Glaeser," "Glaeser et al.," "Glaeser and colleagues," and "trickle-down housing supply fundamentalists," or "fundamentalists," interchangeably.

2. This fundamentalist story also ignores the facts on the ground as to how unemployed Rust Belt workers think and behave when they lose their jobs. Nobel Prize–winning economist Esther Duplo reported that affected workers juggle complex trade-offs between several variables: the need for proximity to long-established family and neighborhood connections, their age, the weak possibility of capturing a fleeting new job opportunity if one moves, and a host of other life-cycle variables. She also found that Rust Belt workers "were substantially more likely to die in the years immediately after" a job loss, as Duflo found in Pennsylvania (Duflo and Banerjee 2019).

3. "Learning from Hong Kong" was a popular notion among those sympathetic to Glaeser's way of thinking, people who sought to promote more vertical density in New York City. In fact, the "Skyscraper Museum" in Manhattan held a multi-day conference on the subject in 2011, an archive of which is available on the museum's website.

4. Opportunity zones are areas where real estate investment was granted a special tax break: zero capital gains taxes if the investment is held for ten years (Melby 2019).

5. See the tables in the appendix to the economic study appended to the Environmental Impact Statement for De Blasio's "Zoning for Quality and Affordability" (BAE Urban Economics Inc. 2013)

6. Social costs refer to the costs to society that a transaction imposes and where the producer of the cost does not have to bear those costs himself. An example might be the cost to the larger society of drunk driving, a cost that the manufacturers of alcohol do not have to bear. Externalities refer to costs and benefits, often by-products of a manufacturing process, which get imposed on others as a side effect of the transaction or manufacturing process. An example would be the release of radioactive substances into the air. They are a negative "externality" of the process of manufacturing nuclear power.

7. For school overcrowding generally, see (Martinez 2019). To learn about the lead problem, be aware that 80 percent of city school buildings in one test had a lead problem in at least one outlet (Matthews 2019). For examples of overcrowded sidewalks, parks, and swimming pools and the problems of trash mountains in the Financial District, see journalist Winnie Hu's coverage in the *New York Times* (Haag and Hu 2019; Hu 2018a; Hu 2016; Hu 2018b). For the general environmental dilemmas of New York City's massive trash problem, see the *New York Times* Editorial Board's essay concluding that the trash problem in NYC is a model of market failure (Board 2019).

8. While there is plenty of natural gas in the United States (at least temporarily), gas pipelines to transport them are not in infinite supply.

9. See Brad Lander's comments on this video from a seminar produced by City Limits: https://citylimits.org/2019/05/24/video-does-nyc-need-a-comprehensive-plan/.

10. Another effort to use weak subsidies to induce developers to build low-income housing also has mixed results. Some researchers have found, for example, that housing produced by "Low Income Tax Credits" can just as often raise the prices of housing around it.

11. The U.S. Census reports the presence of 1,983 housing units in one of the more densely built-out census tracts near the Grand Concourse filled with six-story tenement buildings. If we round that off to 2,000 units per census tract, the calculations follow, assuming a conservative 50 percent loss rate for the forty-four census tracts Flood reports on.

12. I am not considering conversion to be the same as demolition.

13. Readers may recall that Mandatory Inclusionary Housing (MIH) policies use upzoning subsidies to developers if they reserve a portion of their new units as "affordable," vaguely defined. The portion is typically 30 percent, but can go lower, and some cities have gotten developers to do as much as 50 percent of affordable units.

3. The Costs of Towerization and the Problem of Density

1. Personal communication, Michael Sorkin email to Lynn Ellsworth, 2018.

2. See https://en.wikipedia.org/wiki/Arrondissements_of_Paris.

3. For this section, I use data from a variety of sources, often Wikipedia essays on individual cities or neighborhoods, the Zip Code Atlas (http://zipatlas.com/us/zip-code-comparison/population-density.htm), Statistical Atlas that uses census data and American Household Survey (https://statisticalatlas.com/zip/10014/Overview), the World Population Review, a UN database, or https://en.wikipedia.org/wiki/Demographics_of_New_York_City

4. See https://en.wikipedia.org/wiki/Manhattan.

5. See http://zipatlas.com/us/zip-code-comparison/population-density.htm

6. See Jane Jacobs, chapter 11 of *The Death and Life of Great American Cities*. See also https://statisticalatlas.com/zip/10014/Overview and https://en.wikipedia.org/wiki/Greenwich_Village.

7. Caveat for this comparison: I am not sure that the surface area Jacobs was measuring for Brooklyn Heights in 1960 is exactly congruent to the surface area of Brooklyn Heights area that Wikipedia is now measuring as of 2020.

8. See https://en.wikipedia.org/wiki/Arrondissements_of_Paris.

9. See https://worldpopulationreview.com/world-cities/barcelona-population/.

10. See https://www.wehoville.com/2016/05/12/west-hollywood-17th-densely-populated-city-us/#comments.

11. See https://www.areavibes.com/geneva-il/demographics/.

12. See Open Data Network here: https://www.opendatanetwork.com/entity/1600000US3642081-1600000US4242928/Levittown_NY-Levittown_PA/geographic.population.density?year=2018.

4. Economics of the Urban Commons

1. My general practitioner informs me that in Manhattan, most of her patients are chronically deficient in Vitamin D since they don't get enough exposure to sunlight in the fall, winter, and spring.

2. This confirms James McWhorter's well-known view that redlining is a far more complicated story than is popularly assumed. He pointed out that the majority of residents of redlined neighborhoods nationwide were white (McWhorter 2021). They were just poor.

5. The Curse of New York: The Real Estate Lobby as the Demolition Machine

1. Big money sloshes around this sector. To give some indicators: The largest commercial landlords in the city squeeze $7.5 billion a year in net income from Manhattan (mostly in rents) from vast portfolios of properties. Or, consider that Blackstone, an investment firm active in New York City, "closed" its real estate investment fund in 2017 with a mere $20 billion to put into play for real estate investments (TRD Staff 2017). Journalist Rich Bochman notes that in 2018, private equity firms nationally had $278 billion in "dry powder" of uninvested money looking for a real estate investment deals anywhere, with preference for New York, Los Angeles, San Francisco, and Vancouver, B.C. (Parker 2018).

2. This chapter adds to an abundant literature describing the nefarious doings of the city's powerful real estate industry. See books describing various aspect of the city's growth machine (Moskowitz 2018; Angotti 2008; Fitch 1996; Moss 2018; Ward 2014; Schachtman 1991).

3. The years 1992 and 1993 also saw a flurry of failed efforts to reform the much-criticized zoning code (Dunlap 1992; Bressi 1993).

4. As reported to me by CNU co-founder and author John Massengale (*Street Design*) who attended those meetings.

5. Interview with Eugene Sinigalliano, a member of the working group and the lone representative of a community of residents on West 31st Street whose homes EDC threatened with seizure by eminent domain and demolition.

6. How Big Real Estate Stays on Top

1. For a discussion of this undermining of democracy and the twisting of public policies and agendas to favor the donor class at the national level, see Jane Mayer's book *Dark Money: The Hidden History of the Billionaires Behind the Rise of the Radical Right* (Knopf Doubleday Publishing Group, 2017), or David Callahan's book *Fortunes of Change: The Rise of the Liberal Rich and the Remaking of America* (Wiley, 2010) or Lawrence Lessig's book *Republic, Lost: How Money Corrupts Congress and a Plan to Stop It* (Twelve Books, 2015).

2. For those seeking more in-depth understanding look at the work by Timothy Collins (Collins 2013). His is a historical overview. Good summaries and updates can be found in articles by Michael Cavadias (Cavadias 2017).

3. There are small businesses that specialize in harassing rent-stabilized tenants on behalf of a developer to encourage "voluntary" self-eviction. One of those firms in Brooklyn featured a logo of a shadowy character wielding a baseball bat. These businesses have a harder time now that rent reforms have taken place.

4. Much of the Tkaczyk story recounted here is pieced together from excellent investigative work done by stellar ProPublica journalists Cezary Podkul, Derek Kravitz, Will Parker, and their colleagues, along with reporting from *Real Deal*, *New York Times*, *Daily News*, and Susan Lerner of Common Cause.

5. ICAP supplied tax abatements for up to twenty-five years for improvements to commercial buildings. The second Relocation program gave tax abatements to real estate companies that could move jobs to certain areas of Manhattan.

6. Many thanks to journalist and WBAI radio producer Jillian Jonas for collecting many of these examples from industry newspapers, LinkedIn, and press releases.

7. The Mackinac Institute of Public Policy describes the Overton window (named after the person who first promoted the idea) as a concept describing the situation when politicians pursue a limited set of policies that they believe society finds acceptable and ignore alternatives that are "outside" the Overton window.

7. Demonizing Historic Districts and the Capture of the Landmarks Preservation Commission

1. I could not find out why he drafted the report or at whose request.

2. The legislation is available at the New York City Council website: https://legistar.council.nyc.gov/LegislationDetail.aspx?ID=2271110&GUID=A66556A6-1DEA-4D5F-8535-92C31B2B2379.

8. The Architecture of Rupture and Nihilism

1. There are whole bookshelves of brilliant analysis and research attacking modernist architecture, and I am deeply indebted to those authors. For the interested reader, start with books by Tom Wolfe, Steven Semes, James Curl, Nikos Salingaros, Roger Scruton, Alice Coleman, James Kunstler, Alain de Botton, Christopher Alexander, Jan Michl, and John Silber. David Brussat's well-known blog, *Architecture Here and There*, covers the same problem and is full of wit, rage, and intelligence.

2. See the book by Steven Semes (2009) for an elaboration of the possibilities of infill in historic districts.

3. It's the oldest tavern in the city, but it suffered a couple of fires in its history and was extensively renovated, in a way persnickety Huxtable disapproved of. Nobody is sure what the original looked like.

9. What Policies for a Human-Scale City?

1. Personal communication from David Gruber.

2. Personal communication from sources in CB1 and CB6 in Manhattan, who have asked me not to report their names.

REFERENCES

"2019 Charter Revision Commission Hearing Testimony of Marisa Lago, Chair of City Planning Commission." 2019. New York: Charter Review Commission.

Ackerman, Frank, and Lisa Heinzerling. 2005. *Priceless: On Knowing the Price of Everything and the Value of Nothing*. New York: New Press; Signature Books Services (distributor).

Adams, Eric. 2020. "Response to Village Independent Democrats Candidate Questionnaire." Document was online in 2020 election cycle at VID website https://www.villagedemocrats.org/.

Ahad-Legardy, Badia. 2021. *Afro-Nostalgia: Feeling Good in Contemporary Black Culture*. Champaign: University of Illinois Press. https://www.press.uillinois.edu/books/catalog/85dec5fw9780252043666.html.

Ahfeldt, G., E. Pietrostefani, A. Schumann, and T. Matsumoto. 2018. *Demystifying Compact Urban Growth*. https://read.oecd-ilibrary.org/development/demystifying-compact-urban-growth_bbea8b78-en.

AIA-NY. 2020. AIA New York—American Institute of Architects, New York Chapter. AIA New York. 2020. https://www.aiany.org/.

Alexander, Christopher, and Peter Eisenman. 1982. "Contrasting Concepts of Harmony in Architecture: The 1982 Debate between Christopher Alexander and Peter Eisenman." *Katarxis*, no. 3. http://www.katarxis3.com/Alexander_Eisenman_Debate.htm.

Alexander, Christopher, and Hansjoachim Neis. 2012. *The Battle for the Life and Beauty of the Earth: A Struggle between Two World-Systems*. New York: Oxford University Press.

Allen, Joseph G., Piers MacNaughton, Usha Satish, Suresh Santhanam, Jose Vallarino, and John D. Spengler. 2016. "Associations of Cognitive Function Scores with Carbon Dioxide, Ventilation, and Volatile Organic Compound Exposures in Office Workers: A Controlled Exposure Study of Green and Conventional Office Environments." *Environmental Health Perspectives* 124 (6): 805–12. https://doi.org/10.1289/ehp.1510037.

Allison, Eric. 2005. "Gentrification and Historic Districts: Public Policy Considerations in the Designation of Historic Districts in New York City." Master's thesis, Columbia University, New York.

Amato, Rebecca. 2018. "Board to Death?" Urban Omnibus, March 8, 2018. https://urbanomnibus.net/2018/03/board-to-death/.

Anderson, Martin. 1967. *Federal Bulldozer: A Critical Analysis of Urban Renewal 1949–1962*. New York: McGraw-Hill.

Angotti, Tom. 2008. *New York for Sale: Community Planning Confronts Global Real Estate*. Cambridge, Mass.: MIT Press.

Angotti, Tom, and Sylvia Morse. 2016. *Zoned Out! Race, Displacement, and City Planning in New York City*. 1st ed. New York: Terreform.

Appellate Division, First Department Department Kahn, J., J. 2018. Matter of Stahl York Ave. Co., LLC v. City of New York 2018. NY Slip Op 03653. Decided on May 22, 2018. Appellate Division, First Department, Kahn, J., J.

Appellate Division, First Judicial Department. 2018. Matter of Real Estate Bd. of N.Y., Inc. v. City of New York. Appellate Division, First Judicial Department.

Arch2O. n.d.. "10 Unpredictable Facts You Never Knew About Zaha Hadid—Arch2O.Com." https://www.arch2o.com/10-unpredictable-facts-never-knew-zaha-hadid/.

Asquith, Brian, Evan Mast, and Davin Reed. 2019. "Supply Shock versus Demand Shock: The Local Effects of New Housing in Low-Income Areas." Upjohn Institute Working Papers, December 19, 2019. https://doi.org/10.17848/wp19-316.

Associated Press. 1989. "Maid Testifies Helmsley Denied Paying Taxes." *New York Times*, July 12, 1989, sec. New York. https://www.nytimes.com/1989/07/12/nyregion/maid-testifies-helmsley-denied-paying-taxes.html.

BAE Urban Economics Inc. 2015. "Market and Financial Study: NYC Mandatory Inclusionary Housing." New York City Housing Development Corporation.

Baca, Alex, Patrick McAnaney, and Jenny Schuetz. 2019. "'Gentle' Density Can Save Our Neighborhoods." December 4, 2019. https://www.brookings.edu/research/gentle-density-can-save-our-neighborhoods/.

Baccash, Benjamin. 2010. "Enforcement and the New York City Landmarks Law: Past, Present, and Future." Master's thesis, Columbia University. https://www.nypap.org/wp-content/uploads/2016/03/Enforcement_and_the_New_York_City_Landmarks_Law_Ben_Baccash.pdf.

Bagli, Charles V. 2000. "Plan to Revise Zoning Laws Seems to Face an Early Death." *New York Times*, November 24, 2000, sec. N.Y. / Region. https://www.nytimes.com/2000/11/24/nyregion/plan-to-revise-zoning-laws-seems-to-face-an-early-death.html.

Bagli, Charles V. 2003. "Battle Nears Over Rezoning in Seaport." *New York Times*, January 22, 2003, sec. N.Y. / Region. https://www.nytimes.com/2003/01/22/nyregion/battle-nears-over-rezoning-near-seaport.html.

Bagli, Charles V. 2016. "A Trump Empire Built on Inside Connections and $885 Million in Tax Breaks." *New York Times*, September 17, 2016, sec. New York. https://www.nytimes.com/2016/09/18/nyregion/donald-trump-tax-breaks-real-estate.html.

Baker, Peter, and Jesse Drucker. 2017. "Trump Wrote Off $100 Million in Losses in 2005, Leaked Forms Show." *New York Times*, March 14, 2017, sec. Politics. https://www.nytimes.com/2017/03/14/us/politics/donald-trump-taxes.html.

Balint, Nadia. 2018. "High-End Apartments Are 87% of Rentals Built in 2018." *RENTCafé Rental Blog* (blog). September 21, 2018. https://www.rentcafe.com/blog

/apartmentliving/luxury-apartments/8-out-of-10-new-apartment-buildings-were-high-end-in-2017-trend-carries-on-into-2018/.

Bankoff, Simeon. 2011. Interview with Simeon Bankoff. Transcript. New York Preservation Archive Project.

Banks, John. 2018. "Next Landmarks Chair Must Continue Balancing the City's Various Interests." *Crain's New York Business*, June 3, 2018. http://www.crainsnewyork.com/article/20180424/OPINION/180429944/letter-to-the-editor-next-landmarks-preservation-commission-chairman-must-continue-balancing-new-york-citys-various-interests.

Banner, James. 2008. *Who Owns the Sky? The Struggle to Control Airspace from the Wright Brothers On*. Abridged edition. Cambridge, Mass: Harvard University Press.

Barbanel, Josh. 2006. "As New York Apartments Become Condos, Tenants Are Stuck in the Middle." *New York Times*, April 30, 2006, sec. N.Y. / Region. https://www.nytimes.com/2006/04/30/nyregion/as-new-york-apartments-become-condos-tenants-are-stuck-in-the.html.

Barker, Kim. 2018. "Behind New York's Housing Crisis: Weakened Laws and Fragmented Regulation." *New York Times*, May 20, 2018, sec. New York. https://www.nytimes.com/interactive/2018/05/20/nyregion/affordable-housing-nyc.html.

Barr, Jason M. 2016. *Building the Skyline: The Birth and Growth of Manhattan's Skyscrapers*. New York: Oxford University Press.

Bartik, Timothy J. 2018. "'But For' Percentages for Economic Development Incentives: What Percentage Estimates Are Plausible Based on the Research Literature?" SSRN Scholarly Paper ID 3227086. Rochester, NY: Social Science Research Network. https://papers.ssrn.com/abstract=3227086.

Baruch College. 2017. "NYCdata | Income and Taxes." Accessed March 15, 2024. https://www.baruch.cuny.edu/nycdata/income-taxes/hhold_income-numbers.htm.

Barwick, Kent. 2011. "Reminiscences of Kent Barwick." New York Preservation Archive, 2011.

Been, Vicki. 2018. "City NIMBYs." *Journal of Land Use and Environmental Law*, August. https://furmancenter.org/research/publication/city-nimbys.

Been, Vicki, and Ingrid Gould Ellen. 2018. "Supply Skepticism: Housing Supply and Affordability." November 2018. http://furmancenter.org/research/publication/supply-skepticismnbsp-housing-supply-and-affordability.

Been, Vicki, Ingrid Gould Ellen, Michael Gedal, Edward Glaeser, and Brian J. McCabe. 2014. "Preserving History or Hindering Growth? The Heterogeneous Effects of Historic Districts on Local Housing Markets in New York City." Working Paper 20446. Cambridge, Mass.: National Bureau of Economic Research. http://www.nber.org/papers/w20446.

Been, Vicki, John Infranca, Josiah Madar, and Jessica Yager. 2014. "Unlocking the Right to Build: Designing a More Flexible System for Transferring Development Rights." Furman Center, New York University. https://wagner.nyu.edu/impact/research/publications/unlocking-right-build-designing-more-flexible-system-for-transferring.

Berg, Nate. 2021. "Is Building Tall Really Best? Researchers Dispel the Myth of Climate-Friendly Skyscrapers." *Fast Company*, August 18, 2021. https://www.fastcompany.com/90666746/is-building-tall-really-best-researchers-dispel-the-myth-of-climate-friendly-skyscrapers.

Berman, Andrew. 2023. "Village Preservation's Research on Affordability." Humanscale NYC Webinar on City of Yes, February 2, 2023. https://vimeo.com/795593356, summarizing reports found on www.villagepreservation.org.

Bernstein, Andrea, dir. 2015. "Cuomo's Six New Port Authority Appointees: All White, Male, Bankers and Real Estate Titans | WNYC | New York Public Radio, Podcasts, Live Streaming Radio, News." *WNYC News.* https://www.wnyc.org/story/cuomos-six-appointees-port-authority-all-white-male-bankers-and-real-estate-titans/.

Bernstein, Zachary, dir. 2019. *Mapping The Future: The City's Planning Process.* https://www.youtube.com/watch?v=LKYAexH-dmE.

Beyer, Scott. 2022. "Why Jersey City Is Becoming New York City's 6th Borough." *Catalyst* (blog), October 12, 2022. https://catalyst.independent.org/2022/10/12/jersey-city-new-york-borough/.

Bhagwati, Jagdish. 1958. "Immiserizing Growth: A Geometrical Note." *Review of Economic Studies* 25 (3): 201–5. https://doi.org/10.2307/2295990.

Bindelglass, Evan. 2016. "NYC's 10 Biggest Preservation Battles of 2016." *Curbed NY* (blog). December 21, 2016. https://ny.curbed.com/maps/nyc-historic-preservation-landmarks-battles.

Bishop, Peter. 2007. "Superdensity—Recommendations for Living at Superdensity (2007)." *Issuu*, July 2007. https://issuu.com/design4homes/docs/dfh_-_superdensity.

Blackmar, Elizabeth. 1991. *Manhattan for Rent, 1785–1850.* 1st ed. Ithaca, N.Y.: Cornell University Press.

Blackstone, William. *Blackstone's Commentaries on the Laws of England.* Avalon Project. Accessed March 13, 2024. https://avalon.law.yale.edu/subject_menus/blackstone.asp.

Blain, Glenn. 2013. "Special State Corruption Commission Subpoenas New York City Real Estate Developers over Valuable Tax Breaks." *Nydailynews.Com*, August 8, 2013, sec. News, U.S. https://www.nydailynews.com/news/national/state-corruption-commission-subpoenas-nyc-real-estate-developers-tax-breaks-article-1.1420994.

Blair, Jayson. 2000. "Zoning Revisions Are Widely Supported at Planners' Meeting." *New York Times*, April 26, 2000, sec. New York. https://www.nytimes.com/2000/04/26/nyregion/zoning-revisions-are-widely-supported-at-planners-meeting.html.

Bloom, Nicholas Dagen, and Matthew Gordon Lasner, eds. 2015. *Affordable Housing in New York: The People, Places, and Policies That Transformed a City.* Princeton, N.J.: Princeton University Press.

Blumenthal, Ralph. 2008. "Low Rent, East Side Location: See Landlord If You're Famous." *New York Times*, July 21, 2008.

Board of Estimate of New York City. 1913. *Report of the Heights of Buildings Commission.*

Brahinsky, Rachel. 2014. "The Death of the City?" *Boom: The Journal of California* 4 (2): 9.

Brash, Julian. 2011. *Bloomberg's New York: Class and Governance in the Luxury City.* Athens: University of Georgia Press. https://ugapress.org/book/9780820336817/bloombergs-new-york.

Brenzel, Kathryn. 2017. "Ex-DOB Official Arrested for Alleged Cocaine Parties Is Back Pulling Agency's Strings." *Real Deal New York*, April 17, 2017. https://therealdeal.com/2017/04/17/ex-dob-official-arrested-for-alleged-cocaine-parties-is-back-pulling-agencys-strings/.

Brenzel, Kathryn. 2019. "REBNY Throws Support behind CHIP, RSA Rent Law Challenge | News Break." *Real Deal*, December 20, 2019. https://therealdeal.com/new-york/2019/12/20/rebny-throws-support-behind-chip-rsa-rent-law-challenge/.

Brenzel, Kathryn, and Ashley McHugh-Chiappone. 2017. "NYC's Next Wave of Dynasties." *Real Deal New York*, September 1, 2017. https://therealdeal.com/issues_articles/nycs-next-wave-of-dynasties/.

Bressi, Todd W. 1993. *Planning and Zoning New York City Yesterday, Today and Tomorrow.* New Brunswick, N.J.: Center for Urban Policy Research.

Brown, Eliot. 2010. "Steve Roth, Uncorked." *Observer*, March 4, 2010. https://observer.com/2010/03/steve-roth-uncorked/.

Brown, L. 2023. "New Yorkers Never Came 'Flooding Back.' Why Did Rents Go Up So Much?" *Curbed*. January 27, 2023. https://www.curbed.com/2023/01/nyc-real-estate-covid-more-apartments-higher-rent.html?utm_source=sailthru&utm_medium=email_reg&utm_campaign=retargeting_curbedregi_982022&utm_term=NYMag%20-%20Paywall.

Browning, Lynnley. 2019. "Big Real Estate Moguls Win as Smaller Investors Denied Tax Break." *Accounting Today* (blog). January 31, 2019. https://www.accountingtoday.com/articles/big-real-estate-moguls-win-as-smaller-investors-denied-pass-through-tax-deduction.

Bubbins, Harry. 2016. "What Is the Board of Standards and Appeals?" *GVSHP | Preservation | Off the Grid* (blog), July 18, 2016. https://gvshp.org/blog/2016/07/18/what-is-the-board-of-standards-and-appeals/.

Buckley, Cara. 2013. "In the Shadow of Rising Towers, Laments of Lost Sunlight in New York." *New York Times*, December 19, 2013, sec. N.Y. / Region. https://www.nytimes.com/2013/12/20/nyregion/in-the-shadow-of-rising-towers-laments-of-lost-sunlight-in-new-york.html.

Buettner, Russ, Susanne Craig, and Mike McIntire. 2020. "Trump's Taxes Show Chronic Losses and Years of Income Tax Avoidance." *New York Times*, September 27, 2020, sec. U.S. https://www.nytimes.com/interactive/2020/09/27/us/donald-trump-taxes.html.

Bumiller, Elisabeth. 1999. "Skyline Shaper Widens His Own Horizons." *New York Times*, May 5, 1999.

Buntin, John. 2015. "The Myth of Gentrification." *Slate*, January 15, 2015. https://slate.com/news-and-politics/2015/01/the-gentrification-myth-its-rare-and-not-as-bad-for-the-poor-as-people-think.html.

Cabello, Maxwell. 2019. "Zoning and Racialized Displacement in New York City." Churches United for Fair Housing, New York, December 2019.

Cameron, Christopher. 2014. "Aby Rosen Scores Demolition Permits at 67 Vestry." *Real Deal New York*, August 2, 2014. http://therealdeal.com/blog/2014/08/02/aby-rosen-scores-demolition-permits-at-67-vestry-street/.

Campanile, Carl. 2020. "Lobbyists Made $113M in 2019 Wooing NYC City Hall, Council, Report Says." *New York Post* (blog). March 2, 2020. https://nypost.com/2020/03/01/lobbyists-made-113m-in-2019-wooing-nyc-city-hall-council-report-says/.

Campbell-Dollaghan, Kelsey. 2013. "Do We Have a Legal Right to Light?" *Gizmodo*. October 31, 2013. https://gizmodo.com/do-we-have-a-legal-right-to-light-1455302177.

Campoli, Julie, and Alex S. MacLean. 2007. *Visualizing Density*. Cambridge, Mass.: Lincoln Institute of Land Policy.

Carlson, Jen. 2014. "Photo: The Story Behind the Loneliest Brownstone Ever." *Gothamist* (blog). January 28, 2014. https://gothamist.com/arts-entertainment/photo-the-story-behind-the-loneliest-brownstone-ever.

Caro, Robert A. 1975. *The Power Broker: Robert Moses and the Fall of New York*. New York: Vintage.
Carpenter, Dick, and John Ross. 2015. "Robin Hood in Reverse." *City Journal*, December. https://www.city-journal.org/html/robin-hood-reverse-10676.html.
Cavadias, Michael. 2017. "A Brief History of Rent Regulation in New York." *Hypocrite Reader*, no. 81. December 2017. http://hypocritereader.com/81/rent-regulation-nyc.
Chakrabarti, Vishaan. 2013. *A Country of Cities: A Manifesto for an Urban America*. New York: Metropolis Books.
Chase, W. Parker. 1932. *The Wonder City*. New York: Wonder City Publishing.
Chinco, Alex, and Christopher Mayer. 2014. "Misinformed Speculators and Mispricing in the Housing Market." Working Paper 19817. National Bureau of Economic Research. https://doi.org/10.3386/w19817.
City of New York. 1971. "Mount Morris Park Historic District Designation Report." Landmarks Preservation Commission Designation Report.
City of New York. 2020. *New York City Charter*.
City of New York. 2021. "Map of Greenhouse Emissions." https://www.aeintelligence.com/city-of-new-york.
Coleman, Alice. 1985. *Utopia on Trial: Vision and Reality in Planned Housing*. London: H. Shipman.
Collins, Timothy. 2013. "An Introduction to the NYC Rent Guidelines Board and the Rent Stabilization System." Rev. ed. January 2013. https://web.archive.org/web/20130928033447/http://www.housingnyc.com/html/about/intro/toc.html.
Community Board 5 Planning Fellows. 2017. "The Wrecking Ball: Assessing the Pace of Demolition of the Build Environment in CB5."
Community Board 11. 1999. "East Harlem Land Use." *Eastharlem.Com*. 1999.
Conrads, Ulrich. 1971. *Programs and Manifestoes on 20th-Century Architecture*. Cambridge, Mass.: MIT Press.
Corcoran, Cate. 2018. "Neighborhood Groups Call for Ouster of Landmarks Chair Srinivasan and a Halt to LPC Rule Changes." *Brownstoner*, March 27, 2018. https://www.brownstoner.com/architecture/landmarks-chair-ouster-landmarks-preservation-commission-meenakshi-srinivasan-rules-changes/.
Cosman, Jacob, and Luis Quintero. 2018. "Market Concentration in Homebuilding." SSRN Scholarly Paper ID 3303984. Rochester, N.Y.: Social Science Research Network.
Craig, Susanne, William K. Rashbaum, and Thomas Kaplan. 2014. "Cuomo's Office Hobbled Ethics Inquiries by Moreland Commission." *New York Times*, July 23, 2014. http://www.nytimes.com/2014/07/23/nyregion/governor-andrew-cuomo-and-the-short-life-of-the-moreland-commission.html.
Craven, Jackie. 2019. "Biography of Adolf Loos, Belle Epoque Architect and Rebel." *ThoughtCo* (blog). August 20, 2019. https://www.thoughtco.com/adolf-loos-architect-of-no-ornamentation-177859.
Craver, Scott E. 2010. "Urban Real Estate in Late Republican Rome." *Memoirs of the American Academy in Rome* 55: 135–58.
Cullen, Gordon. 1961. *Concise Townscape*. London: Routledge.
Cullen, Terence. 2015. "Peebles' Corp. Hit With $10M Suit for Shafting Partner in Deal." *Commercial Observer*, September 3, 2015, sec. Sales. https://commercialobserve.com/2015/09/don-peebles-hit-with-50m-suit-for-shafting-partner-in-lower-manhattan-deal/.

Curl, James Stevens. 2018. *The Making of Dystopia: The Strange Rise and Survival of Architectural Barbarism*. Vol. 5. Oxford: Oxford University Press.
Daglioglu, Esin. 2015. "The Context Debate: An Archaeology." *Architectural Theory Review* 20 (2): 266–79. https://doi.org/10.1080/13264826.2016.1170058.
Dal Bó, Ernesto. 2006. "Regulatory Capture: A Review." *Oxford Review of Economic Policy* 22 (2): 203–25. https://doi.org/10.1093/oxrep/grj013.
De Botton, Alain. 2006. *The Architecture of Happiness*. New York: Pantheon.
Deffenbaugh, Ryan. 2020. "De Blasio Not Throwing Support behind Push for New Housing in SoHo." *Crain's New York Business*, January 24, 2020, sec. Politics. https://www.crainsnewyork.com/politics/de-blasio-not-throwing-support-behind-push-new-housing-soho.
Derbyshire, Ben, Matthew Goulcher, Andrew Beharrell, and Andy Von Bradsky. 2015. "Superdensity: The Sequel." London. http://www.superdensity.co.uk/.
Doctoroff, Daniel. 2017. *Greater Than Ever: New York's Big Comeback*. New York: Public Affairs.
Dolkart, Andrew. n.d. "The Architecture and Development of New York City with Andrew S. Dolkart."
Dotzour, Mark, Terry Grissom, Crocker Liu, and Thomas Pearson. 1990. "Highest and Best Use: The Evolving Paradigm." *Journal of Real Estate Research* 5 (1): 17–32.
Drucker, Jesse, and Emily Flitter. 2018. "Jared Kushner Paid No Federal Income Tax for Years, Documents Suggest." *New York Times*, October 13, 2018, sec. Business. https://www.nytimes.com/2018/10/13/business/jared-kushner-taxes.html.
Duflo, Esther, and Abhijit Banerjee. 2019. "Opinion | Economic Incentives Don't Always Do What We Want Them To." *New York Times*, October 26, 2019, sec. Opinion. https://www.nytimes.com/2019/10/26/opinion/sunday/duflo-banerjee-economic-incentives.html.
Duggan, William R. 2004. *Napoleon's Glance: The Secret of Strategy*. New York: Thunder's Mouth Press/Nation Books.
Dunlap, David W. 1987. "Landmarks Commission Member Losing Post." *New York Times*, January 23, 1987, sec. New York. https://www.nytimes.com/1987/01/23/nyregion/landmarks-commission-member-losing-post.html.
Dunlap, David W. 1991. "Developer Agrees to Plan to Cut 12 Floors from a Too-Tall Tower." *New York Times*, April 23, 1991, sec. New York. https://www.nytimes.com/1991/04/23/nyregion/developer-agrees-to-plan-to-cut-12-floors-from-a-too-tall-tower.html.
Dunlap, David W. 1992. "The Quest for a New Zoning Plan." *New York Times*, April 12, 1992, sec. Real Estate. https://www.nytimes.com/1992/04/12/realestate/the-quest-for-a-new-zoning-plan.html.
Dunlap, David W. 1996. "Lawyers Who Mold the Shape of a City." *New York Times*, February 25, 1996, sec. Real Estate. https://www.nytimes.com/1996/02/25/realestate/lawyers-who-mold-the-shape-of-a-city.html.
Dunlap, David W. 2012. "Samuel H. Lindenbaum, Lawyer to Major New York Developers, Dies at 77." *New York Times*, August 21, 2012, sec. N.Y. / Region. https://www.nytimes.com/2012/08/22/nyregion/samuel-h-lindenbaum-lawyer-to-major-new-york-developers-dies-at-77.html.
Durkin, Erin. 2015. "NYCHA Is 'Sitting on' 2,300 Empty Apartments despite High Demand for Housing: Audit." *Nydailynews.Com*. June 24, 2015. https://www.nydailynews.com/new-york/nycha-sitting-2-300-empty-apartments-audit-article-1.2270080.

Durning, Alan. 2013. *Unlocking Home: Three Keys to Affordable Communities*. Cork: Sightline Institute.

Dwyer, Jim. 2012. "Survival Skill Abandoned by Schools." *New York Times*, June 15, 2012, sec. New York. https://www.nytimes.com/2012/06/15/nyregion/schools-have-abandoned-a-skill-swimming-education-that-could-save-lives.html.

Easterly, William R. 2001. *The Elusive Quest for Growth: Economists' Adventures and Misadventures in the Tropics*. 1st ed. Cambridge, Mass: MIT Press.

Editors. 2019. "Owners Magazine 2019 Q&A. Talking with the Top Developers and Owners of NYC," *Commercial Observer* (blog). November 5, 2019. https://commercialobserver.com/2019/11/owners-magazine-2019-talking-with-the-top-developers-and-owners-of-nyc/.

Eberle, W. David, and Gregory Hayden. 1991. "Critique of Contingent Valuation and Travel Cost Methods for Valuing Natural Resources and Ecosystems." *Journal of Economic Issues* 25 (3): 649–85.

Ehrenfreund, Max. 2016. "How Donald Trump and Other Real-Estate Developers Pay Almost Nothing in Taxes." *Washington Post*, October 4, 2016. https://www.washingtonpost.com/news/wonk/wp/2016/10/04/how-donald-trump-and-other-real-estate-developers-pay-almost-nothing-in-taxes/.

Ellerman, David. 2009. "Numeraire Illusion: The Final Demise of the Kaldor Hicks Principle." In *Theoretical Foundations of Law and Economics*, edited by Mark White, 96–118. New York: Cambridge University Press.

Ellerman, David. 2014. "On a Fallacy in the Kaldor-Hicks Efficiency—Equity Analysis." *Constitutional Political Economy* 25 (2): 125–36. https://doi.org/10.1007/s10602-014-9159-x.

Ellickson, Robert C., and Dan Tarlock. 1981. *Land Use Controls: Cases and Materials*. Boston, Mass.: Little Brown.

Epstein, Sophia. 2019. "Everyone Needs to Stop Building Giant Glass Skyscrapers Right Now." *Wired UK*, November 11, 2019. https://www.wired.co.uk/article/stop-building-glass-skyscrapers.

Equity Residential. 2017. "Investor Update." Found in 2018 at www.equityresidential.com.

Escot, Alfred. 2017. "Jean Nouvel: 'L'architecture est là pour émouvoir.'" *Grazia*, November 30, 2017. https://www.grazia.fr/culture/arts-architecture/jean-nouvel-l-architecture-est-la-pour-emouvoir-874981.

Fainstein, Susan, and Norman Fainstein. 1992. "The Changing Character of Community Politics in New York City: 1968–1988." In *Dual City: Restructuring New York*, edited by John H. Mollenkopf and Manuel Castells, 315–58. New York: Russell Sage Foundation.

Fanelli, James. 2016. "City Investigating de Blasio Bundler Who Sits on Mayor's Fund Board." DNAinfo New York, October 17, 2016.

Feider, Matthew. 2020. "Classical or Modern Architecture? For Americans, It's No Contest." *Harris Poll* (blog). October 19, 2020.

Fermino, Jennifer, and Matt A. V. Chaban. 2014. "Sky's the Limit: Mayor de Blasio Says He Would OK Affordable Housing Buildings at Any Size." *New York Daily News*, February 20, 2014. https://www.nydailynews.com/news/politics/sky-limit-affordable-housing-mayor-de-blasio-article-1.1620714.

Financial Times. 2011. "Lunch with the FT: Rem Koolhaas." January 7, 2011. https://www.ft.com/content/e29e2c94-19e0-11e0-b921-00144feab49a.

Finch, Elise. 2011. "Plan: Extend Manhattan to Governors Island, With Help from Army Corps of Engineers." November 23, 2011. *CBS*. https://newyork.cbslocal.com/2011/11/23/plan-extend-manhattan-to-governors-island-with-help-from-army-corps-of-engineers/.

Finn, Robin. 2013. "The Great Race for Manhattan Air Rights." *New York Times*, February 22, 2013. http://www.nytimes.com/2013/02/24/realestate/the-great-race-for-manhattan-air-rights.html.

Fisher, Ken. 2017. Private Meeting with City Club and Attorney Ken Fisher, attended by author.

Fiske, Diane M. 2013. "Haven: Making a Louis Kahn Their Own." *Inquirer.Com*, June 9, 2013, sec. Real Estate. https://www.inquirer.com/philly/business/real_estate/20130609_Haven__Making_a_Louis_Kahn_their_own.html.

Fitch, Robert. 1996. *The Assassination of New York*. London; New York: Verso.

Flood, Joe. 2010. "Why the Bronx Burned." *New York Post* (blog). May 16, 2010. https://nypost.com/2010/05/16/why-the-bronx-burned/.

Flood, Joe. 2011. *The Fires: How a Computer Formula, Big Ideas, and the Best of Intentions Burned Down New York City—and Determined the Future of Cities*. Reprint. New York: Riverhead Books.

Ford, George B. 1916. "How New York City Now Controls the Development of Private Property." *City Plan*, October 1916.

Forsyth, A. 2003. *Measuring Density: Working Definitions for Residential Density and Building Intensity*. Design Brief, no. 8. College of Architecture and Landscape Architecture, University of Minnesota.

Frankel, Max. 2015. "Opinion | Make Them Pay for Park Views." *New York Times*, December 30, 2015, sec. Opinion. https://www.nytimes.com/2015/12/31/opinion/make-them-pay-for-park-views.html.

Fraser, C. Gerald. 1991. "Many in Harlem Want Longer Landmarks List." *New York Times*, July 15, 1991.

Freedman, Robert. 2014. "Mid-Rise: Density at a Human Scale." *Planetizen—Urban Planning News, Jobs, and Education* (blog). March 12, 2014. https://www.planetizen.com/node/67761.

Freeman, Lance, and Frank Braconi. 2004. "Gentrification and Displacement New York City in the 1990s." *Journal of the American Planning Association* 70 (1): 39–52. https://doi.org/10.1080/01944360408976337.

Freemark, Yonah. 2019. "Upzoning Chicago: Impacts of a Zoning Reform on Property Values and Housing Construction." *Urban Affairs Review* 56 (3). https://doi.org/10.1177/1078087418824672.

Frey, William H. 2015. "Black Flight to the Suburbs on the Rise." *Brookings* (blog). July 31, 2015. https://www.brookings.edu/blog/the-avenue/2015/07/31/black-flight-to-the-suburbs-on-the-rise/.

Gan, Vincent J. L., C. M. Chan, K. T. Tse, Irene M. C. Lo, and Jack C. P. Cheng. 2017. "A Comparative Analysis of Embodied Carbon in High-Rise Buildings Regarding Different Design Parameters." *Journal of Cleaner Production* 161 (September): 663–75. https://doi.org/10.1016/j.jclepro.2017.05.156.

Gartland, Michael. 2019. "De Blasio Rakes in Big Cash from Crony Lawyer and Allies; Not Much $$ from Grassroots." *Nydailynews.Com*, July 17, 2019, sec. Politics, News.

https://www.nydailynews.com/news/politics/ny-metro-de-blasio-carone-podolsky-abrams-fensterman-20190717-trjmvtsmmfg3raueo4lwgqrdxq-story.html.

Gayle, Margot, and Carol Gayle. 1998. *Cast-Iron Architecture in America: The Significance of James Bogardus*. New York: W. W. Norton.

Gehl, Jan. 2010. *Cities for People*. Illustrated edition. Washington, D.C.: Island Press.

Geiger, Daniel. 2012. "Sandy Lindenbaum, Beloved Zoning Attorney for a Generation of Major Developers, Dies At 77." *Commercial Observer* (blog). August 17, 2012. https://commercialobserver.com/2012/08/sandy-lindenbaum-beloved-zoning-attorney-for-a-generation-of-major-developers-dies-at-77/.

Gelman, Eric. 2019. "Real Estate Tycoons Get a Host of Special Breaks Not Available to Most Other Investors." *Bloomberg Businessweek*, April 29, 2019.

Gevurtz, Franklin. 1977. "Obstruction of Sunlight as a Private Nuisance." *California Law Review* 65 (1): 94. https://doi.org/doi:10.15779/Z38546R.

Gewen, Barry. 2019. "Nathan Glazer, Urban Sociologist and Outspoken Intellectual, Dies at 95." *New York Times*, January 19, 2019. https://www.nytimes.com/2019/01/19/obituaries/nathan-glazer-dead.html.

Gewertz, Ken. 2004. "Kayden Named Frank Backus Williams Professor." *Harvard Gazette* (blog). February 5, 2004. https://news.harvard.edu/gazette/story/2004/02/kayden-named-frank-backus-williams-professor/.

Giedion, Sigfried. 1980. *Space, Time, and Architecture: The Growth of a New Tradition*. Cambridge, Mass.: Harvard University Press.

Gifford, Robert. 2007. "The Consequences of Living in High-Rise Buildings." *Architectural Science Review* 50 (1): 2–17. https://doi.org/10.3763/asre.2007.5002.

Giordano, Margaret. 1988. "Over-Stuffing the Envelope: The Problems with Creative Transfer of Development Rights." *Fordham Urban Law Journal* 16 (1): 43.

Glaeser, Edward L. 2006. "Bonfire of the Landmarks." *New York Sun*, November 29, 2006.

Glaeser, Edward. 2010. "Preservation Follies." *City Journal*.

Glaeser, Edward. 2011a. "How Skyscrapers Can Save the City." *The Atlantic*, March 2011. http://www.theatlantic.com/magazine/archive/2011/03/how-skyscrapers-can-save-the-city/308387/.

Glaeser, Edward. 2011b. "How Riots Start, and How They Can Be Stopped: Edward Glaeser." *BloombergView.Com* (blog). August 2011.

Glaeser, Edward. 2012. *Triumph of the City: How Our Greatest Invention Makes Us Richer, Smarter, Greener, Healthier, and Happier*. New York: Penguin Books.

Glaeser, Edward, and Joseph Gyourko. 2002. "The Impact of Zoning on Housing Affordability." Working Paper 8835. Cambridge, Mass.: National Bureau of Economic Research. http://www.nber.org/papers/w8835.

Glaeser, Edward, and Joseph Gyourko. 2003. "The Impact of Building Restrictions on Housing Affordability." *FRBNY Economic Policy Review*, June 21–39, 2003. https://www.newyorkfed.org/medialibrary/media/research/epr/03v09n2/0306glae.pdf.

Glaeser, Edward, Joseph Gyourko, and Raven Saks. 2003. "Why Is Manhattan So Expensive? Regulation and the Rise in House Prices." Working Paper 10124. National Bureau of Economic Research. https://doi.org/10.3386/w10124.

Glaeser, Edward, Joseph Gyourko, and Raven Saks. 2005. "Why Have Housing Prices Gone Up?" Working Paper 11129. Cambridge, Mass.: National Bureau of Economic Research. *AEA Papers and Proceedings* 95 (2). https://doi.org/10.3386/w11129.

Glaeser, Edward, and Bryce A. Ward. 2008. "The Causes and Consequences of Land Use Regulation: Evidence from Greater Boston." *Journal of Urban Economics* 65 (2008): 265–78.

Glazer, Nathan. 2007. "From a Cause to a Style." *New York Times*, June 3, 2007, sec. Books. https://www.nytimes.com/2007/06/03/books/chapters/0603-1st-glaz.html.

Glick, Mark, and Gabriel A. Lozada. 2021. "The Erroneous Foundations of Law and Economics." *Institute for New Economic Thinking Working Paper Series*, February 15, 2021, 1–114. https://doi.org/10.36687/inetwp149.

Goldberg, Leo. 2015. "Game of Zones: Neighborhood Rezonings and Uneven Urban Growth in Bloomberg's New York City." Master's thesis, MIT. https://dspace.mit.edu/bitstream/handle/1721.1/98935/921891223-MIT.pdf?sequence=1&isAllowed=y.

Goldberger, Paul. 1979. *The City Observed, New York: A Guide to the Architecture of Manhattan*. New York: Vintage.

Goldberger, Paul. 1985. "Architecture View: Modernism Reaffirms Its Power." *New York Times*, November 24, 1985. https://www.nytimes.com/1985/11/24/arts/architecture-view-modernism-reaffirms-its-power.html.

Goldberger, Paul. 1989. "When Developers Change the Rules during the Game." *New York Times*, March 19, 1989.

Goldberger, Paul. 2010. "Lecture: Why Architecture Matters." *Paulgoldberger.Com* (blog). September 5, 2010. https://www.paulgoldberger.com/lectures/why-architecture-matters/.

Goldberger, Paul. 2015. *Building Art: The Life and Work of Frank Gehry*. New York: Knopf.

Goldensohn, Rosa. 2019. "After Amazon Loss, Economic Development Corp. Hired Big Guns for Local Battles." *The City*, August 28, 2019. https://www.thecity.nyc/economy/2019/8/28/21210846/after-amazon-loss-economic-development-corp-hired-big-guns-for-local-battles.

Gonzalez, David. 1998. "About New York: Architecture Doesn't Stop At 96th Street." *New York Times*, January 21, 1998, sec. New York. https://www.nytimes.com/1998/01/21/nyregion/about-new-york-architecture-doesn-t-stop-at-96th-street.html.

Goodwin, Michael. 1982. "Zoning Plan Bends under Lobbying." *New York Times*, May 6, 1982, sec. New York. https://www.nytimes.com/1982/05/06/nyregion/zoning-plan-bends-under-lobbying.html.

Gorney, Douglas. 2011. "City Limits: A Conversation with Edward Glaeser." *The Atlantic*, February 8, 2011. https://www.theatlantic.com/national/archive/2011/02/city-limits-a-conversation-with-edward-glaeser/70351/.

Gould, Jessica, and WNYC. 2021. "Dozens of NYC Public School Buildings May Not Be Able to Fit Their Students at 3 Feet Apart This Fall." *Gothamist*. August 5, 2021.

Gourarie, Chava. 2018. "Extell Lands $530M Loan Package for Brooklyn Point Development." *Real Deal New York*. July 30, 2018. https://therealdeal.com/2018/07/30/extell-lands-530m-loan-package-for-brooklyn-point-development/.

Graaskamp, James. 1972. "A Rational Approach to Feasibility Analysis." *Appraisal Journal*, October, 513–21.

Gratz, Roberta. 1973. "Landmarks Law a Threat to City's Heritage." *New York Post*, January 8, 1973.

Gravel, Nicolas, and Alessandra Michelangeli. 2006. "Measuring the Impact of Historic District Designation on Real Estate in New York City." *Applied Economics* 38 (16): 1945–61.

Gray, Christopher. 2012. "Thieves of Light, Built by Barbarians." *New York Times*, June 7, 2012, sec. Real Estate. https://www.nytimes.com/2012/06/10/realestate/thieves-of-light-built-by-barbarians.html.

Haag, Matthew, and Luis Ferré-Sadurní. 2021. "To Save Penn Station, New York Wants to Build 10 Skyscrapers." *New York Times*, May 5, 2021, sec. New York. https://www.nytimes.com/2021/05/05/nyregion/penn-station-redevelopment.html.

Haag, Matthew, and Winnie Hu. 2019. "1.5 Million Packages a Day: The Internet Brings Chaos to N.Y. Streets." *New York Times*, October 27, 2019, sec. New York. https://www.nytimes.com/2019/10/27/nyregion/nyc-amazon-delivery.html.

Haimson, Leonie, and Emily Carrazana. 2019. "Class Size Presentations of Citywide and District Trends Since 2006." Presented at Class Size Matters, New York. https://www.classsizematters.org/class-size-presentations-of-citywide-and-district-trends-since-2006/.

Hardy, Lee. 2019. "How Le Corbusier's American Dream Became a Nightmare." *American Conservative*, April 19, 2019. https://www.theamericanconservative.com/urbs/how-le-corbusiers-american-dream-became-a-nightmare/.

Harris, Richard. 1992. "The Geography of Employment and Residence in New York since 1950 (Chapter 5)." In *Dual City: Restructuring New York*, edited by John H. Mollenkopf and Manuel Castells. New York: Russell Sage Foundation.

Hausman, Jerry D. 2012. "Contingent Valuation: From Dubious to Hopeless." *Journal of Economic Perspectives* 26 (4): 43–56.

Hawthorne, Christopher. 2004. "The Architect Designing Daniel Libeskind's Apartment." *New York Magazine*, April 1, 2004.

Heffelmire, Jason. 2014. "The Challenge: Tall and Super-Tall Buildings: HVAC." *Consulting—Specifying Engineer*. July 28, 2014. https://www.csemag.com/articles/the-challenge-tall-and-super-tall-buildings-hvac/.

Hempling, Scott. 2014. "'Regulatory Capture': Sources and Solutions | Emory University School of Law | Atlanta, GA." *Emory University School of Law* Vol 17. http://law.emory.edu/ecgar/content/volume-1/issue-1/essays/regulatory-capture.html.

Hicks, J. R. 1939. *Value and Capital*, 2nd ed. http://archive.org/details/in.ernet.dli.2015.223876.

Hinsdale, Jeremy. 2016. "By the Numbers: Air Quality and Pollution in New York City." Earth Institute. *State of the Planet* (blog). June 6, 2016. https://blogs.ei.columbia.edu/2016/06/06/air-quality-pollution-new-york-city/.

Hobbes, Thomas. 1651. *Leviathan*. https://www.gutenberg.org/files/3207/3207-h/3207-h.htm.

Hofmann, Tess. 2015. "Peebles Corporation | Daniel Newhouse | Tawan Davis." *Real Deal New York*. June 23, 2015.

Honan, Katie. 2022. "Adams Economic Czar Likely Pick Had Secret Sideline Securing City Real Estate Deals." *The City*, January 11, 2022. https://www.thecity.nyc/2022/1/11/22879122/adams-economic-czar-pick-city-real-estate-deals.

Hong, Emily K., Constantine Sedikides, and Tim Wildschut. 2020. "Nostalgia Strengthens Global Self-Continuity through Holistic Thinking." *Cognition and Emotion* (December): 1–28. https://eprints.soton.ac.uk/445641/.

Hsieh, Chang-Tai, and Enrico Moretti. 2018. "Housing Constraints and Spatial Misallocation." SSRN Scholarly Paper ID 3184219. Rochester, NY: Social Science Research Network.

Hu, Winnie. 2016. "Want to Relax in a New York City Park? Join the Crowd." *New York Times*, August 3, 2016, sec. New York. https://www.nytimes.com/2016/08/04/nyregion/want-to-relax-in-one-of-new-york-citys-parks-join-the-crowd.html.

Hu, Winnie. 2017. "A Tiny Park Fights for Sunlight among New York City Skyscrapers." *New York Times*, May 22, 2017. https://www.nytimes.com/2017/05/22/nyregion/greenacre-park-sunlight-skyscrapers-new-york.html?searchResultPosition=100.

Hu, Winnie. 2018a. "Harlem's Trash Bins Were Overflowing. So the City Took 223 Away." *New York Times*, August 19, 2018, sec. New York. https://www.nytimes.com/2018/08/19/nyregion/harlem-litter-baskets-sanitation-department-nyc.html.

Hu, Winnie. 2018b. "Crossing Guards for Grown-Ups? Yes, Traffic Is That Bad." *New York Times*, December 27, 2018, sec. New York. https://www.nytimes.com/2018/12/27/nyregion/ny-traffic-walking-pedestrians.html.

Hubert, Craig. 2018a. "Preservationists Raise Alarm on Proposed Landmarks Rule Changes." *Brownstoner* (blog). March 21, 2018. https://www.brownstoner.com/architecture/landmarks-rule-changes-lpc-proposal-mas-greenwich-village-landmarks-preservation-commission/.

Hubert, Craig. 2018b. "Public Rips Proposed Changes to Landmarks Rules in Contentious Public Hearing Tuesday." *Brownstoner* (blog). March 28, 2018. https://www.brownstoner.com/architecture/landmarks-rule-changes-public-hearing-landmarks-preservation-commission-lpc-chair-meenakshi-srinivasan/.

Hudson, Erin. 2019. "220 CPS: Against the Odds." *Real Deal New York*, April 1, 2019. https://therealdeal.com/issues_articles/220-central-park-south/.

Hudson, Erin. 2020. "William Zeckendorf Planning New York City Homeowner Association." *Real Deal New York*, January 27, 2020. https://therealdeal.com/2020/01/27/william-zeckendorf-wants-to-build-an-army-of-nyc-homeowners/.

Hughes, C. J. 2013. "The Mayor Elect's Short List." *Real Deal New York*, December 1, 2013. https://therealdeal.com/magazine/new-york-december-2013/the-mayor-elects-short-list/

Hughes, C. J. 2015. "NYC's Biggest Real Estate Law Firms." *Real Deal New York*, September 2015. https://therealdeal.com/issues_articles/nycs-biggest-real-estate-law-firms/.

Hughes, Jazmine. 2021. "Does SoHo, Haven for Art and Wealth, Have Room for Affordable Housing?" *New York Times*, April 4, 2021, sec. New York. https://www.nytimes.com/2021/04/04/nyregion/soho-gentrification-racism-wealth.html.

Hutchins, Ryan. 2015. "Interest Groups Push as 421-a Expiration Nears." *ALIGN* (blog). June 9, 2015. Accessed October 21, 2020. https://alignny.org/press/interest-groups-push-as-421-a-expiration-nears/.

Hutson, Matthew. 2016. "Why Nostalgia Is Good for You." *Scientific American*, November 1, 2016. https://doi.org/10.1038/scientificamericanmind1116-8b.

Huxtable, Ada Louise. 1961. "To Keep the Best of New York." *New York Times*, September 10, 1961.

Huxtable, Ada Louise. 1962. "Our New Buildings: Hits and Misses; A Survey of the Construction That Has Given New York a New Face Shows Too Few Departures from the Characterless and the Imitative. Our New Buildings." *New York Times*, April 29, 1962. http://select.nytimes.com/gst/abstract.html?res=F70917FC3E55107A93CBAB178FD85F468685F9.

Huxtable, Ada Louise. 1965. "Lively Original versus Dead Copy." *New York Times*, May 9, 1965.

Huxtable, Ada Louise. 1969. "Boston's New City Hall: A Public Building of Quality." *New York Times*, February 8, 1969. http://timesmachine.nytimes.com/timesmachine/1969/02/08/79946927.html?login=smartlock&auth=login-smartlock.

Huxtable, Ada Louise. 1984. *The Tall Building Artistically Reconsidered: The Search for a Skyscraper Style*. New York: Pantheon Books.

Independent Budget Office. 2015. "From Tax Breaks to Affordable Housing: Examining the 421-a Tax Exemption for One57." New York City: Independent Budget Office.

Ingram, Paul, and Hayagreeva Rao. 2004. "Store Wars: The Enactment and Repeal of Anti-Chain-Store Legislation in America." *American Journal of Sociology* 110 (2): 446–87. https://doi.org/10.1086/422928.

Isserman, Dominique. 2015. "Jean Nouvel Is a Master without a Style." *Intelligencer* (blog), July 1, 2015. http://nymag.com/daily/intelligencer/2015/06/architect-jean-nouvel-profile.html.

Jacobs, Jane. 1992. *The Death and Life of Great American Cities*. New York: Vintage Books. Originally published in 1961.

Janes, George. 2019. Personal Conversation with George Janes by Phone.

Jarvis, Helen, and Alastair Bonnett. 2013. "Progressive Nostalgia in Novel Living Arrangements: A Counterpoint to Neo-Traditional New Urbanism?" *Urban Studies* 50 (11): 2349–70. https://doi.org/10.1177/0042098013478235.

Jayson, Sharon. 2019. "Welcome Home North Texas Tells Companies," *US News & World Report*, February 8, 2019. https://www.usnews.com/news/best-states/articles/2019-02-08/corporations-move-in-to-north-texas-suburbs.

Jeanneret-Gris, Charles Edouard. 1943. *The Athens Charter*. 1973. New York: Grossman.

Jenkins, Simon. 2015. "What Are Cities Doing So Right—and So Wrong? Edward Glaeser Talks to Simon Jenkins." *The Guardian*, May 21, 2015, sec. Cities.

Jerome, Sara. 2015. "Deadly Parasites Take $5 Billion Bite Out of Big Apple." *Water Online* (blog). July 10, 2015. https://www.wateronline.com/doc/deadly-parasites-take-billion-bite-out-of-big-apple-0001.

Johnson, Matthew. 2020. "Architecture Doesn't Need Rebuilding, It Needs More Thoughtful Critics." *ArchDaily*. January 29, 2020. http://www.archdaily.com/586834/architecture-doesn-t-need-rebuilding-it-needs-more-thoughtful-critics/.

Jonas, Andrew E. G., and David Wilson. 1999. *The Urban Growth Machine: Critical Perspectives Two Decades Later*. Albany: SUNY Press.

Juhl, J., T. Wildschut, C. Sedikides, X. Xiong, and X. Zhou. 2021. "Nostalgia Promotes Help Seeking by Fostering Social Connectedness." *Emotion* 21 (3): 631–43. https://doi.apa.org/doiLanding?doi=10.1037%2Femo0000720.

Kaldor, Nicholas. 1939. "Welfare Propositions of Economics and Interpersonal Comparisons of Utility." *Economic Journal* 49, no. 195 (1939): 549–52.

Kallos, Ben. 2014. "Policy Report: Improving Community Boards in New York City." Accessed June 4, 2018. https://www.google.com/search?q=policy+repoft+improving+community+hboards+in+nyc&rlz=1C5CHFA_enUS793US795&oq=policy+repoft+improving+community+hboards+in+nyc&aqs=chrome.69i57.5574j0j4&sourceid=chrome&ie=UTF-8.

Kallos, Ben. 2015. "Testimony on Landmarks Bill, New York City Council—File #: Int 0775-2015." https://legistar.council.nyc.gov/LegislationDetail.aspx?ID=2271110&GUID=A66556A6-1DEA-4D5F-8535-92C31B2B2379.

Kallos Testimony at Hearing on Affordable Housing Development: To Examine Programs Supporting Affordable Housing Development, Including Policies Relating to Building Density. 2019. https://benkallos.com/press-release/kallos-testimony-hearing-affordable-housing-development-examine-programs-supporting.

Kamping-Carder, Leigh. 2018. "Hit the NYC Jackpot: How to Get an Affordable Mitchell-Lama Apartment to Call Your Own." Brick Underground. March 15, 2018. https://www.brickunderground.com/blog/2014/10/mitchell_lama_affordable_housing_guide.

Kane, Tim J. 2010. "The Importance of Startups in Job Creation and Job Destruction." *SSRN Electronic Journal.* https://doi.org/10.2139/ssrn.1646934.

Kaysen, Ronda. 2014. "Divided by a Windfall." *New York Times*, November 14, 2014, sec. Real Estate. https://www.nytimes.com/2014/11/16/realestate/affordable-housing-in-new-york-city-sparks-debate.html.

Kazin, Alfred. 1951. *A Walker in the City.* New York: Harcourt Brace.

Keenan, Jesse, and Vishaan Chakrabarti. 2013. *NYC 2040: Housing the Next One Million New Yorkers.* Sponsored by the Carnegie Foundation. Center for Urban Real Estate (CURE): Columbia University Department of Architecture.

Kennedy, Shawn G. 1991. "Landmarks: Now, It's Harlem's Turn." *New York Times*, May 12, 1991, sec. Real Estate. https://www.nytimes.com/1991/05/12/realestate/landmarks-now-it-s-harlem-s-turn.html.

Keshner, Andrew, and Greg Smith. 2018. "De Blasio Donor Harendra Singh Testifies the Mayor Told Him 'Do What You've Got to Do' with Illegal Contributions." *Nydailynews.Com*, March 22, 2018, sec. Politics, New York. https://www.nydailynews.com/news/politics/de-blasio-donor-turned-blind-eye-illegal-contributions-article-1.3890675.

Khorsandi, Sean. 2020. "Update on West 66th Street Battle." *Landmark West!* (blog). January 2020.

Kim, Elizabeth. 2019a. "Powerful NYC Landlords Secretly Met with Affordable Housing Advocates to Seek Rent Reform Compromise." *Gothamist* (blog). May 29, 2019. https://gothamist.com/news/powerful-nyc-landlords-secretly-met-with-affordable-housing-advocates-to-seek-rent-reform-compromise.

Kim, Elizabeth. 2019b. "New State Law Seeks to Unmask Property Owners Behind LLCs." *Gothamist* (blog). October 9, 2019. https://gothamist.com/news/new-state-law-seeks-unmask-property-owners-behind-llcs.

Kim, Joon H. 2017. "Acting U.S. Attorney's Statement on de Blasio." *New York Times*, March 16, 2017, sec. New York. https://www.nytimes.com/interactive/2017/03/16/nyregion/city-hall-investigation-statement.html.

Knakal, Robert. 2019. "Foreign Investment: Down but Not Out." *Commercial Observer* (blog). March 20, 2019. https://commercialobserver.com/2019/03/foreign-investment-down-but-not-out/.

Kober, Eric. 2020. "Zoning That Works." *City Journal of the Manhattan Institute*, October. https://www.city-journal.org/nyc-zoning-reform-needed-for-housing-growth?utm_source=Twitter&utm_medium=Organic_Social.

Koeppel, Gerard T. 2015. *City on a Grid: How New York Became New York.* Boston: Da Capo Press.

Koolhaas, Rem. 1994. *Delirious New York: A Retroactive Manifesto for Manhattan.* New York: Monacelli Press.

Koolhaas, Rem. 1998. *Small, Medium, Large, Extra-Large*. New York: Monacelli Press. https://www.google.com/books/edition/S_M_L_XL/7PmPDwAAQBAJ?hl=en&gbpv=1&dq=rem+koolhaas&printsec=frontcover.

Kramer Levin. 2013. "Kramer Levin Wins Dismissal for JP Morgan Chase of Case Claiming First Amendment Right to Demonstrate in Plaza." Corporate. Kramer Levin. October 8, 2013. https://www.kramerlevin.com/en/perspectives-search/kramer-levin-wins-dismissal-for-jp-morgan-chase-of-case-claiming-first-amendment-right-to-demonstrate-in-plaza.html.

Kramer, Robin. 2018. "Buying and Selling Air Rights In New York City: Part 1." Portfolio Media.

Krisel, Brendan. 2019. "East Harlem District Nominated for Historic Designation." *Harlem, NY Patch* (blog). March 27, 2019. https://patch.com/new-york/harlem/east-harlem-district-recommended-historic-designation.

Kroessler, Jeffrey A. 2018. "Losing Its Way: The Landmarks Preservation Commission in Eclipse." *Environmental Law in New York* 29 (8). https://academicworks.cuny.edu/jj_pubs/245.

Krugman, Paul. 2015. "Opinion | Inequality and the City." *New York Times*, November 30, 2015, sec. Opinion. https://www.nytimes.com/2015/11/30/opinion/inequality-and-the-city.html.

Krugman, Paul. 2020. "Opinion | Have Zombies Eaten Bloomberg's and Buttigieg's Brains?" *New York Times*, February 17, 2020, sec. Opinion. https://www.nytimes.com/2020/02/17/opinion/bloomberg-buttigieg-economy.html.

Kunstler, James Howard. 1994. *The Geography of Nowhere: The Rise and Decline of America's Man-Made Landscape*. New York: Simon & Schuster.

Kusisto, Laura, and Eliot Brown. 2012. "Midtown's New Look Unveiled." *Wall Street Journal*, July 12, 2012, sec. New York. https://www.wsj.com/articles/SB10001424052702303919504577521411010664218.

Kwartler, Michael. 2015. "Shadow, Sunlight and Zoning Analysis Done for the East Fifties Zoning Proposal of EFRA." This is a printout of a PowerPoint presentation he did for EFRA, January 6, 2015 (document in author's library).

Kwartler, Michael, and Raymon Masters. 1984. "Daylight as a Zoning Device for Midtown." *Energy and Buildings* 6 (2): 173–89. https://doi.org/10.1016/0378-7788(84)90072-0.

La Guardia, Fiorello. 1938. *The Tenement Era and the Dawn of Public Housing | The Brian Lehrer Show*. https://www.wnyc.org/story/pg2p-history-public-housing/.

Landmarks Preservation Commission. 2015. "Mount Morris Park Historic District Extension Designation Report." http://s-media.nyc.gov/agencies/lpc/lp/2571.pdf.

Landmark West! 2018. "The Next Step: LPC to Hold Hearing for Revised Rules Changes." *Landmark West!* (blog). July 31, 2018. https://www.landmarkwest.org/the-next-step-lpc-to-hold-hearing-for-revised-rules-changes/.

Lavdas, Alexandros A., Nikos A. Salingaros, and Ann Sussman. 2021. "Visual Attention Software: A New Tool for Understanding the 'Subliminal' Experience of the Built Environment." *Applied Sciences* 11 (13): 6197. https://doi.org/10.3390/app11136197.

Layous, K., J. L. Kurtz, T. Wildschut, and C. Sedikides. 2022. "The Effect of a Multi-Week Nostalgia Intervention on Well-Being: Mechanisms and Moderation." *Emotion* 22 (8): 1952–68. https://doi.org/10.1037/emo0000817.

Le Corbusier. 1923. *Towards a New Architecture*. Kindle edition. New York: Dover.

Le Corbusier, and Frederick Etchells. 1929. *The City of Tomorrow and Its Planning*. 8th ed. Kindle edition. New York: Dover.

Lehrer, Brian, dir. 2017. "Preet Bharara's Take on the News | The Brian Lehrer Show." WNYC. New York. October 25, 2017. https://www.wnyc.org/story/preet-bhararas-take-news/.

Leland, John. 2019. "Real Estate Thought It Was Invincible in New York. It Wasn't." *New York Times*, December 2, 2019, sec. New York. https://www.nytimes.com/2019/11/29/nyregion/real-estate-industry-nyc.html.

Leonhardt, David. 2011. "A Conversation with Edward L. Glaeser." *New York Times: Economix* (blog). February 15, 2011. https://economix.blogs.nytimes.com/2011/02/15/a-conversation-with-edward-l-glaeser/.

Lerner, Susan. 2013. "Jobs for NY Scorecard: PAC Underperforms $5 Million Investment." Press Release. *Common Cause*, September 12, 2013. https://www.commoncause.org/new-york/press-release/jobs-for-ny-scorecard-pac-underperforms-5-million-investment/.

Lerner, Susan. 2014. "'Moreland Monday' Analysis of REBNY Contributions Raises Serious Issues for Commission to Consider." *Common Cause*, February 27, 2014. https://www.commoncause.org/new-york/press-release/moreland-monday-analysis-of-rebny-contributions-raises-serious-issues-for-commission-to-consider/.

Levine, Jon. 2021. "Corey Johnson Looking into Government Relations Consulting." *New York Post*, December 18, 2021. https://nypost.com/2021/12/18/corey-johnson-looking-into-government-relations-consulting/.

Levine, Larry. 2019. "A Wet 2018 Saw Sharp Rise in NYC Sewage Alerts: 1 in 3 Days." NRDC. April 12, 2019. https://www.nrdc.org/experts/larry-levine/wet-2018-saw-sharp-rise-nyc-sewage-dumping-1-3-days.

Lewis, Christina S. N. 2010. "Boston Mayor Blasts Vornado's Roth over 'Blight' Speech." *Wall Street Journal*, March 8, 2010, sec. Developments Blog. https://www.wsj.com/articles/BL-DVB-10035.

L'Heureux, Catie. 2015. "Why I Live in an All-Women Boardinghouse in New York City." *New York Magazine*, March 24, 2015. http://nymag.com/thecut/2015/03/why-i-live-in-an-all-women-boardinghouse.html.

Li, Xiaodi. 2019. "Do New Housing Units in Your Backyard Raise Your Rents?" New York: Furman Center for Real Estate and Urban Policy, New York University.

Lindgren, James M. 2014. Preserving South Street Seaport: The Dream and Reality of a New York Urban Renewal District. New York: NYU Press.

Lipton, Eric, and Jesse Drucker. 2019. "Symbol of '80s Greed Stands to Profit from Trump Tax Break for Poor Areas." *New York Times*, October 26, 2019, sec. Business. https://www.nytimes.com/2019/10/26/business/michael-milken-trump-opportunity-zones.html.

Logan, John R., and Harvey Molotch. 2007. *Urban Fortunes: The Political Economy of Place*. 20th anniv. ed. Berkeley: University of California Press.

Logue, Edward. 1973. "Another Chance for Housing: Low-Rise Alternatives." New York: Museum of Modern Art; distributed by New York Graphic Society.

Long, Christopher. 2018. "Apostle and Apostate: Josef Frank's Modernist Vision." *Places Journal*, February 6, 2018. https://doi.org/10.22269/180206.

Loos, Ted. 2020. "At Home with Rem Koolhaas." *Wall Street Journal*, January 9, 2020, sec. Magazine. https://www.wsj.com/articles/at-home-with-rem-koolhaas-11578576867.

Loum, Mary. 2013. "The Verdict on Environmental Harm: Leave It to the Jury." *Ecology Law Quarterly* 40 (2): 385–410. https://doi.org/doi:10.15779/Z380S0R.

Lubove, Roy. 1963. *The Progressives and the Slums: Tenement House Reform in New York City, 1890–1917*. Pittsburgh, Penn.: University of Pittsburgh Press.

Lusvardi, Wayne. "A Critique of the Position Papers on the Valuation of Land Suitable for Habitat Preservation or Mitigation." *Right of Way*. November/December 1996, 23–31.

Magill, M. Elizabeth. 2011. "Courts and Regulatory Capture." SSRN Scholarly Paper ID 1926736. Rochester, N.Y.: Social Science Research Network. http://papers.ssrn.com/abstract=1926736.

Makielski, S. J. 1966. *The Politics of Zoning: The New York Experience*. New York: Columbia University Press.

Mahoney, Bill. 2015a. "REBNY Members Gave a Tenth of All N.Y. Campaign Money." Politico PRO (blog), April 15, 2015. https://www.politico.com/states/new-york/albany/story/2015/04/rebny-members-gave-a-tenth-of-all-ny-campaign-money-021345.

Mahoney, Bill. 2015b. "Real Estate Invests in Wright Congressional Bid." Politico PRO (blog), October 2015. https://www.politico.com/states/new-york/albany/story/2015/10/real-estate-invests-in-wright-congressional-bid-026843.

Mallonee, Laura. 2016. "The Unreal, Eerie Emptiness of China's 'Ghost Cities.'" *Wired*, February 4, 2016. https://www.wired.com/2016/02/kai-caemmerer-unborn-cities/.

Mandzy, Orest. 2017. "Apartment REITs with New York Exposure Competing with New Supply." *Urban Land Magazine*. May 1, 2017. https://urbanland.uli.org/capital-markets/apartment-reits-new-york-exposure-competing-new-supply/.

Mangin, John. 2014. "The New Exclusionary Zoning." *Stanford Law & Policy Review* (Urban Law and Policy) 25 (1): 91.

Manhattan Borough President's Office. 2019. "Envision Soho/Noho: Summary of Findings and Recommendations." New York: Department of City Planning.

Manrodt, Alexis. 2020. "The Real Deal Residential Brokerage Ranking Expands beyond Manhattan." *Real Deal New York*. June 22, 2020.

Marcus, Norman. 1992. "New York City Zoning—1961–1991: Turning Back the Clock—But with an Up-to-the-Minute Social Agenda Essay." *Fordham Urban Law Journal* 19: 707–26.

Marohn, Charles. 2014. "A Case for Height Restrictions." *Strong Towns* (blog). November 3, 2014. https://www.strongtowns.org/journal/2014/11/3/the-case-for-height-restrictions.

Marsh, Julia. 2020a. "De Blasio Pushes 'Racial Justice' Soho Development Plan for 3,200 New Apartments." *New York Post*, October 7, 2020. https://nypost.com/2020/10/07/de-blasio-pushes-soho-development-plan-that-would-create-3200-new-apartments/.

Marsh, Julia. 2020b. "Real Estate Firm with Deep Ties to de Blasio Poised to Profit from Soho Rezoning." *New York Post*, October 16, 2020. https://nypost.com/2020/10/16/real-estate-firm-with-de-blasios-ties-expected-to-profit-from-rezoning/.

Martin, Will. 2016. "'You Can Concrete over the Entire Length and Breadth of the UK and House Prices Would Still Rise.'" *Business Insider*. April 23, 2016. https://www.businessinsider.com/societe-generales-albert-edwards-on-the-uk-housing-market-2016-4.

Martin, Will. 2017. "The Key Driver of Britain's Wildly Inflated Property Market Might Not Be What We Think It Is." *Business Insider*. April 11, 2017. https://www.businessinsider.com/britains-housing-market-is-not-being-driven-by-a-supply-and-demand-imbalance-2017-4.

Martinez, Edwin. 2019. "Overcrowding in NYC Public Schools: A Growing Problem." CUNY School of Journalism, Voices of New York. March 29, 2019.

Mason, Randall. 1999. "Economics and Heritage Conservation: Concepts, Values, and Agendas for Research." In *Economics and Heritage Conservation*, 63. Los Angeles: Getty Conservation Institute.

Mason, Randall. 2002. "Assessing Values in Conservation Planning: Methodological Issues and Choices." In *Assessing the Value of Cultural Heritage*. Los Angeles: Getty Conservation Institute.

Mast, Evan. 2019. "The Effect of New Market-Rate Housing Construction on the Low-Income Housing Market," Journal of Urban Economics 133: 103383. 10.17848/wp19-307.

Mathurin, Desiree. 2016. "Tawan Davis." *Real Deal New York*, April 27, 2016. https://therealdeal.com/2016/04/27/tawan-davis-jumps-to-re-investment-firm-after-messy-break-with-peebles/.

Matthews, Joan Leary. 2019. "Still High Levels of Lead in Drinking Water in NYC Schools." NRDC. August 20, 2019. https://www.nrdc.org/experts/joan-leary-matthews/still-high-levels-lead-drinking-water-nyc-schools.

Mayer, Martin. 1978. *The Builders: Houses, People, Neighborhoods, Governments, Money*. 1st ed. New York: Norton.

Mays, Jeffery C. 2019. "De Blasio to Developers: Donate to My Nonprofit. $125,000 Came." *New York Times*, September 19, 2019, sec. New York. https://www.nytimes.com/2019/09/19/nyregion/de-blasio-2020-ethics.html.

Mays, Jeff, and Murray Weiss. 2016. "De Blasio Asked Me for $20K And It Was Hard to Say No, Developer Says." *DNAinfo New York*, May 4, 2016. https://www.dnainfo.com/new-york/20160504/civic-center/de-blasio-asked-me-for-20k-it-was-hard-say-no-developer-says.

McCloskey, Deirdre N. 1998. *The Rhetoric of Economics*. Madison: University of Wisconsin Press.

McCloskey, Deirdre Nansen. 2009. "Bourgeois Dignity and Liberty: Why Economics Can't Explain the Modern World." MPRA Paper No. 16805, August 22, 2009.

McCloskey, Deirdre Nansen. 2015. "Max U vs. Humanomics: A Critique of Neo-Institutionalism." *Journal of Institutional Economics* 12 (1): 1–17.

McEnaney, Liz. 2011. "Jennifer Raab Interview." *New York Preservation Archive* (blog). Accessed May 8, 2022. https://www.nypap.org/oral-history/jennifer-raab/.

McFadden, Robert D. 2017. "Leonard Litwin, New York Real Estate Mogul, Dies at 102." *New York Times*, April 3, 2017, sec. New York. https://www.nytimes.com/2017/04/03/nyregion/leonard-litwin-dead-real-estate-developer-glenwood-new-york.html.

McMahon, E. J. 2006. "Defusing New York's Pension Bomb." *Empire Center for Public Policy* (blog). June 7, 2006. https://www.empirecenter.org/publications/defusing-new-yorks-pension-bomb/.

McWhorter, John. 2021. "Opinion | What's Missing from the Conversation about Systemic Racism." *New York Times*, September 28, 2021, sec. Opinion. https://www.nytimes.com/2021/09/28/opinion/redlining-systemic-racism.html.

Mehaffy, Michael. 2010. "The Landscape Urbanism: Sprawl in a Pretty Green Dress?" *Planetizen*, October 4, 2010. https://www.planetizen.com/node/46262.

Mehaffy, Michael, and Rachelle Alterman. 2019. "White Paper on Tall Buildings Reconsidered: The Growing Evidence of a Looming Urban Crisis." Stockholm: Centre for the Future of Places.

Meiggs, Russell. 1963. "The Political Implications of the Parthenon." *Greece & Rome* 10: 36–45. https://www.jstor.org/stable/826894.

Melby, Caleb. 2019. "Trump's 'Opportunity Zones' Tax Break under Assault in New York." *Bloomberg News*, February 6, 2019. https://www.bloomberg.com/news/articles/2019-02-06/trump-s-opportunity-zones-tax-break-is-under-assault-in-n-y.

Melton, Paula. 2018. "The Urgency of Embodied Carbon and What You Can Do about It." *Building Green*. August 20, 2018. https://www.buildinggreen.com/feature/urgency-embodied-carbon-and-what-you-can-do-about-it.

Meyer, David. 2022. "NY State Agency Approves Penn Station Tax Breaks for Hochul Donor Steve Roth." *New York Post*, July 21, 2022. https://nypost.com/2022/07/21/ny-agency-approves-penn-station-tax-breaks-for-hochul-donor/.

Michl, Jan. 2014. "A Case against the Modernist Regime in Design Education." *International Journal of Architectural Research* 8 (2): 36–46.

Michl, Jan. 2015. "Towards Understanding Visual Styles as Inventions without Expiration Dates." *ARS* 48 (1): 19.

Miklovic, Susan. 2016. "Saving Grand Central Station." *NBX Express*, December 16, 2016. https://www.thenbxpress.com/saving-grand-central-station/.

Miller, Justin. 2016. "How the Real Estate Lobby—and Trump—Got a Huge Tax Break." *American Prospect*, October 7, 2016. https://prospect.org/api/content/b3d5f45e-7d5f-5554-8544-303d2ed09232/.

Mitchell, Joseph. 2008. *My Ears Are Bent*. New York: Vintage Books.

Molotch, Harvey. 1976. "The City as a Growth Machine: Toward a Political Economy of Place." *American Journal of Sociology* 82 (2): 309–32. http://www.jstor.org/stable/2777096.

Moreland Commission to Investigate Public Corruption. 2013. "Preliminary Report." New York: State of New York.

Moskowitz, P. E. 2018. *How to Kill a City: Gentrification, Inequality, and the Fight for the Neighborhood*. Reprint. New York: Bold Type Books.

Moss, Jeremiah. 2018. *Vanishing New York: How a Great City Lost Its Soul*. Reprint. New York: Dey Street Books.

Moss, M. L., and C. Qing. 2012. *The Dynamic Population of Manhattan*. Rudin Center for Transportation Policy and Management Wagner School of Public Service, New York University.

Moss Spatt, Beverly. 2011. "Leading the Commission: Interviews with the Former Chairs of the NYC's Landmarks Preservation Commission." New York: New York Preservation Archive Project. https://www.nypap.org/wp-content/uploads/2016/11/Spatt_Beverly_2011.pdf.

Mumford, L. 1962. "The Sky Line." *New Yorker*. December 1, 1962. http://archives.newyorker.com/?i=1962-12-01#folio=CV1.

Murphy, Jarrett, with reporting by Annamarya Scaccia. 2018. "Coming to Grips with the Two-Decade Deluge of LLC Money into New York's Democracy." *City Limits* (blog). September 7, 2018. https://citylimits.org/2018/09/07/coming-to-grips-with-the-two-decade-deluge-of-llc-money-into-new-yorks-democracy/.

Muschamp, Herbert. 2001. "ART/ARCHITECTURE; Measuring Buildings without a Yardstick." *New York Times*, July 22, 2001, sec. Arts. https://www.nytimes.com/2001/07/22/arts/art-architecture-measuring-buildings-without-a-yardstick.html.

Muschamp, Herbert. 2003. "A Building's Bold Spirit," *New York Times*, November 24, 2003.
Nahmias, Laura. 2016. "Campaign for One New York, Disbanded and under Investigation, Raised Money through February." *Politico PRO* (blog). July 15, 2016. https://politi.co/2JWKnVd.
Nahmias, Laura. 2017. "Disgraced Donor Lays out Explosive Testimony in City Corruption Trial." *Politico*, October 26, 2017, New York edition.
Natali, Marcos Piason. 2004. "History and the Politics of Nostalgia." *Iowa Journal of Cultural Studies* 5 (1): 10–25. https://doi.org/10.17077/2168-569X.1113.
Navarro, Mireya. 2014. "Affordability Will Be Focus for New Housing Leaders." *New York Times*. February 8, 2014. https://www.nytimes.com/2014/02/09/nyregion/affordability-will-be-focus-for-new-housing-leaders.html.
Neuman, William. 2019. "Landlords Get a $173 Million Deal from City as Their Lawyer Raises Funds for de Blasio." *New York Times*, April 4, 2019, sec. New York. https://www.nytimes.com/2019/04/04/nyregion/homeless-buildings-sold-de-blasio-democrats.html.
Neuman, William, and J. David Goodman. 2017. "The Mayor Sought Money, a Donor Sought Access: Both Said 'Yes.'" New York Times, November 2, 2017, sec. N.Y. / Region. https://www.nytimes.com/2017/11/02/nyregion/de-blasio-rechnitz-donor-nyc.html.
Neumeyer, Fritz. 1991. *The Artless Word: Mies van der Rohe on the Building Art*. Cambridge, Mass.: MIT Press.
New York City Council Land Use Committee. 2016. "Landmarks for the Future: Learning from 50 Years of Preservation." New York. http://nyccouncillabs.wpengine.com/press/wp-content/uploads/sites/56/2016/06/landmarks.pdf.
New York City Department of City Planning. n.d. "Unified Bulk Program." Accessed October 3, 2017.
New York City Department of Housing Preservation and Development. 2020. "Where We Live NYC Final Plan." October 20, 2020. http://www1.nyc.gov/site/hpd/news/045-20/new-york-city-releases-final-where-we-live-nyc-plan-blueprint-advance-fair-housing-the.
New York City Department of Investigation. 2016. "Examination of the City's Removal of the Deed Restriction 45 Rivington Street in Manhattan." New York City Department of Investigation.
New York City Independent Budget Office. 2017. "An Efficient Use of Public Dollars? A Closer Look at the Market Effects of the 421-a Tax Breaks for Condos." Independent Budget Office. https://ibo.nyc.ny.us/iboreports/an-efficient-use-of-public-dollars-a-closer-look-at-the-market-effects-of-the-421-a-tax-break-for-condos.pdf.
New York City Rent Guidelines Board. 2019. "2019 Housing Supply Report." New York. https://rentguidelinesboard.cityofnewyork.us/wp-content/uploads/2019/08/2019-HSR.pdf
New York Senate, dir. 2022. *Economic Development—Subsidies and Tax Incentives*. https://www.youtube.com/watch?v=CoVEz8tokiA.
New York Times. 1902. "To Protect Skyscrapers." *New York Times*, February 16, 1902.
New York Times Editorial Board. 2000. "Opinion | Battling Over the Cityscape." *New York Times*, April 25, 2000, sec. Opinion. https://www.nytimes.com/2000/04/25/opinion/battling-over-the-cityscape.html.

New York Times Editorial Board. 2019. "Opinion | Why New York Can't Pick Up Its Trash." *New York Times*, October 29, 2019, sec. Opinion. https://www.nytimes.com/2019/10/29/opinion/nyc-sanitation.html.

New York Times Editors. 1906. "Tall Buildings." Editorial. *New York Times*, August 13, 1906.

New York University, Furman Center. 2015. "The Challenge of Rising Rents." Report. https://furmancenter.org/thestoop/entry/report-the-challenge-of-rising-rents.

New York University, Furman Center. 2020. "Bedford Stuyvesant Neighborhood Profile." *Furman Center Neighborhood Profiles* (blog). 2020. https://furmancenter.org/neighborhoods/view/bedford-stuyvesant.

New Yorker. 1967. "Preservation." *New Yorker*, February 25, 1967.

Newfield, Jack, and Paul Du Brul. 1981. *The Permanent Government: Who Really Rules New York?* New York: Pilgrim Press.

Newman, David, Matthew Sachs, Arthur Stone, and Norbert Schwarz. 2020. "Nostalgia and Well-Being in Daily Life: An Ecological Validity Perspective." *Journal of Personality and Social Psychology* 118 (January): 325–47. https://doi.org/10.1037/pspp0000236.

Oldfield, Philip, Dario Trabucco, and Antony Wood. 2009. "Five Energy Generations of Tall Buildings: An Historical Analysis of Energy Consumption in High-Rise Buildings." *Journal of Architecture* 14 (5): 591–613. https://doi.org/10.1080/13602360903119405.

O'Leary, Amy. 2012. "How Many People Can Manhattan Hold?" *New York Times*, March 1, 2012. http://www.nytimes.com/2012/03/04/realestate/how-many-people-can-manhattan-hold.html.

Ostrom, Elinor. 2012. *The Future of the Commons: Beyond Market Failure and Government Regulation*. Institute of Economic Affairs.

Packes, Nancy. 2018. "Third Quarter Triboro Rental Report." New York: Nancy Packes Signature Marketing Services.

Parker, Will. 2019. "City to Revoke Permits for Extell's Kazakh-Backed Tower at 50 West 66th." *Real Deal New York*, January 17, 2019. https://therealdeal.com/2019/01/17/city-revokes-permits-for-extells-kazakh-backed-tower-at-50-west-66th-street/.

Parker, Will, and Kathryn Brenzel. 2018. "Recasting Cuomo." *Real Deal New York*, October 1, 2018. https://therealdeal.com/issues_articles/recasting-cuomo/.

Parker, Will, and Konrad Putzer. 2017. "Unlikely Allies: How NYC Real Estate Got Minority Advocacy Groups to Lobby for Its Cause." *Real Deal New York*, November 2017.

Partnership for New York City. 2020. "A Call for Action and Collaboration." https://pfnyc.org/research/a-call-for-action-and-collaboration/.

Passell, Aaron. 2016. "Historic District Designation and Neighborhood Change: Exploring the Preservation and Gentrification Question."

Paulsen, Sherida. 2011. "Leading the Commission: Interviews with the Former Chairs of the NYC's Landmarks Preservation Commission." New York: New York Preservation Archive Project.

Pearson, Marjorie. 2010. "New York City Landmarks Preservation Commission 1962–1999." James Marston Fitch Charitable Foundation. https://www.nypap.org/wp-content/uploads/2017/11/320367933-Marjorie-Pearson-pdf.pdf.

Peck, Jamie. 2016. "Economic Rationality Meets Celebrity Urbanology: Exploring Edward Glaeser's City." *International Journal of Urban and Regional Research* 40 (1): 1–30. https://doi.org/10.1111/1468-2427.12321.

Pennington, Kate. 2021. "Does Building New Housing Cause Displacement?" In Dropbox. Department of Agricultural and Resource Economics, University of California Berkeley, 2021. https://www.dropbox.com/s/oplls6utgf7z6ih/Pennington_JMP.pdf?dl=0.

Pereira, Sydney. 2018. "The Shadows Megatowers Cast on a Light-Starved City." *The Villager*, May 31, 2018.

Peterson, Iver. 1988. "The Anatomy of a Co-Op Conversion." *New York Times*, March 27, 1988, sec. Real Estate. https://www.nytimes.com/1988/03/27/realestate/the-anatomy-of-a-co-op-conversion.html.

Petry, Ann. 2019. "Harlem." In *The Street, the Narrows*. New York: Library of America.

Piano, Renzo. 2013. "The Fussiest Clients—." *Wall Street Journal, Eastern Edition*, January 11, 2013. https://www.proquest.com/docview/1268632805/abstract/AF5211F38DB042F0PQ/11.

Pierce O'Brien, Dianne. 2013. "Measuring the Full Economic Impacts of Local Historic District Designations." M.A. thesis, Columbia University. https://doi.org/10.7916/D86Q24DX.

Pincus, Adam. 2013. "Meet the Family Dynasties That Rule New York Real Estate." *Business Insider*. October 3, 2013. https://www.businessinsider.com/meet-the-family-dynasties-that-rule-new-york-real-estate-2013-10.

Pincus, Adam. 2019. "Affordable Housing Landlords among City's Most Active Evictors." *PincusCo* (blog). May 22, 2019. https://www.pincusco.com/affordable-housing-landlords-among-citys-most-active-evictors/.

Plunz, Richard. 2016. *A History of Housing in New York City*. Rev. ed. New York: Columbia University Press.

Podkul, Cezary, Derek Kravitz, and Will Parker. 2016. "Why Developers of Manhattan Luxury Towers Give Millions to Upstate Candidates." *ProPublica* (blog). December 30, 2016. https://www.propublica.org/article/developers-of-manhattan-luxury-towers-give-millions-to-upstate-candidates.

Podkul, Cezary, Will Parker, and Derek Kravitz. 2016. "The Inside Story of How 421a Developers Sway Albany." *Real Deal*, December 30, 2016.

Pogrebin, Robin. 2010. "Commissioner Is Removed from Landmarks Panel." *City Room* (blog). November 3, 2010. https://cityroom.blogs.nytimes.com/2010/11/03/commissioner-is-removed-from-landmarks-panel/.

Polevoy, Jason. n.d. "Biography | Jason T. Polevoy." Patterson Belknap Webb & Tyler LLP.

Popper, Karl. 1944. "The Poverty of Historicism, I." *Economica* 11 (42): 86–103. https://doi.org/10.2307/2549642.

Poretz, Ted, and Alyson Weiss. 2000. "Terminating Sponsor Leases: Regaining Control of Your Garage." *The Cooperator*, August 2000. https://cooperator.com/article/terminating-sponsor-leases.

Porter, Michael E. 2003. "The US Homebuilding Industry and the Competitive Position of Large Builders."

Poteete, Amy R., Marco A. Janssen, and Elinor Ostrom. 2010. *Working Together: Collective Action, the Commons, and Multiple Methods in Practice*. Princeton, N.J.: Princeton University Press.

Powell, M. 2005. "Harlem's New Rush: Booming Real Estate; Historic District Is Undergoing Transformation." *Washington Post*, March 12, 2005. http://search.proquest.com/news/docview/409780357/34BCF2482FC54C47PQ/1?accountid=10226.

Powell, Sherida. 2014. "Explaining Gentrification: The Role of Dwelling Age, Historic Districts, and the Redevelopment Option." Ph.D. diss., George Washington University.

Pratt Center for Community Development. 2015. "Making Room for Housing and Jobs." https://prattcenter.net/our_work/making_room_for_housing_and_jobs.

Powell, Sherida. 2014. "Explaining Gentrification: The Role of Dwelling Age, Historic Districts, and the Redevelopment Option." Ph.D. diss., George Washington University.

Putzier, Konrad. 2018. "Top Commercial Mortgage Firms." *Real Deal New York*. May 1, 2018.

Quigley, John, and Larry Rosenthal. 2005. "The Effects of Land Use Regulation on the Price of Housing: What Do We Know? What Can We Learn?" *Cityscape: A Journal of Policy Development and Research* 8 (1): 69–137.

Rabiyah, Sam. 2020. "Examining the Myth of the 'Mom-and-Pop' Landlord." *Medium*, June 28, 2020. https://medium.com/justfixnyc/examining-the-myth-of-the-mom-and-pop-landlord-6f9f252a09c.

Ramey, Corinne. 2018. "Michael Shvo, Manhattan Real-Estate Developer and Art Collector, Pleads Guilty to Tax Evasion." *Wall Street Journal*, April 26, 2018, sec. U.S. https://www.wsj.com/articles/michael-shvo-manhattan-real-estate-developer-and-art-collector-pleads-guilty-to-tax-evasion-1524782893.

Ransom, Jan. 2019. "'Liar,' and Star Witness in City Graft Cases, Gets 10-Month Sentence." *New York Times*, December 19, 2019, sec. New York. https://www.nytimes.com/2019/12/19/nyregion/jona-rechnitz-corruption-sentencing.html.

Rashbaum, William K. 2017. "No Charges, but Harsh Criticism for de Blasio's Fund-Raising." *New York Times*, March 16, 2017, sec. New York. https://www.nytimes.com/2017/03/16/nyregion/mayor-bill-de-blasio-investigation-no-criminal-charges.html.

Raskin, Sam. 2018. "The YIMBY Movement Comes to New York City." *Curbed New York*. September 17, 2018. https://ny.curbed.com/2018/9/17/17869546/open-new-york-yimby-rezoning-brooklyn-nimby.

Real Deal, The, dir. 2020. *Dan Doctoroff & Alicia Glen: The Future of Urban Development*. Video Zoom Interview. New York. Available as of 2023 at https://www.youtube.com/watch?v=Iw_MJlkOLlI.

Real Estate Bd. of NY, Inc. v. City Council of City of New York. 2007.

REBNY. 2013a. "An Analysis of Landmarked Properties in Manhattan." New York. This may be behind a paywall, as REBNY took the paper down after a few years. Author has printouts in home library.

REBNY. 2013b. "Landmarking Curtails Affordable Housing Development in Manhattan, REBNY Study Reveals." REBNY. www.rebny.com. This may be behind a paywall, as REBNY took it down sometime after 2016. Author has a printout in home library.

Rebong, Kevin. 2020. "Ranking New York's Most Active Investment Sales Brokerages." *Real Deal New York*. March 19, 2020. https://therealdeal.com/issues_articles/the-investment-sales-scuffle/.

Regional Plan Association. 2016. Charting a New Course, May 2016 report. New York. https://rpa.org/work/reports/charting-a-new-course.

Reinvent Albany. 2019. "Report: Assembly Leaders Get Few Contributions from People in Districts. Heastie—One in District Human Donor." *Reinvent Albany* (blog). May 23, 2019. https://reinventalbany.org/2019/05/only-16-of-campaign-donations-assembly-leadership-receives-are-from-people-in-their-districts/.

Rennix, Adrian, and Nathan J. Robinson. 2017. "Why You Hate Contemporary Architecture." *Current Affairs*, October 31, 2017. https://www.currentaffairs.org/2017/10/why-you-hate-contemporary-architecture.

RERG (Real Estate Record and Guide). 1896. "Real Estate." *Real Estate Record and Guide*, February 29, 1896, V. 57, #1459 edition.

RERG. 1897. "Real Estate Update." *Real Estate Record and Guide*, March 13, 1897, V 57 edition.

RERG. 1917. "Legislative Concerns." *Real Estate Record and Guide*, February 3, 1917.

RERG. 1920. "Excess Profits Tax." *Real Estate Record and Guide*, December 25, 1920.

Rice, Andrew. 2013. "How the Podolsky Family Turns Subpar Real Estate into For-Profit Homeless Shelters." *New York Magazine*, November 30, 2013. https://nymag.com/news/features/podolsky-homeless-shelters-2013-12/.

Richardson, Lynda. 1996. "29 Arrested in Tax Fraud Scheme Described as New York's Largest." *New York Times*, November 22, 1996, sec. New York. https://www.nytimes.com/1996/11/22/nyregion/29-arrested-in-tax-fraud-scheme-described-as-new-york-s-largest.html.

Rizzo, Jovana. 2008. "Rangel Not Only Famous Rent-Stabilized Tenant." *Real Deal New York*, July 15, 2008. https://therealdeal.com/2008/07/15/decoding-new-york-city-s-rent-stabilized-mysteries/.

Roberson, Jerry D. 1997. "Tradition or Stagnation? In Defense of Non-Economic Highest and Best Use." *Appraisal Journal* 65 (2).

Robbins, Lionel. 1945. An Essay on the Nature and Significance of Economic Science. London: Macmillan.

Rochabrun, Marcelo. 2016. "How Rudy Giuliani Helped Landlords Get a Tax Break with No Strings Attached." *ProPublica*, May 20, 2016. https://www.propublica.org/article/how-rudy-giuliani-helped-landlords-get-a-tax-break-with-no-strings-attached.

Rodríguez-Pose, Andrés, and Michael Storper. 2019. "Housing, Urban Growth and Inequalities: The Limits to Deregulation and Upzoning in Reducing Economic and Spatial Inequality." SSRN Scholarly Paper ID 3383971. Rochester, NY: Social Science Research Network. https://papers.ssrn.com/abstract=3383971.

Rose, Joseph B. 1999. "Reforming the New York City Zoning Resolution." http://www.tenant.net/land/zoning/unifiedbulk/reforming.html.

Rose, Sarah. 2014. "How One Family Passes It On, and On . . ." *Wall Street Journal*, April 7, 2014, sec. New York. https://online.wsj.com/article/SB10001424052702304640104579485840796072468.html.

Rosenfeld, Clarissa. 2014. "Frank Gehry Claims Today's Architecture Is (Mostly) 'Pure Shit.'" *ArchDaily*, October 23, 2014. https://www.archdaily.com/560673/frank-gehry-claims-today-s-architecture-is-mostly-pure-shit.

Rosengaard, Mikkel. 2015. "Rising from the Ashes of 9/11 Is Not a Phoenix, but a $4 Bn White Elephant." *Architectural Review*, August 2015.

Ross, John K., and Dick Carpenter. 2015. "Robin Hood in Reverse." *City Journal*, December. https://www.city-journal.org/html/robin-hood-reverse-10676.html.

Roth, Steven. 2020. "2020 Chairman's Letter: Vornado Realty Trust." http://books.vno.com/books/qybn/#p=1.

Rypkema, Donovan D. 1994. *The Economics of Historic Preservation: A Community Leader's Guide*. Washington, D.C.: National Trust for Historic Preservation.

Rypkema, Donovan D. 2016. "Historic Preservation: At the Core of a Dynamic New York City—Place Economics—Neighborhood Revitalization." New York: Landmarks Conservancy. https://www.placeeconomics.com/resources/historic-preservation-at-the-core-of-a-dynamic-new-york-city-2/.

St. John, Alexa. 2019. "National Grid Isn't Providing New Gas Hookups in New York." *Wall Street Journal*, July 24, 2019, sec. U.S. https://www.wsj.com/articles/national-grid-isnt-providing-new-gas-hookups-in-new-york-11564003583.

Sadeghi, Akbar, David Talan, and Richard Clayton. 2016. "Small Business and Job Creation." *Monthly Labor Review*, November.

Salant, Katherine. 2011. "Peter Eisenman, an Architect at Home." *Sarasota Herald-Tribune*, May 20, 2011. https://www.heraldtribune.com/story/news/2011/05/20/peter-eisenman-an-architect-at-home/29018628007/.

Salonen, Heidi J., Anna-Liisa Pasanen, Sanna K. Lappalainen, Henri M. Riuttala, Tapani M. Tuomi, Pertti O. Pasanen, Beatrice C. Bäck, and Kari E. Reijula. 2009. "Airborne Concentrations of Volatile Organic Compounds, Formaldehyde and Ammonia in Finnish Office Buildings with Suspected Indoor Air Problems." *Journal of Occupational and Environmental Hygiene* 6 (3): 200–209. https://doi.org/10.1080/15459620802707835.

Salpukas, Agis. 1994. "Irving M. Felt, 84, Sports Impresario, Is Dead." *New York Times*, September 24, 1994, sec. Obituaries. https://www.nytimes.com/1994/09/24/obituaries/irving-m-felt-84-sports-impresario-is-dead.html.

Samtani, Hiten. 2014a. "Property Lobbyists Expect to Gain Ground under de Blasio." *Real Deal*, February 10, 2014.

Samtani, Hiten. 2014b. "REBNY's Influence over Cuomo Laid Bare." *Real Deal New York*, July 24, 2014. https://therealdeal.com/2014/07/24/rebnys-influence-over-cuomo-laid-bare/.

Sanders, Anna. 2018. "City Hall Finally Discloses Lobbyist Meetings—and the Results Are Eye-Opening." *New York Post*, August 11, 2018. https://nypost.com/2018/08/11/city-halls-top-brass-took-136-lobbyist-meetings-in-3-months/.

Sant'Elia, Antonio. 1914. "Manifesto of Futurist Architecture." R/D. https://www.readingdesign.org/manifesto-futurist.

Sassen, Saskia. 2001. *The Global City: New York, London, Tokyo*. Princeton, N.J.: Princeton University Press.

Sassen, Saskia. 2015. "Who Owns Our Cities—and Why This Urban Takeover Should Concern Us All." *The Guardian*, November 24, 2015, sec. Cities. http://www.theguardian.com/cities/2015/nov/24/who-owns-our-cities-and-why-this-urban-takeover-should-concern-us-all.

Saunders, Pete. 2017. "The Millennial Housing Shortage Fallacy." *Strong Towns*, August 8, 2017. https://www.strongtowns.org/journal/2017/8/4/the-millennial-housing-shortage-fallacy.

Saval, Nikil. 2018. "Philip Johnson, the Man Who Made Architecture Amoral." *New Yorker*, December 12, 2018. https://www.newyorker.com/culture/dept-of-design/philip-johnson-the-man-who-made-architecture-amoral.

Sen, Amartya. 2017. "Collective Choice and Social Welfare: An Expanded Edition." In *Collective Choice and Social Welfare*. Cambridge, Mass.: Harvard University Press.

Schachtman, Tom. 1991. *Skyscraper Dreams: The Great Real Estate Dynasties of New York*. Boston: Little Brown.

Schill, Michael H., Ioan Voicu, and Jonathan Miller. 2007. "The Condominium versus Cooperative Puzzle: An Empirical Analysis of Housing in New York City." *Journal of Legal Studies* 36 (2): 275–324. https://doi.org/10.1086/519421.
School of Life. 2020. "Why Is the Modern World So Ugly?" May 13, 2020. https://www.theschooloflife.com/thebookoflife/why-is-the-modern-world-so-ugly/.
Schram, Lauren Elkies. 2019. "Power Landlords: The Guys Who've Got the Biggest Portfolios in New York." *Commercial Observer* (blog). April 23, 2019. https://commercialobserver.com/2019/04/power-landlords-the-guys-whove-got-the-biggest-portfolios-in-new-york/.
Schumacher, Patrik. 2008. "Parametricism." *AD Architectural Design Digital* Cities 79 (4).
Schwartz, Joel. 1993. *The New York Approach: Robert Moses, Urban Liberals, and Redevelopment of the Inner City*. 1st ed. Columbus: Ohio State University Press.
Scruton, Roger. 2013. *The Aesthetics of Architecture*. Rev. ed. Princeton, N.J.: Princeton University Press.
Scully, Vincent, Jr. 1969. *American Architecture and Urbanism*. New York: Praeger.
Sears Archives. 2012. "History of Sears Modern Homes." March 21, 2012. http://www.searsarchives.com/homes/history.htm.
Semes, Steven W. 2009. *The Future of the Past: A Conservation Ethic for Architecture, Urbanism, and Historic Preservation*. New York: W. W. Norton.
Semple, Kirk, and Jeffrey E. Singer. 2015. "On a Block of Single-Story Homes, a 'Monstrosity' in Queens Draws Ire." *New York Times*, June 2, 2015. http://www.nytimes.com/2015/06/03/nyregion/on-a-block-of-single-story-homes-a-monstrosity-in-queens-draws-ire.html.
Sert, J. L. 1947. *Can Our Cities Survive?* Cambridge, Mass.: Harvard University Press.
Shelton, Tracey, Christina Zhou, and Pan Ning. 2018. "'An Incredible Amount of Waste': What China's Eerie Ghost Cities Say about Its Economy." ABC News. June 26, 2018. https://www.abc.net.au/news/2018-06-27/china-ghost-cities-show-growth-driven-by-debt/9912186.
Siegel, Charles. 2010. *An Architecture for Our Time: The New Classicism*. Berkeley, Calif.: Preservation Institute.
Silber, John. 2007. *The Architecture of the Absurd: How Genius Disfigured a Practical Art*. New York: Quantuck Lane.
Sitte, Camillo. 1946. *City Planning According to Artistic Principles*. New York: Phaidon Press.
Skyscraper Museum. 2019. *Housing Density: From Tenements to Towers, an Exhibit*. https://skyscraper.org/housing-density/
Slater, Tom. 2006. "The Eviction of Critical Perspectives from Gentrification Research." *International Journal of Urban and Regional Research* 30 (4): 737–57. https://doi.org/10.1111/j.1468-2427.2006.00689.x.
Small, Eddie. 2018. "Who Owns All of New York?" *Real Deal New York* (blog). September 1, 2018. https://therealdeal.com/issues_articles/who-owns-all-of-new-york/.
Small Business and Entrepreneurship Council. 2018. "Get the Facts." https://sbecouncil.org/about-us/facts-and-data/.
Smith, Greg B. 2018. "Blaz's Secret Donor Deal." *Daily News*, April 10, 2018. https://www.pressreader.com/usa/new-york-daily-news/20180410/281479276991057.
Smith, Greg B. 2015. "NYC Buildings Show Connection between Albany Corruption and Real Estate Industry, with Developers Saving Millions on Taxes." *Nydailynews.Com*,

May 9, 2015, sec. Politics, NYC Crime. https://www.nydailynews.com/news/politics/nyc-buildings-show-albany-corruption-real-estate-connection-article-1.2216861.

Smith, Greg B. 2016. "Lobbyist Who Steered $50,000 to Mayor de Blasio Turned Lower East Side Nursing Home into Luxury Condos." *Nydailynews.Com*, March 26, 2016, sec. Politics, New York, News. https://www.nydailynews.com/news/politics/de-blasio-lobbyist-helped-turn-nursing-home-condos-article-1.2578230.

Smith, Stephen Jacob. 2013. "Jed Walentas Plants a Tree (or Two) in Williamsburg." *Observer* (blog). March 4, 2013. https://observer.com/2013/03/jed-walentas-plants-a-tree-or-two-in-williamsburg/.

Solomont, E. B., and Kevin Sun. 2019. "NYC's Ghost Towers." *Real Deal New York*. April 1, 2019. https://therealdeal.com/issues_articles/ghost-towers-new-york-city/.

Somerville, C. Tsuriel. 1999. "The Industrial Organization of Housing Supply: Market Activity, Land Supply and the Size of Homebuilder Firms." *Real Estate Economics* 27 (4): 669–94. https://doi.org/10.1111/1540-6229.00788.

Sorkin, Michael. 2013. "The Fungibility of Air." *The Nation*, 2013. https://www.thenation.com/article/archive/fungibility-air/.

Sorkin, Michael. 2014. "Critical Mass: Why Architectural Criticism Matters." *Architectural Review* (blog). May 28, 2014. https://www.architectural-review.com/essays/critical-mass-why-architectural-criticism-matters.

Sparago, Mary. 2022. "Jersey City Now the Most Expensive U.S. City for Renters." *New Jersey Digest* (blog), September 28, 2022. https://thedigestonline.com/news/jersey-city-most-expensive-rent-in-us/.

Spectrum News NY1 Staff. 2020. "REBNY to File Lawsuit Challenging Rule That Waives Broker Fee for NY Tenants," February 7, 2020. https://www.ny1.com/nyc/all-boroughs/news/2020/02/07/lawsuit-challenges-rule-waving-broker-fee-for-tenants.

Spinola, Steven. 2014. "State Budget Extends Incentive Programs for Industry." *REBNY Watch* (blog). April 4, 2014.

Stellin, Susan. 2011. "You Don't Have to Pay It." *New York Times*, January 28, 2011, sec. Real Estate. https://www.nytimes.com/2011/01/30/realestate/30cov.html.

Stern, Robert A. M, Thomas Mellins, and David Fishman. 1997. *New York 1960: Architecture and Urbanism between the Second World War and the Bicentennial*. New York: Monacelli Press.

Stevenson, Alexandra, and Jin Wu. 2019. "Tiny Apartments and Punishing Work Hours: The Economic Roots of Hong Kong's Protests." *New York Times*, July 22, 2019, sec. World. https://www.nytimes.com/interactive/2019/07/22/world/asia/hong-kong-housing-inequality.html.

Stewart, Lindsey. 2021. *The Politics of Black Joy: Zora Neale Hurston and Neo-Abolitionism*. Evanston, Ill.: Northwestern University Press.

Stiglitz, Joseph E. 1991. "The Invisible Hand and Modern Welfare Economics." Working Paper 3641. Cambridge, Mass.: National Bureau of Economic Research. http://www.nber.org/papers/w3641.

Storper, Michael. 2013. *Keys to the City*. Princeton, N.J.: Princeton University Press.

Storper, Michael, and Allen J. Scott. 2016. "Current Debates in Urban Theory: A Critical Assessment." *Urban Studies Journal* 53 (6): 1114–36. https://doi.org/10.1177/0042098016634002.

Stringham, Edward. 2001. "Kaldor-Hicks Efficiency and the Problem of Central Planning." Quarterly Journal of Austrian Economics 4 (2): 41–50.

Sugarman, Alan. 2010. "Lowering the Variance Bar: New York City Board of Standards and Appeals Further Eases Requirements for Variance Applications." Landmark West! November 4, 2010. http://protectwest70.org/2010-docs/BSA_lowering_the_variance_bar.pdf.

Sullivan, Brian J., and Jonathan Burke. 2013. "Single-Room Occupancy Housing in New York City: The Origins and Dimensions of a Crisis." *CUNY Law Review* 17 (1): 113. https://doi.org/10.31641/clr170104.

Sullivan, Paul. 2019. "The Perks of Being a Real Estate Mogul." *New York Times*, May 11, 2019.

Sun, Kevin. 2018. "These Are NYC's Biggest Rental Landlords." *Real Deal New York*. December 24, 2018. https://therealdeal.com/2018/12/24/these-are-nycs-biggest-rental-landlords/.

Talen, Emily. 2018. *Neighborhood*. New York: Oxford University Press.

Tabuchi, Hiroko. 2022. "He's an Outspoken Defender of Meat. Industry Funds His Research, Files Show." *New York Times*, October 31, 2022, sec. Climate. https://www.nytimes.com/2022/10/31/climate/frank-mitloehner-uc-davis.html.

Taibbi, Matt. 2010. "The Great American Bubble Machine." *Rolling Stone*, April 5, 2010. https://www.rollingstone.com/politics/politics-news/the-great-american-bubble-machine-195229/.

Teachout, Zephyr. 2016. *Corruption in America: From Benjamin Franklin's Snuff Box to Citizens United.* Cambridge, Mass.: Harvard University Press.

Tharpe, Cody. 2017. "Architects and Structural Engineers: Can't We All Just Get Along?" *ArchDaily*, June 18, 2017. https://www.archdaily.com/873824/architects-and-structural-engineers-cant-we-all-just-get-along.

Tierney, John. 2013. "What Is Nostalgia Good For? Quite a Bit, Research Shows." *New York Times*, July 8, 2013, sec. Science. https://www.nytimes.com/2013/07/09/science/what-is-nostalgia-good-for-quite-a-bit-research-shows.html.

Trangle, Sarina. 2016. "Emails Reveal Close Relationship between REBNY Execs and de Blasio Administration." *City and State NY* (blog). August 26, 2016.

TRD Staff. 2017. "In Box." *Real Deal*, March 2017.

TRD Staff. 2019a. "NYC's Top Property Owners | TRD Data Book." Rankings. New York: Real Deal. https://therealdeal.com/databook2019/2019/commercial/nycs-top-property-owners-2/.

TRD Staff. 2019b. "In Their Words." *Real Deal*, September 2019.

TRD Staff. 2020a. "Blackstone Is World's Largest Commercial Landlord: Fortune." *Real Deal New York*, February 18, 2020. https://therealdeal.com/2020/02/18/how-blackstone-became-the-worlds-biggest-commercial-landlord/.

TRD Staff. 2020b. "Top Construction Firms in NYC." *Real Deal New York*. Accessed October 4, 2020. https://therealdeal.com/issues_articles/renovation-kings-the-citys-30-leading-general-contractors/.

Tung, Anthony Max. 2002. *Preserving the World's Great Cities: The Destruction and Renewal of the Historic Metropolis.* New York: Three Rivers Press.

University College of London. 2017. "High-Rise Buildings Much More Energy Intensive than Low-Rise." June 29, 2017. https://phys.org/news/2017-06-high-rise-energy-intensive-low-rise.html.

Urbach, Peter. 1985. "Good and Bad Arguments against Historicism." In *Popper and the Human Sciences*, edited by Gregory Currie and Alan Musgrave, 133–46. Nijhoff

International Philosophy Series, vol. 19. Dordrecht: Springer Netherlands. https://doi.org/10.1007/978-94-009-5093-1_9.

Vandell, Kerry, and Charles Carter. 2000. "Graaskamp's Concept of Highest and Best Use." In *Essays in Honor of James A. Graaskamp: Ten Years After*, edited by James R. Delisle and Elaine Worzala, 6:307–19. Research Issues in Real Estate. https://doi.org/10.1007/978-1-4615-1703-0.

Velsey, Kim. 2015. "A Taxing Matter: Looking Back on the History of 421-a." *Observer*, May 28, 2015. https://observer.com/2015/05/a-taxing-matter-looking-back-on-the-history-of-421-a/.

Venturi, Robert. 2011. *Complexity and Contradiction in Architecture*. New York; Boston: Museum of Modern Art. Distributed by New York Graphic Society.

Villa Valmarana. 2016. "Villa Valmarana ai Nani." June 2, 2016. https://it-it.facebook.com/villavalmaranaainani/posts/944969565558344.

Village Preservation. 2021a. "Study: City's Proposed SoHo/NoHo Upzoning Would Make Neighborhoods Richer, Whiter, and More Expensive." New York: Village Preservation, March 5, 2021. https://www.villagepreservation.org/campaign-update/study-citys-proposed-soho-noho-upzoning-would-make-neighborhoods-richer-whiter-and-more-expensive/.

Village Preservation. 2021b. "Mapping the Incentive to Demolish." New York.

Village Preservation. 2021c. "Upzoning SoHo and NoHo Report." New York. Found on Report section of www.villagepreservation.org.

Violette, Zachary J. 2019. *The Decorated Tenement: How Immigrant Builders and Architects Transformed the Slum in the Gilded Age*. Illustrated edition. Minneapolis: University of Minnesota Press.

Vitale, Alex S. 2009. *City of Disorder*. New York: New York University Press.

Voorhies, Stephen, Ralph Walker, Perry Smith, and Benjamin Smith. 1958. *Zoning New York City: A Proposal for a Zoning Resolution*. New York.

Vornado Realty Trust. 2022. "Vornado Realty Trust (VNO) Q3 2022 Earnings Call Transcript | Seeking Alpha." November 1, 2022. https://seekingalpha.com/article/4551681-vornado-realty-trust-vno-q3-2022-earnings-call-transcript.

Walker, Alissa. 2014. "Why Tall Buildings Make Cities Hotter." *Gizmodo*. June 9, 2014. https://gizmodo.com/why-tall-buildings-make-cities-hotter-1588242736.

Walker, Nathaniel Robert. 2016. "American Crossroads: General Motors' Midcentury Campaign to Promote Modernist Urban Design in Hometown U.S.A." *Buildings & Landscapes: Journal of the Vernacular Architecture Forum* 23 (2): 89–115. https://doi.org/10.5749/buildland.23.2.0089.

Wallace, Deborah, and Rodrick Wallace. 2017. "Benign Neglect and Planned Shrinkage." *Versobooks.Com* (blog). March 25, 2017. https://www.versobooks.com/blogs/3145-benign-neglect-and-planned-shrinkage.

Walunas, Rosie. 2017. *The Monolith*. https://www.rosiewalunas.com/themonolith.

Ward, Vicky. 2014. *The Liar's Ball: The Extraordinary Saga of How One Building Broke the World's Toughest Tycoons*. New York: Wiley.

Wang, Vivian. 2017. "'We Were Friends': De Blasio Donor Describes a Direct Line to City Hall." *New York Times*, October 26, 2017, sec. N.Y. / Region. https://www.nytimes.com/2017/10/26/nyregion/de-blasio-donor-favors-rechnitz.html.

Weinstock, Charles. 2022. "Petitioner's Memorandum of Law for a Judgment Pursuant to CPLR Article 78 against New York State Urban Development Corporation d/b/a Empire State Development." Supreme Court of the State of New York.

Weiss, Howard. 2010. "Navigating a Development Project through Multiple Land Use Controls." Conference Lecture presented by a land use attorney with Davidoff and Hutcher LLP. https://www.scribd.com/document/294697280/00536178.
Weiss, Howard. 2019. "Every Square Foot Matters." *City and State*, April 1, 2019.
Weiss, Lois. 1999. "New Zoning Plan Released." *Real Estate Weekly*, December 15, 1999.
Weiss, Lois. 2019. "REBNY Furious That City Is Going Ahead with New Zoning Laws." *New York Post* (blog). February 13, 2019. https://nypost.com/2019/02/12/rebny-furious-that-city-is-going-ahead-with-new-zoning-laws/.
Weiss, Marc. 1992. "Density and Intervention: New York's Planning Traditions." In: *New York City 1900–1940*. Baltimore: John Hopkins University Press.
Wilson, Donald C., and Craig D. Hungerford. 1995a. "Public Interest Value: Toward an Analytic Understanding of the Appraisal Institute's Proposed Definition of Value for Environmentally Significant Real Estate." *Right of Way*, February/March 1995.
Wilson, Donald C., and Craig D. Hungerford. 1995b. "Economic Preservation Use—Is It Highest and Best Use?" *Right of Way*, 1995.
Wolf, Michael Allan. 2008. *The Zoning of America: Euclid v. Ambler*. Lawrence: University Press of Kansas.
Wolfe, Tom. 1982. *From Bauhaus to Our House*. New York: Pocket Books.
Wolfe, Tom. 2006. "Opinion | The (Naked) City and the Undead." *New York Times*, November 26, 2006, sec. Opinion. https://www.nytimes.com/2006/11/26/opinion/26wolfe.html.
Wood, Anthony C. 2008. *Preserving New York: Winning the Right to Protect a City's Landmarks*. New York: Routledge.
Wright, Gwendolyn. 1983. *Building the Dream: A Social History of Housing in America*. Reprint. Cambridge, Mass: MIT Press.
Wright, Valerie. 2015. "Red Road and Pearl Jephcott's 'Homes in High Flats.'" *University of Glasgow* (blog). October 11, 2015. http://glasgowhousing.academicblogs.co.uk/red-road-and-pearl-jephcotts-homes-in-high-flats/.
Yao, Kim. 2020. "Advocacy." AIA New York. June 2020. https://www.aiany.org/membership/advocacy/.
Zahirovic-Herbert, Velma, and Karen M Gibler. 2012. "Historic District Influence on House Prices and Marketing Duration." *Journal of Real Estate Finance and Economics*, May 2012.
Zielinska-Dabkowska, Karolina M., and Kyra Xavia. 2019. "Protect Our Right to Light." *Nature* 568 (7753): 451–53. https://doi.org/10.1038/d41586-019-01238-y.

INDEX

Abyssinian Development Corporation, 224–25
activism, 223, 225, 244–45
Adams, Eric, 38, *141*, 187, 245
Adams, Michael Henry, 226
advertising, real estate industry, 207–8
aesthetic value, building heights and, 214
affordable housing, 8, 24, 34–35, 250, 313; controversial plans for, 204; demolition of, 61; destruction of, 37–38; finding sources of money for, 314; gentrification and, 127; historic districts and, 123–24; human-scale affordable housing policy, 311–17; low-rise, 316; new towers and, 56–57; New York State Association for Affordable Housing, 147; policy crisis creating, 60–62; problem, 36, 37; towers and, 248–49; upzoning and, 247, 247–48; in wealthier areas, 245–46
AIA. *See* American Institute of Architects
air rights, 154, 313; better regulation of, 296–99; transfers, 118, 297
airspace, 97
Alexander's department store, 165–66
Algiers, *19*
Allied Realty Interests, 139
Allure Group, 205

Amazon company, 157, 290
Amedore, George, 180, *181*
"amenities," privatized, 32
American Craftsman bungalow, 271, *272*
American Institute of Architects (AIA), 148–49, 255
American Museum of Natural History, 149
ancient light law, 117
anti-chain store law, 309
anti-landmarking, 234
anti-urban streets, 78
anti-zoning, 111–112
apartments: co-operatives, 61; empty, 49, 62; luxury, 48–49; single owner limits, 308
appointees, community board, 301–2
Appraisal Institute of the United States, 112–113
appraisals, real estate, 112–13
Appraisal Standards for Federal Land Acquisitions, 114
architects: as artists, 273–76; European, 256; homes of, 278–85; as influential, 148; lobby, 148; in LPC, 194; modernist, 245–55, 257–59, 261–67; starchitects, 278–85. *See also specific architects*
architectural exhibitionism, 29

architecture, 1, 11–12; AIA, 148–49, 255; copying of, 268–69; critics of, 274–76; historic styles as "dead," 267–69; landscape, 163; nature in, 14; nostalgia and, 277–78; starchitecture, 29; traditional, 31–32; vernacular, 18, 31, 260, 275. *See also* modernist architecture movement
Arrow, Kenneth, 106–7
Asian cities, 22
Asian residents, 246
Association for a Better New York, 144, 146
The Athens Charter (Jeanneret-Gris), 17, 252, 260
Atlantic Yards project, 24–25, 25
AT&T, 113
"austerity budget," Cuomo, 199
Austria, 26

backlog controversy, LPC, 234–38
Bancroft Building, *189*
Banks, John, 186–87
Bar Association committees, 146–47
Barcelona, Spain, 88, 89
Barnett, Gary, 49
Barwick, Kent, 229
Bassett, Edward, 152
Battery Park City, 50
beauty, measuring, 265
Beckelman, Laurie, 225, 230
Bed-Stuy, 126–27
Been, Vicki, 40–41, 54, 57, 111, 248–49
Bells Are Ringing (film), 197
below-market housing, for powerful, 197–99
Benfatto, Robert, 190
Bernstein, Zachary, 56
Bharara, Preet, 173, 202
bicycles, 32, 33
BIDs. *See* business improvement districts
Big Real Estate, 173–75
Black experience, 277–78
Black families, 73, 83
Black homeowners, 119, 127
Black Manhattanites, 223
Black residents, 59, 73, 124, 125–28; LPC and, 224–26

Blackstone, William, 115–16
De Blasio, Bill, 55, 111, *141*, 165, 233; donor base 2017, 183–86, *184*, *185*; influence in regulatory agencies and, 192–93
Blaug, Marc, 110
blighting, 165–66
Bloomberg, Michael, 4, 7, 38, 128, 188; "Seaport City" and, 238
"boarding houses," 127
Board of Standards and Appeals (BSA), 159, 193–94
border vacuums, 161–63
Borelli, Anthony, 190
borough presidents, 300
Boston, Massachusetts, 90–91
Boston City Hall, 264, *265*
de Botton, Alain, 266
Brahinsky, Rachel, 129
Brewer, Gale, *141*, 188, 242–43
bribery, 175, 180, 202–5
British townscape movement, 26
brokers, 138–39, 142
Bronx, "burning" of the, 61
Brooklyn, New York: density of, 94–95; gentrification of, 126; Gowanus neighborhood, 196
Brooklyn Heights, 88
Brownstone neighborhoods, 88
Bruges, Belgium, 265
BSA. *See* Board of Standards and Appeals
building permits, 51–52
buildings. *See* skyscrapers; towers; *specific buildings*
Burney, David, 193
business improvement districts (BIDs), 149–50, 195, 299–305
Byford, Andy, 292
by-products, of production process, 67–68

California, 87–88, 89
campaign contributions, 176; to mayor, 183–86; rent laws controlled and, 177–83
Campaign Finance Board, 183
Campbell, Valerie, 188, 231

INDEX · 361

Campoli, Julie, 93
campuses, modernist, 261–62
Canada, 101–3, *102*, *103*
Can Cities Survive? (Le Corbusier), 19
Capalino and Company, 190
capitalism, 12, 129, 222
Cappelli, Allen, 192
capture. *See* regulatory capture
carbon emissions, 75–76
carbon-filled aluminum, 75–76
carrying capacity, 53–54, 66
cars, designing for, 18–19, 30, 31
Center for an Urban Future, 144
Center for Climate Solutions non-profit, 170–71
Central Park, *71*, *72*
Cerullo, Alfred, 193
Chakrabarti, Vishaan, 7, 11, 80, 82, 251; on Atlantic Yards project, 24–25, *25*; Governor's Island proposal, *168*; hyperdensity and, 21–26; RPA and, 146
Chance, W. Parker, 5–6
Chanda, Shampa, 193–94
Charter reforms (2019), 192
"Charting a New Course" (paper), 82
Chicago, Illinois, 74
Chin, Margaret, 242
Chin, Yuien, 225–26
China, 24, 25
Chinatown, *16*, 56
CHIP. *See* Community Housing Improvement Program
CHPC. *See* Citizens Housing and Planning Council
Church of St. John the Baptist, 162–63
CIAM. *See* International Congress for Modern Architecture
Citizens Budget Commission, 147
Citizens Housing and Planning Council (CHPC), 144, 229, 244
Citizens Union nonprofit, 193
City Charter, 300; amendments, 197; reforms, 139
City Council, zoning and, 55–56
City Hall, 186
"City of Tomorrow" (diorama), 20

The City of Tomorrow and Its Planning (Le Corbusier), 11, 13–15
City Planning According to Artistic Principles (Sitte), 26
City Planning Commission, New York City, 115
climate change, 81
Clinton, Bill, 158
Clocktower Building, 203
cloverleaf highways, 15
coffin homes, 69
college-educated workers, 64
college graduates, 81
Commandment #70, *The Athen's Charter*, 260
Commentaries on the Laws of England (Blackstone), 115, 116
Commercial Rent Control bill, 308–9
Commercial Rent Reform Act, 159–60
common-pool resources, 99–100, 129, 132
commons. *See* urban commons
community board members, lobbyists as, 195–96
community boards, BIDs merged with, 299–305
Community Housing Improvement Program (CHIP), 142
conflict of interest rules, 301, 305
Congress for the New Urbanism, 31–32
construction, 140, 219–20
construction companies, lobbying by, 196
construction unions, 200
"context," idea of, 253–56
contingent valuation, 100, 106–7
convenience, 28
co-operatives, apartments, 61–62
copying, of architecture, 268–69
corporation locations, 213
corporatism, 76
corruption, 180
cost-benefit analyses, 107
cost-benefit proposals, 97–98
costs, social, 67, 68–69
A Country of Cities (Chakrabarti), 21, 22
courtyards, 27
Covid. *See* pandemic

Cozen O'Connor firm, 188
crime, high-rise living and, 79
Criterion Four, Appraisal Institute of the United States, 113
critics, of architecture, 274, 276
Cuomo, Andrew, 147, 163, 176–77, 182; "austerity budget," 199
Cupertino, California, 89

Dallas, Texas, 47
Daly City, California, 87–88
"dark money," 176
Davis, Ali, 187
The Death and Life of Great American Cities (Jacobs), 4, 27–28, 89–91
The Decorated Tenement (Violette), 36
La Defense, Paris, 24
demand, ignoring, 43–46
democracy, 76, 104, 303, 324n1
demographics, of residents, 73
demolished building, 135
demolition, 6, 43, 136, 137, 322n12; of affordable housing, 61; of historic properties, 59, 210, 212; moratorium on, 313–14; pace of, 135–37
"Demolition Machine," "growth machine" as, 134–37, 138
density: benefits of, 95–96; of Brooklyn, 94–95; census report on, 322n11; FAR, 85, 115, 216, 295; as height limit, 165; human-scale design and, 34, 88; "ideal," 92, 94; in-between densities, 91–92; of Manhattan, 94–95; manifestos on, 10; measures of, 84–85; "missing middle" urban, 65; natural limit to, 83; net, 85–86; New York City levels of, 87–89; of Paris, 88–89; policy making and, 96; problem with, 50; safety and, 30; skyscrapers and, 93–94; as social cost, 68; suburban, 89; units of, 24, 32; zoning codes and, 294–95. *See also* hyper-density
Density Wars, 84
Department of Buildings, 296
Department of City Planning, 130–31
Department of Transportation (DOT), New York, 28, 129

"despotic dominion," 115–17
Detroit, Michigan, 25, 41
developers, 45–46, 203; air rights transfers and, 298; campaign contributions by, 181; competition among, 47–50; fines for, 201–2; Glossary of Tax Breaks and Giveaways, 158, 159; historic districts stalked by, 218; Manhattan, 139–40; plazas and, 131; private, 40; profiting, 42–43; skydome and, 118; supply shock and, 72
Dharvi slum, 87
disciplinary autonomy, 255
discrimination, housing, 249
displacement, 57, 73–74
diversity, 28; racial, 244–46; suppression of, 92–93
Dobson, Ellen, 133
Doctoroff, Dan, 73, 143, 187
dominion, despotic, 115–17
Domino Sugar Factory project, 149
donations: from real estate industry, 185–86; unethical, 202–6
Donovan, Shaun, 97
DOT. *See* Department of Transportation
Douek, Joseph, 192
Duany, Andrés, 31–32
Duflo, Esther, 64
Duggan, William, 268
dynastic character, of real estate industry, 48

East Harlem rezoning, 193
East River, 82
EB-5 green card program, 158
Economic Development Corporation (EDC), 143–44, 162–66, 189, 323n5; real estate development deals and, 195; Seaport Historic District and, 238–40
economic development strategy, 290–91
economic geographers, 62–63
economic growth, 290
economics, 104, 106
EDC. *See* Economic Development Corporation
Edelman firm, 189

Edison Properties, in SoHo and NoHo, 242–43
Edwardian building, 281
Eichner, Ian Bruce, 202
80 South Street, 297
Eisenman, Peter, 251, 280
elected officials, as lobbyists, 191–92
election, of community boards members, 303–5
Electoral College, 303
11th Arrondissement of Paris, 282
Ellerman, David, 110–111
Emergency Tenant Protection Act, 179
Emigrant Savings Bank Building, 203
Empire State Development Corporation (ESD), 143, 144, 159, 163–65, 192; Vornado towers, 164
engineering, social, 249
England: "despotic dominion" and, 117; period of industrialization in, 109–10
environmentally sustainable buildings, 75
Environmental Protection Agency (EPA), 174
environmental toxins, skyscrapers, 75–76
"Envision SoHo/NoHo" report, 243
EPA. *See* Environmental Protection Agency
Equity Residential, 46
ESD. *See* Empire State Development Corporation
ethics, 104, 109
European architects, 256
European cities, 22
evictions, 179
"Exclusionary Zoning" (paper), 54
exhibitionism, architectural, 29
extremists, hyper-density, 84
eye level planning, 30
"eyes on the street" phrase, 29

facades, 31
Fainstein, Susan, 55
Fair Housing Act, 249
FAR. *See* floor area ratio
Federal Housing and Rent Act (1947), 178
Federal Post Office, 160, 161
Felt, Irving, 160–61

Felt, James, 152, 160–61
15 Penn Plaza, 153
Fifth Avenue Committee, 192
50 West 66th Street tower, 202
Figuera, Héctor, 200
filtering, upward process, 40
finance industry, 6
finance rules, for politicians, 306–7
Financial District, 151, 168
financialization, of housing, 315
financing, of new towers, 49
1st Arrondissement, Paris, 89
First Nation People, 108–9
fisheries, regulations, 99
Fishman, Torrey, 190
519 Fifth, 135
floor area ratio (FAR), 85, 115, 216, 295
Ford, George, 151–52
foreign investors, 45
forests, value of, 101–3
Fortune 500 companies, 213–14
Fox & Jacobs, 47–48
fraud, tax, 203
Freedman, Robert, 32
Freemark, Yonah, 74
free market, 44
freestanding buildings, 31
Frick Museum, 149
Friends of Governors Island organization, 170
fronts and surrogates, 199–201
Fulton Fish Market, 237
fundamentalism, trickle-down housing supply, 40–43, 65
fundamentalists: cost-benefit proposals, 97–98; historic districts and, 122; NIMBY and, 54–65
Furman Center, 124, 144
"Future City" (sideshow), 20

Garden City idea, 91–92
Garment District buildings, 162
Gateway Tunnel, 164
GDP. *See* Gross Domestic Product growth
Geddes, Norman Bel, 20
Gehl, Jan, 30–32
Gehry, Frank, 30, 275, 280

364 · INDEX

General Motors (GM), 20, 262
gentrification, 60, 124–28, 132, 178
geographers, economic, 62–63
geographic-information-systems (GIS), 305
Gerhards, Basha, 187
German house, 272
gerrymandering, 180
Giedion, Sigfried, 19
Gifford, Robert, 79
GIS. *See* geographic-information-systems
Giuliani, Rudy, 153, 155, 230–32
Glaeser, Edward, 7–8, 38–40, 41–43, 201; critics of, 62–65; elite influenced by, 79–83; on historic districts, 122, 214–18; on LPC, 209–10; NIMBYs and, 54–55, 56; "Preserving History or Hindering Growth" (paper), 210–12, 214–18; problematic assumptions in trickle-down theory, 44; sky space, New York City and, 52–53; on towers for young people, 72–73; on zoning codes, 50–52
glass curtain walls, 261–62
Glazer, Nathan, 266
Glen, Alicia, 170, 195
Glen/Weisbrod plan, for Governor's Island, 170–71
Glenwood real estate firm, 180
Glossary of Tax Breaks and Giveaways, 158, 159
GM. *See* General Motors
Goldberger, Paul, 133, 201, 262–63, 267–68; on architecture as art, 274
Goldman Sachs Investment Bank, 144
Good Cause Eviction Act, 315
Google, 213
government, 17; as clients, 13; real estate ties to, 186–92
Governors Island, 167–72, *168*, *169*, *171*
Governors Island Preservation and Education Corporation, 169
Gowanus, 193, 196
Graaskamp, James, 113
Grand Central Station proposal, 23
granny units, 312
Gratz, Roberta, 157
Greenfield, David, 235

Greenpoint, New York City, 59
Greenwich Village, 29, 64, 88, 103
grid layouts, 27, 138
Gropius, Walter, 257–58, 279
Gross Domestic Product (GDP) growth, 41, 107, 113
growth: economic, 290; historic districts hindering, 212–13; infinite, 53, 134; measuring, 84; population rates, 80–81
"growth machine," as "Demolition Machine," 134–37, 138, 232
Gumowitz, Arthur, 166
Gutman family, 242

Hadid, Zaha, 20, 282
Hagelgans, Andrea, 188–89
Halloran, Daniel, 176
Hamilton Heights, 225
Harlem, 124, 126, 223–26
Hasidic Williamsburg, 312
Hasson, Cory, 189
Hausman, Jerry, 107
Haussmannian buildings, 93, 260
HBU. *See* highest and best use
Hearst Tower, *10*
Heastie, Carl, 177
"heat island" effect, 76
Hegel, G. W. F., 269, 270
height bonuses, 159
height caps, elimination of, 83, 180
height limits, 296; aesthetic value and, 214; Seaport Historic District, 237–38; for skyscrapers, 150–51, 154, 165; zoning codes for, 53
height restrictions, of buildings, 38
Heights of Buildings Commission, 150, 151
"heritage" tourism jobs, 213
Herzog, *284*
Hicks, John, 109
"high-low" design pattern, 24
High Rise City (*Hochhausstade*), 20
high-rise living, income level and, 79
high-rises, housing prices and, 58–59
highest and best use (HBU), 111–14
highways, cloverleaf, 15
Hilberseimer, Ludwig, 20

Hinkson-Carling, Susan, 190, 194
historical context, architecture, 261
Historic Buildings Committee, 148
historic districts, 119–28, 131, 132, 250; anti-, 214; attacks on, 209–11; developers stalking, 218; erosion of, 157; Glaeser on, 122, 214–18; housing prices influenced by, 211–12; new construction and, 219–20; profiting from, 211–12; real estate lobby wars on, 218–23; Seaport, 237–40; SoHo and NoHo, 60, 240–49; upzoning of, 244–45; values of, 120–21, 216; white residents in, 221–26
historic properties, demolition of, 59, 210, 212
Hoboken, 59
Hochhausstade (High Rise City), 20
Hochul, Kathy, 141, 166, 167
Holden, Robert, 190
homeowners, 3, 34–35
Hong Kong, 21, 22–23, 69, 321n3
Hotel Pennsylvania, demolition of, 160, 162, 167
hotels, SRO, 37
household earnings, average, 306
housing: Chakrabarti on, 21–23; demand for, 7; determining pricing of, 42; luxury, 24, 40; Mitchell-Lama program, 62; prefabricated modular, 24–25; Pruitt-Igoe towers, 22; "supply shock," 38; towers and, 246; trickle-down supply fundamentalism, 40–43, 44, 65; young people looking for, 64. *See also* affordable housing
housing court, 179
housing discrimination, 249
Housing Justice for All coalition, 182
housing market: barriers to entry, 47–50; supply side, 42
housing prices: building new towers and, 56–60; gentrification and, 124; high-rises and, 58–59; in historic districts, 122–23; historic districts influence on, 211–12; inflation, 57; studies on, 58–60; zoning codes and, 51–52, 63–64
housing shortage, 62

Housing Stability and Protection Act (2019), 182–83
How Innovation Really Happens (Duggan), 268
"How Skyscrapers Can Save the City" (article), 38, 210
Hudson Square, 155
Hudson Yards, 7, 23, 80
Hughes, Howard, 238–39
Hughes, Kara, 189
human-scale affordable housing policy, 311–17
human-scale design, 26–32; density and, 34, 88; framework principles for, 287–89; hyper-density compared with, 32–35; Manhattan, 34
human-scale economic development strategy, 291
human-scale neighborhoods, 2–3, 87–88
human-scale urbanism, 32
The Hunger Games (film), 115
hutongs, 24
Huxtable, Ada Louise, 74, 262
hyper-dense political economy, 33
hyper-density, 21, 86; Chakrabarti and, 21–26; human-scale compared with, 32–35; ideology of, 2, 7–10; Le Corbusier on, 14; origins of, 11–17
hyper-density extremists, 84
hyper-density persuasion, 80

ICAP. *See* Industrial and Commercial Abatement Program
IDC. *See* Independent Democratic Conference
Illinois Institute of Technology campus plan (1941), 20
immigrant neighborhoods, 37
immigrants, 5, 85, 87
in-between densities, 91–92
income level, 37, 79, 246
Independent Democratic Conference (IDC), 181
India, 87
Industrial and Commercial Abatement Program (ICAP), 182
industrialization, 5, 109–10

industries, regulated, 174
infinite growth, 53, 134
inflation, housing prices, 57
influential simulation model, 41
in-migration, of young people, 81
"integrity," idea of, 253, 254
Interagency Land Acquisitions Conference (1995), 114
International Congress for Modern Architecture (CIAM), 19
Intro 775 bill, 233
investment, in public realm, 289–92
investment demand, 45
investors, foreign, 45
Inwood, 88, 115

Jackson Heights, 88
Jacobs, Jane, 3, 4, 17–18, 27–30, *105*; on border vacuums, 161–62; on density, 89–95; value of urban commons and, 103–4
Jamaica (Queens) Community Development Corporation, 145
Jane Jacobs School of Urban Planning, 29
Jeanneret-Gris, Charles-Edouard ("Le Corbusier"), 11–15, 17–19, 22, 257; "Let's Demolish everything and Rebuild" plan, *18*; Ville Radieuse fantasy, 20
Jenga building, 77, *131*, *256*, *284*
"Jobs for New York" campaign, 182
Johnson, Philip, 256–57
Jonas, Jillian, 187
JP Morgan, 144

Kahn, Louis, *284*
Kaldor, Nicholas, 109
Kaldor-Hicks efficiency test (KH test), 110–12
Kallos, Ben, 235
Kartal Masterplan, 20
Kasirer, Suri, 189–90
Keenan, Jesse, 80–82
Kent, Carolyn, 225
KH test. *See* Kaldor-Hicks efficiency test
kids: high-rise living and, 79; Le Corbusier on, 15; playground for, 17; raising, 2–3; schools and, 54

Kim, Joon, 205–6
Kimball, Andrew, 143
Kimball, Kyle, 145
Kirkpatrick, Steven, 146–47
Klein, Jeff, 180–82
Knakal, Robert, 45
Koch, Ed, 229–30
Koolhaas, Rem, 74–75, 251, 261, 279, *281*
Kramer Levin firm, 187, 188, 237, 244
Kruger, Liz, 133
Krugman, Paul, 124

labor, semi-slave, 264
labor unions, 24–25
Lafayette Towers, Detroit, 25
Lago, Marisa, 192
La Guardia, Fiorello, 60–61
laissez-faire attitudes, 113
land "elasticity," 52
Lander, Brad, 57, 196
landlords, New York City, 48, 127, 323n1; Glossary of Tax Breaks and Giveaways, 158, 159; rent regulations and, 177–80
landmark designations, 223, 225–26, 235–37
landmarking, anti-, 234
landmarks, 155–57
Landmarks Laws, 155–57, 194
Landmarks Preservation Commission (LPC), 38, 97, 119, 148, 156–57, 169, 175; architects in, 194; backlog controversy, 235–37; Black residents and, 224–26; capture and, 174; Glaeser on, 209–11; on public policy, 226–27; REBNY capturing, 226–28, 232; requests of, 212; Seaport Historic District and, 237–40; what to do about, 310–11
landowners, 112
landscape architecture, 163
Land Use Controls (Ellickson and Tarlock), 111–12
land-use policy, 289
Langer, Barry, 165
Las Vegas, 52
Latino residents, 59, 73–74
lawsuits, 206–7
Leach, Gwyneth, 70

"Le Corbusier." *See* Jeanneret-Gris, Charles-Edouard
"LEED" certifications, 75
Leicht, Holly, 160, 165
Lenox Terrace houses, 198
"Let's Demolish Everything and Rebuild" plan, *18*
Levin, Anna, 193
Li, Sylvia, 190
libertarianism, 38–39, 41–42, 109–110, 147–48
Libeskind, Daniel, 280
lifespan, of buildings, 220
limited liability corporations (LLCs), 176, 307
Lindenbaum, Samuel "Sandy" H., 153, 232
Litwin, Leonard, 180
LLCs. *See* limited liability corporations
loan brokers, 142
lobby: architect, 148; real estate, 3, 138–42, 175
lobbying, 187–92, 218–19; by construction companies, 196; as corporate power tool, 197; reforms to reduce, 307–8
lobbyist law firms, 139
lobbyists: as community board members, 195–96; elected officials as, 191–92; Open New York, 2, 201; at real estate firms, 196; spending big on, 196–97
localized housing prices, 122
Loeb, Rachel, 195
"loft law," 126
London, 10–11
Long Island, New York, 89
Long Island Hospital site, 204
Loos, Adolf, 258–59
Lower Manhattan Expressway rendering, *105*
low-income families, 46, 129
low-income neighborhoods, supply shock and, 58
low-income workers, 64
low-rise housing, 79, 316, 322n10
LPC. *See* Landmarks Preservation Commission
luxury apartments, 48–49
luxury housing, 24, 40

Macklowe, Harry, 202
MacLean, Alex, 93
MacLear, Christy, 201
mainstream press, 207–8
Mandatory Inclusionary Housing (MIH), 56–57, 65, 128, 322n13
Mangin, John, 54
Manhattan, New York, 36, 39, 52, 77, 86; Black Manhattanites, 223–24; density of, 94–95; developers, 139–40; gentrification and, 124–26; Hearst Tower, *10*; Hudson Yards project in, 7; human-scale design, *34*; Lower, 5; Midtown East, 45; segregation of, 221–22; Thomas Street building, *8*; Trump City, *16*; "white-ification" of, 221
Manhattan Institute, 147–48
manifestos: on density, 10; by modernist architects, 257, 259
manufacturers, reforms to, 308–10
Marohn, Charles, 78
Martin, Dean, 197
Martin, Nicholas, 189
Marxists, 277
M.A.S. *See* Municipal Art Society
Mason, Randall, 121, 122
mass transit, 37
Mast, Evan, 57
mayor, New York City, 174–75, 183–86
McCloskey, Deirdre, 109–10
McFadden, Robert, 202
McMansions, 51
McMillan, Joe, 200
Meiggs, Russell, 276
mental health, 267
Mercury Public Affairs, 199–200
Meridian Capital, 142
MetLife building, 258
de Meuron, *284*
micro-zoning, 314–15
middle-class, 6, 34, 36, 125, 129
Midtown East, 45, *185*, 185–86
Mies, Ludwig, 258, 271, 272, *281*
Miesian skyscrapers, 271
migration, 81–83
MIH. *See* Mandatory Inclusionary Housing
Millennium Partners, 145

Milstein real estate family, 237–38
Miner, Dorothy, 230–31
"missing middle" urban densities, 65
Mitchell, Joseph, 6
Mitchell-Lama housing program, 62, 126, 223–24
mixed-use neighborhoods, 30
modernist architects, 253, 254–55, 257–59; how they won, 261–67
modernist architecture movement, 6, 17–21, 251–52, 267; as art, 273–76; on campuses, 261–62; "commandments" of, 259–60; Le Corbusier and, 11–12; gurus of, 263; ideology, 254–55, 256–61; towers, 261
modernist buildings, 120
modernists, 17–21, 255
modernity, 8, 12, 32
Mohawk First Nation, 101–3, *102*, *103*, 114
Molotch, Harvey, 134
Mom and Pop stores, 157, 310
monetary value, assigning, 106–7, 114
money and power, 104
money prices, assigning, 111
The Monolith (documentary), 70
monopoly, 47–48
Moreland Commission to Investigate Public Corruption, 202, 176
Morgan Library, 231, *231*
Moses, Robert, 60–61, 92, 104, *105*, 134
Moskowitz, Ross, 147
Moss, Jeremiah, 98
Moss, Mitchell, 86–87
Mount Morris Park, 224
Moynihan Train Hall, 160
Mulligan, Jeff, 187
Multiple Dwelling Law, 51, 298–99
Municipal Art Society (M.A.S.), 200–201
Muschamp, Herbert, 278

natural gas, 322n8
nature: in architecture, 14; separation from, 23–24; Sitte on, 27
negative externalities, 67–68, 73–75, 79

neighborhoods: "context" of, 253–54; as historic districts, 119–20; human-scale, 2; immigrant, 37; mixed-use, 30; of New York City, 7. *See also specific neighborhoods*
neo-classical stables, 283, *283*
neo-classical style apartment building, *281*
net density, 85–86
New Jersey waterfront, 59
Newtown Creek Sewage Treatment Plant, 53–54
New York Association of Realtors, 182
New York City Planning Commission, 21
New York residents, 2
New York State Association for Affordable Housing, 147
NIMBYs ("Not In My Backyard"), 3, 43, 245, 304; fundamentalists and, 54–56
9/11 disaster, 232
9/11 shock, on housing, 217
1990 Oka Crisis, *102*, 102–3, *103*
NoHo. *See* SoHo and NoHo historic districts
Norman, Gene, 230
North End, Boston, 90–91
nostalgia, architecture and, 277–78
"Not In My Backyard." *See* NIMBYs
Nouvel, Jean, 281–82, *282*
numeraire illusion, 108
NYC 2040 (report), 80–83

Obama, Barack, 97
Olnick real estate family, 198
111 West 57th Street, 98, *98*
1031 exchange program, 159
one-sided supply-side theory, 43
Open New York, lobby group, 2, 201, 244–45
Opportunity Zones, 158, 321n4
Organisation for Economic Co-operation and Development (OECD) study, 95–96
Ortiz, Larisa, 192
Ostrom, Elinor, 100
outdoor dining, 129–30, *130*

out-migration, 83
"overbuilding," 134
overcrowding, 53
overdevelopment, 1–2, 207

PACB. *See* Public Authorities Control Board
Packes, Nancy, 48
pandemic, 87, 129
Pareto, Vilfredo, 108
"Pareto Efficient," 109
Pareto Optimality, 107–11
Paris, 6, 11, 85; La Defense, 24; density of, 88–89; Le Corbusier on, 13–15; "Let's Demolish Everything and Rebuild" plan, *18*
Park Avenue Historic District Extension, 148–49
parking: lots for, 30; street, 129–30
parking lots, Edison, 242–44
parks, 14, 23, 30; regulations for, 131
Park Slope, 59
"parochialism," 24, 26
Partnership for New York City organization, 146
patent production, 96
Paterson, David, 198–99
"PAU" architecture firm, 21
Paulsen, Sherida, 231–32
Pearson, Marjorie, 232
pedestrians, 31
Peebles, Don, 203–4
Penn Central law case, 228
"Penn Plaza," 161–62
Penn Station project, 55, 70, *70*, 153, 160–67, *161*
Pennsylvania Station, 160–61, *161*
people of color, 6
Peppers, Briana, 190
permits, building, 51–52
Petry, Ann, 6, 126
Philadelphia row house, *284*
Piano, Renzo, 278–79, *279*
pilotis (towers), 15
planners, NYC, 83–84
playground, for kids, *17*

plazas, 26–27, 31; building heights in exchange for, 154; public private, 130–31
Podolsky Brothers, 204–5
Polevoy, Jason, 147
policy crisis, affordable housing and, 60–62
policymaking, density and, 96
politicians, 173, 175–77, 306–7
poor people, 73, 81
population growth, 63, 82; prediction of, 83; rate of, 80–81
postmodernists, 255
Potential Pareto Improvement (PPI), 109, 110
power and money, 104
PPI. *See* Potential Pareto Improvement
practice hearing, for Seaport Historic District, 239–40, *241*
prefabricated modular housing, 24–25
"Preservation Follies," 209–10
"Preserving History or Hindering Growth" (paper), 210–13, 214–18
presidents, of boroughs, 300
press, mainstream, 207–8
price markups, as regulatory tax, 46–47
price premiums, 123
prices, shadow, 100. *See also* housing prices
private developers, 40
privatization, 118
privatized "amenities," 32
privatized rentals, 62
production process, by-products of, 67–68
profit: leaving New York City, 46; price markups as, 46–47
property ownership, 36, 48, 115, 116
property taxes, 241
Provisional Typology of Values Relevant in "Heritage Analysis," adapted and expanded from Randall Mason, *121*
Pruitt-Igoe towers, 9, 22
Public Authorities Control Board (PACB), 166
public goods, 100, 132
public infrastructure, 34
public land bank, 315
public policy, LPC on, 226–27
public private plazas, 130–31

public realm, investment in, 33
public transit, 4, 28, 316
public transportation, 291–92

Queens, 53–54, 61, 127, 145

Raab, Jennifer, 225, 230–31
racial diversity, 244–45
racial equity, 247–48
racial injustice, 221
racism, 128
The Radiant City (Le Corbusier), 18–19
Rampershad, Raj, 193
Reagan, Ronald, 113–14
real estate appraisals, 112–13
real estate battles, 55
Real Estate Board of New York (REBNY), 56, 133–34, 138–40, *141*, 142, 304; campaign contributions by, 181–82; complaints from, 219–21; De Blasio cabinet, 233; government and, 186–92; lawsuits and, 206–7; LPC backlog controversy and, 234–37; LPC captured by, 226–28, 232; Open New York and, 201; organizations with ties to, 143–48; rent control and, 180–81; rent reforms and, 183; towerization and, 155; war on historic districts, 218–23
real estate brokers, 138–39
real estate industrial complex, 7, 134, 287; branches of, 142–50; De Blasio funded by, *184*
real estate industry, 1–2, 135, 323n2; advertising, 207–8; corruption and, 202–3; donations made by, 186; dynastic character of, 48; government ties to, 186–92; historic districts and, 132; in New York City, 3–4; public good of, 119–20
Real Estate Investment Trusts (REITs), 45–46
real estate lobby, 3, 138–42, 218–23
REBNY. *See* Real Estate Board of New York
Rechnitz, Jona, 204
recreation places, 15
redlining, 126–27, 323n2

reforms, to community boards, 302–3
Regional Plan Association (RPA), 82–83, 145–46
regulatory agencies, influence appointment to, 192–96
regulatory capture, 173–76, 287
regulatory tax, price markups as, 46–47
Reinvent Albany, 177
REITs. *See* Real Estate Investment Trusts
Related Company, 21
rent, cost of, 36; market-rate rental tower and, 58; for politically powerful, 197–99; rising, 48–49
rentals, privatized, 62
rent control, 37, 178
Rent Guidelines Board, 178
rent laws, controlling, 177–83
rent regulations, 177–78
rent stabilization, 37, 49, 61–62, 126; laws, 315; small business, 157–60
Rent Stabilization Association (RSA), 142, 180, 183
Requests for Evaluation (RFEs), 233–34
residential constructions, 50
residential towers, 78–79
resources, common-pool, 99–100
restaurants, sidewalk access for, 129, *130*
"revolving door" issues, 186–92, 307–8
rezoning, 55, 73; East Harlem, 193
RFEs. *See* Requests for Evaluation
RG Group, 190
rich people, preferences of, 128–29
Right of Way (magazine), 114
Rivington case, 206
Rivington House building, 205
roadways, 130
Robbins, Lionel, 108–9
"Robin Hood in reverse," 143
Robinson, Nathan, 251, 266
Rockefeller, David, 146
Rockefeller, Nelson, 178
Rodríguez-Pose, Andrés, 62–63
van der Rohe, Ludwig Mies, 20
Romans, 97
roofs, 13
Rose, Joe, 118, 135, 153–55
Roth, Steven, 162, 163, 165–67

row-houses, 37
RPA. *See* Regional Plan Association
RSA. *See* Rent Stabilization Association
Rudin Management Company, 189
Rudin real estate family, 198
Rudolf, Paul, *105*
Rust Belt workers, 64, 321n2
Rypkema, Donovan, 73, 212

safety, density and, 30
La Sagrada Familia, 89
Samuel, Michael, 170
Sanders, Anna, 173
San Francisco, 59, 90, 118
Santa Barbara, 119
Sant'Elia, Antonio, 11, 15
Sassen, Saskia, 21
Saunders, Pete, 64–65
Scarpa, Carlo, 283, *283*
schools, 54, 322n7
Schumacher, Patrik, 263
Schumer, Chuck, *141*, 166, 189
Scott, Allen J., 63
Seagram building, *281*
Seaport Historic District, 237–38; practice hearing for, 239–40, *241*
Seaport Museum, funding for, 239
Seattle, Washington, 307
Section 8 housing, 224
segregation: of Manhattan, 221–22; of urban centers, 22
SEIU-32BJ, non-construction union, 200
semi-slave labor, 264
Sen, Amartya, 108
sewage, 53–54
shadow fan illustration, *70, 70*
shadowing, from buildings, 67–68, 70, *70, 71*
shadow laws, 118
shadow prices, 100
"Shard" building, 278, *279*
SHoP Architects, 190
shortage, housing, 62
"side payments," 202–6
sidewalks, 54, 129, *130*
Siegel, Charles, 32
Silberman, Mark, 239

Silicon Valley, California, 89
Sillerman, Michael, 153
Simmons, Emily, 188
Singh, Harendra, 204
single-family homes, 36, 37
single-family zoning, 66
single-room occupancy (SROs), 37, 61
Sitte, Camillo, 26–27
16th Arrondissement of Paris, 85
Skelos, Dean, 180, 181–82
Skidmore, Owings, and Merrill (SOM), 23
skydome, 52, 66, *116*, 132; developers and, 118; rendering of, *115*; as urban commons, 114–19
sky exposure plane, 151
Skyscraper Museum, 145
skyscraper phenomenon, 117–18
skyscrapers, 9–10, 13, 14, 34, 39, *118*; density and, 93–94; economics and, 213; environmental toxins and, 75–76; financing for, 49; height limits for, 150–51, 154; historic buildings replaced by, 219; lifespan of, 220; NIMBY battles for, 55; shadowing from, 67–68, 70, *70, 71*; small cities damaged by, 78; weather changed by, 76; "wedding cake," 151
slavery, 108, 264
Sloan House YMCA, 160
slum, of Mumbai, 87
slumlords, 46, 204
Small Business Congress, 157–58
small businesses, reforms to, 308–10
Small Business Jobs Survival Act, 146, 158, 308
small business rent stabilization, 157–60
smaller cities, 78
Small Property Owners of New York (SPONY), 142
small-scale homeowners, 35
Smith, Stephen Jacob, 251
social cost analyses, 53
social costs, 67, 68–69, 74, 322n6
social engineering, 249
sociologists, 78
SoHo and NoHo historic districts, 60, 240–49
SoHo Cast Iron District, 242

Solow, Robert, 106–7
SOM. *See* Skidmore, Owings, and Merrill
Sorkin, Michael, 84, 263–64
Soros, George, 181
spatial competition, 64
spatial equilibrium theory, 63
Spatt, Beverly Moss, 228–29
speculative value, of properties, 211
Spinola, Steven, 186–87
SPONY. *See* Small Property Owners of New York
squares. *See* plazas
Srinivasan, Meenakshi, 233–35
SROs. *See* single-room occupancy
stables, neo-classical, 283, *283*
St. Albans, 127–28
standardization, of buildings, 28–29
starchitects, 278–85
starchitecture, 29
Starr, Roger, 228–29
State Multiple Dwelling Law, 177, 180
Staten Island, 87
State Senate, 179–81
Stiglitz, Joseph, 49–50
stilts, legalized, 155
Stitt, Joseph, 145
St. Louis, Missouri, 22
stores, Mom and Pop, 157
Storper, Michael, 62–64
St. Paul de Vence, 282
The Street (Petry), 6
StreetEasy, search engine, 182
street parking, 129–30
streets, curved, 27
streetscape, visual impact of, 29
streetscape standards, 295
"streetwall," 30
Stringer, Scott, 190, 245
studies, on housing prices, 58–60
suburban densities, 89
suburban living, 6–7
suburbs, 52, 125, 127–28
subway system, in New York City, 5, 54
Sugarman, Alan, 194
sunlight, 100–101, 152; ancient light and, 117; exposure to, 323n1
Sunnyside Gardens Historic District, 92
superblocks design, 24, 27

supply shock, 35, 38, 57–58
supply side, of housing market, 42
"Supply Skepticism" (Been), 57
surrogates, fronts and, 199–201
"sweetheart" arrangements, 159
Swig, Kent, 200

Tarlock, Dan, 111–12
tax credits, 312
taxes, property, 241
tax fraud, 203
tax incentives, 312–13
tax liabilities, erased, 203
Taxpayers for an Affordable New York group, 199
TDR. *See* transfer of development rights
tech industries, 41
technocrats, 1
Teitelbaum, Bruce, 189
tenement buildings, 36, 60–61, 85
Theater District, 229
Thomas Street building, 8
3M company, 265–66
Thypin, Ben Carlos, 201, 245
Times Square, 229
Tkaczyk, Cecilia, 181–82
Tomorrowland (fantasy city), 2, *2*
Toronto, 32
Toro-Vaca, Omar, 190
Torre Agbar, 282
Towards a New Architecture (Sant'Elia), 11, 13–15
towerization, 2, 8, 14–15, 65, 68; Glaeser's program of, 79–83; REBNY, 155
towers, *135*; affordable housing and, 248–49; as diversity suppressors, 92–93; financing of, 49; housing and, 246; housing prices and building new, 56–60; marketed to wealthy, 76; market-rate rental, 58; modernist, 261; residential, 78–79; shadowing from, 67–68, *70*, *70*, *71*; views from, 77; Vornado, 162–64, *164*; for young people, 72–73
toxins, environmental, 75–76
traditional architecture, 31–32
tragedy, of the commons, 100
trains, 161

transfer of development rights (TDR) policy, 296
transit, public, 4, 28
transportation, public, 291–92
Tribeca, 72, *116*, 125–26, 131, *131*; demolition in, 137, *137*
Tribeca Trust, 186
trickle-down housing supply fundamentalism, 39–43, 44, 65, 97; negative externalities and, 67–68
Tri-State region, 37
Triumph of the City (Glaeser), 38, 209–10
Trump, Donald, 153, 158, 174, 194; tax fraud and, 203
Trump City, *16*
Trump World Tower, 153
Trust for Governors Island, 170–71
Tung, Anthony, 230
tunnel, Gateway, 164
Turkey, 20
Twin Towers, 72
215 East 68th, *198*
217 West 57th, *156*
Two Bridges Tower, 78
The Two-by-Two Model of "Heterogeneous" Effects, 214–15, *215*

ULURP. *See* Uniform Land Use Review Procedure
unemployed workers, 41
unethical donations, 202–6
Unified Bulk reform proposal, 154
"Uniform Land Use Review" applications, 55
Uniform Land Use Review Procedure (ULURP), 56, 243
unions, construction, 200
"Unité d'Habitation" (housing project), *17*
Upper East Side, 87
Upper Manhattan Empowerment Zone, 224–25
Upper West and East Sides, New York City, 40–41
upward filtering process, 40
upzoning, 60, *247*; of NoHo and SoHo, 244–46
urban centers, segregated, 22
urban commons, 98–99; historic districts as assets to, 119–28; regulations for,

129–31; skydome as, 114–19; standard of value for, 107–11; types of value in, 100–106
Urban Design for the City of Toronto organization, 32
urbanism, 31–32, 120; anti-urban streets, 78; human-scale, 32
urbanists, 22
urban monoculture, 129
urban planning, 28
urban renewal, 60–61
Urstadt, Charles, 314

"vacancy decontrol cap," 180
Vacancy Decontrol Law, 178
valuation, 100, 104, 111, 122
values: assigning monetary, 106–7, 114; categorization of, 101; of historic districts, 120–21, 216
ventilation, in buildings, 76
vernacular architecture, 18, 31, 260, 275
views, loss of, 70
Viggiano, Matthew, 189–90, 235, 240
Village Care, 205
Village Preservation, 60, 245–46
Villa Savoye, 257
Ville Radieuse fantasy, 20
Violette, Zachary, 36
Virginia suburbs, 51
Visualizing Density (Campoli and MacLean), 93
visual monotony, 28
vitality, loss of, 28, 78–79
voids, 155, *156*
Vornado, 49, 70, *70*; Penn Station Project and, 160–67
Vornado towers, 163, 164, *164*

Wagner, Robert, 152
Washington Market Park, 72
waterfronts, 131
wealthy, towers marketed to, 76
weather, skyscrapers changing, 76, 77
"wedding cake" skyscraper, 151
Weinstock, Charles, 165
Weisbrod, Carl, 170
West Hollywood North, California, 89
Wharton Regulatory Index, 52

Whelan, James, 140, 187
"Where We Live Now" (report), 248
white residents: gentrification and, 124, 125–28; in historic districts, 221–26
Whyte, William H., 30
Wiley, Maya, 245
Williamsburg, New York City, 59, 73–74, 312
windows, 76, 220
Wolfe, Tom, 232
"Wonder City," New York as, 5–7, 286
Wood, Anthony, 236
World Trade Center, 9, 31, 217, 315

Yamasaki, Minoru, 9
Yao, Kim, 148
Yes In My Backyard (YIMBY), 41–42
young people: in-migration of, 81; looking for housing, 64; towers for, 72–73

Zeckendorf, William, 199
zeitgeist, 270–73

zoning codes, 50–52, 65, 292–96, 323n3; anti-zoning, 111–12; for building heights, 53; housing prices and, 51–52, 63–64; micro-, 314–15; modify, 243; NoHo and SoHo districts, 60, 242–43; penalties for, 312; public purpose of, 53; real estate industry subverting, 150–55; rezoning, 55, 73, 193; rezoning Governor's Island, *171*, *172*; single-family, 66; for small businesses, 309–10; upzoning, 60, 244–46, 247
zoning experts, 293
Zoning for Quality and Affordability/Mandatory Inclusionary Housing plan, 55
Zoning for Quality and Affordability project, 148
zoning reform, 292–96
Zoning Resolution (1916), 139, 150–53
Zoning Resolution (1961), 292–93
zoning rules, 24, 26, 33

Lynn Ellsworth is an economist, mother, New Yorker, and founder of Humanscale NYC, the Tribeca Trust, the Empire Station Coalition, the Citywide Land-use Coalition, and the Friends of Duane Park. She is on the advisory board of the historic preservation program at the University of Notre Dame and lives in Lower Manhattan.

EMPIRE STATE EDITIONS   SELECT TITLES FROM EMPIRE STATE EDITIONS

Patrick Bunyan, *All Around the Town: Amazing Manhattan Facts and Curiosities, Second Edition*

Daniel Campo, *The Accidental Playground: Brooklyn Waterfront Narratives of the Undesigned and Unplanned*

Joseph B. Raskin, *The Routes Not Taken: A Trip Through New York City's Unbuilt Subway System*

Phillip Deery, *Red Apple: Communism and McCarthyism in Cold War New York*

R. Scott Hanson, *City of Gods: Religious Freedom, Immigration, and Pluralism in Flushing, Queens*. Foreword by Martin E. Marty

Dorothy Day and the Catholic Worker: The Miracle of Our Continuance. Edited, with an Introduction and Additional Text by Kate Hennessy, Photographs by Vivian Cherry, Text by Dorothy Day

Mark Naison and Bob Gumbs, *Before the Fires: An Oral History of African American Life in the Bronx from the 1930s to the 1960s*

Robert Weldon Whalen, *Murder, Inc., and the Moral Life: Gangsters and Gangbusters in La Guardia's New York*

Joanne Witty and Henrik Krogius, *Brooklyn Bridge Park: A Dying Waterfront Transformed*

Sharon Egretta Sutton, *When Ivory Towers Were Black: A Story about Race in America's Cities and Universities*

Pamela Hanlon, *A Wordly Affair: New York, the United Nations, and the Story Behind Their Unlikely Bond*

Britt Haas, *Fighting Authoritarianism: American Youth Activism in the 1930s*

Nandini Bagchee, *Counter Institution: Activist Estates of the Lower East Side*

Susan Celia Greenfield (ed.), *Sacred Shelter: Thirteen Journeys of Homelessness and Healing*

Susan Opotow and Zachary Baron Shemtob (eds.), *New York after 9/11*

Andrew Feffer, *Bad Faith: Teachers, Liberalism, and the Origins of McCarthyism*

Colin Davey with Thomas A. Lesser, *The American Museum of Natural History and How It Got That Way*. Forewords by Neil deGrasse Tyson and Kermit Roosevelt III

Wendy Jean Katz, *Humbug: The Politics of Art Criticism in New York City's Penny Press*

Lolita Buckner Inniss, *The Princeton Fugitive Slave: The Trials of James Collins Johnson*

Mike Jaccarino, *America's Last Great Newspaper War: The Death of Print in a Two-Tabloid Town*

Angel Garcia, *The Kingdom Began in Puerto Rico: Neil Connolly's Priesthood in the South Bronx*

Jim Mackin, *Notable New Yorkers of Manhattan's Upper West Side: Bloomingdale–Morningside Heights*

Matthew Spady, *The Neighborhood Manhattan Forgot: Audubon Park and the Families Who Shaped It*

Marilyn S. Greenwald and Yun Li, *Eunice Hunton Carter: A Lifelong Fight for Social Justice*

Jeffrey A. Kroessler, *Sunnyside Gardens: Planning and Preservation in a Historic Garden Suburb*

Jean Arrington with Cynthia S. LaValle, *From Factories to Palaces: Architect Charles B. J. Snyder and the New York City Public Schools*. Foreword by Peg Breen

Boukary Sawadogo, *Africans in Harlem: An Untold New York Story*

Alvin Eng, *Our Laundry, Our Town: My Chinese American Life from Flushing to the Downtown Stage and Beyond*

Stephanie Azzarone, *Heaven on the Hudson: Mansions, Monuments, and Marvels of Riverside Park*

Ron Goldberg, *Boy with the Bullhorn: A Memoir and History of ACT UP New York*. Foreword by Dan Barry

Peter Quinn, *Cross Bronx: A Writing Life*

Mark Bulik, *Ambush at Central Park: When the IRA Came to New York*

Brandon Dean Lamson, *Caged: A Teacher's Journey Through Rikers, or How I Beheaded the Minotaur*

Raj Tawney, *Colorful Palate: Savored Stories from a Mixed Life*

Joseph Heathcott, *Global Queens: An Urban Mosaic*

Francis R. Kowsky with Lucille Gordon, *Hell on Color, Sweet on Song: Jacob Wrey Mould and the Artful Beauty of Central Park*

Jill Jonnes, *South Bronx Rising: The Rise, Fall, and Resurrection of an American City*, Third Edition

Barbara G. Mensch, *A Falling-Off Place: The Transformation of Lower Manhattan*

David J. Goodwin, *Midnight Rambles: H. P. Lovecraft in Gotham*

Felipe Luciano, *Flesh and Spirit: Confessions of a Young Lord*

Maximo G. Martinez, *Sojourners in the Capital of the World: Garifuna Immigrants*

Jennifer Baum, *Just City: Growing Up on the Upper West Side When Housing Was a Human Right*

Davida Siwisa James, *Hamilton Heights and Sugar Hill: Alexander Hamilton's Old Harlem Neighborhood Through the Centuries*

Annik LaFarge, *On the High Line: The Definitive Guide*, Third Edition. Foreword by Rick Dark

Marie Carter, *Mortimer and the Witches: A History of Nineteenth-Century Fortune Tellers*

Alice Sparberg Alexiou, *Devil's Mile: The Rich, Gritty History of the Bowery*. Foreword by Peter Quinn

Carey Kasten and Brenna Moore, *Mutuality in El Barrio: Stories of the Little Sisters of the Assumption Family Health Service*. Foreword by Norma Benítez Sánchez

Kimberly A. Orcutt, *The American Art-Union: Utopia and Skepticism in the Antebellum Era*

Jonathan Butler, *Join the Conspiracy: How a Brooklyn Eccentric Got Lost on the Right, Infiltrated the Left, and Brought Down the Biggest Bombing Network in New York*

Nicole Gelinas, *Movement: New York's Long War to Take Back Its Streets from the Car*

Jack Hodgson, *Young Reds in the Big Apple: The New York Young Pioneers of America, 1923–1934*

Walter Zev Feldman, *From the Bronx to the Bosphorus: Klezmer and Other Displaced Musics of New York*

Larry Racioppo, *Here Down on Dark Earth: Loss and Remembrance in New York City*

Bonnie Yochelson, *Too Good to Get Married: The Life and Photographs of Miss Alice Austen*

For a complete list, visit www.fordhampress.com/empire-state-editions.